THE FIRST THEOLOGIANS

The First Theologians

A Study in Early Christian Prophecy

Thomas W. Gillespie

WILLIAM B. EERDMANS PUBLISHING COMPANY
GRAND RAPIDS, MICHIGAN

© 1994 Wm. B. Eerdmans Publishing Co.
255 Jefferson Ave. S.E., Grand Rapids, Michigan 49503
All rights reserved

Printed in the United States of America

00 99 98 97 96 95 94   7 6 5 4 3 2 1

Library of Congress Cataloging-in-Publication Data

Gillespie, Thomas W., 1928-
 The first theologians: a study in early Christian prophecy / Thomas W. Gillespie.
  p.   cm.
 Includes bibliographical references.
 ISBN 0-8028-3721-2
 1. Prophecy — Christianity — History of doctrines — Early church, ca. 30-600.
 2. Theology — History — Early church, ca. 30-600.   I. Title.
BR195.P74G55 1994
231.7′45′09015 — dc20   94-34746
                                                CIP

Contents

Foreword, by Michael Welker	ix
Acknowledgments	xi
Abbreviations	xiii
Introduction	1
God's Voice	2
Words of the Risen Jesus	5
Sentences of Holy Law	6
Hermeneuts of the Gospel	9
Four Criticisms	11
An Unsuccessful Salvaging Operation	17
Beyond the Oracle	20
A Prophetic Sermon?	23
Prophetic Pastoral Preaching	25
Prophecy and Kerygma	28
Prospectus	32
1. Prophecy and Gospel	33
1 Thessalonians 5:20 and Romans 12:6	
Despise Not Prophesyings: 1 Thessalonians 5:20	36

The Text as Paraenetic Tradition	39
An Early Church Order?	40
A Liturgical Order?	41
Paul's Use of the Tradition	43
The Ecclesial Setting of the Text	44
Summary: 1 Thessalonians 5:20	48
According to the Analogy of the Faith: Romans 12:6	50
A Fence around Pride	54
The Norm of Prophecy	56
What Faith Believes	58
The Faith and the Gospel	59
The Traditioned Faith	61
Summary: Romans 12:6	62
Conclusion	63

2. Prophecy and Confession
1 Corinthians 12:1-3 — 65

The Question of the Question	66
Concerning Spiritual Gifts?	68
Concerning Spiritual People?	74
Who Speaks by the Spirit of God?	78
Confessing Jesus as a Theological Norm	85
Cursing Jesus as an Instance of False Prophecy	90
Conclusion	95

3. Prophecy and Spirit
1 Corinthians 12:4-31a — 97

A Theme and Its Thesis	98
A Thesis Illumined	100
A Thesis Illustrated	105

Utterances of Wisdom and Knowledge	107
A Crucial Disjunction	109
A Traditioned List?	112
To Each . . . for the Common Good	113
One Spirit — One Body	118
God's Ecclesial Order	122
Conclusion	127

4. Prophecy and Tongues
1 Corinthians 14:1-40 — 129

Theme and Argument	129
In Terms of a Tradition	132
Covenant Prophets Old and New	134
In a Manner of Speaking	137
What Prophets Speak	140
Prophetic Edification	142
Prophetic Exhortation	144
Prophetic Encouragement	148
Ecstasy and Inspiration	150
Tongues as a Sign	156
A God of Peace and Not Disorder	160
Conclusion	164

5. Prophecy and Wisdom
1 Corinthians 2:6-16 — 165

Quarrels and Divisions	166
Wisdom/Power and Foolishness/Weakness	170
Corinthian Verbal Wisdom	175
Wisdom and the Mystery of Christ Crucified	178
Speaking Wisdom by the Spirit	183

A Prophetic Wisdom?	187
Revelation of the Gospel	189
Paul's Prophetic Gospel	193
A Commentary on Prophecy	196
Conclusion	197

6. Prophecy and Kerygma
1 Corinthians 15:1-51 — 199

Resurrection and Prophecy	200
Deniers of the Resurrection of the Dead	205
Belief in a Realized Resurrection	211
Paul's Prophetic Discourse	218
Creed or Kerygma?	221
A Revelation of a Mystery	226
An Argument from Revelation	229
Conclusion	235

Conclusion — 237

Theology as Prophetic Interpretation	237
Criteria of the Spirit	241
A Rhetoric of Glory	245
How It Played in Corinth	248
Resurrection and Death	252
An Apocalyptic Theology	255
Israel's Resurrection God	258
Summation	262
Bibliography	265
Index	283

Foreword

"Prophets" and "prophetic speech" — until just a few years ago I accepted these expressions as substantively appropriate only with regard to the prophetic books of the Biblical traditions. By contrast, the general notion of "prophecy," especially of contemporary "prophecy," seemed to me always to smack of pretentiousness, moral self-righteousness, or even soothsaying. I was first challenged in this opinion by studies in the theology of law, which made two things clear to me. First, classical prophecy oriented itself on the basis of complex, systematic interconnections of law and wisdom: that is, on the basis of religious and normative forms that can at least in part be clearly reconstructed even today. Second, the great prophets were astute analysts and diagnosticians of the processes of social development and decay in their day. Taken together, those two points mean that classical prophecy combined substantive theology and substantive cultural and social criticism in ways that are, at least in principle, clear and comprehensible, even to us today.

In doing preparatory work for my book *God the Spirit*, it became clear to me that we must not content ourselves with understanding and interpreting the complex of "the prophetic" as a phenomenon of past cultures. According to key texts of both Testaments, the "pouring out of the Spirit" is connected with a complex interplay of experiences of God and perceptions of reality on the part of diverse people and groups of people. This "proclamatory" interaction is characterized both directly and indirectly as "prophetic speech." This means that anyone who wants to grasp the forces at work in the creative and critical spiritual interaction of women and men, of old and young, and of persons from diverse social and cultural spheres, will have to try to work out a clear understanding of "the prophetic."

In this situation, I came upon the dissertation of Thomas W. Gillespie, "Prophecy and Tongues." I was very impressed by the insistence, persistence, and clarity with which the work poses the question, "How did Paul understand 'Christian prophecy?'" The version now before you, reworked and significantly expanded, shows the same questioning insistence: "What were the function and location of the prophets in early Christianity? What were the nature and authority of their prophesying? What were the form(s) and content of their prophecy?" Gillespie uses clear structural articulations, anticipatory observations and conclusions, to illuminate the many-faceted interconnections of "the prophetic" with the Gospel, confession, the Spirit and the activity of the Spirit, speaking in tongues, wisdom, and the kerygma.

As in the earlier version, Paul's theology provides the decisive theological and historical field of reference. Using Paul's theology as a focus, Gillespie draws in and discusses a broad spectrum of European and North American positions. He is aware that the complex phenomena and the corresponding "loaded" concepts that he relates to each other require a special navigational art. Between the Scylla of reductionistic generalizations and trivializations and the Charybdis of unresolved ambiguity and withheld judgment, Gillespie steers toward the coast of a "typology of early Christian proclamation."

The book does theology as exegesis carried through to its logical conclusions (Karl Barth's *konsequente Exegese*). But the book also speaks to practical and systematic theologians concerning the issues of their disciplines. Gillespie wants to work out standards with regard to "early Christian prophecy" that enable theology in general to recognize its task and obligation as well as its freedom and dignity. Theology demonstrates itself to be a prophetic power inasmuch as it aids in interpreting the "inherent implications of the kerygma" — indeed, inasmuch as it aids the recognition of those implications and helps them to become public.

MICHAEL WELKER

Acknowledgments

This volume, like many others of its genre, is a revision of a doctoral dissertation. The original version, entitled *Prophecy and Tongues,* was presented to, and accepted by, the faculty of the Claremont Graduate School in 1971. I remain grateful to James M. Robinson and Hans Dieter Betz for their guidance of that project, and to Herman C. Waetjen of San Francisco Theological Seminary for his contribution as the external examiner.

Twenty years later, Michael Welker of the University of Heidelberg read a library copy of the work while visiting the campus of Princeton Theological Seminary and urged me to update the study for publication. His confidence in the theological significance of the central thesis was more encouragement than could be responsibly ignored. I am grateful to him for the impetus that initiated the task of revision.

Not surprisingly, the literature on early Christian prophecy had multiplied over the intervening two decades. Whereas in 1971 only two monographs on the topic were identifiable (one by Erich Fascher and the other by H. A. Guy), the resources available in 1991 included numerous dissertations and books, as well as essays. From these new conversation partners I have learned a great deal, even on points of disagreements, and I acknowledge my indebtedness to them. Because of their labors, the original thesis has been re-argued here in a radically different and more informed way.

My thanks also to J. Christiaan Beker and Ulrich Mauser for reading parts of the manuscript; to Donna Kline and Jan Rosenberger for their constant support in numerous ways amidst the demands of the president's office; to Kathy Matakas and Johnny Awwad for creating order in the footnotes and bibliography; to Brent Strawn for correcting the galley proofs; and to Davis Perkins for suggesting the title of this book while we visited theological schools in central and eastern Europe. The preparation of this volume would have been impossible without the enduring encouragement and encouraging endurance of my wife Barbara, to whom it is (again) dedicated with gratitude.

Princeton, New Jersey THOMAS W. GILLESPIE
August 1994

Abbreviations

ABR	The American Benedictine Review
Bib	Biblica
BJRL	Bulletin of the John Rylands University Library of Manchester
BZ	Biblische Zeitschrift
CBQ	Catholic Biblical Quarterly
CTM	Concordia Theological Monthly
DBSup	Dictionnaire de la Bible, Supplément
EVQ	Evangelical Quarterly
ExpTim	The Expository Times
HBT	Horizons in Biblical Theology
HTR	Harvard Theological Review
Int	Interpretation
JBL	Journal of Biblical Literature
JR	Journal of Religion
JTC	Journal for Theology and the Church
JTS	Journal of Theological Studies
KD	Kerygma und Dogma
LB	Linguistica Biblica
MTS	Marburger theologische Studien
MTZ	Münchener theologische Zeitschrift
NovT	Novum Testamentum
NTS	New Testament Studies
PRS	Perspectives in Religious Studies
RAC	Reallexikon für Antike und Christentum
RevExp	Review and Expositor
RTJ	The Reformed Theological Journal
SBLDS	SBL Dissertation Series

SEÅ	*Svensk exegetisk årsbok*
ST	*Studia theologica*
STU	*Schweizerische theologische Umschau*
SWJTh	*Southwestern Journal of Theology*
TDNT	G. Kittel and G. Friedrich (eds.), *Theological Dictionary of the New Testament*
TExH	*Theologische Existenz Heute*
TLZ	*Theologische Literaturzeitung*
TZ	*Theologische Zeitschrift*
WTJ	*Westminster Theological Journal*
ZkWkL	*Zeitschrift für kirchliche Wissenschaft und kirchliches Leben*
ZNW	*Zeitschrift für die neutestamentliche Wissenschaft*

Introduction

EARLY Christian prophecy is a topic that continues to vex New Testament scholarship. David Hill, a major contributor to the investigation, offers anecdotal testimony to the quandary:

> One of my colleagues teaching in the field of Old Testament studies has indicated to me on several occasions that one of the questions which most interests him in connection with classical prophets is, "What was the prophet doing when he was not prophesying?" To which, with unfailing regularity, I respond by saying (out of my interest in early Christian prophecy), "And I would like to know what New Testament prophets were doing when they *were* prophesying!"[1]

Hyperbole aside, the question entails other questions that have yet to evoke answers commanding widespread assent. What were the function and location of the prophets in early Christianity? What were the nature and authority of their prophesying? What were the form(s) and content of their prophecy? Such questions focus the issues of the inquiry as it has developed, but to date no consensus on the specifics has emerged among those who have proposed resolutions.[2] The question of what

---

1. David Hill, "Christian Prophets As Teachers or Instructors in the Church," ed. J. Panagopoulos, *Prophetic Vocation in the New Testament and Today* (1977), 108.

2. Monographs include: Erich Fascher, *Prophētēs* (1927); H. A. Guy, *New Testament Prophecy* (1947); Theodore M. Crone, *Early Christian Prophecy* (1973); J. Reiling, *Hermas and Christian Prophecy* (1973); Gerhard Dautzenberg, *Urchristliche Prophetie* (1975); Ulrich B. Müller, *Prophetie und Predigt im Neuen Testament* (1975); E. Earle Ellis, *Prophecy*

early Christian prophets were doing when they were prophesying thus remains *open*.

The question is *pressing* because modern research has recovered an appreciation of the central leadership role these prophetic figures exercised in the churches of the New Testament period. Long overshadowed by the apostles in ecclesial consciousness — which has tended to focus exclusively upon issues of apostolic authority, tradition, and succession — the prophets of primitive Christianity have been recognized increasingly in modern biblical scholarship as major players in the historical and theological development of the early church. Since the presence of prophets in the embryonic Christian communities is given such broad attestation in the Pauline corpus, the Acts of the Apostles, the Revelation of John, and, some would say, the Synoptic Gospels, such recognition is not only warranted but long overdue. That the prophets' historical presence enjoyed theological significance is affirmed in the Ephesian Letter by the remembrance that the household of God is "built upon the foundation of the apostles and prophets" (2:20). This New Testament assessment of the foundational role played by Christian prophets in the early church is sufficient cause for pressing the question of what these prophetic agents were doing when they were prophesying. It is somewhat surprising, therefore, that the question was evoked not by the biblical evidence itself but by the discovery of an important noncanonical document that necessitated a reassessment of the New Testament data.

God's Voice

Scholarly interest in the ministry of early Christian prophets was occasioned by the discovery (1873) and publication (1883) of the full text of *The Teaching of the Twelve Apostles* (The *Didache*) by Metropolitan Philotheos Bryennios. The contents of this early second-century docu-

---

and *Hermeneutic in Early Christianity* (1978); David Hill, *New Testament Prophecy* (1978); M. Eugene Boring, *Sayings of the Risen Jesus* (1982); Wayne A. Grudem, *The Gift of Prophecy in I Corinthians* (1982); David E. Aune, *Prophecy in Early Christianity and the Ancient Mediterranean World* (1983); Antoinette Clark Wire, *The Corinthian Women Prophets* (1990); and M. Eugene Boring, *The Continuing Voice of Jesus* (1991). Important dictionary articles are: G. Friedrich, "prophētēs," *TDNT* VI, 828-61; E. Cothenet, "Prophetisme dans le Nouveau Testament," *DBSup* VIII, 1222-1337.

INTRODUCTION

ment led in the following year to the publication of the first comprehensive treatment of early Christian prophecy in modern biblical scholarship, a two-part essay written by N. Bonwetsch.[3] More provocative, however, was Adolf von Harnack's interpretation of the fresh data in his 1884 critical edition of the *Didache* text.[4]

Harnack calls attention to the preeminence attributed to the prophets and teachers along with the apostles in the church order of the *Didache* (XI–XV). This new information, he argues, makes it impossible to ignore any longer the evidence of the presence and activity of apostles, teachers, and prophets in the even older sources found in the New Testament, and thus necessitates a reconstruction of the origins and development of the Christian ministry in the first two centuries without focussing myopically upon the traditional offices of bishop, elder, and deacon.

Accordingly, Harnack advances the thesis of a two-tier ministry in early Christianity — one catholic and charismatic, the other parochial and pedestrian.[5] The apostles, prophets, and teachers were Spirit-endowed itinerants who served all of the churches and operated independently of the local bishops, elders, and deacons.[6] These church offices *(Kirchenämter)* were distinguished from the community offices *(Gemeindeämter)*, as he later designates them,[7] by their respective natures and functions. Whereas the local officials were elected by their particular congregation for administrative, jurisdictional, and liturgical tasks, the peripatetic leaders were mandated directly by the Spirit and endowed with charisma for the ministry of the word of God (*Did.* IV, 1). As ministers of the gospel, the apostles, prophets, and teachers occupied the early church's highest rung on the ministerial ladder, and together signified its unity.[8]

---

3. N. Bonwetsch, "Die Prophetie im apostolischen und nachapostolischen Zeitalter," *ZkWkL* 5 (1884): 408-24; 460-77. The novelty of the project is indicated by the fact that the author found it necessary to cite only one previous study of the subject, that by N. Ch. Elend, *De illis qui prophetae vocantur in novo foedere* (1732).

4. Adolf von Harnack, "Die Lehre der zwölf Apostel: Prolegomena," in *Texte und Untersuchungen zur Geschichte der altchristlichen Literatur* (1884), II, 5-268.

5. *Ibid.*, 88-158.

6. *Ibid.*, 96, 103.

7. Adolf von Harnack, *Die Mission und Ausbreitung des Christentums in den ersten drei Jahrhunderten* I (4th ed. 1924), 354.

8. Harnack, *Die Lehre der zwölf Apostel*, 103.

Within this charismatic triad, Harnack distinguishes two orders: (1) the apostles, who were the professional missionaries, and (2) the prophets and teachers, whose task was the upbuilding and spiritual strengthening of the churches.[9] Yet he recognizes that in the *Didache* the prophets are associated with the apostles (XI, 3) on the one hand, and with the teachers (XIII, 1-2) on the other. This ambivalence is occasioned by the fact that the prophets shared with the apostles the task of preaching (rather than teaching) the word of God, and with the teachers the function of upbuilding (in distinction from founding) churches. What thus emerges from the *Didache* is the image of the Christian prophet as the community preacher *(Gemeindeprediger)*.[10]

As such the prophets enjoy a certain prominence in the church order of the *Didache*. The term *prophētēs* occurs fifteen times in this text, Harnack notes, while *apostolos* and *didaskalos* appear only three times each. This implies that the spiritual building of the local congregation through prophetic preaching was the supreme ministerial task, an evaluation confirmed by the designation of the prophets as the high priests of the community (*Did*. XIII, 3).[11] Further, the prophets alone are depicted as "speaking in the Spirit" *(lalein en pneumati; Did.* XI, 7-9, 12), an expression that signifies to Harnack an intense form of inspiration in which the Spirit is the actual speaker and the rational and reflective consciousness of the prophet is submerged.[12] Such inspiration qualifies prophetic discourse as the word of God and designates the prophet as "God's voice."[13] When recognized, the authority of the prophet's message is unchallenged.

Harnack's thesis thus attributes to the early Christian prophets a central place in the catholic ministry of the word in early Christianity. As itinerants they served the purpose of building up the local congregations. As charismatics they were directly inspired by the Holy Spirit. And as preachers they declared the word of God. Subsequent studies have challenged the itinerant status of the prophets[14] and confirmed

---

9. *Ibid.*, 97.
10. *Ibid.*, 119.
11. *Ibid.*, 120.
12. *Ibid.*
13. Harnack, *Die Mission und Ausbreitung des Christentums*, 345.
14. H. Greeven, "Propheten, Lehrer, Vorsteher bei Paulus," *ZNW* 44 (1952-53): 1-43, reads the New Testament evidence to mean that prophecy began as a community phenomenon that was only over time associated with certain individuals who were

INTRODUCTION

their charismatic character.[15] The issue resisting resolution to date is the specificity of their designation as the proclaimers of God's word. If the prophets were the primary preachers of the early Christian congregations, as the *Didache* clearly intimates, then this fact raises historical and theological matters of more than casual interest. What was the content of the prophet's message? What recognizable linguistic forms (if any) did their proclamation assume? Are there New Testament texts that may be identified legitimately as instances of such prophetic utterance?

Words of the Risen Jesus

These questions received an innovative answer from Rudolf Bultmann in his *History of the Synoptic Tradition* (1921), and with his proposal the investigation of early Christian prophecy entered a second stage by taking a form-critical turn. In this study of the historical origins and linguistic forms of the Gospel material, Bultmann suggests that certain logia attributed to Jesus in the Synoptics are in fact the oracles of early Christian prophets that were gradually assimilated into the dominical tradition.[16] The early church drew no sharp distinction between the utterances of the Spirit through the prophets and the traditioned sayings of the earthly Jesus, Bultmann argues, because the latter were not "the pronouncements of a past authority, but sayings of the risen Lord, who

---

eventually given the title of prophet. Even then, however, they remained community based, the wandering prophet being a later development. So also Hans Freiherr von Campenhausen, *Ecclesiastical Authority and Spiritual Power* (1969), 62. For a critique of this view, see J. Reiling, *Hermas and Christian Prophecy* (1973), 7-12.

15. See Hermann Gunkel, *Die Wirkungen des heiligen Geistes nach der populären Anschauung der apostolischen Zeit und der Lehre des Apostels Paulus* (1888); Heinrich Weinel, *Die Wirkungen des Geistes und der Geister im nachapostolischen Zeitalter bis auf Irenäus* (1899); Ernst Käsemann, *Essays on New Testament Themes* (1964), 63-94; and Ulrich Brockhaus, *Charisma und Amt* (1972).

16. Rudolf Bultmann, *The History of the Synoptic Tradition* (1963), 127-28; see also 163. Included are the "Prophetic and Apocalyptic Sayings," 108-30; "Legal Sayings and Church Rules," 130-50; and the "'I' Sayings," 150-63. His reference to the similar suggestion made previously by Hans von Soden and Herman Gunkel (127 n. 1) indicates that Bultmann is not claiming originality in proposing this thesis.

is always a contemporary for the Church."[17] But apart from two references to putative prophetic oracles in the first person singular (Rev. 16:15 and *Odes Sol.* 42:6), Bultmann makes no effort to ground his assumptions in what is known of Christian prophecy from other sources. As M. Eugene Boring, himself a friendly critic, concedes:

> Bultmann's statement about Christian prophecy did not derive from a study of the prophetic phenomenon in early Christianity, but from a need to account for what he saw as extensive elements in the synoptic sayings-tradition which did not derive from Jesus. Although his works repeatedly appeal to Christian prophecy as an explanation for the growth of the tradition, he never describes the prophets, their place in the church and relation to the tradition, nor does he even present evidence to support his identification of a particular saying as having originated from a Christian prophet.[18]

While this criticism does not necessarily invalidate Bultmann's intuitions, it does demonstrate that his proposal remains a speculation until supported by historical evidence.

Sentences of Holy Law

Ernst Käsemann attempted to provide this evidence in his essay "Sentences of Holy Law" (1954).[19] Among the "Legal Sayings and Church Rules" attributed by Bultmann to the early Christian prophets are "a group of sayings which are formulated in legal style, i.e. they are sentences whose first clause contains a condition (*ean, hotan, hos an, hostis*, etc., or instead a participle) and whose second part is an imperative or an assertion (sometimes in the future), and which has the sense of a legal prescription."[20] Picking up on this observation, Käsemann calls attention to a similar form of speech found in the Pauline letters that is characterized by a juridical restriction in the major premise (the

---

17. *Ibid.*, 128.
18. M. Eugene Boring, "Christian Prophecy and the Sayings of Jesus: The State of the Question," *NTS* 29 (1983): 104.
19. Ernst Käsemann, *New Testament Questions of Today* (1967), 66-81.
20. Bultmann, *History of the Synoptic Tradition*, 132.

protasis) — introduced by the casuistic law form *ei tis* (interchangeable with *ean tis* or *hos d' an*) — in correlation with an eschatological curse or blessing in the minor premise (the apodosis).[21] An example of such speech in its purist form is 1 Corinthians 3:17: "If any one destroys God's temple, God will destroy him" (cf. 1 Cor. 14:38; 16:22; Gal. 1:9).[22]

These "surprisingly overlooked utterances," Käsemann argues, are derived stylistically from Old Testament models that pair talion and chiasmus (e.g., Gen. 9:6),[23] and may thus be designated as declarations of an eschatological *jus talionis*. As such they represent dialectic, charismatic, and kerygmatic manifestations of the divine action of the Last Day, directed to a community that knows itself determined by such a future and lives in the imminent expectation of its occurrence. This eschatological law of God is *dialectical* in that it anticipates the verdict of the ultimate Judge and thus determines the present situation without rendering superfluous the future tribunal of the Last Day; it is *charismatic* in that God remains the actor in this law through the Spirit's revelation of the criterion of the final judgment to its mediators; and it is *kerygmatic* in that it is bound to the exclusive medium of the word and is fulfilled solely in its proclamation.[24]

Käsemann connects such formal utterances with the prophets on the basis of Revelation 22:18-19, a text in which the eschatological law of retaliation is declared twice with specific reference to Christian prophecy.

> I warn every one who hears the words of the prophecy of this book: if any one adds to them, God will add to him the plagues described in this book, and if any one takes away from the words of the book of this prophecy, God will take away his share in the tree of life and in the holy city, which are described in this book.

From this text Käsemann infers that prophetic proclamation is the *Sitz im Leben* for sentences of this kind.[25] Further evidence of this prophetic

---

21. Käsemann, *New Testament Questions*, 67.
22. These further texts represent variations of the form, the future tense of the apodosis being replaced in 1 Cor. 14:38 by the passive voice of the verb that conveys in Semitic fashion the divine action in its effect upon the transgressor, and in 1 Cor. 16:22 and Gal. 1:9 by the explicit curse (*ibid.*, 68-70).
23. *Ibid.*, 67; cf. 76, 79.
24. *Ibid.*, 68-74.
25. *Ibid.*, 76.

Sitz im Leben is educed from the fact that such proleptic pronouncements assume a knowledge of the criterion of God's eschatological judgment, a knowledge that only the Spirit can and does provide through charismatically endowed figures, whom Käsemann identifies as the prophets.[26] The proclamation of "sentences of holy law" expresses, therefore, the leadership function of the prophets that was exercised primarily within the small Jewish-Christian communities — communities that existed apart from Jerusalem where a tighter organization under the apostles and a presbyterate was in effect.[27]

These prophetic utterances are connected with the Synoptists by the fact that such logia as Matthew 10:32-33 are cast in the same form: "Every one who acknowledges me before others, I also will acknowledge before my Father in heaven; but whoever denies me before others, I also will deny before my Father in heaven" (cf. Mark 8:38; 4:24; Matt. 5:19; 6:14, 15).[28] These texts, in Käsemann's judgment, represent a very primitive stage of the tradition from "the time after Easter, with its apocalyptic expectation of an imminent end and its prophet-leaders."[29] The function of such prophetic discourse was not only to keep alive the hope of the Parousia in a community under persecution, but also to call, admonish, warn, and punish those beset by temptation by proclaiming God's recompensing action of the Last Day. Again, Käsemann infers from the form of such logia that the proper *Sitz im Leben* of this eschatological divine law "is the situation in which primitive Christian prophecy 'judges' the messianic people of God, as once the old prophets 'judged' Israel."[30]

Using the results of this essay as a heuristic clue to identify further Synoptic logia attributable to the early Christian prophets, Käsemann developed his thesis with primary reference to the Gospel of Matthew in an ensuing article, "The Beginnings of Christian Theology" (1960).[31] In addition to the "sentences of holy law" identified previously in Matthew (5:19; 6:14, 15; 10:32, 33), Käsemann here cites other texts in which the form is "diluted" and yet recognizable (Matt. 19:28f.; 10:42; cf.

---

26. *Ibid.*, 68.
27. *Ibid.*, 79.
28. *Ibid.*, 77-78.
29. *Ibid.*, 78.
30. *Ibid.*, 79.
31. *Ibid.*, 82-107.

INTRODUCTION

10:13f.). Arguing further that "these sentences are by no means the sole determinant of the prophetic proclamation of the enthusiasm of the period after Easter," he draws into their orbit other texts that are "equally couched in the eschatological future" (Matt. 10:15; 11:22, 24; 6:4, 6, 18).[32] On this basis the evidence is extended to include prophetic paraenesis (Matt. 7:2; 13:12; 23:12; 25:29),[33] aphorisms that have been given an eschatological twist (Matt. 10:26f., 39; 16:25),[34] and pronouncements of curse and blessing (Matt. 7:22f.; 8:11f.; 11:20-24),[35] the latter category including all of the beatitudes (Matt. 5:3-12).[36]

Hermeneuts of the Gospel

Beyond claiming a variety of Synoptic logia for the early Christian prophets, however, Käsemann's form-critical analysis yields *a proclamation tradition* that is characterized materially as well as formally by "a basically apocalyptic outlook."[37] This perspective coheres in certain recurrent themes attested in the prophetic utterances.[38] One such is the apocalyptic principle that the End and the Beginning of history correspond: "As were the days of Noah, so will be the coming of the Son of man" (Matt. 24:37; cf. 12:41, 42; 5:12; 10:15; 11:22). Such eschatological references to the Beginning mirrored in Old Testament events not only give the scriptures an apocalyptic interpretation but also evidence thereby the earliest Christian understanding of history. Indeed, Käsemann argues, it was this principle that first made historical thinking possible for Christians: "Since for apocalyptic the world has a definite

---

32. *Ibid.*, 95.
33. *Ibid.*, 98.
34. *Ibid.*, 99.
35. *Ibid.*, 100.
36. *Ibid.*, 101.
37. *Ibid.*, 93.
38. J. Christiaan Beker, *The Triumph of God* (1990), 114, speaks of the coherence of Paul's apocalyptic gospel in terms of "a field of meaning" that is "determined by the apocalyptic coordinates of Paul's 'linguistic world,'" a "network" of "symbolic relations" analogous to "the coherent field of interlocking circles on the Olympic logo." *Mutatis mutandis*, this is an apt description of the apocalyptic proclamation tradition identified by Käsemann.

beginning and a definite end, the course of history therefore takes a definite direction and is irrevocable, articulated into a series of epochs clearly distinguishable from each other."[39]

Moreover, because the individual being receives its place — "its particularity and co-ordinates" — in such a historical scheme, it was apocalyptic that necessitated the narration rather than the mere proclamation of the kerygma of Jesus.[40] Out of this necessity emerged the unique literary form of the Gospels which, although definitely not biography, presents us with "something like the life of a man, from an eschatological perspective and according to an eschatological interpretation."[41] In this context Käsemann, in search of a criterion for determining what is authentically Christian, calls attention to the "I am come" sayings (Matt. 5:17; 9:13; 10:34; 18:11; 20:28; Luke 12:49), sayings that represent prophetic "extracts" from the commission and work of Jesus. As such these sayings function as "the first summaries of the Gospel" and provide "a basis for the development of the narrative element in the Gospel tradition, a development shaped by the kerygma itself."[42]

Here the early Christian prophets appear not vaguely as the community preachers but concretely as the original interpreters of Jesus and thus the formulators and expositors of the gospel. Käsemann acknowledges that this raises the issue which determines all New Testament theology: the relation of the proclamation about Jesus to the message of Jesus. The problem is intensified for Käsemann by his conviction that the preaching of Jesus "did not bear a fundamentally apocalyptic stamp but proclaimed the immediacy of the God who was near at hand."[43] Yet his analysis of the prophetic proclamation tradition leads him to the firm conclusion that "the earthly Jesus and the *ipsissima verba* do not come out on top."[44] The reason is simply that "Easter and the reception of the Spirit caused primitive Christianity to respond to the preaching of Jesus about the God at hand and, in a certain sense, to replace it with

---

39. Käsemann, *New Testament Questions*, 96.
40. *Ibid.*, 96-97.
41. *Ibid.*, 97. Käsemann adds: "The Gospel cannot maintain its identity without the Gospels. The kerygmatic proclamation becomes the proclamation of an idea only, unless it is narration as well: and unless it is always being grasped afresh in the very process of narration, it becomes a document of mere history."
42. *Ibid.*
43. *Ibid.*, 101.
44. *Ibid.*, 103.

INTRODUCTION

a new apocalyptic."[45] Such an apocalypticism means that the mission and message of Jesus were viewed in light of the End — inaugurated by his resurrection from the dead and the reception of the Spirit, and interpreted by the prophets in accordance with the expectation of his imminent Parousia as world judge and redeemer. The dominant theme of primitive Christian apocalyptic is, accordingly, "the accession to the throne of heaven by God and by his Christ as the eschatological Son of Man — an event which can also be characterized as proof of the righteousness of God."[46] On the basis of this historical reconstruction Käsemann sets forth the provocative thesis that apocalyptic was "the mother of all Christian theology,"[47] the implication being that the early Christian prophets were the first theologians.[48] A more crucial role in the development of the earliest church is difficult to imagine.

Four Criticisms

As impressive as Käsemann's *tour de force* is, however, it is not without its inherent difficulties. David E. Aune faults Käsemann's proposal on four grounds: (1) it assumes rather than demonstrates the connection between the pronouncement of sacral law and early Christian prophecy; (2) it involves a generic identification of such utterances as a legal-apocalyptic form of speech that cannot be sustained; (3) it claims that the texts in question represent a stable form of speech that was consistently used in an identifiable setting in the life of the early church — a claim that can be falsified; and (4) it assumes that the presence of all or many of the features of this form may be used to deny the authenticity of a saying of Jesus that exhibits such a structure.[49] Each of these objections is based on technical arguments that require elaboration.

Aune's first criticism implies that Käsemann falls into the same trap as Bultmann by assuming rather than demonstrating that particular

---

45. *Ibid.*, 102.
46. *Ibid.*, 105.
47. *Ibid.*, 102.
48. *Ibid.*, 105.
49. Aune, *Prophecy in Early Christianity*, 166-68, 237-40.

logia, in this case the "sentences of holy law," are characteristic of, and thus attributable to, prophetic proclamation. Aune, in voicing this objection, is not alone. David Hill also complains that "the position and the necessary presuppositions are simply affirmed, or reaffirmed, virtually without argument of any kind."[50] Käsemann does appeal to Revelation 22:18-19 as evidence of the connection between this form of eschatological law and the early prophets. But Hill argues that this text provides "very feeble" support for the claim made by Käsemann because, while it demonstrates the *use* of the form by the Seer of Patmos, it does not establish its *characteristic use* in Christian prophecy.[51] Gerhard Dautzenberg concurs with Hill, noting that apart from "the allusion to the late witness of Revelation, the theory of Käsemann lacks any connection with the prophets elsewhere mentioned in the New Testament, especially with 1 Cor. 12–14."[52] Actually, Käsemann does appeal to this passage, citing 1 Corinthians 14:38 as a primary instance of the form he identifies, as well as its perceived variants in 14:13, 28, 30, 35, 37.[53] Missing from his argument, however, is any reference to the discussion of Christian prophecy in chapters 12–14 in support of the identification of these Pauline pronouncements as forms of *prophetic* utterance. Thus even Boring, who believes the connection can be made between the prophets and these sayings, expresses the wish "that Käsemann had supported his view that *chiasmus* and *jus talionis* are formal marks of prophetic speech with more evidence from outside the Synoptics before relying so heavily on them as indicators of prophetic material in the synoptic tradition."[54]

If Revelation 22:18-19 constitutes, in Aune's words, "a slim link"

---

50. David Hill, "On the Evidence for the Creative Role of Christian Prophets," *NTS* 20 (1973-74): 271-74. See also his *New Testament Prophecy*, 171.

51. Hill, *New Testament Prophecy*, 172.

52. Dautzenberg, *Urchristliche Prophetie*, 25.

53. Käsemann, *New Testament Questions*, 74, writes with regard to these latter texts: "Here there is no longer any talk of guilt and punishment, but some contingency which may occur in the course of worship is set out (introduced by *ean* or some equivalent participle) and there follows the Pauline ruling on the case expressed in the decretal jussive. The eschatological aspect thus loses its prominence. Nevertheless, it would not be correct to say that it is absent. I Cor. 14:38 shows in fact that it is just those decisions of the Apostle which are pronounced here which are put under the sanction of the divine law."

54. M. Eugene Boring, "How May We Identify Oracles of Christian Prophets in the Synoptic Tradition? Mark 3:28-29 as a Test Case," *JBL* 91 (1971-72): 514.

connecting the pronouncements of sacral law to Christian prophecy,[55] the same is true of Käsemann's inference that these sayings represent prophetic proclamation because they assume revealed knowledge of the criterion of the Last Judgment that is dependent upon charismatic endowment. This argument depends, of course, upon the validity of Käsemann's identification of these sentences as instances of an eschatologically oriented legal genre. As Aune's second criticism indicates, however, this is at best debatable. But even if the legitimacy of the proposed genre analysis is conceded for the sake of argument, Hill's questions on this point require an evidential response: "Does it require charismatic endowment to recognise the criterion of the divine judgment and proclaim it? And why has it to be proclaimed with prophetic authority? Were there not others in the Church, besides prophets, to speak, instruct and warn?"[56] If the so-called "sentences of holy law" *can* be connected with the early Christian prophets, it is clear that Käsemann has not made the case convincingly by appealing to a single text and drawing an inference from a presumed *Sitz im Leben*.

Aune's second criticism of Käsemann's proposal, that the so-called "sentences of holy law" do not represent a legal genre derived from Old Testament models and pitched in an apocalyptic key, is made in acknowledged dependence upon Klaus Berger's extensive form-critical analysis of the relevant material, primarily the Synoptics.[57] The test of Käsemann's thesis, according to Berger, is twofold: do the designated sentences belong to an identifiable Old Testament legal genre, and are they necessarily eschatological in orientation?[58] Chiding Käsemann, and Bultmann before him, for mixing form, content, and *Sitz im Leben* in their analyses of the tradition, Berger focusses solely on the grammatical-syntactical forms of the various types of sayings that predicate certain consequences upon specified deeds.[59] The results of his investiga-

---

55. Aune, *Prophecy in Early Christianity*, 238.
56. Hill, *New Testament Prophecy*, 173.
57. Klaus Berger, "Zu den sogenannten Sätzen heiligen Rechts," NTS 17 (1970-71): 10-40.
58. *Ibid.*, 14.
59. *Ibid.*, 16-18. The conditional clauses used to introduce the first of the two-part formal structure (the protasis) include *hos (gar) ean; pas ho* + present participle or *pas (oun) hostis; hotan;* and *ean* + conjunction + aorist imperative or *kai ean* + aorist imperative. The second part (the apodosis) is cast in either the present or future tense.

tion demonstrate that the forms in question have no connection with the Old Testament legal tradition of talion, but depend rather upon the moral instruction of the wisdom literature, according to which every deed has its corresponding recompense. The great majority of such texts simply correlate human behavior with its historical consequence in the moralistic manner of the wisdom tradition; and even those that cast the recompense in the future tense presuppose, for the most part, not a genuine eschatology but an inner-worldly future in which the *eschata* represent merely the end of life.[60] In the earliest stages of the tradition of this form there is thus no relationship to the Last Judgment of the world. Accordingly, the forms designated by Käsemann as "sentences of holy law," being neither generically legal nor intrinsically eschatological, are more appropriately termed "sentences of wisdom instruction."[61] The form-critical basis of Käsemann's thesis is thus effectively eroded.

Boring seeks to dismiss these negative implications of Berger's study by charging that he "did not sufficiently consider the fact that prophets used wisdom materials and that, though the 'sentences of holy law' are expressed according to wisdom *forms,* the *content* of such sayings is often of an eschatological nature impossible in the teaching of a sage."[62] Given Berger's explicit acknowledgment that this wisdom form was "suitable" for apocalyptic usage and that it was in fact transposed into a genuinely eschatological conceptuality at a later stage of its development (as in 1 Cor. 3:17; 14:38; 2 Cor. 9:6; Rev. 13:10; 18:6; 22:18-19),[63] Boring's charge cannot be sustained. But the fact that the form was, at a point in time, "apocalypticized," as Eduard Schweizer puts it,[64] does not salvage Käsemann's thesis. For the transposition of the wisdom dogma of moral retribution to an eschatological plane where God effects the inevitable recompense at the turn of the ages

---

60. *Ibid.*, 20-21.
61. *Ibid.*, 23-24.
62. Boring, *Sayings of the Risen Jesus,* 131.
63. Berger, "Zu den sogenannten Sätzen heiligen Rechts," 23.
64. Eduard Schweizer, "Observance of the Law and Charismatic Activity in Matthew," *NTS* 16 (1969-70): 226 n. 2. Schweizer is here responding not to Berger, but to a similar criticism of Käsemann's thesis by Georg-Christoph Kähler in an unpublished paper, "Das Matthäusevangelium als Rekonstruktionsbasis für die 'Anfänge christlicher Theologie'?" (August, 1969). Like Boring, he argues that despite the origins of the form of the "sentences of holy law" in the wisdom tradition, the pattern has been taken over into apocalyptic in such texts as 1 Cor. 3:17; Mark 8:38; Matt. 5:19.

INTRODUCTION

results, according to Berger, not in "sentences of holy law" but in "sapiential apocalyptic instruction" *(weisheitliche apokalyptische Belehrung)*.[65] Consequently, such sayings lie in no proximity to either a prophetic function or an inspired expression. Their authority depends not upon the status of their proclaimer, but upon their own inner logic which affirms that every human deed has its corresponding recompense, even when that occurs only at the Last Judgment.[66] While this sapiential understanding does not preclude the possibility of prophets having uttered such eschatological paraenesis, it clearly invalidates the assumption that prophetic activity may be inferred from the form *alone*.[67] Those who claim these sayings for the prophets must, as U. B. Müller concedes, shoulder the responsibility of showing the connection on a case by case basis.[68]

Aune's third criticism against Käsemann's thesis is directed also to Berger's subsequent counter-proposal — that the texts which exemplify this peculiar form have their *Sitz im Leben* in the catechetical instruction of the early missionary church.[69] Whether they are identified as "sentences of holy law" or as "sentences of wisdom instruction," both Käsemann and Berger "assume that the form of speech they are analyzing has stable formal features and that it was consistently used in one original identifiable setting in the life of the early church."[70]

Aune's point regarding the issue of stability is confirmed by recalling the qualifying terms "pure," "diluted," and "variant," terms that Käsemann is required to employ to bring under one rubric the various sayings identified as "sentences of holy law." Even the four Pauline texts cited as primary instances of such a form (1 Cor. 3:17; 14:38; 16:22; Gal. 1:9) are characterized more by formal diversity than by uniformity. Features such as the same verb in the protasis and apodosis, the chiastic structure, and the introductory conditional clause appear to be optional. Given such diversity, is it legitimate to speak of a common rhetorical form? Aune concludes that the only distinctive feature of the sayings identified by Käsemann and Berger

---

65. Berger, "Zu den sogenannten Sätzen heiligen Rechts," 31.
66. *Ibid.*, 32.
67. Crone, *Early Christian Prophecy*, 243-44.
68. Müller, *Prophetie und Predigt*, 180.
69. Klaus Berger, "Die sog. 'Sätze heiligen Rechts' im N.T.: Ihre Funktion und ihr Sitz im Leben," *TZ* 28 (1972): 305-30.
70. Aune, *Prophecy in Early Christianity*, 238.

is "the principle of retributive justice,"[71] a feature that is not a formal but a material characteristic.

But even if a stable rhetorical form was established, it would not be possible to relate it demonstrably to a specific life setting within the early church. Here Aune cites Erhardt Güttgemanns's warning against facile attempts to locate such life settings because of the discontinuity between oral and written tradition as well as the sociological, historical, and literary meanings of the phrase *Sitz im Leben*.[72] The most that can be said is that such sayings may have been uttered by prophets, but the form itself in no way guarantees that this was the case.

Aune's final objection to Käsemann's proposal is that it fails to demonstrate, on formal and material grounds, why these sayings may not be attributed to the earthly Jesus.[73] Käsemann argues that Jesus "proclaimed the immediacy of the God who was near at hand," and "no one who took this step can have been prepared to wait for the coming Son of Man, the restoration of the Twelve Tribes in the Messianic kingdom and the dawning of the Parousia . . . in order to experience the near presence of God."[74] But this judgment is theological rather than form-critical. It depends, moreover, upon Käsemann's denial of the authenticity of all sayings attributed to Jesus that betray an apocalyptic perspective. The argument is thus circular. Because Käsemann assumed that an apocalyptic perspective is characteristic of the early Christian prophets but not Jesus, he inferred that all genuinely eschatological logia originated with the former rather than the latter.[75] Berger's case for identifying the majority of these texts as sapiential paraenesis further weakens Käsemann's argument by eroding its basic assumption of the prophetic character of such speech. Yet even if these sayings were in fact prophetic in the sense claimed by Käsemann, there is no compelling reason why Jesus could not have uttered them as a prophet himself. Thus if it is improper to locate such sayings in a particular setting in life, it is equally inappropriate to assign or deny authorship on the sole basis of a rhetorical form of speech.

---

71. *Ibid.*, 238-39.
72. Erhardt Güttgemanns, *Offene Fragen zur Formgeschichte des Evangeliums* (1969), 167-73.
73. Aune, *Prophecy in Early Christianity*, 240.
74. Käsemann, *New Testament Questions*, 101.
75. See Fritz Neugebauer, "Geistsprüche und Jesuslogien," *ZNW* 53 (1962): 218-28.

While these criticisms of the proposal made by Bultmann and developed by Käsemann do not rule out the possibility of certain logia in the Synoptic tradition having their origin in the proclamation of early Christian prophets,[76] they do show that criteria for identifying such sayings have yet to be established. If the case is to be argued convincingly, rhetorical forms must be identified from sources other than the Synoptic tradition that are, with some degree of probability, characteristic of Christian prophetic proclamation and uncharacteristic of the preaching of Jesus.

An Unsuccessful Salvaging Operation

In his *Sayings of the Risen Jesus,* M. Eugene Boring seeks to meet this requirement.[77] His methodological approach is to provide a provisional and functional definition of the early Christian prophet which is used heuristically to characterize the prophetic phenomenon,[78] including its chief forms of speech, on the basis of the evidence provided by Christian sources.[79] Thus Boring postulates that the early Christian prophet was "an immediately inspired spokesman for the risen Jesus, who received intelligible messages that he felt impelled to deliver to the Christian community."[80] When filtered through the grid of this definition, the

---

76. Thus James D. G. Dunn, "Prophetic 'I'-Sayings and the Jesus Tradition," *NTS* 24 (1977-78): 175-97.

77. Boring's subsequent volume, *The Continuing Voice of Jesus: Christian Prophecy and the Gospel Tradition,* represents "a complete rewriting" of his earlier monograph cited above. Because the new edition is "less technical than its predecessor" and is "directed to a more general readership," our exposition of his argument will follow the original work, which was "concerned with method and evidence in order to make a scholarly case" (13).

78. Boring, *Sayings of the Risen Jesus,* 12-13: "*Any new attempt to deal with the problem of Christian prophecy and the Synoptic tradition should define its terms and characterize the prophetic phenomenon as exactly as possible, making historical distinctions*" (emphasis his).

79. *Ibid.,* 22-52. Boring finds evidence of early Christian prophecy in Revelation, Paul's letters, the Deutero-Pauline letters, Luke-Acts, the Gospel of Matthew, the *Didache,* and *Hermas.* In *The Continuing Voice of Jesus,* 68, 77-79, he adds the Gospel of Mark as well as the Gospel and Letters of John.

80. *Ibid.,* 16. This definition is expanded in *The Continuing Voice of Jesus,* 38: "*The early Christian prophet was an immediately inspired spokesperson for the risen Jesus, who*

textual evidence yields a composite description of the early Christian prophet as (1) a church figure, (2) a pneumatic, (3) a hermeneut of Scripture and tradition, and (4) an eschatological preacher, who (5) mediated oracles of the risen Jesus "according to intentional patterns."[81] Of these prophetic features, the last mentioned is the crux of Boring's effort to rescue Bultmann's thesis. The question is whether the "particular formal characteristics" of the oracles of the early Christian prophets can be specified convincingly.[82]

Boring contends that four such formal characteristics of Christian prophetic utterance are recoverable: (1) "Speaking for the risen Lord in the first person," (2) "'Sentences of holy law'/'eschatological correlative,'" (3) "Initial *amēn*," and (4) "Blessing and curse."[83] Despite the evidence Boring provides to support his claim that these rhetorical forms characterized Christian prophecy, his argument is tenuous. The fact that Paul speaks prophetically "with the ego of the prophet, not in the first-person form of 'I-sayings' spoken with the ego of the risen Christ" compels Boring to admit that "the absence of this form in Paul is significant."[84] His unwarranted dismissal of Berger's criticism of Käsemann's "sentences of holy law" has been noted.[85] And his appeal to the "eschatological correlative," a form analyzed and labeled by R. A. Edwards,[86] is compromised by the concession that this form is only "somewhat characteristic" of prophetic speech, and even then "not unique to Christian prophets."[87] With regard to the initial *amēn (legō*

---

received intelligible messages that he or she felt impelled to deliver to the Christian community or, as a representative of the community, to the general public."

81. Ibid., 127.
82. Ibid., 127-28.
83. Ibid., 58-136.
84. Ibid., 130.
85. In *The Continuing Voice of Jesus*, 163, Boring gives away his case by conceding (1) that the form identified as "sentences of holy law" "was not used *exclusively* by Christian prophets"; (2) that it is "*somewhat* characteristic of prophetic speech but is not unique to Christian prophets"; and (3) that "no saying in the Gospel tradition may be attributed to a Christian prophet on the basis of this form *alone*" (emphasis added).
86. R. A. Edwards, *The Sign of Jonah in the Theology of the Evangelists and Q* (n.d.), 47-58; idem, "The Eschatological Correlative as a *Gattung* in the New Testament," *ZNW* 60 (1969): 9-20. The basic example of the form is found in Luke 11:30: "For *as* Jonah became a sign to the men of Nineveh, *so* will the Son of man be to this generation" (emphasis added).
87. Boring, *Sayings of the Risen Jesus*, 132.

hymin/soi), originally identified by Jeremias as "an indication of Jesus' prophetic self-consciousness,"[88] Boring can say only that it is "appropriate" on the lips of "a Christian bearer of revelation."[89] As for unconditional pronouncements of blessing and curse in the New Testament, they are "almost entirely limited to the synoptic sayings of Jesus and to those who claim to speak by the inspiration of the risen Lord: Paul and the prophet John of Revelation."[90] Yet in actuality the non-Synoptic sources are here limited to the Seer of Patmos, for Boring is compelled to acknowledge that the blessing-and-cursing form "is not explicitly present in Paul's own prophetic speech."[91] A rhetorical form characteristic of an individual prophet, however, should not be claimed for the phenomenon itself. Boring's arguments, accordingly, fail to establish a single rhetorical form as uniquely characteristic of early Christian prophecy.

This failure may well be attributable more to the nature of the phenomenon itself than to the lack of scholarly ingenuity. The remarkable conclusion of David Aune's exhaustive study of the subject is that the institution of Christian prophecy "does not readily lend itself to categorical conceptualization." This negative conclusion "indicates that Christian prophecy, in all its various forms and manifestations, did not possess a dominant form or structure (or a relatively small number of dominant forms or structures); i.e. early Christian prophecy was a relatively *unstable and unstructured institution within early Christianity*" that "*produced no distinctive speech forms which would have been readily identifiable as prophetic speech.*"[92] Note well that Aune is not denying the use of rhetorical forms in the proclamation of the prophets. To the contrary, he himself proposes a typology of six basic forms of prophetic speech and three complex forms. His point is rather the "essential indistinguishability" of these forms from other similar discourse in the early church. It is only the imposition of "formal framing devices"[93]

---

88. Joachim Jeremias, *New Testament Theology* (1971), 79.
89. Boring, *Sayings of the Risen Jesus*, 132.
90. Ibid., 133.
91. Ibid., 134. In *The Continuing Voice of Jesus*, 166, Boring speculates that "Paul deliberately avoided" this form because it "was perhaps being abused by his gnosticizing opponents" or that its absence "is simply accidental and related to the epistolary form and function, rather than a result of intentional disavowal of the form."
92. Aune, *Prophecy in Early Christianity*, 231.
93. By "framing devices" Aune means "linguistic markers" or "formulas" commonly

upon the texts that "betrays the possible presence of Christian prophetic speech." Aune concedes, therefore, that there is "no such thing as a distinctively characteristic form of Christian prophetic discourse that is recognizable apart from the presence of formal framing devices."[94] This being the case, Bultmann's proposal, especially as developed by Käsemann, remains both an unconfirmed and unconfirmable hypothesis. As Theodore M. Crone concludes in a summary statement of his own investigation of this issue, "Thus we must remain satisfied with the *possibility* that certain sayings of Christian prophets are contained in the gospels as sayings of Jesus, but are not *recoverable* with any degree of certainty."[95]

The quest for an answer to the question of the *content* of early Christian prophetic proclamation through its identifiable *forms* has led the investigation into a cul-de-sac. Aune claims that one positive implication of this impasse is the recognition that "the distinctive feature of prophetic speech was not so much its *content* or *form*, but its *supernatural origin*." If this is in fact the case, however, prophetic speech is definable merely as "Christian discourse presented with divine legitimation."[96] But without knowledge of how this legitimizing action was performed, prophetic speech that may be represented in the available sources remains unidentifiable.

Beyond the Oracle

The conclusion that prophetic speech is unidentifiable assumes, of course, that the only way to recognize prophetic speech is by its characteristic rhetorical forms. A contributing factor to this assumption is scholarship's captivity to the unexamined notion that early Christian prophecy was typically *oracular* in nature and character. Aune's exhaustive study of the

---

used to introduce or conclude oracles and which serve to "mark off prophetic discourse from other forms of Christian discourse." He identifies six types: (1) messenger formulas, (2) commission formulas, (3) proclamation formulas, (4) legitimation formulas, (5) oath formulas, and (6) the "mystery" formula. See *ibid.*, 327-33 for the full analysis.

94. *Ibid.*, 338.
95. Crone, *Early Christian Prophecy*, 247 (emphasis added).
96. Aune, *Prophecy in Early Christianity*, 338.

phenomenon exemplifies this hypothesis at work in determining the course and thus the results of the investigation. In his proper endeavor to locate early Christian prophecy in its broad historical and cultural milieu, Aune first examines the prophetic utterances of the Greco-Roman religious tradition which are characteristically articulated in the form of oracles.[97] Two features typify this genre: oracles were *brief,* ordinarily "consisting of one to four lines,"[98] and composed in *verse,* "usually dactylic hexameter."[99] With regard to the latter feature, Aune notes: "The poetic form of oracles was regarded as an indication of their divine origin in the Hellenistic and Roman periods, since the Greeks widely accepted the divine inspiration of poetry."[100] Turning to ancient Israelite prophecy, Aune calls attention to the fact that it too was "couched in poetic form."[101] Although somewhat masked by their preservation in literary collections, the brevity of oracles in the classical tradition of Hebrew prophecy at the oral stage of their history is nonetheless discernible.[102] Given this history-of-religions background, Aune seems justified in taking up the subject of early Christian prophecy under the rubric of the oracle, and assuming thereby that it too was typically brief in length and poetic in form.[103] The first of these features, brevity, prejudices the case in favor of terse dicta; the second trait, a rhythmic and thus patterned type of rhetoric, encourages the quest for recognizable forms of prophetic utterance.[104] If

---

97. *Ibid.,* 23. Aune here defines oracles as "messages from the gods in human language, received as statements, usually in response to inquiries."

98. *Ibid.,* 49.

99. *Ibid.,* 50. Other forms included iambic trimeter, iambic tetrameter, trochaic tetrameter, and anapestic tetrameter.

100. *Ibid.,* 51.

101. *Ibid.,* 89.

102. *Ibid.,* 101.

103. *Ibid.,* 334-36. That Aune forces the evidence into the procrustian bed of his assumption of its poetic form is acknowledged in this summary statement of his findings: "Of the 107 prophetic texts which we have analyzed, *some* are written in a poetic style (i.e. using Semitic parallelism as a basic poetic structure) and are for that reason easier to divide into constituent stichoi or sense lines. The more *prosaic* oracles I have resolved into stichoi on the basis of clauses *(I recognize the relative arbitrariness of this procedure).* The following statistics emerge: oracles of one line: twenty-three; oracles of two lines: sixteen; oracles of three lines: nine; oracles of four lines: nine; oracles of five lines: seven; oracles of six lines: five; oracles of seven lines: one; oracles of eight lines: four; oracles of ten to fifteen lines: nine; oracles of eighteen to twenty-four lines: six; oracles of twenty-six to thirty lines: five; oracles of thirty-one lines: one; oracles of forty-four lines: one" (emphasis added).

104. See Amos Wilder, *Early Christian Rhetoric* (1964), 89-117, who identifies

these are in fact the criteria, however, the negative results produced by the application of the criteria required by Aune's assumption to the available sources are indeed puzzling. Aune's conclusion that "Christian prophecy produced no distinctive speech forms which would have been readily identifiable as prophetic speech" may well say more about the validity of his hypothesis regarding the formal nature of such utterance than it does about the phenomenon itself.[105]

This conception of early Christian prophecy is neither original with, nor unique to, Aune. It was introduced early into the discussion by Heinrich Weinel, who noted the comment in the *Shepherd of Hermas* that the false prophet is one who "chatters" (*Herm. Man.* XI, 12) and inferred from this that "genuine pneumatic words are abrupt short sentences, often in poetic or its approximate form."[106] Ulrich B. Müller correctly observes, however, that this far-reaching conclusion is not supported by the text of *Hermas*. Weinel has simply read into the text his own conception of prophetic speech.[107] Nonetheless, this preunderstanding of the formal character of early Christian prophecy has oriented the investigation to individual sayings *(logia)* rather than to that type of discourse which Müller designates as "the phenomenon of the prophetic sermon" *(Predigt)*, meaning "a linguistic unity of prophetic speech developed out of several individual parts."[108]

Contributing to the neglect of this alternative conception of prophetic speech in early Christianity is yet another assumption regarding the nature of prophetic inspiration. Because inspiration has been understood primarily in terms of *ecstasy,* the possibility of the Spirit effecting an extended discourse, characterized by rational reflection and the logical development of a theme, has been excluded on the ground that it is incompatible with divine inspiration of the kind postulated. Yet the apostle Paul demonstrates, as Müller wryly observes,[109] that the inspiration of prophetic utterance can be con-

---

rhythm as the one reliable test for distinguishing between poetry and prose. That this dynamic criterion includes patterned speech is attested by this definition: "A good poem in any cultural epoch is a combination of convention and novelty, of received structure and improvisation" (89).

105. Aune, *Prophecy in Early Christianity,* 231.
106. Weinel, *Die Wirkungen des Geistes und der Geister,* 89.
107. Müller, *Prophetie und Predigt,* 13.
108. *Ibid.,* 12.
109. *Ibid.,* 14.

INTRODUCTION

ceived otherwise than by ecstasy, namely, in a manner that includes rather than excludes the mind (1 Cor. 14:13-19) and effects understanding expressible in rational speech (1 Cor. 2:10-13). There is no a priori reason, therefore, to deny the possibility of *a prophetic sermon* in early Christianity. Indeed, Harnack's identification of the Christian prophet as the *community preacher* encourages the investigation of such a hypothesis.

A Prophetic Sermon?

In pursuing this project in his *Prophetie und Predigt im Neuen Testament*, Müller remains methodologically within the form-critical paradigm and thus subject to its noted limitations. He first seeks to establish the paraenetic function of early Christian prophecy on the basis of Paul's statement that the prophet "speaks edification, exhortation and comfort" (1 Cor. 14:3). This "emphatically ordered" text expresses both "the sense and significance" of prophecy in the apostle's opinion and warrants the conclusion that "exhortation was a catchword that characterized the task of prophecy."[110] From this conclusion Müller infers that prophetic sermons were expressed either as a "repentance speech" *(Bussrede)* or as an "exhortation speech" *(Mahnrede)*.[111]

In the second part of his work, Müller cites examples of both speech forms from the open letters of the prophet John to the seven churches of Asia Minor (Rev. 2–3), and categorizes them according to their formal and material characteristics.[112] The third part of his book is devoted to an analysis of alleged prophetic passages in the Pauline correspondence, which he groups into three categories: (1) the proclamation of the imminence of the eschaton (or the end of this world) as *a part* of a prophetic exhortation sermon (Rom. 13:11-14; 1 Thess. 5:1-11; 1 Cor. 7:29-31);[113] (2) prophetic judgment preaching by Paul (Rom. 16:17-20; Phil. 3:17–4:1; Gal. 1:6-9);[114] and, (3) prophetic proc-

---

110. *Ibid.*, 24.
111. *Ibid.*, 26.
112. *Ibid.*, 47-108.
113. *Ibid.*, 140-74.
114. *Ibid.*, 175-214.

lamation of salvation for the purpose of comfort (1 Thess. 4:13-14; 1 Cor. 15:51-52; Rom. 11:25-26).[115] The second part of Müller's argument is more successful than the third, according to Aune, because it does establish the prophetic character of the seven letters in the Apocalypse of John,[116] and thus the thesis of a prophetic sermon.

A striking feature of the texts Müller cites as instances of this genre, especially in view of his expressed intention of moving the conception of prophetic speech beyond the limited scope of individual logia, is their relative *brevity*. It is thus clear that his objection to Weinel's designation of such inspired utterances as "abrupt short sentences" is not as severe as the term *sermon* might suggest. In this connection it should be noted that Müller characterizes the prophecy of the Corinthian enthusiasts in precisely Weinel's terms, arguing that it was "the abounding fullness" of such prophetic expression in Corinth that required the apostle Paul to restrict the number of prophets allowed to speak in the worship service to "two or three" (1 Cor. 14:29).[117] But if the prophetic sermons anticipated by the apostle were no longer in duration than the examples cited by Müller, the need for this liturgical restriction is a cause for wonder.

Even more problematic in such circumstances is the succeeding rubric, "If a revelation is made to another sitting by, let the first be silent" (1 Cor. 14:30). Why it would be necessary for a prophet to yield the floor to another while in the midst of delivering either an oracle (typically one to four lines) or a sermon as brief as those represented in the seven letters of John is not easily imagined. On the contrary, these two Pauline rubrics suggest that the prophecy envisioned was, as David Hill claims, "expressed in sustained utterance."[118] In noting Hill's argument on the implications of these two verses, Aune acknowledges that the reforms proposed by Paul "probably resulted in the development of *longer, more homiletic forms of prophetic speech*";[119] but his commitment to the oracular form of Christian prophecy does not allow him to explore this insight.

---

115. *Ibid.*, 214-33.

116. Aune, *Prophecy in Early Christianity*, 276. With regard to the Pauline texts cited, Aune comments: "The greatest difficulty with Müller's study, and one which he should have faced head-on given the title of the book, is the problem of distinguishing between prophecy and parenesis in early Christian literature" (262).

117. Müller, *Prophetie und Predigt*, 16.

118. Hill, *New Testament Prophecy*, 123.

119. Aune, *Prophecy in Early Christianity*, 334 (emphasis added).

Even so, two historical observations by Aune on the character of prophecy in the religious world of early Christianity may be cited in support of this possibility. With regard to the form and function of Greco-Roman oracles, he writes:

> From one perspective Greek oracles exhibit a striking uniformity of style. They are short and written in verse, usually dactylic hexameter. Other meters were used after the fifth century B.C., and *prose oracles became common during the first and second centuries* A.D.[120]

When he takes up the subject of prophecy in early Judaism, Aune calls attention to the absence of the more characteristic formal features of Old Testament prophecy (including poetic form) from the various types of revelatory speech and writing represented: *"Prose, not poetry, becomes the rule."*[121] This does not preclude the use of other revelatory formulas, conventions, and genres in early Jewish prophecy, but it does locate such usage in the context of ordinary discourse that is nonetheless prophetic in character in spite of its prosaic rather than poetic nature. Further, it invites consideration of the possibility that early Christian prophecy, being closer in historical proximity to its Jewish counterpart than to its Old Testament antecedents, also expressed itself in extended prose style.

Prophetic Pastoral Preaching

The kind of "sustained utterance" that Hill has in mind is "prophetic *paraklēsis*,"[122] signifying "*pastoral preaching* which, by its very nature, offers guidance and instruction to the community."[123] The basis of this designation is the functional definition of prophecy provided by the apostle Paul that also informs Müller's understanding of the purpose of prophetic speech (1 Cor. 14:3). Arguing that the terms "exhortation" (*paraklēsis*) and "consolation" (*paramythia*) are not coordinate with

---

120. *Ibid.*, 50 (emphasis added).
121. *Ibid.*, 106 (emphasis added).
122. Hill, *Prophetic Vocation*, 112. The argument is repeated in his *New Testament Prophecy*, 123.
123. *Ibid.*, 114.

"edification" *(oikodomē)* in this verse but indicative of its nature,[124] and discerning no significant semantic distinction between these two words, Hill employs *paraklēsis* to designate the character of prophetic proclamation and thereby orients it to paraenesis. It is admonition, therefore, "addressed to those already within faith and designed to lead them to conduct worthy of the Gospel." Or again, "It is exhortatory preaching: it constantly refers back to the work of salvation as its presupposition and basis; its locus is normally in the worshipping congregation and it contributes to the guidance, correction, encouragement, in short, the *oikodomē* of the community."[125]

Such prophetic *paraklēsis* serves a teaching or instructional purpose. Hill notes Paul's comment in the immediate context that prophecy provides learning and exhortation (1 Cor. 14:31), as well as the apostle's express desire to speak five words with his mind "in order to instruct *(katechein)* others, than a thousand words in a tongue."[126] From this he concludes: "As *pastoral* preachers the New Testament prophets teach and give instruction on what the Christian way requires of individual believers and of the community."[127]

Although convinced that "there is no word or passage in the New Testament which can . . . be classified beyond doubt or question as a prophetic utterance," Hill acknowledges that the "one possible exception is the content of the book of the Revelation and especially the letters of Rev. 2–3."[128] Müller's form-critical analysis of this epistolary material is thus cited with approval. "This is prophetic *paraclesis*," Hill affirms: "It is, as Müller is concerned to make clear, *Predigt*; but it is *pastoral* preaching or instruction, designed not to proclaim the gospel but to call or recall Christians to a path of life and witness which is worthy of the Lord who gives them a share in his kingdom and glory."[129]

The distinction Hill makes here, between prophetic pastoral

---

124. *Ibid.*, 112 n. 10.
125. *Ibid.*, 115.
126. *Ibid.*, 114.
127. *Ibid.*, 116-17.

128. *Ibid.*, 130. Hill qualifies this concession by adding the proviso that the words and experience of John "are so remarkably unlike those of other New Testament speakers or writers and so strikingly like those of Old Testament prophets that one may be justified in regarding him as unique: at the very least, it is unwise to regard him as typical of New Testament prophets."

129. *Ibid.*, 121.

preaching and the proclamation of the gospel, seems artificial in view of his previous statements that exhortatory preaching is addressed to the faithful and "designed to lead them to conduct worthy of the Gospel," and that it "constantly refers back to the work of salvation as its presupposition and basis."[130] Hill's point, of course, is simply that prophetic *paraklēsis* assumes but does not articulate the gospel. This way of conceptualizing the distinction is a familiar one since C. H. Dodd's classical formulation of the relation between the apostolic *didache* and the *kerygma*.[131] But the relation of the gospel to prophetic preaching is more than presuppositional, as 1 Corinthians 14:24-25 clearly attests. Commenting on this text, which describes the potential effects of prophesying on the "unbeliever" or "outsider" present in the service of worship, Hill recognizes "that prophetic speech could bring about conviction, conversion and the acknowledgement of the divine presence in the midst of the congregation."[132] Here "Paul demonstrates his desire to affirm the missionary function of the word, even in the case of the prophetic word spoken in worship." Further, "It is not without significance that for Paul the term *oikodomein/oikodomē* can refer to his apostolic, missionary activity (2 Cor. 10:8; 12:19; and 13:10) and to the building up of the congregation as well."[133]

Such warranted comments on this text suggest that prophetic proclamation, at least according to Paul, was related to the gospel mate-

---

130. *Ibid.*, 115.

131. C. H. Dodd, *The Apostolic Preaching and Its Development* (1951), 7-9: "The New Testament writers draw a clear distinction between preaching and teaching. . . . Teaching *(didaskein)* is in a large majority of cases ethical instruction. . . . Preaching, on the other hand, is the public proclamation of Christianity to the non-Christian world." The New Testament letters, being addressed to readers already Christian, "have the character of what the early Church called 'teaching' or 'exhortation.' They presuppose the Preaching. They expound and defend the implications of the Gospel rather than proclaim it."

132. Hill, *Prophetic Vocation*, 112.

133. *Ibid.*, 112 n. 12. In his treatment of the same text in *New Testament Prophecy*, 123-25, Hill refers positively to the claim of Eduard Schweizer "that in the last resort Paul would allow no distinction to be drawn between prophetic proclamation to Church members and to those from outside: what happens to the latter, according to 14:25, is not fundamentally different from what happens to every Church member when he really hears God's word afresh and accepts again what he has already learnt. In this way the individual believer is edified by the prophetic utterance whilst the congregation as a whole is edified by the response to the word by the outsider" (125).

rially in a way that escapes attention when it is defined as pastoral preaching, and is thus tilted in the direction of moral exhortation that merely presupposes the basic kerygma of the early church. In the summary of his essay "Christian Prophets as Teachers or Instructors in the Church," Hill sounds the caveat that his purpose is "not to discover something novel, but to correct an imbalance in some recent writing on the prophet's role" and thus "simply to stress that *much* of their preaching was pastorally oriented, aimed at building up the Church by exhortation, warning and encouragement."[134] Bending over backwards to help others stand up straight is sometimes a necessary corrective, but it can contribute to distortion as well. When Paul's functional description of prophesying in 1 Corinthians 14:3 is understood predominantly in terms of paraenesis, such distortion occurs and can even lead to the trivialization of early Christian prophecy.[135]

Hill's insight into the extended sermonic character of prophetic discourse, however, invites consideration of the relationship between this prophetic form of Christian proclamation and the foundational kerygma of the church.

Prophecy and Kerygma

Gerhard Dautzenberg addresses the issue of this relationship in his monograph *Urchristliche Prophetie*, explicitly asking the question of how and where the christological kerygma and apocalyptic prophecy met and were melded in early Christian theology.[136] Dautzenberg's answer,

---

134. Hill, *Prophetic Vocation*, 128 (emphasis added).
135. Grudem succumbs to this danger in his 1981 Cambridge dissertation, *The Gift of Prophecy in 1 Corinthians*. The author distinguishes between a divine authority of "exact words" (attributed to the OT prophets and the NT apostles) and of "general content" (attributed to the NT prophets). Like Müller and Hill, he finds the clue to the role of prophecy in the early church in 1 Cor. 14:3, and thus places it under the rubric of "edification." He writes: "Here I am using 'edify' in an extremely broad sense, to include anything which contributes to the spiritual growth of anyone present, or anything implied by *oikodomē, paraklēsis* and *paramythia* in 1 Cor. 14:3" (221). The examples provided on the preceding page (220) in a discussion of the content of "revelation" amply demonstrate the banality of early Christian prophecy as Grudem understands it.
136. Dautzenberg, *Urchristliche Prophetie*, 225.

INTRODUCTION

given at the conclusion of his study, is that these discrete forms of proclamation are materially and formally unrelated.[137] Since this judgment is predicated upon Dautzenberg's idiosyncratic views on the nature and purpose of early Christian prophecy, it must be assessed in light of his interpretation of the phenomenon.

Contra Müller and Hill, Dautzenberg contends that edification and exhortation, attributed by Paul to Christian prophecy in 1 Corinthians 14:3, should be understood as the *result* of prophetic proclamation but not its *object*.[138] This text, in his view, tells us nothing about the essential nature or material content of prophecy. The clue to these matters is found rather in 1 Corinthians 13:2, 8-12. In the first of these texts (13:2), prophecy is correlated with and defined as (revealed) knowledge *(gnōsis)* of the (divine) mysteries *(mysteria)*. As in Jewish apocalyptic and at Qumran, revelation is conceived here as the mediation of understanding that is oriented to the comprehensive object of divine knowledge.[139] The second citation (13:8-12), however, introduces the proviso that prophetic knowledge is "imperfect" (v. 9), and is so in a sense analogous to our seeing "through a mirror dimly" (v. 12).

Dautzenberg connects the latter metaphor with the Jewish exegetical tradition on Numbers 12:6-8 which locates the origin of prophecy in "dark dreams and visions." Although mediated to the seer through such revelatory experiences, prophetic knowledge is necessarily opaque because it penetrates into the sphere of the divine, i.e., into the mysteries (see 2 Cor. 12:1-7).[140] By emphasizing the visionary character of early Christian prophecy, Dautzenberg distinguishes between the prophetic experience of revelation and its subsequent linguistic expression.[141] The latter corresponds to the former in the sense that it takes the form of an equally obscure oracle that requires illumination.

This subsequent and necessary interpretation of prophecy, accord-

---

137. *Ibid.*, 302.
138. *Ibid.*, 298.
139. *Ibid.*, 223-24.
140. *Ibid.*, 224.
141. *Ibid.*, 224-25. Dautzenberg observes that the visionary character of early Christian prophecy lends itself to the forms of discourse typical of the apocalypse, but argues that its oral and literary expressions may not be limited to this genre. The orientation of prophetic knowledge to the divine mysteries makes it reasonable to assume that it is present also in those texts that speak explicitly of revealed mysteries (such as 1 Cor. 2:6-16; 15:51-58; Rom. 11:25-36).

ing to Dautzenberg, is provided by the discrete charisma of *diakrisis pneumatōn* (1 Cor. 12:10; cf. 14:29). In a novel (and dubious) translation, the phrase is rendered as "interpretation of Spirit revelations" rather than the conventional "discernment of spirits." This charisma is then related to prophecy in the same way that the text correlates interpretation *(hermeneia)* with tongues. The phrase thus denotes a charismatic interpretation or explanation, but not a judgment or evaluation, of the prophetic oracle. As the dream in antiquity and the vision in early Jewish apocalyptic required interpretation, so also Christian prophecy needed the supplementary illumination provided by the Spirit.[142]

Dautzenberg concludes that 1 Corinthians 12:10, 13:2, and 14:29, thus understood, exclude the possibility of an original unity or material identity between the christological kerygma and early Christian prophecy.[143] The former, having the redemptive events as its content and being expressed in intelligible speech, is directed to the past. The latter, consisting in the knowledge of eschatological mysteries mediated by visionary experiences and articulated in "dark" oracles requiring interpretation, is oriented to the future.[144] At best, kerygma and prophecy are complementary forms of early Christian proclamation.

This negative conclusion is dependent upon the validity of two theses in Dautzenberg's characterization of early Christian prophecy, both of which are problematic. The first is that prophecy, in Paul's view, consists in the revealed knowledge of the *eschatological* mysteries of God (1 Cor. 13:2). From this plausible premise, the inference is drawn that the kerygma and prophecy have different contents. The question is whether the eschatological "salvation blessings" that constitute the object of prophetic knowledge and proclamation may be distinguished so sharply from the historical "salvation events" that compose the content of the kerygma. Paul's discussion of revealed wisdom in 1 Corinthians 2:6-16, where "God's wisdom hidden in a mystery" (v. 7) has its textual antecedent and material reference in "the word of the cross" (1:18) or "Christ crucified" (1:23), suggests that the apostle would not recognize such a material disjunction between the eschatological realization of God's salvation and its historical ground in the death and resurrection of Jesus.[145] At issue is

---

142. *Ibid.*, 147-48.
143. *Ibid.*, 302.
144. *Ibid.*, 304.
145. See Chapter Five for the exegetical argument in support of this claim.

not the eschatological character of the mysteries, but the exclusion of the events attested in the kerygma from them. Put otherwise, Do not the kerygmatic events include an inherent expectation of their eschatological fulfillment? If the kerygma and prophecy are in fact unrelated forms of proclamation in early Christianity, as Dautzenberg argues, the case for this separation cannot be made by an appeal to a necessary and radical difference of content based upon knowledge of the divine mysteries.

Dautzenberg's second thesis leading to his negative conclusion is that prophecy, unlike the kerygma, was articulated in opaque oracles that required supplementary interpretation. Crucial to this argument is the claim that both *diakrisis* (12:10) and its cognate *diakrinein* (14:29) include within their semantic field the sense of "interpretation"/"explanation" and "interpret"/"explain" respectively, and designate in these texts a distinct charismatic activity that compensates for the initial mysteriousness of prophetic utterance. The implication is that the kerygma was not proclaimed, as was prophecy, in the form of "dark" oracles that required interpretation, and that this formal difference further distinguishes these two forms of proclamation. In an exhaustive study of the linguistic evidence, however, Wayne Grudem has demonstrated that the sense of the terms *diakrisis* and *diakrinein* proposed by Dautzenberg for translating 1 Corinthians 12:10 and 14:29, respectively, "would be unique and unprecedented" for Paul's time.[146] With this loss of synchronic semantic support, the thesis of an "interpretation" of the "dark" oracles of prophecy collapses. Thus prophecy and kerygma may not be separated on the formal grounds postulated by Dautzenberg; such a characterization of prophecy cannot be demonstrated from the texts cited.

---

146. Wayne Grudem, "A Response to Gerhard Dautzenberg on 1 Cor. 12:10," *BZ* 22 (1978): 253-70. "*Diakrisis* and *diakrinō* are never used in Jewish or Christian literature to refer to the interpretation or explanation of prophecies or other obscure words. When we come to seek precise and specific parallels to Dautzenberg's suggested meaning for *diakrisis* and *diakrinō* in 1 Cor. 12:10 and 14:29, we find not one example in all of Jewish and Christian literature: nowhere in more than 200 occurrences are these words used to speak of interpreting prophecies or other kinds of obscure words. Indeed, in all of Greek literature, Dautzenberg has produced no examples of *diakrisis* or *diakrinō* in this way except the one late quotation in Stobaeus. So the sense he proposes for *diakrisis* in 1 Cor. 12:10 would be unique and unprecedented for its time" (262-63).

Prospectus

Dautzenberg's failure to dissociate prophecy from the kerygma on the basis of material and formal differences, of course, does not establish by default a substantive connection between these two types of early Christian proclamation. It does, however, elicit a further investigation into the intrinsic relation between prophecy and the kerygma, a relation firmly established by virtue of their common subject matter. It is the nature of this relationship that is pursued in the present study. The thesis argued in the following chapters is that, according to the apostle Paul, the early Christian prophets were interpreting theologically the inherent implications of the kerygma when they were prophesying. We will seek to recover on alternative grounds, therefore, the intuitive insight of Käsemann that the prophets were the hermeneuts of the gospel and as such the first theologians of the church.

CHAPTER ONE

Prophecy and Gospel:

1 Thessalonians 5:20 and Romans 12:6

THE quest here undertaken for an answer to the question of what the early Christian prophets were doing when they were prophesying focuses primarily upon the conflict over prophecy reflected in canonical 1 Corinthians. Paul explicitly addressed the controversy in chapters 12–14. This passage, as Boring points out, provides the only "extensive discussion" of Christian prophecy in either canonical or noncanonical church literature dating from the first and second centuries and thus represents an invaluable source of information on the topic.[1] But the dispute is evident also in (1) the flap over the decorum of the prophets (male and female) in the community's worship (11:2-16), (2) the debate over authentic words of wisdom (1:18–3:20), and, as will be argued, (3) the sharp disagreement over the eschatological implications of the kerygma (15:1-58).

Full consideration of these Corinthian texts, accordingly, requires sensitivity to the fact that they reflect two views of prophecy: one advocated by the apostle Paul and the other by (at least some of) the Corinthians.[2] Such sensitivity, however, does not deprive them of their evidential value, for controversy often sharpens rather than blurs crucial issues. This study seeks to describe rather than resolve the differences between Paul and his opponents in Corinth on the subject of prophetic

---

1. Boring, *Continuing Voice of Jesus*, 59.
2. Although provocative as well as suggestive at many points, the attempt by Wire, *Corinthian Women Prophets*, to identify this alternative view of early Christian prophecy primarily with the female prophets in Corinth is excessively gender specific.

utterance. No attempt will be made, therefore, to determine the normativity of one view over the other.[3] Such a judgment depends, even as it did in the church at Corinth, upon a theological evaluation of the apostle's arguments as expressions of his claim to authority in matters of faith and practice.[4] Nor will the results be universalized in order to characterize early Christian prophecy in all of its complexity and diversity. As noted in the Introduction, it is methodologically improper to extrapolate uncritically the general features of Christian prophets and their prophesying from a single source.

The aim of this inquiry is thus relatively modest. On the basis of an ecclesial case study from the early fifties of the first century, it seeks to discern how prophecy was conceived and advocated by one apostle in conflict with the contrary views and practices championed by members of a congregation he founded. As a window into this dispute, 1 Corinthians not only positions itself with 1 Thessalonians as one of the two earliest extant witnesses to the phenomenon of early Christian prophecy; it also provides — through the magnitude of its relevant material — the most promising point of departure for an investigation of the nature and purpose of prophecy in primitive Christianity.

The historical particularity of this Corinthian controversy, however, does not disqualify the evidence from enjoying a significance that transcends the situation out of which it arose. For if it is unwarranted to universalize the features of context-specific data, it is equally unjustified to seal off hermetically the evidential value of such information from the larger world of its occurrence. Qualified generalizations may be drawn if they are established critically. The understanding of proph-

---

3. Aune, *Prophecy in Early Christianity*, 10, faults Hill, *New Testament Prophecy*, for making this methodological mistake: "He has not decided if he is presenting a history of early Christian prophetism or a theological normative study in which the NT evidence is regarded prescriptively."

4. Wire, *Corinthian Women Prophets*, 10-11, evidences the contemporary importance of this issue when she writes: "Two appropriate standards for determining a text's authority are the way it claims authority and the authority it actively exercises with the receptive reader." Her own preference is for the latter standard: "Paul's letters' authority depends on free assent to Paul's arguments because they are convincing." Because authority is located "in the event where the persuasive word meets conviction," it is possible that "the Corinthian women prophets may convince us at a point where Paul does not...." Given the similarity between Wire's reconstruction of the basic theological motifs of the women prophets in Corinth and the feminist agenda, it is not surprising that she is convinced by the echoes of their voices on most points vis-à-vis the apostle.

ecy that Paul articulates in 1 Corinthians, for example, represents in all probability his general view of the matter. Had he been asked about prophecy by the church in Thessalonica or Philippi or Ephesus — as he was by the church in Corinth (1 Cor. 12:1) — it is likely that his response, though tailored to the contingent situation that occasioned the question, would have reflected the same basic understanding of the phenomenon that he held for the Corinthians. What then emerges from the apostle's ad hoc treatment of the subject in 1 Corinthians is his view of the intrinsic nature and purpose of Christian prophecy that informs this contextualized discussion. Moreover, the question must be asked whether Paul's version of Christian prophecy was uniquely his own or typical of the views and practices of other apostolic figures and churches outside the Pauline mission field. His concluding appeal to the "practice" recognized by "the churches of God" in his effort to resolve the issue of prophetic decorum at Corinth (1 Cor. 11:16) certainly suggests the possibility of Paul's reliance upon pre-Pauline traditions for his understanding of prophetic utterance.[5]

Likewise, the views of the prophets in Corinth reflected in this correspondence may typify attitudes and practices of believers in other congregations — who also came to faith out of the religious milieu of the Greco-Roman world with all of its distinctive assumptions about the nature of prophecy.[6] To the extent that the Corinthian understanding of this phenomenon was culturally determined, it would not be *sui generis*. Rather the controversy in Corinth would be paradigmatic of the potential conflict over the prophetic word in any church that shared views of prophecy indigenous to the Greco-Roman religious world. While the testimony of 1 Corinthians thus reflects a dispute local and particular, the Corinthian views of prophecy may typify understandings that transcend the Corinthian situation. The issue of the scope of the views on early Christian prophecy represented in 1 Corinthians thus merits serious consideration.

5. Gerhard Dautzenberg, "Botschaft und Bedeutung der urchristlichen Prophetie nach dem ersten Korintherbrief (2:6-16; 12–14)," *Prophetic Vocation*, 132, infers from 1 Cor. 11:2-16 that Paul is not particularly original in his view of prophecy but stands in a broad primitive Christian tradition which can be traced to its origins in Jewish Christianity of Palestinian province. For a fuller treatment of the implications of this text, see also his *Urchristliche Prophetie*, 265-70.

6. For an admirable survey of these views, see Aune, *Prophecy in Early Christianity*, 23-79.

Although controversial in Corinth, prophecy was by no means peculiar to that congregation — as the evidence from the apostle's other correspondence makes clear.[7] Twice Paul encourages the exercise of prophecy in the assembled community: once in a letter to a congregation he founded (1 Thess. 5:20), and again in correspondence to a church unknown to him personally (Rom. 12:6). Significantly, each of these texts also mandates the testing of prophetic utterance on material grounds in order to establish its authenticity. Because 1 Thessalonians pre-dates and Romans post-dates 1 Corinthians, these two references bracket the Corinthian conflict over prophecy chronologically, and thus contextualize it historically. Together the references shed light upon the issues entailed in that controversy which merit prior attention.

Despise Not Prophesyings: 1 Thessalonians 5:20

The exhortation to the Thessalonians, "Do not despise prophesyings" (1 Thess. 5:20), occurs in the context of a paraenetic passage of the letter (5:12-22). Traugott Holtz notes that the "different style" encountered at verse 16 and continuing through verse 22, coupled with a thematic concentration upon the spiritual side of community life, indicates that 5:16-22 must be viewed as a unity in spite of "a certain caesura" between verses 18a and 19.[8] This theme of the Spirit's activity in the community is explicitly stated in 5:19-22, a subsection that expresses its coherence through the logic of its structure. If the quintet of imperatives in this text suggests a fivefold partition stylistically, the flow of the argument requires a threefold division united by the theme of "the manifestation of the Spirit."[9] Structured in this fashion, the text reads:

> Quench not the Spirit;
> do not despise prophesyings, but test everything;
> hold fast to the good, abstain from every form of evil.[10]

---

7. For methodological purposes, the genuine Pauline corpus is limited here to the seven undisputed letters (Romans, 1 and 2 Corinthians, Galatians, Philippians, 1 Thessalonians, and Philemon).
8. Traugott Holtz, *Der erste Brief an die Thessalonicher* (1986), 240.
9. *Ibid.*, 258.
10. I. Howard Marshall, *1 and 2 Thessalonians* (1983), 156, assesses the inherent

According to this analysis, the first exhortation (v. 19) refers to the Spirit *(to pneuma)* as the agent of divine actions that Paul terms *charismata* in 1 Corinthians 12:4-11. This identification is assured by the second exhortation (v. 20), which specifies the particular activity of the Spirit in view as prophetic utterances *(prophēteia)*.[11] Syntactically, as Ernst von Dobschütz explains, these two verses may be understood either as synonyms (in which case the Spirit represents prophetic activity and "despise not" interprets the metaphorical "quench not") or as coordinates (in which case the Spirit designates the genus and prophesyings the species).[12] Both construals, however, make the point that the Spirit and prophetic utterances are intrinsically related. The third injunction (v. 21a) is conjoined to the second by *de* (but) in its adversative sense. As the only conjunction in 5:19-22, *de* strongly emphasizes the connection between these two mandates.[13] This exhortation to "test the genuineness" *(dokimazein)*[14] of "all things" *(panta)* thus refers specifically to prophetic utterances and not generally to all manifestations of the Spirit — the antecedent of *panta* being *prophēteia* (v. 20) rather than *to pneuma* (v. 19).[15] The concluding two sentences, according to Holtz, "unfold the results of testing."[16] Thus

---

structure of the text similarly: "There are five statements in the imperative. The first two (vv. 19, 20) stand in parallelism with each other; the third (v. 21a) is in effect a repetition of the second, but expressed positively; the fourth and fifth (vv. 21b, 22) fill out the content of the third."

11. Charles A. Wanamaker, *Commentary on 1 & 2 Thessalonians* (1990), 202, notes that this noun "may refer either specifically to the gift of prophecy or to the utterances of a person prophesying. The accusative plural form of the noun here and the lack of an article favor the latter."

12. Ernst von Dobschütz, *Die Thessalonicher-Briefe* (1974), 225. Cf. Bartholomäus Henneken, *Verkündigung und Prophetie im 1. Thessalonicherbrief* (1969), 109, who views the sequence Spirit–prophesyings as a transition from the general to the particular which represents a constructive or a synthetic parallelism.

13. Holtz, *Der erste Brief an die Thessalonicher*, 261.

14. Leon Morris, *The First and Second Epistles to the Thessalonians* (1959), 178, notes: "The verb 'prove' is often connected with the testing of metals, and it is not unlikely that this is the basic meaning of the verb."

15. Ernest Best, *A Commentary on the First and Second Epistles to the Thessalonians* (1977), 240, thinks that *panta* refers to "*all* charismata, not prophecy alone." This ignores, however, the close connection between vv. 20 and 21a established by the conjunction *de*.

16. Holtz, *Der erste Brief an die Thessalonicher*, 261. Cf. Marshall, *1 and 2 Thessalonians*, 157: "In analysing the structure in this way we are assuming that the reference throughout the section is the same subject, the gifts of the Spirit, and rejecting the view that the last two commands are more general and ethical in content."

the Thessalonians are enjoined to "hold fast to the good" and to "abstain from every form of evil," the two injunctions being related through paronomasia (*katechete/apechesthe:* "hold fast"/ "abstain from"). While these commands may have a general sense and a universal applicability, in this context they refer to the results of testing prophetic utterances.[17] The "good" *(kalon)* is that which is in accordance with the will of God. Conversely, "every form of evil" is that which is contrary to the will of God as discerned by the testing of prophecy.[18] As Holtz concludes: "There are only two possibilities: either the word of prophecy is 'good' and thus has binding power; or it is 'evil' and must be refused by the community."[19]

With evident caution, Aune derives three salient points from this text: "In spite of the brevity of these statements, several tentative conclusions regarding Christian prophecy may be drawn from them: (1) the Holy Spirit and prophesying have an intimate, cause-and-effect relationship, (2) prophesying was a normal congregational activity, and (3) prophesying had, for whatever reason, become a factor in intramural conflict."[20] As a provisional summary, this is an adequate assessment. Further observations regarding the probable tradition character of 1 Thessalonians 5:16-22, however, will not only permit but require greater specificity.

---

17. Dobschütz, *Die Thessalonicher-Briefe*, 225, arguing that the five members of 1 Thess. 5:19-22 "belong strictly together and treat all of the working of the Spirit," contends that it is not permissible to separate the last or the last two commands from the preceding ones and understand them as referring to good and evil in a general moral sense, unless one also does that with the third. Marshall, *1 and 2 Thessalonians*, 159, observes that in its present context "a sudden transition to a general ethical principle is improbable" in 1 Thess. 5:22. "But the generality of the language may suggest that a broader principle has been applied to a more specific area, namely prophecy."

18. With reference to 1 Thess. 5:22, F. F. Bruce, *1 & 2 Thessalonians* (1982), 126, comments: "The present injunction could also refer to prophetic utterances; indeed, it is possible to treat *ponērou* as attributive to *eidous* (rather than a genitive dependent upon it) and translate 'abstain from every evil kind [of utterance].' An utterance which is 'evil' would be one running contrary to gospel faith and practice; such an utterance is to be rejected."

19. Holtz, *Der erste Brief an die Thessalonicher*, 262.

20. Aune, *Prophecy in Early Christianity*, 191.

The Text as Paraenetic Tradition

The testimony to early Christian prophecy provided by 1 Thessalonians 5:19-22 very likely represents views and practices that pre-date the letter. The text occurs in the larger context of a paraenetic passage (5:12-22) which, because of its formal characteristics, has been identified as a piece of early church tradition cited by the apostle. With regard to verses 14-22, F. F. Bruce comments:

> The outstanding feature of this subsection is the triple series of short cola (each colon comprising a verb in the imperative with an object or an adverbial amplification). Colon 1 (v 14) consists of four pastoral injunctions; colon 2 (vv 16-18a) of three directions for manifesting the will of God in one's spiritual life; colon 3 (vv 19-22) of five exhortations relating to the prophetic ministry.[21]

This combination of formal and material characteristics suggests to Bruce the possibility that "instruction was given in this form to serve as an easily memorized catechesis."[22]

Ernest Best sees "an obvious parallel" to 1 Thessalonians 5:12-22 in Romans 12:9-13, a passage in which "we have the same succession of brief sentences but with the difference that they are constructed around participles and not imperatives."[23] Best argues, depending upon David Daube,[24] that this stylistic variation represents the Semitic convention, common in the New Testament, of using the participle for the imperative. From this he infers that "behind Rom. 12:9-13 lies material originating in a Semitic environment, presumably the Palestinian Jewish community." Also noting that Romans 12:14-21 features the same type of material as in 12:9-13 but without the use of imperatival participles, Best endorses C. H. Talbert's suggestion[25] that here tradition, originally similar in form to 12:9-13, "has been heavily edited in a Hellenistic Christian context to produce vv. 14-21," and posits that "the same has probably taken place in respect of the material

---

21. Bruce, *1 & 2 Thessalonians*, 122.
22. Ibid.
23. Best, *The First and Second Epistles to the Thessalonians*, 241-42.
24. David Daube, "Participle and Imperative in 1 Peter," in E. G. Selwyn, *The First Epistle of St. Peter* (1952), 467-88 (esp. 480f.).
25. Charles H. Talbert, "Tradition and Redaction in Rom. xii. 9-21," *NTS* 16 (1969/70): 83-93.

in 1 Th. 5:12-22." To these formal similarities he adds "the striking parallels in content between Rom. 12:9ff and 1 Th. 5:12ff; 1 Th. 5:13b and Rom. 12:18; 1 Th. 5:15 and Rom. 12:17a; 1 Th. 5:16 and Rom. 12:12a; 1 Th. 5:17 and Rom. 12:12c; 1 Th. 5:19 and Rom. 12:11b; 1 Th. 5:21b-22 and Rom. 12:9b."[26] From this analysis of form and content, Best concludes "that in 1 Th. 5:12ff Paul has used traditional material, probably of Jewish-Christian origin."[27]

An Early Church Order?

The discussion of the use of tradition in 1 Thessalonians 5:12-22 becomes even more interesting for this study when it moves to the question of genre identification. Noting that 1 Thessalonians 5:16-22 is structured uniformly by the location of the verb at the end of each line, preceded by an adverbial definition of the subject, James M. Robinson suggests that this passage as a subsection of the cited tradition represents an embryonic *church order*.[28] When these formal features of the Greek text are observed in English translation, the passage (as structured by Robinson) reads:

> Always rejoice;
> constantly pray;
> in everything give thanks;
> (for this is the will of God in Christ Jesus for you.)[29]
> the Spirit do not quench;

---

26. See also Wanamaker, *Commentary on 1 & 2 Thessalonians*, 191, for a similar list of material parallels between the two passages.
27. Best, *A Commentary on the First and Second Epistles to the Thessalonians*, 241-42. For an analysis of Paul's use of tradition throughout the letter, see Traugott Holtz, "Traditionen im 1 Thessalonicherbrief," in Ulrich Luz und Hans Weder, eds., *Die Mitte des Neuen Testaments* (1983), 55-78. Holtz does not include 5:12-22 among the texts suspected of employing traditional material, but this is attributable to his initial caveat that the essay treats "only a few sections" in the interest of a closer examination of those cited (55). It is significant, however, that he attributes the apocalyptic tradition in 4:13-18 and its sequel in 5:1-11 to a Semitic groundwork ("eine semitische Grundlage"; 67).
28. James M. Robinson, "Die Hodajot-Formel in Gebet und Hymnus des Frühchristentums," in Walther Eltester, ed., *Apophoreta* (1964), 222-24.
29. Robinson, *ibid.*, 222 n. 56, designates the parenthetical clause that interrupts the otherwise uniformly composed list "a Pauline commentary."

prophesying do not despise;
but everything test, the good hold fast;
from every form of evil abstain.

In addition to the parallel form of these seven exhortations, Robinson notes that the second and third offer the same combination of prayer and thanksgiving that provides the clamps of Paul's treatment of glossolalia in 1 Corinthians 14:13-17. That discussion is then connected by Robinson with prophecy in 1 Corinthians 14:27-32, which is also encountered in the fifth exhortation of 1 Thessalonians 5:16-22. Prophecy for its part is bound in the sixth exhortation with criticism, as it is in 1 Corinthians 14:29. Between the paired concepts of prayer/thanksgiving and prophecy/testing stands the fourth exhortation not to quench the Spirit. Robinson sees a parallel to this in *Didache* X, 7: "Allow the prophets to give thanks as they will," and notes that this injunction likewise stands between passages dealing with prayer (*Did.* IX-X) and the testing of prophecy (*Did.* XIff.). Further, the verb *chairein* (rejoice) in the first exhortation, which Robinson associates with the hymnic praise characteristic of both sectarian Judaism and early Christianity,[30] stands in strict relation to *eucharistein* (give thanks) in the third, even as the two activities are bonded in Philippians 1:3-4 and 4:4-6. The concluding exhortation to "abstain from every form of evil" has as its primary reference such abuses of charismatic activity as are proscribed in the *Didache:* overstaying one's welcome as a peripatetic prophet (XI, 5 and XII, 3); ordering a meal under the guise of inspiration (XI, 9); and asking for money "in a spirit" (XI, 6, 12). Robinson concludes that "1 Th. 5:16-22 appears in fact to be a preliminary stage of later church orders. . . ."[31]

A Liturgical Order?

More recently, Ralph P. Martin has modified Robinson's proposal by identifying 1 Thessalonians 5:16-22 as a list of "headings" of a church

---

30. See *ibid.*, 194-201 for the discussion of the Hodayot formula that Robinson believes characterized both sectarian Jewish and early Christian praise.
31. *Ibid.*, 223.

service that begins with the note of glad adoration and concludes with an admonition to let nothing unseemly enter the assembly.[32] To the formal characteristics of the passage noted by Robinson, Martin adds "the predominance of words beginning with the Greek letter 'p', thus giving it a rhythm." He notes with Robinson the parallels to this passage in the apostolic counsels on the subject of congregational worship in 1 Corinthians 14:

> The custom of praise and 'hymning' is mentioned (verses 14, 15), and both practices are inspired by the Spirit (as we are to infer from 1 Thessalonians v. 19). Prayer and thanksgiving are found in that order (verses 13-18) and prophecy and the testing of utterances (verses 27ff.) are also linked, as in the Letter to the Thessalonians. It is true that the injunction 'Quench not the Spirit' is not alluded to, but this omission may be explained by the fact at Corinth there was not the danger that the Spirit's more spectacular gifts in worship were being neglected — quite the reverse!

Martin infers from these texts "that the Church is moving out of a situation in which the pattern of worship is pliant and free, under the direct afflatus of the Holy Spirit and with each believer making a contribution as seems good to him (with all the attendant perils which surround such a liberty) into an area of experience that comes with organization and development, and where the worship (though no less Spirit-inspired and real) will be offered according to recognized 'canons.'"[33] Similarly, Wayne A. Meeks argues that in the "verbal formulas" of 1 Thessalonians 5:12-27 we discover "a very free, charismatic order, but an order nonetheless: there are customary forms."[34] If such is in fact the case,[35] then prophesying is rooted in *a liturgical tradition* that pre-dates 1 Thessalonians. This tradition represents not only the ordering of worship advocated by Paul among his churches but, if Best's conjecture is valid, observed by earlier Jewish Christian congregations as well. The import of these observations is that the view of early Christian prophecy presented here is not unique to the apostle Paul.

---

32. Ralph P. Martin, *Worship in the New Testament* (1964), 135-36.
33. *Ibid.*, 137.
34. Wayne A. Meeks, *The First Urban Christians* (1983), 150.
35. Martin's thesis is considered worthy of consideration by Bruce, *1 & 2 Corinthians*, 122, and cited with approval by Hill, *New Testament Prophecy*, 119-20.

Paul's Use of the Tradition

While there is significant support among commentators for the thesis *that* Paul used tradition in composing 1 Thessalonians 5:12-22, the thesis is qualified by estimates of *how* he used it. The issue is whether this text expresses only the generalities of traditional paraenesis, thus allowing no inferences pertaining to the actual situation in Thessalonica, or whether the tradition cited by the apostle has been tailored to conditions existing in the church, thus illuminating the ecclesial environment of those to whom Paul directs his counsel.[36] Holtz observes that the exhortations in 1 Thessalonians 5:12-14 clearly have a concrete community situation in view — a factor that enhances the possibility that the same relation of tradition to situation may also characterize 5:16-22 without that excluding the general validity of the exhortations. Because the Thessalonian church, as Holtz puts it, belonged to the comprehensive circle of Christian congregations and participated in their weaknesses and strengths, such a particular application of the tradition is appropriate. Thus even when applied to a specific situation, such exhortations remain part of the paraclesis that is valid generally among Christians.[37] At the same time, however, the *way* the tradition is cited here illumines the situation addressed.

A clue to the possible alteration of the tradition cited in 1 Thessalonians 5:16-22 (functionally intended to sharpen its applicability to the Thessalonian situation) is suggested by the negative formulation of the two injunctions in verses 19 and 20. Prohibition is not uncommon in paraenesis, of course, as the parallel material in Romans 12 demonstrates

---

36. The ambiguity of the issue is attested by the following observations. Marshall, *1 and 2 Thessalonians*, 146, acknowledges "a common basis in tradition" between 1 Thess. 5:12-24 and Rom. 12, but insists that "Paul handles it quite freely," adding, "it is arguable that he shaped the teaching to suit the needs of each individual community. This is particularly obvious in vv. 12-13a, 14, 19, 20, 21a, where the parallels with Romans are weakest." Wanamaker, *Commentary on 1 & 2 Thessalonians*, 191, however, is ambivalent. While he agrees with Marshall that "Paul has shaped this material in light of his knowledge of the situation at Thessalonica," the tidal pull of tradition away from the specific to the general compels him to observe: "On the whole the information in 5:12-22 has greater value for determining general characteristics of community life and personal relations within the Pauline mission than the specific situation prevailing at Thessalonica."

37. Holtz, *Der erste Brief an die Thessalonicher*, 241.

(vv. 11, 14, 16, 19, 21). Yet verses 19 and 20 in tandem, the only exceptions to the otherwise positively stated exhortations in this paraenetic section, call attention to themselves in a way inviting explanation for their location in a tradition that probably represents either a church order (Robinson) or a liturgical order (Martin). In either case, positive rubrics would seem more appropriate. Both mandates may be formulated positively, and indeed are so expressed elsewhere in Paul's correspondence. Holtz calls attention to the positive formulation of verse 19 ("Quench not the Spirit") in Romans 12:11b ("Be aglow with the Spirit").[38] Heinz Schürmann suggests that verses 19 and 20 together have their affirmative counterpart in 1 Corinthians 14:1 ("Earnestly desire the spiritual gifts, especially that you may prophesy").[39] Given the greater suitability of positively stated rubrics in a tradition intended to order the communal or liturgical life of churches, a plausible explanation of the apostle's shift to negative formulations in the text is that the Thessalonian church *required* such specific prohibitions. The Spirit was in fact being "quenched" in the worship of the community, and this precisely because prophetic utterances were being "despised."[40] What Paul is challenging here is thus the conscious suppression of the Spirit that effects prophecy.[41]

The Ecclesial Setting of the Text

The Thessalonian resistance to the Spirit's manifestation in prophetic speech is customarily explained by commentators as a reaction to the excesses of an element in the congregation given to *Spirit-enthusiasm*.[42]

---

38. *Ibid.*, 260.
39. Heinz Schürmann, *The First Epistle to the Thessalonians* (1969), 75.
40. With reference to v. 19, Bruce, *1 & 2 Thessalonians*, 125, comments: "As the context goes on to make plain, the activity chiefly in view here is prophecy. In this respect the Spirit may be quenched when the prophet refuses to utter the message he has been given, or when others try to prevent him from uttering it." Morris, *The First and Second Epistles to the Thessalonians*, 176 n. 53, notes that in v. 20, "The verb, *exoutheneo*, is a strong one, with the meaning 'to make absolutely nothing of.'"
41. S. Dobschütz, *Die Thessalonicher-Briefe*, 226.
42. Much confusion in the discussion of this broad phenomenon of human preternatural experiences in the ancient world is caused by the loose use of such terms as "enthusiasm" *(enthysiasmos)*, "ecstasy" *(ekstasis)*, "possession" *(entheos)*, and "inspiration" *(en pneumati)*. The extensive survey of the relevant texts from the Greco-Roman

Neil posits that "some of the more critical members were inclined to frown on any kind of supernatural manifestation," particularly "speaking in tongues."[43] Apart from reflecting attitudes more typical of a "mainline" Protestant congregation than a first-century Hellenistic church, Neil's assessment must be faulted on two textual grounds: (1) it assumes without warrant that "the Spirit" *(to pneuma)* in verse 19 refers to glossolalia;[44] and (2) it fails to explain why a reaction to speaking in tongues would entail a rejection of prophesyings. Best attributes the scorn of prophetic utterance in Thessalonica to the ecstatic character of prophecy itself, which "might too easily both become uncouth and appear too similar to pagan practices."[45] Here again modern sensitivities are imposed upon ancient believers. But even more damaging is Best's failure to establish the assumption that early Christian prophecy was manifested in ecstasy, particularly of the kind associated with "pagan practices." Further, even if it could be demonstrated that prophetic utterance was an ecstatic phenomenon familiar to the Thessalonians from their religious environment, Best does not explain why it would have been deemed "uncouth" by at least a significant number in that community.[46]

Equally problematic is Walter Schmithals's argument — based on

---

world by Aune, *Prophecy in Early Christianity*, 23-79, is the exception. The common denominator of these words, he argues, is "an altered state of consciousness" that connotes the "irrational," in distinction from "a normal state of mind" *(ennous)*, and evidences itself typically by "frenzied, hysterical behavior" (33). Gordon D. Fee, *First Corinthians* (1987), 575 n. 25, agrees with Aune's definition of "ecstasy" (and its synonyms) as "a trance of some kind," but rightly distinguishes that kind of experience from "other kinds of spiritually inspired activity or speech." Thus it is both possible and necessary to speak of "inspiration" and "inspired utterance" in a sense other than that required by the technical terms "enthusiasm," "possession," and "ecstasy."

43. William Neil, *The Epistles of Paul to the Thessalonians* (1950), 130.

44. Thus Dobschütz, *Die Thessalonicher-Briefe*, 225. Holtz, *Die erste Brief an die Thessalonicher*, 259, rightly objects to this tendency to distinguish between "Spirit" and "prophecy" on the basis of 1 Cor. 14 and thus to identify the former with the phenomenon of "tongues."

45. Best, *A Commentary on the First and Second Epistles to the Thessalonians*, 239.

46. Commenting on v. 20, Best, *ibid.*, 239, writes: "Scorn of ecstasy would have appeared easily in Jewish-Christian circles and if, as we have suspected, the material goes back to Jewish Christianity this then is probably its meaning." In addition to the questionableness of this assessment of attitudes among Jewish Christians toward ecstasy, this statement does not explain how such an attitude could have been operative in a predominantly Hellenistic church such as that at Thessalonica.

his well-known thesis that incipient Gnosticism is Paul's nemesis in the majority of his genuine correspondence — that 1 Thessalonians 5:19-22 represents the apostle's polemic against "an exaggerated reaction" to the excesses of "Gnostic pneumatics" that "have brought members of the community into their defensive position against any spiritual gifts at all."[47] The question of a Gnostic presence in the church at Thessalonica aside, the basic deficiency of this proposal, as Wanamaker points out, is that in 1 Thessalonians "the evidence is totally lacking to prove that a pneumatic problem of any sort was a serious factor."[48] Wanamaker's is a valid assessment of the textual data, however, only if it implies a lack of evidence for a pneumatic issue involving excesses of *ecstatic behavior*. For the quenching of the Spirit by the despising of prophetic speech was evidently a negative practice requiring correction. But if the cause of the reaction against prophecy cannot be identified with behavioral demonstrations of Spirit-inspired ecstasy, then the logical alternative is that the reaction was occasioned by the *content* of the prophetic messages delivered in Thessalonica. The ecclesial setting that would account for this possibility is portrayed by Robert Jewett in his monograph, *The Thessalonian Correspondence*.

Jewett argues persuasively that the situation addressed by Paul in both 1 and 2 Thessalonians is best understood as an instance of millenarian piety. Characterized by an intense apocalyptic expectation of imminent salvation that encouraged the proleptic celebration of the coming freedom by experiences of ecstasy,[49] such piety was vulnerable to a radical interpretation oriented toward realized eschatology. The actual exploitation of this vulnerability, according to Jewett, led some in the congregation to resist "on principle the structures of everyday life including the work ethic, the sexual ethic, and the authority of congregational leadership." As he explains, "They refused to prepare for a future *parousia* of Christ because in principle they were experiencing and embodying it in their ecstatic activities."[50]

In this context Jewett interprets 1 Thessalonians 5:19-22.[51] On his reading of the text, it "confirms the presence of *conflicts over ecstatic*

---

47. Walter Schmithals, *Paul and the Gnostics* (1972), 174.
48. Wanamaker, *Commentary on 1 & 2 Thessalonians*, 201.
49. Robert Jewett, *The Thessalonian Correspondence* (1986), 174.
50. *Ibid.*, 176.
51. *Ibid.*, 101-2 (emphasis added in the ensuing quotations).

manifestations in the congregation." Paul's urging of its leaders not to "quench the Spirit" or "despise prophesying," on the one hand, "indicates there were tendencies to stamp out such *ecstatic expressions* entirely." His insistence that "all things" be tested "according to the *moral standards* of good and evil," on the other hand, "indicates there were some who felt these *ecstatic manifestations* were beyond evaluation." As with the previously discussed proposals, Jewett emphasizes the behavioral evidence of Spirit-inspired ecstasy without any support from the text. This lack of textual support undoubtedly accounts for his equally unwarranted limitation of the testing mandated by the apostle to activity approached through "the moral standards of good and evil." The testing of "all things" (v. 21), as noted above, refers to "prophesyings" (v. 20), a term that may or may not imply ecstatic states in the expression of prophetic utterances — though it clearly entails those utterances' material content.[52]

Jewett is compelled to deal with the issue of substance in prophetic speech, however, when he discusses the sense and significance of 2 Thessalonians 2:2, a text he deems genuinely Pauline.[53] He correctly perceives that the declaration, "The Day of the Lord has come" (direct address introduced by *hōs hoti*), has as its primary source an inspired utterance ("through a spirit") representing a "prophetic oracle"[54] or an "ecstatic message."[55] "There is a much clearer indication of ecstatic conflicts in 2 Thess 2:2," he observes, "showing that by the time of writing the second letter Paul had become concerned over the *kind* of ecstatic prophecies that could proclaim the end of time had already arrived."[56] It is necessary to distinguish, however, between the time *the apostle became concerned* about such a prophetic word and the chronological point at which prophecies of this "kind" *became problematical in the Thessalonian church*. Ascribing this oracle to the period between the composition of 1 and 2 Thessalonians, Jewett views it as evidence of the "deepening radicalism" in the congregation: "What had hitherto been

---

52. Holtz, *Der erste Brief an die Thessalonicher*, 259-60, aptly remarks, "Apparently Paul did not see the danger that the gift of prophecy in itself was despised, but rather that the prophetic *word* was despised and so received no value" (emphasis added).
53. See Jewett, *The Thessalonian Correspondence*, 3-60, for a discussion of this issue and the strong case made for Pauline authorship of 2 Thessalonians.
54. *Ibid.*, 176.
55. *Ibid.*, 177.
56. *Ibid.*, 101 (emphasis added).

merely implicit in the activities of the radicals was now stated in final form: the millennium has come."[57] In other words, the millenarian piety of the Thessalonians, according to Jewett, evoked at last the prophetic word that baldly confirmed its intrinsic inclination toward realized eschatology. But a more likely interpretation, given the conflict over prophetic utterances already attested to in 1 Thessalonians 5:19-20, is that the millenarian piety of the Thessalonian church had its origins in just this ilk of eschatological prophecy.

There is, then, a total lack of textual evidence that the pointed prohibitions in 1 Thessalonians 5:19 and 20 were necessitated by ecstatic manifestations of the Spirit. Moreover, 5:19-22 focuses on the testing of the content of Spirit-inspired speech. These two points, taken together, generate the inference that in Thessalonica the quenching of the Spirit by the despising of prophetic speech was occasioned by the content of prophetic utterances that authorized confidence in the presence of the millennium and encouraged the freedom from the structures of everyday life that characterized the church's piety. At issue in this conflict was nothing less than the validity of the content of the "prophesyings" in Thessalonica.

Summary: 1 Thessalonians 5:20

In the light of this discussion of 1 Thessalonians 5:19-22 as cited tradition and the application of that tradition to the Thessalonian situation, Aune's three tentative conclusions regarding the information this text provides on early Christian prophecy may be confirmed and expanded. The first, his inference that the Holy Spirit and prophesying have "an intimate, cause-and-effect relationship," distinguishes early Christian prophecy from its counterpart in the Greco-Roman religious world and locates it in the tradition of classical Israelite and early Jewish prophetism. "Unlike early Christianity and early Judaism, where *pneuma* is primarily a theological concept and a central means for explaining the phenomenon of divine inspiration," Aune observes, "among Greco-Roman authors the term has no theological significance and is marginal for their understanding of divine inspiration."[58] That Christian proph-

---

57. Ibid., 177.
58. Aune, *Prophecy in Early Christianity*, 34.

ecy is grounded in the Spirit's activity is thus an important characteristic of the phenomenon. Further, the prohibition against quenching the Spirit in verse 19 also attests to the conviction that the Spirit does not operate in the community as an irresistible force, but rather is susceptible to human resistance. The undergirding assumption beneath "Quench not the Spirit" is that the activity of the Spirit may in fact be, metaphorically speaking, extinguished like the flame of a fire.[59] This assumption is evident also in the liturgical rubrics Paul enjoins upon the Corinthian prophets (1 Cor. 14:29-33), particularly in the principle that "the spirits of prophets are subject to prophets" (v. 32).

Aune's second conclusion, that "prophesying was a normal congregational activity," dates the prophetic phenomenon as early as the composition of 1 Thessalonians, considered the first of Paul's preserved correspondence and the oldest of the New Testament documents.[60] Holtz infers from 1 Thessalonians that "the phenomenon of prophecy had been given to the community at its founding";[61] but this is chronologically insignificant in view of the historical probability that the founding of the Thessalonian community occurred only six to eight months prior to the composition of 1 Thessalonians.[62] What is significant, however, is the strong possibility that the tradition cited here by the apostle reflects "the normal congregational activity" of Jewish-Christian churches that pre-dates the Pauline mission. If so, then 1 Thessalonians reflects a community practice of prophecy characteristic of early Christianity itself.

The third conclusion drawn by Aune establishes not only that prophesying was "a factor in intramural conflict" in the church at Thessalonica, even as it was later in Corinth, but also that Christian prophecy was intrinsically problematic. This is not to argue that the conflict over

---

59. Morris, *The First and Second Epistles to the Thessalonians*, 175, notes that the verb "quench" denotes literally the putting out of the flame of a fire (Mark 9:48) or a lamp (Matt. 25:8), and is used metaphorically in the New Testament only here.

60. Helmut Koester, *Introduction to the New Testament* (1982), II, 112, voices the consensus of scholarship in stating that "the letter must have been written from Corinth, probably still in the year 50 CE. It is therefore the oldest preserved Pauline letter and as such the oldest writing of the New Testament."

61. Holtz, *Der erste Brief an die Thessalonicher*, 260.

62. Gerd Lüdemann, *Paul, Apostle to the Gentiles* (1984), 201-38, dates the founding of the church in Thessalonica in A.D. 40, but the basis of this hypothesis has been convincingly criticized by Robert Jewett, *A Chronology of Paul's Life* (1979), 82f.

prophecy was in every case, such as at Thessalonica and at Corinth, uniformly occasioned. The point is that the cited tradition regarding prophecy makes it evident that from an early period the prophetic word required and was subjected to "testing" (cf. 1 Cor. 12:10; 14:29). "The gift of prophecy lent itself to imitation," F. F. Bruce observes, "and it was important that counterfeit prophets should be detected."[63] How the apostle intended this task to be executed is unclear. For, as Bruce further notes, "No criteria are suggested here for distinguishing genuine prophecy from false. . . ." Nonetheless, it is clear that the apostle shared the expectation of the tradition he cites that prophesying is subject to critical evaluation and that he assumed the church had the necessary resources to conduct such criticism. What criteria these resources afforded is specified in Romans 12:6, the other text here under consideration.

According to the Analogy of the Faith: Romans 12:6

Paul's explicit reference to early Christian prophecy in his Letter to the Romans (12:6) occurs, as in 1 Thessalonians, in its paraenesis (12:1–15:13), specifically in the first subsection (12:3-8) of the general exhortations (12:1–13:14). Here, at the head of an exemplary list of different charismatic gifts given to the church as the Body of Christ through its many members (vv. 6b-8), Paul mentions the charism of "prophecy" *(prophēteia)* and qualifies it by the enigmatic phrase "according to the analogy of the faith" *(kata tēn analogian tēs pisteōs)*. As brief as this reference to early Christian prophecy is, it indicates nonetheless that prophetic utterance is here being subjected to some kind of regulation.[64] This text, accordingly, designates how the apostle expected the testing of prophecy mandated in 1 Thessalonians 5:20f. to be carried out. Because the interpretative key to the qualifying phrase in Romans 12:6b is often found in the perceived parallel phrase "a measure of faith" *(metron pisteōs)* of verse 3, each locution must be unpacked semantically within the context of the unit as a whole.

63. Bruce, *1 & 2 Thessalonians*, 125-26.
64. This characteristic of the passage leads Ernst Käsemann, *Commentary on Romans* (1980), 332, to the conclusion that here "direction is being given in respect to church order." More emphatically, "We have the start of a first community order, a more advanced stage being offered in the Pastorals in relation to public functions in the community."

Käsemann identifies the unifying theme of Romans 12:3-8, expressed in verse 3 by a Hellenistic play on words,[65] as that sober-minded judgment *(sōphronein)* of oneself required by the immediately preceding exhortation: be "transformed by the renewal of the mind."[66] The norm of this sober-mindedness is the "measure of faith" *(metron pisteōs)* apportioned *(emerisen)* by God to each believer. Semantic ambiguity shrouds the precise meaning of this norm, however. As Cranfield formulates the puzzle, "There are three basic questions which confront us here: (i) In what sense is *metron* used? (ii) In what sense is *pistis* used? and (iii) What kind of genitive is *pisteōs?*"[67] His own analysis produces several possible answers to each question and multiple choices among their various combinations.[68] Only an abbreviated summary of the major options is presented here. The noun *metron* can denote either *(a)* a means of measurement (a norm or standard) or *(b)* a result of measuring (a portion or amount). The semantic range of *pistis* includes *(a)* faithfulness, *(b)* the human act of believing *(fides qua creditur), (c)* a special *charisma,* (d) what is believed *(fides quae creditur),* and *(e)* trust. With regard to the genitive construction, the primary grammatical candidates are *(a)* an appositive genitive (a measure, which is faith) and *(b)* a partitive genitive (a part or portion of faith itself).

Cranfield discusses and dismisses the "two most generally favoured explanations" of this exegetical conundrum.[69] The one, represented most recently by Barrett,[70] resolves the issue by reading *metron* as "a measured quantity" or "portion" of *pistis,* which is understood as charismatic "wonder working faith." The other, advocated by Schlatter,[71] also takes *metron* to mean "a measured quantity," but interprets *pistis* in terms of the basic Christian act of believing. Each of these interpretations entails a partitive genitive construction. Cranfield objects to both

---

65. Impossible to duplicate in English translation, the three terms that constitute the wordplay in v. 3 are *hyperphronein* ("to think of oneself too highly"), *phronein* ("to think"), and *sōphronein* ("to think soberly").
66. Käsemann, *Commentary on Romans,* 332.
67. C. E. B. Cranfield, *The Epistle to the Romans* (1979), II, 613.
68. For the full discussion, see C. E. B. Cranfield, "*Metron Pisteōs* in Romans XII.3," *NTS* 8 (1961-62): 345-51.
69. Cranfield, *The Epistle to the Romans,* II, 614.
70. C. K. Barrett, *The Epistle to the Romans* (1957), 235.
71. Adolf Schlatter, *Gottes Gerechtigkeit: ein Kommentar zum Römerbrief* (3rd ed. 1959), 336f.

proposals on the ground that they make the quality of one's faith dependent upon its quantity, and thereby invite the very invidious comparisons among believers that the exhortation "to think with sober judgment" intends to exclude.[72]

Cranfield's alternative proposal is to interpret *metron* as a "means of measurement" (its primary sense), *pistis* as the basic act of believing, and the genitive as appositive; he thus renders the phrase "a standard (by which to measure, estimate, himself), namely, his faith (in the sense of *fides qua*)."[73] It should be noted, however, that even when *metron* is understood as a "portion," as in the two rejected explanations, it *functions* as a "standard" or "norm" of the believer's self-assessment. The only difference is that in Cranfield's reading of the phrase this standard (faith as the act of believing) is uniform for every member of the church. Yet this effort to rescue the phrase "measure of faith" from possible abuse ignores the semantic pull of the controlling verb *merizein* (apportion) — which connotes such notions as dividing something into separate parts, distributing parts of a whole to a series of persons, giving to someone a part of something, or assigning to someone a particular part or aspect of a function or responsibility.[74]

Dunn is thus on firm ground when he insists that, following the verb *merizein*, "the phrase is more naturally taken as an apportioning of *different* measures." Further, the fact "that the *metron* is given to *each* does not imply that all have the same *metron*."[75] His own solution melds the two rejected by Cranfield by regarding *pistis* as "the human act and attitude of believing" and arguing that Paul sees this "common denominator of all Christians" as a "variable in different believers."[76] By this he means:

> Here there is no sharp distinction in fact between "saving faith" and "miracle-working faith" (as in 1 Cor. 12:9). Both indicate that mea-

---

72. Cranfield, *The Epistle to the Romans*, II, 614, aptly notes: "A congregation, the members of which were carefully calculating their relative importance according to the amount of faith (of either sort) which they possessed, would have little chance of being a happy one."
73. *Ibid.*, II, 615.
74. Johannes P. Louw and Eugene A. Nida, *Greek-English Lexicon of the New Testament Based on Semantic Domains* I (1988), pars. 63.23; 57.89; 57.90; 37.100.
75. James D. G. Dunn, *Romans 9–16* (1988), 721.
76. *Ibid.*, 722.

sure of reliance on God which enables *charis* to come to expression in *charisma*. It is the confident trust in God which recognizes that all faith and grace is from God which prevents the misjudgment of *hyperphronein*.[77]

Despite Dunn's assurances that his construal of the phrase meets Cranfield's concerns, it is difficult to see how this is so. For not only does it affirm that some believers are apportioned a greater "measure of reliance on God" than others, but also that this quantitative trust "enables" God's grace to actualize itself in and through believers.

With characteristic exegetical and theological insight, Käsemann makes the same point that Dunn scores — without the detrimental implications.[78] "The call in v. 2 for a renewed and critical reason is applied to the gifts of the Spirit in v. 3," he explains, "under the keyword *sōphronein*." The phrase "measure of faith" expresses this "with a terminology and motivation which stereotypically recur in the context of teaching on charismata," a term Käsemann understands as "the concretion and individuation of grace" (Ridderbos) or "the concretion and individuation of the Spirit" (Bultmann). Since divine distribution is "the essence of charisma" (1 Cor. 12:7), *metron* here has the sense of "a portion," and the genitive is partitive.[79] What saves Käsemann from the inherent dangers of Dunn's interpretation is the semantic value he ascribes to the term faith *(pistis)* in Pauline usage. Faith for the apostle, he contends, is the human act that receives the Spirit given to all Christians in baptism. Put simply:

> The Spirit and faith are reverse sides of the same thing, seen from the standpoint of the giver on the one hand and the recipient on the other. Faith is the pneuma given to the individual and received by him.[80]

Representing the lordship of God, the gift of the Spirit entails "earthly responsibility" in the form of "a non-interchangeable *klēsis*" (calling). It is this personalized responsibility that is denoted by the phrase "mea-

77. Ibid.
78. Käsemann, *Commentary on Romans*, 331-35.
79. Ibid., 335: "Paul is probably following the Jewish principle that God does not give the Spirit totally to anyone."
80. Ibid.

sure of faith," which thus connotes a God-assigned *(emerisen)* task. This assignment determines the "limit" beyond which the believer is not to think in his or her self-assessment *(par' ho dei phronein)*. Transgression of this limit constitutes "both abandonment of reason and disdain of the sovereignty of God who gives concretely."[81] For Käsemann, the emphasis falls not upon the quantity or quality of the human "reliance upon God" (Dunn) but upon the initiative of the Spirit in educing *saving* faith, which is qualified as *serving* faith by the specific responsibility assigned to it. In other words, the human act of believing is contoured to "the grace given to us" (v. 6). Grace for Paul is both the gift of personal salvation and the task of individual service to others in the church who also have been "apportioned" by God their customized "measure of faith."

A Fence around Pride

This line of interpretation is confirmed by the apostle's ensuing appeal to the concept "one body" *(heni sōma)* with its "many members" *(polla melē;* v. 4), and his use of this concept to depict the church metaphorically as "the many" *(hoi polloi)* who are "one body in Christ" *(hen sōma en Christō;* v. 5). This characteristic Pauline metaphor works by the analogical comparison made possible through the notion of an organism — a living whole constituted by its several and diverse parts. The point of the metaphor is the diversity of functions among members of the same body. "Just as *(kathaper)* . . . the many members [of the human body] do not have the same function *(praxin)*" (v. 4), "so also *(houtōs)* the many [members of the one body in Christ]" have "different charisms *(charismata diaphora)* according to the grace given to us" (vv. 5-6a). Another way of saying this is that "God has apportioned to each [member of the one body in Christ] a measure of faith" (v. 3). Because *emerisen metron pisteōs* has its parallel locution in *kata tēn charin dotheisan,* the assertion that "God has apportioned a measure of faith to each one" (v. 3) is restated by the participial phrase "having different charisms according to the grace which has been given to us" (v. 6a).

The diversity effected by this divine act of apportioning faith or

---

81. *Ibid.*

giving grace is illustrated in verses 6b-8. This list, which typifies rather than exhausts the possibilities of grace, is unique among parallel enumerations (1 Cor. 12:8-10, 28, 29-30; cf. Eph. 4:11) in that each gift/task is qualified by a prepositional phrase that conditions its exercise:

> if prophecy, according to *(kata)* the analogy of the faith;
> if service, in *(en)* the serving;
> if the one who teaches, in *(en)* the teaching;
> if the one who exhorts, in *(en)* the exhortation;
> the one who donates, in *(en)* liberality;
> the one who leads, in *(en)* diligence;
> the one who does mercy, in *(en)* cheerfulness.[82]

Ulrich Brockhaus perceives that this qualifying of each example by "a syntactically abbreviated" final clause has the effect of limiting the practice of the respective *charismata* "to the field of activity foreseen by God for them and with that to the task given with each gift."[83] The basic thought is that God binds each gift *(Gabe)* to a definite task *(Aufgabe)*, thereby limiting the exercise of a particular charism to the area of its ordained function. Thus the gift of "service" *(diakonia)* is bound to "the act of serving" *(en tē diakonia)*, "the one who teaches" *(ho didaskōn)* is limited to "the act of teaching" *(en tē didaskalia)*, "the one who exhorts" *(ho parakalōn)* is restricted to "the act of exhorting" *(en tē paraklēsei)*, and so on through the remaining three examples cited.[84] As formulated, therefore, the list of charisms explicates the argument of verse 3 —

---

82. Dunn, *Romans 9–16*, 725, argues correctly that in spite of the almost universal assumption that v. 6 begins a new sentence, with the prepositional phrases supported by a supplied imperative (RSV: "let us use them"), it "reads more naturally as a continuation of the body imagery of vv 4-5 with the meaning of *allēlōn melē* spelled out in terms of different charisms."

83. Brockhaus, *Charisma und Amt*, 201.

84. The shift of the qualifying phrases in v. 8bcd from the definition of the proper sphere of each act to a description of "the spirit and manner" in which they are to be exercised (Cranfield) or to their "character" (Dunn) does not alter the intent of the qualifications. The acts of "donating," "leading," and "doing mercy" (note the continuing use of present participles) are simply qualified further. "The one who donates" is limited to acts of donating that are characterized by "liberality," even as "the one who leads" is bound to acts of leading performed with "diligence" and "the doer of mercy" to merciful acts executed with "cheerfulness."

which John Koenig summarizes as the apostle's warning to his readers that "they must consider their charismata to be limitations as well as powers."[85] "Here the charismata act as a fence around pride," he adds; "they place a check on the believer's potentially arrogant self-image."[86]

The Norm of Prophecy

Koenig's summary makes good sense of the six clauses introduced by the preposition "in" *(en;* vv. 7-8). The question is whether the clause qualifying the charism of prophecy (v. 6b) can be understood properly in quite the same way. Had Paul intended a formal uniformity of the seven qualifying phrases, he could have formulated the first as he does the second, "if prophecy, in the prophecy" *(eite prophēteia, en tē prophēteia),* or even as he does the third and the fourth, "if the one who prophesies, in the prophecy" *(eite ho prophēteuōn, en tē prophēteia).* That he does not do so, but rather introduces the qualifying phrase by the preposition *kata* instead of *en* is sufficient reason to suspect that a different nuance is intended here. Unlike the charisms that are limited to their respective areas of intended actualization, prophecy is restricted in its expression by the phrase "according to the analogy of the faith" *(kata tēn analogian tēs pisteōs).* What is problematical is the nature of the restriction placed upon prophecy.

A possible (and popular) resolution of this exegetical issue is achieved by reading the qualifying phrase in verse 6b as a variation of "a portion of faith" *(metron pisteōs)* in verse 3. This argument assumes (1) that *metron* and *analogia* are virtually synonymous terms, and (2) that *pistis* has the same sense in both expressions. Whether faith is understood as a contingent act of charismatic endowment that effects prophetic utterance or as the Christian act of believing that capacitates the prophet to engage in this special task, prophecy is qualified by "the measure of faith allotted by God."[87] In either case, the restriction placed upon prophecy is basically the same — the quantity of faith given to the prophet.

---

85. John Koenig, *Charismata* (1978), 130.
86. *Ibid.,* 130-31.
87. W. Sanday and A. C. Headlam, *The Epistle to the Romans* (1896), 356.

If, on the one hand, the norm is charismatic faith, as John Ziesler argues, then the qualification of prophecy means "that the prophet must never go beyond the particular faith he or she has for the task of prophecy." As to how an inspired speaker might know when the proper limits of prophetic utterance had been reached, Ziesler appeals to the prophet's "*confidence* that it is God who is really speaking through the prophecy." "When this *confidence* is missing or lapses," he concludes, "the speaker should refrain or cease from speaking."[88] Prophecy is qualified, in other words, by the limitations of the prophet's *experience* of inspiration.

If, on the other hand, the implied standard is the act of Christian faith, then prophecy is qualified by the depth of the prophet's believing or trusting in God. Dunn, who views the list of charisms as descriptive rather than prescriptive of how they function in the church, argues that "according to the analogy of faith" is not only a variation of "a portion of faith" in verse 3 but also parallels and elaborates "according to the grace given to us" in verse 6a — "clearly implying that the faith is the faith exercised by the one who prophesies."[89] Accordingly, the phrase "describes how the prophet functions, or, more precisely, how the act of prophecy comes about — that is, by the prophet speaking forth in proportion to his faith = his dependence on God (the usual sense of *pistis* throughout Romans)." Whether read as description or prescription, however, the significance of the qualifying phrase disappears into an amorphous cloud of pistic subjectivism. For if prophecy is exercised, either descriptively or prescriptively, in proportion to the prophet's "dependence on God," we must (1) infer that some prophetic utterances are more authentic than others because expressed out of a greater portion of faith, and (2) wonder how this difference might be discerned by either the prophet or the community.

A more promising variation of this interpretation of the term *pistis* in verse 6b as the act of believing is provided by Cranfield, who considers the term's objective as well as subjective elements. Faith, for him, functions normatively in its relation to prophecy. He writes: "the prophets are to prophesy in agreement with the standard which they possess in their apprehension of, and response to, the grace of God in Jesus Christ — they are to be careful not to utter (under the impression that they

---

88. John Ziesler, *Paul's Epistle to the Romans* (1989), 299 (emphasis added).
89. Dunn, *Romans 9–16*, 727-28.

are inspired) anything which is incompatible with their believing in Christ."[90] Human experience is acknowledged in the acts of apprehending and responding, but it is subordinate to the object apprehended and responded to by faith — the grace of God in Jesus Christ.[91] It is this object of faith that functions as the "standard" with which prophecy must agree and by which the words of the prophets may be deemed "incompatible with their believing in Christ."

What Faith Believes

In orienting the act of faith *(fides qua)* to its normative object in Romans 12:6b, Cranfield demonstrates that such an exegetical option differs only in degree of emphasis from the alternative view — advocated, among others, by Käsemann[92] — in which "the faith" *(hē pistis)* is understood in terms of its content *(fides quae creditur)*.[93] That the semantic range of *faith* in Paul's discourse includes this sense of the word is evidenced by Galatians 1:23, Romans 10:8, and Philippians 1:27 — three texts that also designate *pistis* with the definite article. On this reading of the term, "the analogy of the faith" in Romans 12:6b is clearly not a variant of "a measure of faith" in verse 3 because *pistis* is nuanced differently in each verse. Further, this reading releases *analogia* from its semantic bondage to *metron* ("portion") and allows it to convey its own proper sense ("proportion").[94]

In their *Greek-English Lexicon of the New Testament Based on*

---

90. Cranfield, *Romans*, II, 621.

91. Rudolf Bultmann, *Theology of the New Testament* (1951), I, 317, in his structural analysis of *pistis* in Paul's usage, concurs: "'Faith' is 'faith in . . .' That is, it always has reference to its object, God's saving deed in Christ." This correspondence between act and object gives faith its character as "confession."

92. Käsemann, *Commentary on Romans*, 341-42. See also Rudolf Bultmann, "*pisteuō*," *TDNT* VI, 213; Campenhausen, *Ecclesiastical Authority*, 62; Aune, *Prophecy in Early Christianity*, 204, 235; Hill, *New Testament Prophecy*, 130; Müller, *Prophetie und Predigt*, 27, 187, 214-15.

93. Ziesler, *Paul's Epistle to the Romans*, 299, notes that the difference between *fides qua* and *fides quae* is "slight."

94. The argument that *analogia* and *metron* may be read here as synonyms because both terms are translated by the same Syriac word in the Peshitta is unconvincing. The instance cited may say more about the limitations of the receptor language than it does about the semantics of Greek terminology.

Semantic Domains, Louw and Nida locate both the preposition *kata* and the noun *analogia* in the semantic domain of "Relations Involving Correspondences (Isomorphisms)." The former serves as "a marker of a relation involving similarity of process — 'in accordance with, in relation to,'"[95] and the latter denotes "a relation of proportion — 'in relation to, in proportion to.'"[96] The full phrase "according to the analogy of the faith" *(kata tēn analogian tēs pisteōs)* thus qualifies prophecy by requiring it to be exercised in accordance with an isomorphic relation to the *content* of faith. But if it is the content of faith that norms prophetic utterance, then it is equally the content of particular prophecies that is conditioned by this standard.

While the "portion" of faith or grace given to the prophet is not irrelevant to the issue addressed in Romans 12:6b, the point is that prophetic inspiration can be assessed only by the material content of the utterances it ostensibly effects. "It makes no sense at all to suggest that the prophet must judge himself by his own faith," Käsemann contends, for this "would open the gates to every abuse and even false teaching."[97] The prophetic word must be evaluated in terms of its "right relation" to, or "correspondence" with, the content of faith, i.e., what faith knows, believes, and confesses. Thus unlike 1 Thessalonians 5:20, which requires the testing of prophecy but provides no criterion for the exercise of this mandate, Romans 12:6b specifies the norm by which the appropriateness of prophetic speech may be discerned.

The Faith and the Gospel

It is noteworthy that each of the other Pauline texts in which *hē pistis* occurs in the sense of *fides quae creditur* relates the term to Christian proclamation. Galatians 1:23 cites a tradition about Paul himself: "'The one who formerly was persecuting us is now proclaiming the faith *(euangelizetai tēn pistin)* he once tried to destroy.'"[98] Romans 10:8 is a

---

95. Louw and Nida, *Greek-English Lexicon,* par. 89.8.
96. *Ibid.,* par. 89.10.
97. Käsemann, *Commentary on Romans,* 341.
98. Hans Dieter Betz, *Galatians* (1979), 81 n. 235: "*pistis* ('faith') here in the absolute state . . . is understood as the content of faith *(fides quae creditur)* rather than the act of believing." See also Bultmann, "*pisteuō,*" *TDNT* VI, 213.

parenthetical comment on a citation of Deuteronomy 30:14, "that is, the word of faith *(to hrēma tēs pisteōs)* that we proclaim *(kēryssomen)*."[99] Philippians 1:27 is a call to stand firm in one spirit, "striving side by side with one mind for the faith of the gospel *(tē pistei tou euangeliou)*."[100] In each case *hē pistis* represents the substance of the basic Christian message. For this reason it functions in the first two instances as a synonym of the more customary Pauline designations of apostolic proclamation: "the gospel" *(to euangelion)* or "the kerygma" *(hē kerygma)*.

This association of faith in its objective sense *(fides quae)* with the act of apostolic preaching is made possible, as Bultmann emphasizes, by the intrinsic relationship recognized in the New Testament between faith and the kerygma.[101] The object of faith *(fides qua)*, whether formulated theologically as "the grace of God in Jesus Christ" (Cranfield) or "God's saving deed in Christ" (Bultmann), is mediated by the message that witnesses to its reality. As the substance of the gospel comes to expression in the particular form and structure of its proclamation, so what faith believes is determined by the message it hears and accepts. The content of faith, in other words, is for Paul "in accordance with an isomorphic relation to the gospel" *(kata tēn analogian tou euangeliou)*.[102] Because faith in this sense corresponds to the kerygma, *hē pistis* may denote the content of this message. What is believed, therefore, is coterminous with what is proclaimed.

---

99. Käsemann, *Commentary on Romans*, 290, with regard to the phrase *to hrēma tēs pisteōs* in Rom. 10:8, comments: "The interpretation in v. 9 shows that the reference is to the faith which is believed *(fides quae creditur)*...."

100. J. B. Lightfoot, *Epistle to the Philippians* (1868), 106: "Thus *hē pistis* is here objective, 'the faith,' 'the teaching of the Gospel'...." Cf. Ralph P. Martin, *Philippians* (1976), 83: "Not by their faith but by their faithfulness to the apostolic teaching ... would they be able to win through in their conflict...." Karl Barth, *The Epistle to the Philippians* (1962), 47, states emphatically, "*Pistis tou euangeliou* (faith of the Gospel) is subjective genitive!"

101. Bultmann, *"pisteuō," TDNT* VI, 209: "Kerygma and faith always go together...." Similarly Hans Conzelmann, *An Outline of the Theology of the New Testament* (1969), 171: "The essential element of the concept [faith] is not ... to be seen in psychological terms, in terms of faith as an attitude, but in the connection of faith with its object, the kerygma."

102. What Conzelmann, *An Outline of the Theology of the New Testament*, 172, says of the formal structure of faith is equally applicable to its content: "The nature of faith cannot be developed through self-analysis, but only through the description of its *inner structure* and *external references*" (emphasis added).

Together Galatians 1:23, Romans 10:8, and Philippians 1:27 suggest that when Paul uses *hē pistis* to denote the content of Christian belief, he has in mind the substance and structure of the gospel. This means that in Romans 12:6b prophecy is (1) drawn into the orbit of gospel proclamation, and (2) subjected to the standard provided by the content of this message. Just as faith *(fides quae)* corresponds to the kerygma, so also prophetic speech must demonstrate its appropriateness in relation to "the faith of the gospel" (Phil. 1:27). The basic principle of Romans 12:6b is, as Müller articulates it, that "Prophecy walks 'in agreement' with the faith.'"[103]

The Traditioned Faith

Such agreement as the standard of Christian prophecy receives a measure of specificity and concreteness from those New Testament texts that, variously designated, represent "the traditioned faith,"[104] "the faith as proclaimed by the apostles,"[105] "preaching schemes,"[106] or the "kerygmatic tradition."[107] Peter Stuhlmacher stresses the point that even Paul's gospel, given by direct revelation for the mission to the Gentiles (Gal. 1:12, 16), both created and adopted proclamation traditions out of necessity.[108] What was revealed required a formulated message for its transmission, a factor that gives Paul's gospel "a quite natural affinity with doctrine and tradition."[109] This is confirmed explicitly in 1 Corinthians 15:1-11 by the apostle's appeal to the gospel "word" *(logos)* which he had "received" as tradition and "delivered" to the Corinthians in his preaching, and which they had "received" in faith. Moreover, it is Paul's contention that this cited tradition forms and

---

103. Müller, *Prophetie und Predigt*, 187.
104. *Ibid.*, 187, 195, 200.
105. Hill, *New Testament Prophecy*, 130.
106. Peter Stuhlmacher, *The Gospel and the Gospels* (1991), 167.
107. Aune, *Prophecy in Early Christianity*, 235.
108. Stuhlmacher, *The Gospel and the Gospels*, 157: "When in Gal. 1:16 Paul mentions that he has received a revelation of the Son of God 'in order that I might preach him among the Gentiles' he is referring to missionary labor that he could only accomplish with the aid of his own, as well as traditional, formulations."
109. *Ibid.*

informs the preaching of all the apostles: "Whether then it was I or they, so we proclaim and so you have come to believe" (v. 11). The issue of the genre of 15:3bff., be it a kerygmatic, catechetical, or creedal formulation, is actually moot given the correspondence between the gospel and what faith believes, knows, and confesses. The point with regard to Romans 12:6b is that such formulations serve as the norm of prophetic utterance. Käsemann's summation of the matter is thus accurate: "Notwithstanding his inspiration the prophet is subject to testing *in this light* by his associates and the assembled community, in which the appropriateness of his message has to be demonstrated."[110]

Summary: Romans 12:6

The information about early Christian prophecy provided by 1 Thessalonians 5:19-22 is confirmed and supplemented by Romans 12:3-8. (1) The identification of the Spirit *(to pneuma)* as the source of prophecy, stated explicitly in 1 Thessalonians 5:19, is made implicitly in Romans 12:6 by the reference to "the different gifts *(charismata)*" which members of the Body of Christ have "according to the grace *(charis)* given to us." Käsemann notes that Paul, according to the context, "could speak equally well of the measure of the Spirit or of grace."[111] This claim is also evident in 1 Corinthians 12:4-11, where the listed *charismata*, again including prophecy, are expressly attributed to the distributive work of the Spirit. (2) Just as 1 Thessalonians 5:20 documents prophecy as a normal congregational activity in the apostle's mission field (and in pre-Pauline Jewish Christian circles as well if the text represents, as argued above, an early tradition), Romans 12:6 evidences Paul's assumption that prophecy would be known equally to a church located in the distant capital of the Empire. These factors together clearly suggest the broad scope of prophecy in early Christianity. (3) If the negative formulation of the mandate in 1 Thessalonians 5:20 signals the fact that prophecy was the occasion of intramural conflict in a particular church, the exhortations in 1 Thessalonians 5:21 and Romans 12:6, requiring the testing of prophetic utterances in terms of their content, intimate

---

110. Käsemann, *Commentary on Romans*, 341-42 (emphasis added).
111. *Ibid.*, 335.

that prophecy was intrinsically problematical. While 1 Thessalonians 5:21 mandates this task without identifying the appropriate criterion of such discernment, Romans 12:6 specifies "the faith" of the gospel as the norm by which the substance of prophecies must be evaluated and to which they will materially correspond if they are genuine communications of the Spirit.

Conclusion

The intrinsic relation established by 1 Thessalonians 5:20 and Romans 12:6 between prophecy and the gospel is significant, for it implies that the former is in some sense an expression of the latter. Only if both are grounded in a common subject matter does it make sense to appeal to the traditioned faith of the gospel as the standard of prophetic speech. The logical inference is that, for Paul at least, prophecy was a form of gospel proclamation. If so, then the provisional answer to the question of what the early Christian prophets were doing when they were prophesying is that they were proclaiming the gospel. In what sense Paul understood this to be the case is discernible in the conflict over prophecy that is attested in canonical 1 Corinthians. Not surprisingly, that controversy centered on the issue of how the authenticity of prophetic utterances was to be tested. It is to this matter that we now turn.

CHAPTER TWO

Prophecy and Confession

1 Corinthians 12:1-3

N. Bonwetsch began his 1884 seminal essay on early Christian prophecy by mining the evidential ore of 1 Corinthians 12–14,[1] and subsequent investigators of the phenomenon have recognized this passage as a rich lode of primary information. According to Greeven, "Who the prophets are, what they do, and what significance prophecy has for the community — all that is answered for Paul most clearly in 1 Cor. 12–14."[2] Hill writes that "most of what Paul had to say concerning [the phenomenon of prophets and prophecy in the Christian congregations] is found in chapters 12 and 14 of 1 Corinthians, chapters separated by — but not at all separable from — the famous hymn in praise of Christian love *(agapē)*."[3] For Aune, chapters 12–14 are "the single most important source for our knowledge of first century Christian prophecy."[4]

In view of such assessments, it is a curious fact that there is no consensus among commentators on the precise identity of the subject addressed in this passage or the logical flow of its argument. Interpreters do agree that 1 Corinthians 12–14 forms an extended and coherent response to one of several issues raised by the Corinthians in a previous letter to Paul and addressed by him *ad seriatum* in his reply (12:1; cf. 7:1, 25; 8:1; 16:1, 12).[5] This agreement extends to the broad gauged

---

1. Bonwetsch, "Die Prophetie im apostolischen und nachapostolischen Zeitalter," 410-16.
2. Greeven, "Propheten, Lehrer, Vorsteher bei Paulus," 3.
3. Hill, *New Testament Prophecy*, 110.
4. Aune, *Prophecy in Early Christianity*, 220.
5. See J. C. Hurd, *The Origin of I Corinthians* (1983), 65-74, for the discussion of

literary structure of the text: an introduction (12:1-3) followed by a section on the unity and diversity of the Spirit's work in the Body of Christ (12:4-31a),[6] another on the "more excellent way" of love (12:31b–14:1a),[7] a final segment on two types of inspired speech, namely, prophecy and tongues (14:1b-36), and a conclusion (14:37-40). But if these three chapters represent the apostle's answer, what was the Corinthian question? On this issue scholarly opinion is sharply divided.

The Question of the Question

Here it becomes painfully evident that we are reading someone else's mail. For the modern interpreter is privy to only half of a conversation between the apostle Paul and one of his churches. Gordon Fee explains why this disadvantage frustrates our attempts to identify the intended subject of 1 Corinthians 12–14:

> When a problem is *reported* to him, Paul feels compelled to tell what he knows (cf. 1:11-12; 5:1; 6:1; 11:17-22); thus we, too, have a better idea of what was going on. When responding to their letter, unless he quotes from it (7:1; 8:1, 4), he picks up right at that point, so we are not always informed as to the precise nature of the problem.[8]

---

the structure of 1 Cor. 7–16, and 186-95 for the arguments in support of the literary unity of chaps. 12–14.

6. Charles H. Talbert, *Perspectives on the New Testament* (1985), 96, notes the establishment of an inclusio by the use of the term *charismata* in vv. 4 and 31a.

7. It is generally recognized that 1 Cor. 12:31b–14:1a interrupts the flow of the argument begun in 12:1-31a and completed in 14:1b-40. Three basic explanations of this break are given by commentators: (1) the text is integral to the argument; (2) it is a Pauline excursus; and (3) it is an editorial insertion of a Pauline text. The first is advocated by Günther Bornkamm, *Early Christian Experience* (1969), 188; F. W. Grosheide, *Commentary on the First Epistle to the Corinthians* (1953), 303; Hans Lietzmann, *An die Korinther I/II* (4th ed., rev. Werner Georg Kümmel, 1949), 64-65; Hans Conzelmann, *1 Corinthians* (1975), 215-16 n. 52; the second by Werner Georg Kümmel, *Introduction to the New Testament* (1966), 199; Fee, *First Corinthians*, 571; C. K. Barrett, *The First Epistle to the Corinthians* (1968), 297, 299, 314; Eduard Schweizer, "The Service of Worship: An Exposition of 1 Corinthians 14," *Int* 13 (1959): 404; and the third by Johannes Weiss, *Der erste Korintherbrief* (10th ed., 1925), 309-13; Walter Schmithals, *Gnosticism in Corinth* (1971), 95 n. 23.

8. Fee, *First Corinthians*, 570 n. 2.

The point at which Paul picks up the query of the Corinthians in 12:1 is located in the opening prepositional phrase, *Peri de tōn pneumatikōn*. Unfortunately, the cryptic character of this expression obscures rather than clarifies the precise nature of the subject being addressed. What makes it enigmatic is the gender ambiguity of the grammatical construction *tōn pneumatikōn* — the genitive plural suffix masking either the masculine adjective *pneumatikoi* (spiritual ones) or its neuter correlative *pneumatika* (spiritual things [understood as gifts of the Spirit]). If the masculine option is exercised, the thematic phrase reads "Now concerning the spirituals. . . ." If the neuter alternative is selected, it means "Now concerning the spiritual gifts. . . ."[9] So which is it?

Some argue that the difference is inconsequential in view of the probability that both Paul and the Corinthians had in mind the people who exercised the gifts.[10] Such a supposition, though warranted, simply dodges rather than bites the exegetical bullet. The price paid for indecision here is the loss of the topical key that unlocks the argument as a whole. Others contend, therefore, that the Corinthian question must

---

9. Ralph P. Martin, *The Spirit and the Congregation* (1984), 7, notes that grammatically *pneumatikōn* may also be feminine. If this were the intended sense, the opening phrase of 12:1 would read, "Now concerning the spiritual women *(hai pneumatikai)*." It is surprising that Wire, *Corinthian Women Prophets*, 135, does not consider this possibility, given her thesis that the people with whom Paul contends in 1 Corinthians were female prophets. Opting rather for the masculine reading (spiritual people), she comments that "Corinth's Christian women prophets are *among* the spiritual Paul discusses in [1 Cor. 12–14]" (emphasis added). Clearly the masculine *pneumatikoi* may be understood generically (males and females) rather than gender specifically (men), and should be so understood in view of the reference in 1 Cor. 11:4-5 to men and women who "pray and prophesy." Thus the fact that women are "among" those identified as "spiritual people" in chaps. 12–14 is not at issue. Wire's claim that the women prophets are the primary, if not exclusive, focus of Paul's rhetoric throughout the letter is further diluted by her concession that in chaps. 12–14 Paul "may be persuading others as well — spiritual people who are not women and perhaps spiritual women who are not prophets — but his last and longest argument dissociating prophecy and tongues shows that he has *people* with these gifts in mind" (emphasis added). No doubt the reason why the feminine option is not considered by commentators is the fact that *pneumatikē*, unlike *pneumatikos* and *pneumatika*, is unattested in either chaps. 12–14 or 1 Corinthians as a whole.

10. Thus Leon Morris, *The First Epistle of Paul to the Corinthians* (1958), 163; cf. Barrett, *First Corinthians*, 278, who comments: "it seems impossible to find objective ground for a decision between the two possibilities, and little difference in sense is involved — spiritual persons are those who have spiritual gifts."

and may be inferred from the apostle's answer.[11] Deductions drawn from the internal evidence ordinarily follow one of two linguistic clues given in the text to the identity of the ambiguous intended theme, and thus to the logical argumentation of the entire passage. The evidence is subtle and the arguments technical, but of such is the realm of exegesis.

Concerning Spiritual Gifts?

The majority of commentaries and all standard English translations prefer an intended *ta pneumatika* (spiritual gifts) in 12:1.[12] The basis of this preference is the unambiguous use of the term in 14:1b where *ta pneumatika* picks up *ta charismata* from 12:31a and resumes the discussion interrupted by 12:31b–14:1a under this alternative rubric. On the ground that the two terms, if not synonyms, at least refer to the same powers of the Spirit, it is argued that the word *charismata* in 12:4 reverses the terminological interchange at 12:31 and 14:1 by taking up the obscured theme of *ta pneumatika* in 12:1. On this reading of the introductory phrase, the argument of the passage moves from the reference to the expressed Corinthian concern about "spiritual gifts" (12:1-3), to Paul's principal discussion of this subject under his preferred term *charismata* (12:4-31a), to the interlude on love (12:31b–14:1a), to the concluding treatment of inspired speech (14:1b-40). According to this analysis, the weight of the argument is carried by 12:4-31a, which speaks directly to the Corinthian question as inferred. But what is the logical connection between this initial discussion of "spiritual gifts" and the two major segments that follow? The purpose of chapter 13 is clearly to qualify the *charismata* by subordinating

---

11. Fee, *First Corinthians*, 570, claims that "both the length and the nature of Paul's response allow for a fairly straightforward reconstruction of the problem." In a footnote, however, he adds a caveat: "Although a glance at the various reconstructions discussed by Hurd [*The Origin of I Corinthians*], 186-87, 190-91, should make one duly cautious as to what seems 'straightforward'" (n. 4).

12. Among the commentators who opt for the neuter reading are: Wilhelm Bousset, *Der erste Brief an die Korinther* (1917), 134; Conzelmann, *1 Corinthians*, 204; Jean Héring, *La Première Épitre de Saint Paul aux Corinthiens* (1949), 106; Archibald Robertson and Alfred Plummer, *First Epistle of St Paul to the Corinthians* (1953), 259; Fee, *First Corinthians*, 575. The standard English translations of the Bible are unanimous in rendering the phrase "spiritual things" or "spiritual gifts."

them to the theological preeminence of *agapē*. It is unclear, however, why the apostle's response to the generic issue of "spiritual gifts" requires the inclusion of specific instructions on prophecy and tongues in chapter 14.

Hans Conzelmann attempts to overcome this difficulty by arguing that the subject of chapter 14 is implicitly included in the announced topic of 12:1, which he reads as *ta pneumatika* in the sense of "spiritual gifts."[13] Noting the "harsh" transition at 14:1 that effects the resumption of the discussion in chapter 12, he comments:

> The tenor is now different: no longer a *crisis* of *pneumatika*, 'spiritual gifts,' in general, but their *regulation*, with reference to the actual condition in Corinth. Now it is only speaking with tongues and prophecy that are discussed as spiritual gifts.[14]

His point is that the substance of chapter 14 is implicit in the announced topic of 12:1 because the *crisis* of "spiritual gifts" in Corinth was occasioned by the activity which Paul addresses and seeks to regulate in this concluding section of his response.

Despite the treatment of both prophecy and tongues in this text, Conzelmann oddly limits "the actual condition in Corinth" that induced the church's question, and thus the focal topic of the answer, to the phenomenon of speaking in tongues. The reason given for this restriction is the "latent criticism" of *glossolalia* in chapter 14. As he explains:

> The presupposition is that in Corinth prophecy does not stand at the head of the list, but ranks after speaking with tongues. Thus the gifts are evaluated in Corinth according to the intensity of the ecstatic outburst; in fact, even according to the degree of unintelligibility. The latter is considered to be an indication of the working of supernatural power.[15]

Thus the culprit lurking in the shadows of 1 Corinthians 12–14 is identified as the Corinthian overevaluation of the ecstatic and unintelligible speech that Paul identifies as *glossolalia*.

---

13. Conzelmann, *1 Corinthians*, 204.

14. Ibid., 233. The English translation of the first sentence is misleading, and has been corrected in accordance with the German original, *Der erste Brief an die Korinther* (1969), 275, which reads: "Der Tenor ist jetz ein anderer, nicht mehr: *Krisis* der *pneumatika* überhaupt, sondern *Ordnung* derselben, in Anknüpfung an den tatsächlichen Befund in Korinth."

15. Conzelmann, *1 Corinthians*, 233–34.

It must be noted, however, that Conzelmann's analysis of the ecclesial situation in Corinth depends upon his assumption that prophecy and tongues were recognized among the Corinthians as differentiated gifts of the Spirit. His reconstruction begs the question of whether the sharp contrast made in chapter 14 between these two types of inspired utterance represents a conventional distinction or a Pauline innovation. Although it is almost universally supposed by commentators that the former is the case, there are significant exceptions. Bornkamm, for one, writes:

> Without doubt, in the ordinary Christian understanding in Corinth the spiritual gifts of prophecy and speaking in tongues were most closely related. Both were ways of speaking, through which the exalted Lord or the Spirit communicated directly. *Here the speaking in tongues was regarded simply as an exalted form of prophecy.*[16]

Müller also argues that the Corinthians did not distinguish between prophecy and *glossolalia:* "This distinction was first created by Paul."[17] The text inferentially argues against the conjecture of the majority.

If prophecy and tongues were recognized in Corinth as discrete gifts of the Spirit, then the terminology Paul uses to designate them would have been known also to the congregation. It seems strange, therefore, that the issue of speaking in tongues would be raised with the apostle in terms of the generic *ta pneumatika* if this particular gift of the Spirit was in fact the occasioning problem. Why was the question

---

16. Bornkamm, *Early Christian Experience*, 38 (emphasis added).

17. Müller, *Prophetie und Predigt im Neuen Testament*, 28. See also the following: Nils I. J. Engelsen, "Glossolalia and Other Forms of Inspired Speech According to I Corinthians 12–14" (Ph.D. diss., Yale University, 1970), 189: "Paul uses *glōssais lalein* where the Corinthians used *pneumati lalein* or the like. Paul seems to have narrowed down the meaning of the term, so that *glōssa* used as a technical term refers only to unintelligible, inspired speech, while the Corinthians . . . seem to have followed a less precise usage, without a real distinction between 'speaking in tongues,' 'speaking in the Spirit,' and prophesying"; Luke Timothy Johnson, "Norms for True and False Prophecy in First Corinthians," *ABR* 22 (1971): 31: "It seems that Paul's concern is that both the Christians in Corinth and their pagan neighbors will equate Christian prophecy with the ecstatic, frenzied prophecy which was well known in the Hellenistic world. . . . Paul is especially concerned to separate the charism of prophecy from any identification with this gift and consequently remove it from any danger of being mistaken for pagan prophecy"; Thomas W. Gillespie, "A Pattern of Prophetic Speech in First Corinthians," *JBL* 97 (1978): 74-95.

asked by the congregation not phrased something like, *Peri de lalōn glōssais* (Now concerning speaking in tongues)? The likely answer is that the Corinthians were unaware of such a distinction and thus did not know the word *glōssa* (tongues) in the specialized sense that Paul uses it here. While Conzelmann preserves the coherence of the argument in 1 Corinthians 12–14 by identifying the explicit subject of chapter 14 as the implicit reason for the Corinthian question, his limitation of the issue to *glossolalia* is dubious.

D. W. B. Robinson concurs with Conzelmann's assessment of the problematic situation in Corinth, but argues the case on other grounds. Assuming that *ta pneumatika* is the proper reading of the Corinthian question (12:1), he writes:

> There is no reason to suppose that the Corinthians had written to ask Paul's advice about *charismata*, that is, about gifts in general; it is much more likely that they had sought his mind about certain types of ecstatic utterance which were occurring at Corinth, and which some of them considered to be a special, perhaps a unique, evidence of Spirit-possession. For in his reply Paul does not at once speak of *charismata*, but of "speaking by the Spirit of God" *(en pneumati theou lalōn)*. What he "wants them to know" *(gnorizō)* is a certain criterion for testing such utterances. That is his short answer to the question of *ta pneumatika*, given in I Cor. 12:1-3.[18]

Here Robinson challenges the canonical status which the virtual equation of *pneumatika* and *charismata* enjoys among exegetes by contending that in 1 Corinthians 12–14 "Paul is using *ta pneumatika*, not for *charismata* in general, but in the limited sense of 'speaking in spirit'" (12:3).

The semantic limitation of *pneumatika* in this context to inspired utterance receives even greater specificity from Robinson's further suggestion that the term represents Corinthian jargon for precisely the type of Spirit-induced ecstatic speech designated as speaking in tongues by Paul. Robinson supports this identification with four arguments. First, he emphasizes that Paul's answer to the Corinthian question begins in 12:1-3 with instruction on the discernment of authentic "speaking in spirit" (v. 3) rather than with the discussion of *charismata* in their unity

---

18. D. W. B. Robinson, "Charismata versus Pneumatika: Paul's Method of Discussion," *RTJ* 31 (1972): 51.

and diversity (v. 4). Second, he argues that the phrase "speaking in spirit" in 12:3 is interpreted by the subsequent definition of tongues in 14:2 as "speaking mysteries in spirit." Third, this interpretation is confirmed, he contends, by the formal parallel between 14:1 and 14:5,[19] where prophesying is contrasted with *ta pneumatika* in the former and speaking in tongues in the latter, thus demonstrating that *pneumatika* and *lalein glōssais* (speak in tongues) are parallel expressions. Finally, he maintains that the terms *prophētēs* (a prophet) and *pneumatikos* (a spiritual) in 14:37 represent respectively the agents of the gifts of prophecy and tongues contrasted by Paul throughout chapter 14 — which implies that the *pneumatikos* is someone who engages in *pneumatika* (speaking in tongues).

Robinson's case, however, is only partially justified. His point that 12:1-3 represents Paul's "short answer" to the Corinthian question is exegetically valid. This introductory text's focus on discerning who is and who is not "speaking in the Spirit of God" does identify the subject being considered in chapters 12–14 as inspired speech. The content of 1 Corinthians 12:1-3, however, does not warrant the limiting of such utterances to the ecstatic and incomprehensible phenomenon of speaking in tongues. For both the negative and positive criteriological examples given in v. 3 for discerning authentic inspiration ("Jesus be cursed" and "Jesus is Lord") are uttered in intelligible rather than unintelligible speech. Robinson's mistake is assuming with Conzelmann that Paul's distinction between prophecy and tongues was conventional wisdom in Corinth. Accordingly, the phrase "speaking in the Spirit of God" (12:3) may not be interpreted exclusively by the description of tongues as "speaking mysteries in the Spirit" (14:2). Paul's correlative claim that "the one who prophesies speaks edification, exhortation and comfort" (14:3) is equally valid as an interpretative key. The plural *ta pneumatika* in 14:1 also makes it risky to restrict the referent of the term to only one type of inspired utterance, in spite of the formal parallel between this verse and 14:5.[20] Finally, his

---

19. *Ibid.* The Greek texts read:

14:1 *zēloute de ta pneumatika,*
mallon de hina prophēteuēte.
14:5 *thelō de pantas hymas lalein glōssais,*
mallon de hina prophēteuēte.

20. Note, however, that *mallon de* is grammatically intensive in 14:1 and adversative in 14:5.

claim that *prophētēs* and *pneumatikos* in 14:37 refer to the distinct agents of prophesying and speaking in tongues is anything but certain. The terms may be understood equally well as alternative designations of the same individuals.

Robinson's attempt to limit *ta pneumatika* to speaking in tongues is thus unsuccessful. What he does achieve, however, is recognition of the possibility that in Corinthian parlance the term, in distinction from *charismata*, designated the work of the Spirit associated with inspired speech. For his observation that Paul's response to the Corinthians' question begins in 12:1-3 clearly focuses the ensuing discussion upon "speaking in the Spirit of God." If the Corinthian question may be inferred from Paul's answer, and if *ta pneumatika* is a valid interpretation of the expressed issue, then the term must denote the phenomenon of Spirit-inspired utterance *per se*.

This inference is supported by E. Earle Ellis, who maintains that *pneumatika* is equally a Pauline idiom for the voice of the Spirit. Ellis calls attention to Rom. 1:11 where *pneumatikon* qualifies *charisma* in expressing Paul's desire to visit Rome in order to impart to the church there "some spiritual charism." With regard to this phrase, Ellis comments:

> The kind of qualification represented by 'spiritual' *(pneumatikon)* becomes clear from Paul's usage. That is, *charisma* can be used of any or all of the gifts while *pneumatikon* appears to be restricted to gifts of inspired perception, verbal proclamation and/or its interpretation. Thus, in 1 Cor. 9,11 the 'spiritual things' that Paul sowed among the Corinthians are defined in the following context as the gospel message. Similarly, in 1 Cor. 12,1 the 'spiritual' gifts (or persons) are connected directly with 'speaking' *en pneumati*. . . .[21]

The same is true, he argues, of the discussion of spiritual gifts in 1 Corinthians 14. Here the *pneumatika* of v. 1 refer not to the gifts of the Spirit in general but more specifically to "the greater gifts *(ta charismata ta meizona)*" of 1 Corinthians 12:31, which, as the ensuing discussion in chapter 14 makes clear, "are concerned with inspired speech. . . ."[22]

David L. Baker supports Ellis's point by examining the content of

---

21. Ellis, *Prophecy and Hermeneutic*, 24.
22. *Ibid.*, 24-25. Koenig, *Charismata*, 107, concurs: "*Pneumatika*, then, are charismata meant to be practiced within the context of congregational worship." See also Martin, *The Spirit and the Congregation*, 8.

1 Corinthians 14. "We learn from 14:1 that the chapter is to be about the *pneumatika*," he writes, "but we find that it is devoted almost entirely to a discussion of the relative merits and uses of prophecy and speaking in tongues." From this he correctly infers, "If we started reading at ch. 14 we would assume that the *pneumatika* were prophecy and speaking in tongues, and if we examine this assumption we shall find that it is consistent with the text of the whole section and sheds new light to its interpretation."[23]

The yield of these arguments by Robinson, Ellis, and Baker is fourfold. They demonstrate (1) that *pneumatika* has a more restricted sense than does *charismata* in Paul's usage, denoting specifically the gifts of inspired speech, and that (2) the case for reading *ta pneumatika* in 12:1 can no longer be made on the ground that it represents the same interchange with *charismata* in 12:4 as that which allegedly occurs in 12:31 and 14:1. Even if the case for *ta pneumatika* in 12:1 could be made on other grounds, such as an appeal to the use of the term in 14:1 not merely to pick up the theme of the "greater" *charismata* from 12:31a but to address the Corinthian question directly, it would (3) transform the issue addressed in this passage from the generic to the specific, and thus (4) shift the center of gravity of the argument as a whole from 12:4-31a to 14:1b-40. The text's coherence would thus be preserved, but on the ground that the subject of chapter 14 is explicit rather than merely implicit in the neuter reading of the introductory phrase in 12:1, "Now concerning speech inspired by the Spirit." The loss of the argument based upon the presumed interchangeability of *pneumatika* and *charismata*, however, makes it necessary to consider seriously the alternative possibility of a masculine reading of *tōn pneumatikōn*.

Concerning Spiritual People?

The counter-argument that the Corinthian question to Paul concerned *hoi pneumatikoi* (spiritual people) is advocated by a strong minority of exegetes.[24] The textual clue followed in this case is found in 14:37 where

---

23. David L. Baker, "The Interpretation of I Corinthians 12–14," *EvQ* 45 (1973): 228.

24. Philipp Bachmann, *Der erste Brief des Paulus an die Korinther* (3rd Aufl. 1921),

Paul draws his discussion to a close: "If anyone thinks he is a prophet or a spiritual, he must acknowledge that what I am writing to you is a command of the Lord." Here the masculine term *pneumatikos* (a spiritual) occurs unambiguously, and in close association with *prophētēs* (a prophet). Two observations on this text lend credence to the claim that it provides the key to the subject of chapters 12–14.

The first observation pertains to its location in the structure of the entire passage. C. K. Barrett points out that 14:37-40 is "a conclusion of the whole argument, and not simply a resumption of the earlier discussion of prophecy."[25] This suggests that Paul ends the discussion where it began, with a reference to one of those in the congregation who styled themselves as *pneumatikoi* (spirituals) and who occasioned the Corinthian question about their status, activity, and role in the life of the church. If this is so, then *hoi pneumatikoi* in the introduction (12:1-3) and *pneumatikos* in the conclusion (14:37-40) form an inclusio that unifies the intervening discussion of this matter.

The second observation is made by Fee, who points up the important role played in 1 Corinthians by the opening phrase of 14:37, "If anyone thinks. . . ." Although this expression occurs only twice elsewhere in the letter (3:18; 8:2), Fee comments that it is "probably no accident that the statement . . . is found in each of the three major sections of the letter (chaps. 1–4; 8–10; 12–14) and reflects these three crucial Corinthian terms ('wisdom,' 'knowledge,' and 'spiritual')."[26] Further, "the argument in each case indicates that by this formula Paul is zeroing in on the Corinthians' perspective as to their own spirituality. They do indeed think of themselves as 'the wise' (3:18) and as 'having knowledge' (8:2), probably in both cases because they also think of themselves as being *pneumatikoi*. . . ."[27] The connection between these three verses, established by their common introductory formulas, gives the term *pneumatikos* in 14:37 an added weight by tying it into the religious ethos in Corinth that occasioned

---

381; F. F. Bruce, *1 and 2 Corinthians* (1976), 116; Hurd, *The Origin of I Corinthians*, 194; Birger A. Pearson, *The Pneumatikos-Psychikos Terminology in I Corinthians* (1973), 47; Schmithals, *Gnosticism in Corinth*, 171f.; Weiss, *Korintherbrief*, 294.

25. Barrett, *First Corinthians*, 333. Cf. Talbert, *Perspectives on the New Testament*, 107, who comments on 14:37-40, "Presumably this covers Paul's directive in the entire thought unit (1 Cor. 12–14)."

26. Fee, *First Corinthians*, 11.

27. Ibid., 711.

1 Corinthians itself.[28] Given the apparent role of the *spirituals* in creating the problematic ecclesial situation, it makes good sense to construe the intended subject of 1 Corinthians 12–14 in terms of such people and the principal function they claimed to serve in the congregation's life.

The question of the relation between the *pneumatikos* and the *prophētēs* in 14:37 thus takes on added significance. While the terms are related in the text by the disjunctive particle *ē* (or), this does not necessarily mean they are adversatives. For the Greek particle *ē* serves to separate not only opposites but also "related and similar terms, where one can take the place of the other or one supplements the other. . . ."[29] Thus the argument that they are to be distinguished in this text, the *spiritual* representing one who speaks in tongues and the *prophet* one who prophesies, depends entirely upon the previously noted assumption that the distinction between these two forms of inspired speech was commonplace. If it is a Pauline innovation, however, then both terms refer to those who speak under the inspiration of the Spirit, *prophētēs* representing Paul's terminology and *pneumatikos* the idiom of the Corinthians.[30] Schmithals thus concludes from 14:37, "The Pneumatics

---

28. The ecclesial circumstances in Corinth at the time 1 Corinthians was written can only be reconstructed from the evidence of the letter itself. While "mirror reading" of the text has its inherent dangers and limitations, it seems evident from the issues addressed by the apostle here that the situation in the church must be characterized by certain religious themes. Conzelmann, *1 Corinthians*, 14, speaks of "a freedom principle" that rests upon "knowledge" that derives from "experience of the Spirit." To these he adds "Christology" and "sacramentalism." The "obvious structural unity of the manifold phenomena," he contends, "is completely explained by the agreement between exaltation Christology and enthusiasm" (15). Fee, *First Corinthians*, 4-15, amplifies the list by including "spiritualized eschatology," an admittedly "inelegant expression" he coins to denote the Corinthians' "overrealized eschatological view of their present existence" (12). Focusing the unifying concept of these themes somewhat differently from, but not in contradiction to, Conzelmann, Fee thinks "the key issue" between Paul and the church "has to do with the Corinthian understanding of what it means to be 'spiritual' (*pneumatikos*)" (6). Similarly Ellis, *Prophecy and Hermeneutic*, 23-44; and John Painter, "Paul and the *Pneumatikoi* at Corinth," in M. D. Hooker and S. G. Wilson, eds., *Paul and Paulinism* (1982), 237-50.

29. Walter Bauer, *A Greek-English Lexicon of the New Testament and Other Early Christian Literature* (4th revised and augmented edition by William F. Arndt and F. Wilbur Gingrich, 1952), 342.

30. Müller, *Prophetie und Predigt im Neuen Testament*, 30, with regard to 14:37, comments: "Here Paul takes up the language of his opponents, likewise what concerns

were simply *prophets.*" What this means, he explains, is that "the Pneumatics in Corinth represented themselves to be prophets when they went into action in the community's gatherings for purposes of worship."[31]

Fee concurs with this assessment of the Corinthian situation, commenting that those addressed in 14:37 "consider themselves to be 'prophets' and 'Spirit people.'" Not only are these two terms "closely linked" in this concluding injunction, he observes, but the noun *prophētēs* "here reverts back to the usage in 12:28, where it refers to those who had a 'ranked' position of ministry in the local assembly."[32] Because God has placed in the church *first* apostles and *second* prophets, Paul is not denying the status of *prophētēs* or *pneumatikos* to those he is addressing in 14:37 so much as he is pulling apostolic rank on them. His assumption is that if they are indeed prophets or spirituals, as they claim,[33] they are obligated to acknowledge that what he is writing to them as an apostle is "a command of the Lord."[34] The inference is therefore warranted that the apostle concludes his response to the Corinthian query by addressing those who had occasioned it. His specific reference to the *prophētēs/pneumatikos* in 14:37 thus provides evidential encouragement for reading the enigmatic *tōn pneumatikōn* in 12:1 as a masculine adjective *(hoi pneumatikoi).*

When the entire passage is read under this supposition, the Corinthian question concerns "the spirituals" who claim the powers of prophetic utterance, and the apostolic answer (1) provides criteria for discerning authentic inspiration (12:1-3), (2) relativizes the value of inspired speech by locating it in the context of the diverse activities of

---

the concept 'prophet'...." The text clearly attests, according to Müller, that the prophet is a spiritual, but this does not permit us to infer that the spirituals did not designate themselves as prophets. Thus v. 37 "does not intend to separate prophets and other ecstatics, perhaps tongue speakers, but sees them together."

31. Schmithals, *Gnosticism in Corinth,* 284-85. Cf. Ellis, *Prophecy and Hermeneutic,* 50: "They are called pneumatics and, broadly speaking, they exercise the role of prophets."

32. Fee, *First Corinthians,* 711.

33. Walter J. Bartling, "The Congregation of Christ — a Charismatic Body," *CTM* 40 (1969): 68, comments wryly on 14:37, "It does not take a skilled exegete to catch the challenge of disguised irony in that use of *pneumatikos.*"

34. The word "command" here, as Fee, *First Corinthians,* 711, rightly notes, "is most likely a collective singular referring to all that [Paul] has written on this present matter," namely, the text that begins at 12:1 and will conclude at 14:40.

the Spirit in the Body of Christ (12:4-31a), (3) qualifies *all charismata* by subjecting them to the proviso of "the more excellent way" (12:31b-14:1a), and (4) addresses directly the problematic issue of those who prophesy and speak in tongues (14:1b-40). If prophecy and tongues were understood in Corinth as intrinsically related components of Spirit-inspired utterances, this construal of Paul's argument in 1 Cor. 12–14 becomes even more illuminating. For the contrast between prophesying and speaking in tongues in chapter 14 opens up the possibility of understanding the underlying cause of the issue addressed by Paul here not simply as an overevaluation of ecstatic speech *per se* but as a misconception of the significance of speaking in tongues in relation to prophetic proclamation.

As attractive and suggestive as this argument on behalf of a masculine reading of *tōn pneumatikōn* in 12:1 is, however, it must be acknowledged that it is not compelling without additional supporting evidence. The structure and content of the introductory section (12:1-3) as a whole provides just such evidence.

Who Speaks by the Spirit of God?

With reference to 1 Corinthians 12:1-3, Nils Engelson comments, "There seems to be no common agreement about the meaning of any one clause within the passage, and the function of the whole is still an open question."[35] In addition to the ambiguity of the opening prepositional phrase in verse 1, the obstinate exegetical issues include: the ungrammatical formulation and the problematic reference of verse 2; the character of the curse pronounced on Jesus in verse 3 and, if actual rather than hypothetical, its historical occasion and context; the question of the relationship between verses 2 and 3; and the problem of the logical connection between the introduction and the ensuing argument as a whole. All is not darkness in 12:1-3, however, and the resolution of these difficult issues may be achieved by moving exegetically from verse 3 where the light shines most clearly.

Having declared his desire that the Corinthians not be ignorant

---

35. Engelson, "Glossolalia and Other Forms of Inspired Speech according to I Corinthians 12–14," 103.

(*agnoein*) about the (to us ambiguous) subject of this section of his letter (v. 1), and having referred them to what they do know (*oidate*) from their pre-Christian experience of idol worship (v. 2), Paul introduces the next sentence (v. 3) with a formula that indicates he is making what Johannes Weiss calls a "solemn declaration" of "an authoritative decision" regarding the issue raised by the congregation, "Therefore I want you to know (*gnōrizō*) that. . . ."[36] Here then the original formulation of the Corinthian question comes into view.[37]

The substance of the apostolic pronouncement identifies the fundamental issue under discussion. What Paul makes known to his readers is that "no one speaking by the Spirit of God says, 'Jesus be cursed' (*Anathema Iēsous*), and no one can say 'Jesus is Lord' (*Kyrios Iēsous*), except by the Holy Spirit." Put simply, this authoritative declaration establishes what someone "speaking by the Spirit of God" (*en pneumati theou lalōn*) cannot say and what only someone speaking "by the Holy Spirit" (*en pneumati hagiō*) can say. Representing the apostle's "short answer" to the Corinthian question,[38] verse 3 designates the issue raised by the church as the problem of the authenticity of divine inspiration in prophetic utterance. In other words, the issue addressed in 1 Corinthians 12:1-3 is precisely the same as that implicit in 1 Thessalonians 5:20 and explicit in Romans 12:6. Both 1 Corinthians 12:3 and Romans 12:6 make it clear that for Paul the problem of genuine Spirit inspiration must be resolved on the ground of the content of such discourse.[39]

---

36. Weiss, *Korintherbrief,* 295. While recognizing that the verb *gnōrizein* also signifies a common communication, Weiss notes that in the New Testament it is often used in the technical sense of making known a revelation (Col. 1:27 and often in Eph.; Rom. 16:26; John 15:15; 17:26; Luke 2:15, 17). See also Bauer, *Lexicon,* 162.

37. Both Grosheide, *First Corinthians,* 280, and Weiss, *Korintherbrief,* 295, designate 1 Cor. 12:3 as the original *Fragestellung* of the ensuing discussion. Norbert Brox, "ANATHEMA IHSOYS (1 Kor. 12,3)," *BZ* 12 (1968): 105, aptly notes: "From the diction of the beginning verses of 1 Cor. 12 one would not hesitate to understand v. 3 as the answer of Paul to a corresponding question of the Corinthians, if the monstrosity of ANATHEMA IHSOYS did not seem to prohibit it . . ." (*peri de tōn . . . gnōrizō hymin . . .*).

38. See n. 18 above.

39. Aune, *Prophecy in Early Christianity,* 221: "While Paul is not formally setting out the criteria for evaluating prophetic speech, it is nevertheless clear that the *content* of such speech is the decisive criterion for determining whether or not it is an authentic utterance inspired by the Spirit of God." Aune does not explain how such clarity about the "decisive criterion" of content is achieved apart from the text being a formal statement of "the criteria for evaluating prophetic speech."

The emphatic "therefore" *(dio)* with which Paul begins 1 Corinthians 12:3 indicates a logical connection between this sentence and its antecedent that depends upon the sense of the latter. Although verse 2 clearly refers the Corinthians to something they know from their pre-Christian experience in the precincts of pagan temples, it is a grammatical nightmare. The sentence as it stands is an *anacolouthon* that may be rendered literally, "You know that *(hoti)* when you were pagans, how you were continually led *(hōs an ēgesthe)* to dumb idols, being carried away *(apagomenoi)*." Fee attributes the grammatical deficiency of the statement to the absence of another main verb. "Either something dropped out in the transmission of the text," he conjectures, "or else Paul himself intended his readers to supply a second 'you were' at some point in the sentence."[40] Another way of resolving the difficulty is to read the phrase "how you were continually led" *(hōs an ēgesthe)* as a resumption of the clause introduced by *hoti* (that), the particle *hōs* having the significance of *hoti* when following a verb of knowing.[41]

The grammatical plot thickens, however. If the particle *an* is not taken in its iterative sense, denoting repeated action in past time with the imperfect indicative,[42] but is prefixed to *agein*, then the verb has the technical sense of being "caught up" into the world of pneumatic powers.[43] Similarly the term *apagein* (lead away) can connote in the passive voice the experience of being "carried away" by divine or demonic forces.[44] Conzelmann warns against reading these verbs in verse 2 as a clear reference to the ecstatic character of the pagan cults,[45] but Fee correctly counters that while neither term on its own necessarily implies ecstasy, "the unusual compounding of the verbs . . . seems to lead in this direction."[46] Thus Aune boldly concludes that "A careful

---

40. Fee, *First Corinthians*, 576.
41. Bauer, *Lexicon*, 907.
42. Ibid., 47.
43. Bauer, *Lexicon*, 52, designates the literal sense of the compound verb as being led "from a lower to a higher point." As a technical term for experiences of the divine, it denotes being "caught up" in the minimum sense of an altered state of human consciousness. More radically, it conveys the ancient concept of the translation of the individual from one place to another under the influence of divine powers, i.e., from earth to heaven. Cf. Georg Strecker, "Entrückung," *RAC* V, 462.
44. Bauer, *Lexicon*, 79.
45. Conzelmann, *1 Corinthians*, 205.
46. Fee, *First Corinthians*, 577-78. Note also Fee's further insight: "The combina-

examination of the context shows that when Paul referred to the pagan background of the Corinthian Christians in 1 Cor. 12:2, he was in all probability referring to pagan religious experiences of possession trance."[47] By this he means a state of "divine possession" or "ecstasy."[48] As an allusion to the Corinthians' pre-Christian ecstatic experiences in pagan temples, verse 2 reads: "You know that, when you were pagans, that you were *caught up* to the dumbs idols, *being carried away*" (emphasis added).[49]

Even if the text is properly construed as referring to the ecstasy known to the Corinthians from their pagan experience of idol worship, however, the question of the purpose of this allusion remains. Obviously the statement functions as a *premise* that warrants the inferential *conclusion* drawn in verse 3, but in what sense is this so? How is the logical connection between the two verses in their literary context to be understood?

Jouette Bassler documents the fact that the commentators typically answer this question by positing a logic of "contrast and comparison."[50] Of this consensus she writes:

> Such an understanding encourages the interpretation of v. 3 as a test or criterion. Since once you were pagans and ignorant of the ways of the Holy Spirit, I will now give you criteria by which to recognize them. Since once you experienced pagan ecstasy, I will now give you criteria to distinguish it from Christian inspiration.[51]

---

tion *ēgesthe apagomenoi*, which is strange at best, seems emphatic, a point generally overlooked" (577 n. 39).

47. Aune, *Prophecy in Early Christianity*, 257.

48. *Ibid.*, 33.

49. Karl Maly, "1 Kor. 12,1-3, eine Regel zur Unterscheidung der Geister?" *BZ* 10 (1966): 83-89, argues on the basis of Deut. 28:36 (LXX) that the participle *apagomenoi* has the meaning of enslavement rather than ecstasy ("being carried away [as prisoners]"). The antithesis for Maly is between the previous enslavement of the pagan Corinthians to the dumb idols and their present freedom to speak in the Spirit. But Conzelmann, *1 Corinthians*, 206 n. 15, observes that Deut. 28:36 in no way determines the meaning of *apagein* in 1 Cor. 12:2. Furthermore, Maly's juxtaposition of enslavement to dumb idols, on the one hand, to freedom to speak in the Spirit, on the other, leaves the text in the lurch. The attribution of muteness to the idols is merely a traditional Jewish polemic against pagan images, and does not imply that the participants in the pagan cults were mute also.

50. Jouette M. Bassler, "1 Cor 12:3 — Curse and Confession in Context," *JBL* 101 (1982): 417 nn. 10, 12.

51. *Ibid.*, 416-17.

Rejecting this reading of the text on the questionable ground that "regarding v. 3 as a test or criterion severs this verse from the rest of the argument of chaps. 12–14," Bassler argues that the unity of the overall argument is maintained only "if the relationship between v. 2 and v. 3 is viewed as one of *analogy*, not contrast."[52]

The basis of the analogy she perceives is the religious experience, common to pagans and Christians, of being under the "compulsion" of supernatural powers, whether demonic or divine. As she explains:

> Paul reminds the Corinthians of an aspect of their pagan past that will illuminate his argument in v. 3. The key to the argument is the emphatic repetition of the verbs *agein* and *apagein* and the sense of compulsion that they impart. Paul appeals to the Corinthians' experience in pagan cults where the *daimōn* exercised total control over their actions. Thus they should recognize that the Christian likewise does not make the confession of faith by his own will, but shows thereby the controlling presence of the Holy Spirit.[53]

The assumption upon which her case rests, however, is the common but dubious view that in 1 Corinthians 12–14 "Paul is concerned to refute those Corinthians who claim their gift of glossolalia is a special, perhaps unique, demonstration of spirit possession," a claim to "pneumatic elitism" which he undermines by noting that "the simple baptismal confession, Jesus is Lord, can only be uttered under the influence of the Holy Spirit (v 3b)." The point of the argument, as Bassler understands it, is that "All Christians make this confession, thus all Christians, not a tongue-speaking few, are *pneumatikoi*."[54]

While this is a sound Pauline argument, it is not the one made by the apostle in 1 Corinthians 12:1-3. Verse 3 focuses, as we have emphasized above, on what one who is "speaking by the Spirit of God" or "by the Holy Spirit" can and cannot say. In view of the fact that Paul includes both prophecy and speaking in tongues among the diverse manifestations of the Spirit listed in 12:4-11, there is absolutely no textual warrant for limiting the inspired utterance attested in verse 3 to the phenomenon of *glossolalia*. On the contrary, the text argues against narrowing the scope of its reference in this way by providing negative and positive

---

52. *Ibid.*, 417 (emphasis added).
53. *Ibid.*
54. *Ibid.*, 416.

criteria of inspired speech that is expressed in intelligible language and thus may be assessed in terms of its material content. Such criteria would be useless for discerning the authenticity of unintelligible utterances. Clearly they are applicable only with regard to determining the genuineness of intelligible prophetic speech.[55]

What then is the connection between this reference to the Corinthians' pre-Christian experience of ecstatic states in pagan temples (v. 2) and the apostle's "solemn declaration" regarding the necessity of assessing intelligible inspired speech in terms of its content (v. 3)? So long as prophecy and tongues are viewed as discrete spiritual gifts recognized as such in Corinth, and verse 3 is understood as an implicit reference to the latter phenomenon only, the logical link between the two statements is limited to contrast or comparison or analogy. Another possibility emerges, however, if Paul's differentiation between prophecy and tongues in 1 Corinthians 12-14 represents a novel distinction hitherto unknown to the church in Corinth where intelligible and unintelligible inspired speech were viewed as intrinsic elements of prophetic utterance.

Two neglected implications of verses 2 and 3 support this alternative view. The first is that Paul's insistence in verse 3 that all speech claiming divine inspiration be tested for its authenticity on the basis of its content intimates that such was not the practice in Corinth. The second is that the emphatic inferential conjunction *dio* (therefore) which initiates verse 3 indicates that it was the type of ecstasy critiqued in verse 2 which actually served as a criterion of genuine inspired speech among the Corinthians.[56] A schematic paraphrase allows the force of the inferential logic that connects the two verses to express itself:

Premise: You know that evidences of ecstasy are an unreliable criterion of authentic divine inspiration because in your pagan past they led you to the dumb idols (v. 2).

Conclusion: Therefore *(dio)* the genuineness of all prophetic utterances must be judged on the basis of their material content alone (v. 3).

---

55. Traugott Holtz, "Das Kennzeichen des Geistes (1 Kor. xii.1-3)," *NTS* 18 (1971/72): 370, emphasizes that attempts to refer 12:3 to speaking in tongues "make no sense," because tongues are an inarticulate speech while the cursing and confessing of Jesus in v. 3 are completely understandable.

56. H. E. Dana and Julius R. Mantey, *A Manual Grammar of the Greek New Testament* (1927), 245, designate *dio* as "the strongest inferential conjunction."

The effect of this tightly argued introduction, accordingly, is the disqualification of ecstatic states from consideration as a validating sign of authentic prophetic speech.[57] While the text itself does not specify that the ecstasy in view was linguistic in character, the logical connection between verses 2 and 3 does suggest that some kind of "speaking in spirit" is implied. The legitimacy of making this inference is supported, rather than denied, by the description of the idols as *aphōna* (dumb). For Duncan Derrett points out that Paul's analogy of tongues in 1 Corinthians 14:10 — "There are doubtless many different languages *(genē phōnōn)* in the world, and none is without meaning *(aphōnon)*" — provides contextual warrant for reading the appellation "dumb" in 12:2 as a statement of the inability of the idols to communicate *intelligibly*.[58] Lietzmann thus calls the phrase "dumb idols," itself an expression of the traditional Jewish polemic against idolatry, "an unfortunate *epitheton ornans*" in view of the ecstatic speech incited by the graven images.[59]

What surfaces here then is a description of the formal Corinthian understanding of the prophetic word. Inspired speech, as conventionally understood in Corinth, was constituted by both intelligible and unintelligible components, the latter serving to validate the authenticity of the former. The apostle's argument in 1 Corinthians 12:2-3, therefore, seeks to undermine not simply the "elitism" of "the glossalalia-flaunting pneumatics" in the congregation, as Bassler argues,[60] but rather the validity of this formal conception.[61]

---

57. Painter, "Paul and the *Pneumatikoi* at Corinth," 243, comes to the same conclusion with regard to the significance of 1 Cor. 12:2-3: "For Paul ecstasy was not an adequate criterion for evaluating the claims of the *pneumatikoi*. His first criterion concerned content. . . . In this way Paul redefines the acceptable meaning of *pneumatikos* by calling the criterion of ecstasy into question. . . . The Corinthian *pneumatikoi* valued ecstasy without distinguishing prophecy from glossolalia (ecstatic = *pneumatikos*) but Paul distinguished prophecy from glossolalia. . . ."

58. J. Duncan M. Derrett, "Cursing Jesus (1 Corinthians XII.3)," *NTS* 21 (1974): +553 n. 9.

59. Lietzmann, *Korinther I/II*, 60-61.

60. Bassler, "1 Cor 12:3 — Curse and Confession in Context," 416.

61. Müller, *Prophetie und Predigt im Neuen Testament*, 30, unfortunately identifies speaking in tongues *per se* with the Corinthian view of prophecy: "Tongues were for them the real, only and suitable form of prophecy."

Confessing Jesus as a Theological Norm

The problematic issues that attend the cursing and confessing of Jesus attested in verse 3 may now be addressed in the light of the Corinthian view of prophecy. While attention has focused primarily upon the troublesome phrase *Anathema Iēsous* (Jesus be cursed), it must be acknowledged that the antithetical acclamation *Kyrios Iēsous* (Jesus is Lord) presents its own set of difficulties for the exegetical argument that Paul intended it to serve as a norm for assessing the validity of prophetic speech in terms of its intelligible content. For this reason we will take up these matters first.

The acclamation *Kyrios Iēsous* occurs twice elsewhere in Paul's letters, each instance indicating that it represents a piece of the pre-Pauline tradition and that its social setting was the worship of the assembled congregation. In Romans 10:9 it is conjoined with what Werner Kramer calls a "pistis-formula," designating a formulation "which has as its content the saving acts of death and resurrection."[62] The combined formulas read, "if you confess with your lips that *(hoti)* Jesus is Lord *(kyrion Iēsoun)* and believe in your heart that *(hoti)* God raised him from the dead, you will be saved." "On both points it is almost certain that Paul cites formulae which would be familiar to his readers," Dunn comments, "formulae which would probably recall their own conversion and initiation into the new movement, formulae in fact which go back to the earliest days of the new movement."[63] For Cranfield "it seems clear that *kyrios Iēsous* was already an established confessional formula." He thinks it "probable that it was used in connexion with baptism . . . , but also in Christian worship generally."[64] Käsemann finds it "natural to take the *hoti* recitatively" (the Greek equivalent of our quotation marks), indicating that "Paul is citing *kyrios Iēsous* as a traditional formula that has its *Sitz im Leben* in worship."[65]

In a modestly expanded form, the acclamation occurs also in the early christological hymn cited by Paul in Philippians 2:6-11.[66] It culmi-

---

62. Werner Kramer, *Christ, Lord, Son of God* (1963), 21.
63. Dunn, *Romans 9–16*, 616.
64. Cranfield, *Romans*, II: 527.
65. Käsemann, *Commentary on Romans*, 291.
66. The thesis that Phil. 2:6-11 represents a pre-Pauline christological hymn, proposed initially by Ernst Lohmeyer in his 1928 monograph *Kyrios Jesus: Eine Unter-*

nates the second stanza, which the New Revised Standard Version renders as follows:

> Therefore God also highly exalted him
> and gave him the name
> that is above every name,
> so that at the name of Jesus
> every knee should bend,
> in heaven and on earth and under the earth,
> and every tongue should confess
> that *(hoti)* Jesus Christ is Lord *(kyrios Iēsous Christos)*
> to the glory of God the Father. (vv. 9-11)

The introductory *hoti recitativum* indicates that the acclamation is here, as in Romans 10:9, being quoted — an instance of a tradition being cited by a tradition, and the hymnic context makes it plain that the *Kyrios* title acclaimed of Jesus is "the name that is above every name," which God "gave him" at his exaltation. In this divine bestowal of the name that is exalted above all other names, as Käsemann rightly insists, "we will have to maintain that here the designation of God in the Greek Old Testament is transferred to Jesus, especially since vs. 10 quotes Isa. 45:25 LXX, where God proclaims Himself as *kyrios*."[67] Some locate the provenance of the hymn in the baptismal rite,[68] and others in the celebration of the eucharist.[69] Either way, it is safe to say that the acclamation is at home in the worship life of the early church.

It is significant that both of these texts speak of *confessing* "Jesus is Lord" (Rom. 10:9, *homologein*; Phil. 2:11, *exhomologein*). Conzelmann has thus coined the term *homologia* (confession) to designate the genre of this acclamation.[70] But what does it entail? Kramer differentiates the *homologia* from the pistis formula on the ground that "it is not con-

---

suchung zu Phil. 2,5-11, enjoys virtually unanimous acceptance among New Testament scholars, although there is no consensus on issues of its poetic structure or possible Pauline redactions of the cited tradition. A survey of the discussion up to 1963 is provided by Ralph P. Martin in *Carmen Christi* (1967), and a supplement that updates the report is found in his commentary, *Philippians* (1976), 109-16.

67. Ernst Käsemann, "A Critical Analysis of Philippians 2:5-11," in Robert W. Funk, ed., *God and Christ* (1968), 77.
68. Jacob Jervell, *Imago Dei* (1960), 206-9.
69. Lohmeyer, *Kyrios Jesus*, 65ff.
70. Hans Conzelmann, "Was glaubte die frühe Christenheit?" *STU* 25 (1955): 64.

cerned with formulating the saving events but with a *direct invocation* in which the Church does obeisance to the Lord by acclaiming his majesty."[71] As he explains:

> By 'acclamation' is meant an act of tribute and submission of this sort. In acclamation the Church is not thinking of any particular saving event but is putting itself into a relationship which holds good in the present.[72]

The *homologia*, in other words, is a confession of *loyalty* to the one acclaimed as Lord, but not a confession of *faith* in the sense of a statement of what is believed. Accordingly, "The *homologia* is not 'preached' but proclaimed with a shout, and thus it is a summons to renewed acclamation and renewed confession."[73] If the characterization of the *Kyrios Iēsous* formula provided by Kramer is accurate, however, it is impossible to imagine how it could function in 1 Corinthians 12:3 as a material criterion of intelligible prophetic speech. For it is not the loyalty of the prophets that requires testing, but the content of their prophecies.

Kramer's analysis is falsified, however, by the textual evidence. His claim that the *homologia* is "not 'preached' but proclaimed with a shout" is refuted by 2 Corinthians 4:5. Commenting on this text, Bultmann observes that "when Paul... declares, 'What we preach is not ourselves, but Jesus Christ as Lord [*Iēsoun Christon Kyrion*],' it is clear that just this is held to be the Christian message: to proclaim Christ as the Kyrios."[74] The point here is not that a declaration of the *homologia* is an act of Christian proclamation in a formal sense, but that it entails the substance of the gospel.

Kramer's further claim that in acclamation "the Church is not thinking of any particular saving event" is equally suspect. Käsemann properly emphasizes that the acts of confessing and believing attested in Romans 10:9 represent a unified response to "the word of the faith which we preach" in verse 8. Thus the reference in verse 9 "is to the faith which is believed *(fides quae creditur)*, i.e., the gospel which is always previously

---

71. Kramer, *Christ, Lord, Son of God*, 66.
72. Ibid., 66-67.
73. Ibid., 67.
74. Bultmann, *Theology of the New Testament*, I, 125. See also J. D. G. Dunn, *Unity and Diversity in the New Testament* (1977), 50: "That Jesus is Lord, is a central affirmation of the Pauline kerygma (II Cor. 4:5; Col. 2:6)."

given to us in the form of *homologia*...." The two verbs *homologein* (confess) and *pisteuein* (believe) in verse 9 both "relate to the content of faith fixed in the confession and consequently they cannot be materially separated."[75] Likewise, the acclamation in the Christ hymn of Philippians 2:6-11 betrays the claim that it is not concerned with saving events. For it is predicated upon such antecedent statements as "he ... became obedient unto death, even death on a cross" (v. 8), and "God has highly exalted him" (v. 9), which together bear witness to a soteriological event. To quote Käsemann again, "The divine act at the enthronement of Christ shows that the action of him who was obedient on earth affects the whole world and is a salvation-event." Moreover, "The scheme of the whole passage as well as the individual motifs disclose the use of mythological language" that is "precisely the language which the early Christian kerygma uses again and again in describing the salvation event."[76] As cited in the hymn, the *homologia* of verse 11 attests to the saving event by its very dependence upon it.

In a word, the confession *Kyrios Iēsous* is not deprived of its theological substance by its acclamatory character. If it is a confession of loyalty to the Lord Jesus, it is equally a confession of faith in the one who is Lord precisely because he is the crucified and exalted Jesus. As such it expresses the gospel to which it corresponds. Because of its substantive character, the *homologia* in 1 Corinthians 12:3 can and, in the judgment of Paul, should serve as a criterion for assessing the validity of prophetic speech on the basis of its content. The only significant difference between this recommendation and the apostle's later counsel to the Romans that prophecy be "in accordance with the faith" (12:6) is that here Paul specifies a particular tradition that expresses the gospel and thus norms prophetic utterances.

The theological assumption undergirding this use of the *homologia* as a means of recognizing the authentic voice of the Spirit is that the Spirit is, so to speak, tethered to Jesus, the crucified, risen, and exalted Lord. Georg Eichholz argues that Paul is so determined to understand the Spirit "as the *presence of Jesus Christ in the community*" that he "binds the Spirit to Christ." This connection is clearly made in 1 Corinthians

---

75. Käsemann, *Commentary on Romans*, 290. He goes on to acknowledge that the phrase *Kyrios Iēsous* is "primarily ... not a confession but acclamation," but adds the caveat that this "naturally includes a confessional element" (291).

76. Käsemann, "A Critical Analysis of Philippians 2:5-11," 77.

12:1-3, according to Eichholz, where "the present Lord in the community is no other than 'Jesus.'" Thus, "The Christian Spirit is recognizable therein, that it confesses Christ, or, more sharply, that it confesses the historical Jesus as the Lord."[77]

Dunn is more specific: "The relation between Christ and Spirit becomes clearer when we realize that Paul regards Jesus as now in some sense *the definition of the Spirit*."[78] The question is, of course, in what sense this is so. Dunn himself proposes that "it is the *Jesus-character* of [Paul's] and his converts' *experiences* of the Spirit which marks them as authentic."[79] Such an appeal to "the Jesus-character" of "experiences of the Spirit" as a mark of authentic inspiration is ambiguous at best, however, and Dunn seeks to overcome this by explaining that 1 Corinthians 12:3 means that "the experience of inspiration is authenticated as an experience of the Holy Spirit when the Lordship of Jesus is affirmed thereby." His point seems to be that "the Lordship of Jesus" defines "the Jesus-character" of Spirit-inspiration. More light is shed on this explanation when elsewhere Dunn declares that the distinctiveness of the *homologia* is its expression of "*the conviction that the historical figure, Jesus the Jew, is now an exalted being* — that this Jesus is and continues to be the *agent of God*."[80] What the *homologia* thus implies with regard to the inspiration of the Spirit is not only that the Spirit affirms the Lordship of Jesus, but that the Jesus who is acclaimed Lord is "the agent of God" who himself works in and through the Spirit.

Prophetic utterance genuinely inspired by the Spirit is thus a form of self-testimony provided by the crucified earthly Jesus now raised from the dead and exalted. Put otherwise, authentic prophecy bears witness to the reality and meaning of the Lordship of Jesus in accordance with the salvation event that effected his exaltation. This then explains why "no one can say 'Jesus is Lord,' except by the Holy Spirit" (v. 3), for the *homologia* is a response to the One who manifests himself in the proclamation of the gospel (cf. 2 Cor. 4:4-6) and thereby calls for the faithful confession.[81]

---

77. Georg Eichholz, *Die Theologie des Paulus im Umriss* (1977), 274.
78. James D. G. Dunn, *Christology in the Making* (1980), 145.
79. *Ibid.* (emphasis added).
80. Dunn, *Unity and Diversity in the New Testament*, 56.
81. James D. G. Dunn, *Baptism in the Holy Spirit* (1970), 151, says too much when he asserts that the *homologia* represents "an inspired or ecstatic utterance which

Cursing Jesus as an Instance of False Prophecy

What then is to be made of the antithetical declaration in verse 3, *Anathema Iēsous* (Jesus be cursed)?[82] Interpretation here depends initially upon whether the imprecation is construed as an *actual* pronouncement reported by the Corinthians in their letter to Paul or as a *hypothetical* alternative to the *homologia* framed by the apostle himself for rhetorical effect. If the curse is taken as an actual occurrence, then it must be determined whether it was pronounced *within* or *without* the Christian assembly. Whichever of the latter options is preferred, the occasion of such a pronouncement in the setting proposed must be demonstrated. Finally, whether hypothetical or actual, the cursing of Jesus must be explained in terms of its literary relation to the reference in verse 2 to the ecstatic states experienced by the Corinthians in their pagan past. As Fee aptly notes: "The solutions are many and varied; none is without difficulties."[83]

Brockhaus calls attention to the sentence structure of verse 3 as an important clue to the resolution of the exegetical issues,[84] constructed as it is by two statements that stand in antithetical parallelism

---

did not originate in the individual's own consciousness." On the other hand, Bultmann, *Theology of the New Testament*, I, 330n., says too little in stating, "When 1 Cor. 12:3 gives the cry, 'Lord Jesus' as the criterion for possession by the Spirit, this does not intend to attribute the confession of faith to the Spirit, but to state the means by which spiritual and demonic ecstasy are to be distinguished." Clearly the qualifying phrase, "except in the Holy Spirit" means that the *homologia* is effected by the Spirit. But this does not imply that it is effected in the individual by an altered state of consciousness. The encounter of the one who acclaims with the One acclaimed through the Spirit's presence in the proclamation of the gospel is a sufficient and, I think, an accurate theological explanation.

82. W. C. van Unnik, "Jesus: Anathema or Kyrios (1 Cor. 12:3)," in *Christ and Spirit in the New Testament*, Barnabas Lindars and Stephen S. Smalley eds. (1973), 115-16, objects to the assumption that the supplied verbal copula is an imperative, arguing that it could be an indicative even as it is presumably in the *homologia* (Jesus is Lord). Fee, *First Corinthians*, 579, concedes the possibility of such an interpretation, but thinks it unlikely in view of the fact that *Anathema Iēsous* "has all the earmarks of an actual curse formula" which is usually characterized by an imperative (see n. 44).

83. Fee, *First Corinthians*, 579. In addition to the concise overview of the various scholarly proposals provided by Fee (580 nn. 50, 51), see Derrett, "Cursing Jesus (I Cor. XII.3)," 544; Ralph P. Martin, *The Worship of God* (1982), 175-78; and Bassler, "1 Cor. 12:3 — Curse and Confession in Context," 415-16.

84. Brockhaus, *Charisma und Amt*, 160. His suggestion is not devalued by the unacceptable way in which he himself pursues it.

to each other and are connected by a simple *kai* (and). Materially they are related by a common subject matter. As the first denies the *Anathema Iēsous* to one "speaking by the Spirit of God," so the second limits the *Kyrios Iēsous* to one who speaks "in the holy Spirit." Each declaration, in other words, has as its textual context the subject of Spirit-inspired utterance. Because the *homologia* is clearly an actual Christian acclamation that demonstrably has its social setting in the worship life of the congregation, the parallelism between the the two statements in verse 3, though antithetical, suggests that the same actuality and situation characterize the imprecation as well. Put otherwise, the sentence structure of verse 3 affords *prima facie* evidence in support of the thesis that the *Anathema Iēsous* here represents an actual rather than a hypothetical occurrence that originated in the worship life of the Christian community rather than in such alternative possibilities as the synagogue,[85] the tribunal,[86] or the pagan cultus.[87]

It is not surprising, therefore, that most commentators on this text at least consider the possibility of the curse actually taking place within the Corinthian assembly. Those who defend the actuality of the anathema but turn to life settings external to the church to account for its occurrence, as well as those who recognize that the literary context of the curse excludes external alternatives and thus conclude that it is a hypothetical construction, do so for the same reason. They are unable to explain satisfactorily either how such a blasphemous declaration could have been uttered by a believer in an ecclesial context or why, if actually said, it would have required special apostolic instruction. Crone summarizes the dilemma, "If we cannot find a likely *Sitz im Leben* for the acclamation 'Jesus be cursed,' we are left with the probability that it is Paul's own formulation."[88]

---

85. Adolf Schlatter, *Die Korintherbriefe* (1962), 333; Moffatt, *First Corinthians*, 178; and Derrett, "Cursing Jesus (I Cor. XII.3)," 544-54, locate the actual cursing of Jesus in the Jewish synagogue and explain its occasion in various ways.

86. Oscar Cullmann, *The Christology of the New Testament* (1963), 218-20, identifies the *Sitz im Leben* of the anathema as the Roman courts where Christians were compelled to confess Caesar and curse Jesus; cf. Vernon H. Neufeld, *The Earliest Christian Confessions* (1963), 63.

87. Fee, *First Corinthians*, 581, thinks the options are, in the final analysis, limited either to the hypothetical or to "something that some of them had actually experienced in their pagan past" while worshipping the idols in their temples.

88. Crone, *Early Christian Prophecy*, 226.

What makes an explanation "likely" is, of course, the issue. An adequate interpretation demands two criteria. It must account for the actuality of the curse in terms of (1) its immediate literary context (12:1-3), and (2) what is known from the letter as a whole about the situation in the Corinthian church at the time 1 Corinthians was written.[89] The proposal of Schmithals that the Corinthian pneumatics were Gnostics who cursed the flesh *(sarx)* of the earthly Jesus under the influence of divine inspiration, for example,[90] meets the first criterion but not the second. As Conzelmann persuasively argues, the hypothesis of a mythological Gnostic system is not essential for the interpretation of this letter. For "the obvious structural unity of the manifold phenomena — Christology, enthusiasm, sacramentalism, the catchwords of knowledge and freedom" can be "completely explained by the agreement between exaltation Christology and enthusiasm."[91]

Yet this very "agreement," plus Conzelmann's subsequent concession that because there are "isolated traces" in the letter of "Gnosticism *in statu nascendi*" the Corinthians could be described as "proto-Gnostics,"[92]

---

89. Conzelmann, *1 Corinthians,* 15: "The position in Corinth cannot be reconstructed on the basis of the possibilities of the general history of religion. Certainty attaches only to what we can learn from the text." Also, "The difficulty of this task is increased further by the problem of how far it is permissible to draw upon 2 Corinthians" in order to "trace out general characteristics of Corinthian thought and life" at the time of the composition of 1 Corinthians (14).

90. Schmithals, *Gnosticism in Corinth,* 124-30. So also Ulrich Wilckens, *Weisheit und Torheit* (1959), 121 n. 1; Brox, "ANATHEMA IHSOUS (1 Kor 12,3)," 105-8, identifies the curse of Jesus as "a gnostic-christological expression," indeed "a negatively formulated homologia to the gnostic Christ."

91. Conzelmann, *1 Corinthians,* 15. Schmithals's thesis has been further weakened by the demonstration of Birger A. Pearson, "Did the Gnostics Curse Jesus?" *JBL* 86 (1967): 301-5, that the two passages in Origen to which Schmithals appeals as parallels to the alleged Corinthian situation (*Contra Celsus* 6.28 and a fragment on 1 Cor. 12:3 from Origen's lost commentary, available in C. Jenkins, "Origen on I Corinthians," *JTS* 10 [1909]: 30) have an entirely different meaning. But see the response to Pearson's critique by Brox, "ANATHEMA IĒSOYS (1 Kor. 12,3)," 103-11 (esp. 107 n. 16).

92. *Ibid.* R. McL. Wilson, *Gnosis and the New Testament* (1968), 16-18, calls attention to the important terminological distinction drawn between pre- and proto-Gnosticism at the 1966 Messina Colloquium on the origins of Gnosticism. Pre-Gnostic refers to "themes and motifs, concepts and ideas" which were "preparing the way" for the development of Gnosticism proper in the classical Gnostic systems of the second century. Proto-Gnostic denotes "the essence of Gnosticism" in its pre-classical forms,

makes his summary dismissal of Schmithals's suggestion as "fantastic" unduly harsh.[93] For if the various themes of Corinthian piety can be united under the rubric of an "exaltation Christology and enthusiasm," even so can the *Anathema Iēsous* in 12:3 be explained on the same terms. The tendency that here devalues the earthly Jesus resurfaces in the dispute over the legitimate implications of the gospel formula in chapter 15, which, as Conzelmann acknowledges, was susceptible to the interpretation "that death is nullified, so to speak, and that faith has now to focus solely on the exalted Lord."[94] Such a christological focus in combination with Spirit-inspiration adequately explains how someone claiming to speak "by the Spirit of God" could actually curse Jesus with a straight face in the context of Christian worship.[95] Dunn surmises that in 12:3 we may have a formulation of a distinctive christology in which "the *earthly* Jesus was of no account, it was the *heavenly* Christ alone that counted." It is not necessary to posit, as Dunn does, that it was "Gnostic" in character in order to make the point.[96] An exaltation christology in combination with a Spirit-enthusiasm is quite adequate.

The imprecation thus has a theological background that provides the context of its interpretation. Norbert Brox posits that the curse formula was not expressed as a theologoumenon without commentary but was exegeted out of the christological context to which it belonged, just as the corresponding Kyrios formula did not remain without explanation.[97] This suggests that what we may have in 1 Corinthians 12:3 are abbreviated summaries of more extensive inspired discourses. If so, this observation would be equally applicable to the so-called Corinthian slogans attested elsewhere in this letter: "All things are lawful for me"

---

i.e., the idea of the divine nature of the spark in humans that is in need of awakening and reintegration into the divine. On these terms, Conzelmann has in mind the pre-Gnostic stage of development.

93. Conzelmann, *1 Corinthians*, 204 n. 10.
94. Ibid., 15.
95. In addition to Schmithals, see: Grosheide, *First Corinthians*, 280-81; Martin, *The Worship of God*, 175-78; Moffatt, *First Corinthians*, 179; Robin Scroggs, "The Exaltation of the Spirit by Some Early Christians," *JBL* 84 (1965): 359-73; R. St. John Parry, *The First Epistle of Paul the Apostle to the Corinthians* (1928), 176; Weiss, *Korintherbrief*, 295.
96. Dunn, *Unity and Diversity in the New Testament*, 278. With the same proviso, see also Eichholz, *Die Theologie des Paulus im Umriss*, 57: "Because it is a matter of the heavenly Spirit-Christ, it can come to an *Anathema Iēsous*, apparently in ecstatic speech, during the community gathering."
97. Brox, "*ANATHEMA IĒSOYS* (1 Kor. 12,3)," 109.

(6:12); "It is well for a man not to touch a woman" (7:1); "All of us possess knowledge" (8:1); "No idol in the world really exists," and "There is no God but one" (8:4); "Food will not bring us close to God" (8:8); and, "There is no resurrection of the dead" (15:12). It is interesting to note in this regard that Paul's response to each of these conceivably inspired utterances is not to deny the truth of their material content, but to interpret them out of a different theological context. The one exception is the denial of the resurrection of the dead, which the apostle dismisses as a patently absurd implication of the cited gospel tradition (1 Cor. 15:3b-5).

It would be a mistake, however, to view the Corinthian church as completely or even predominantly homogeneous in its attitudes and convictions on such matters. Paul's exhortation, "that all of you agree and that there be no dissensions among you, but that you be united in the same mind and the same judgment" (1 Cor. 1:10), is alone sufficient evidence to the contrary. It seems more than likely, therefore, that some in the congregation would take offense at the cursing of Jesus and view it as "unrestrained, excitable blasphemy."[98] The question is why such an occurrence would call for special apostolic instruction on its merits. The answer is implied in verse 2. If, as we have argued above, it was evidence of ecstasy that served to confirm the authenticity of inspired utterance, then the pronouncement of *Anathema Iēsous* accompanied by tongues, the *sine qua non* of authentic Spirit-inspiration, could not readily be dismissed by the church as a whole. Yet the intelligible content of the oracle was so patently outrageous to some that the incident created a crisis of confidence in their formal understanding of prophecy. It was this crisis then that necessitated an appeal to Paul for guidance in the matter.[99]

In his reply, Paul (1) dismisses ecstasy as the test of authentic inspiration on the ground that such states formerly had led the Corinthians to idols and were thus unreliable (v. 2), (2) declares solemnly his "authoritative decision" (Weiss) that "no one speaking by the Spirit of God says, 'Jesus be cursed'"; and (3) designates the confession, "Jesus

---

98. Martin, *The Spirit and the Congregation*, 10.
99. This explanation meets the reasonable insistence of Fee, *First Corinthians*, 579, that an adequate answer to the question of the anathema in 1 Cor. 12:3 "must make sense of two things: (a) how it functions in relationship to v. 2, and (b) how it relates to the larger issue of their apparently inordinate enthusiasm for the gift of tongues."

is Lord," as the material criterion for determining who does and does not "speak by the Holy Spirit" (v. 3). The radical antithesis between the curse and the confession demonstrates what an extreme case of prophetic utterance was required to call into question the legitimacy of ecstasy as the confirming sign of genuine Spirit-inspiration.

Conclusion

Provided that the semantic scope of the term *pneumatika* be limited to spiritual gifts of inspired utterance, in distinction from the designation of spiritual gifts in general by the word *charismata,* and on condition that *pneumatikos* in the context of 1 Corinthians be understood to denote the mediators of inspired utterances (prophets), it indeed may be argued that it is rather inconsequential whether the enigmatic phrase *tōn pneumatikōn* in 1 Corinthians 12:1 that introduces the subject of chapters 12–14 is read as a neuter *(pneumatika)* or masculine *(pneumatikoi)* adjective. For if the topic of the passage is inspired utterances, this necessarily entails the prophets who voiced them. Conversely, if the intended theme is the spirituals who function as prophets, that includes their inspired speech. As Schmitals aptly remarks, "It would be *the height of banality* to say that Paul of his own accord arrives at the idea of telling the Corinthians, who had asked only quite generally for information about the gifts of the Spirit in the community, that in their assemblies no one who wishes to speak in the *pneuma theou* may say *anathema Iēsous.*"[100] Nonetheless, the apostle's emphatic use of the indefinite pronoun "No one" (*oudeis,* twice in v. 3) signals that the focus in the introductory section is not merely upon generic speaking in the Spirit but specifically upon the people who claim so to speak.[101] Here then is the confirming evidence from 12:1-3 that *tōn pneumatikōn* in verse 1 should be read as the substantive use of the masculine plural adjective *hoi pneumatikoi,* meaning "the spirituals" or "the prophets." Such evidence explains why 1 Corinthians 12–14 is a gold mine of information about early Christian prophecy. Put simply, prophecy is its topic.

---

100. Schmithals, *Gnosticism in Corinth,* 124 n. 13 (emphasis added).

101. Painter, "Paul and the *Pneumatikoi* at Corinth," 248-49 n. 37: "That the reference in 12:1 is to people is confirmed by the 'No one . . .' of 12:3 which takes up 12:1."

How then does this interpretation of 1 Corinthians 12:1-3 relate logically to the extended discussion that follows in 12:4–14:40? Very clearly. Paul begins by placing the subject of authentic prophecy in the larger context of the diversity of the work of the Spirit within the unity of the Body of Christ (12:4-31a). Next, in what Fee nicely calls "a theological interlude,"[102] the apostle qualifies all pneumatic manifestations by showing the "more excellent way" of *agapē* (12:31b–14:1a). Finally, he turns to the specific issue of prophecy and tongues, clearly separating the two gifts from each other, establishing tongues as a discrete gift of ecstatic prayer and praise, and ordering both in the worship life of the congregation (14:1b-40). It is to the first of these three major sections of his discussion that we now turn.

---

102. Fee, *First Corinthians*, 571.

CHAPTER THREE

Prophecy and Spirit

1 Corinthians 12:4-31a

PAUL's "short answer" to the Corinthian question about the *pneumatikoi* (spirituals) who function as prophets in the congregation gathered for worship (12:1-3) concludes with a "solemn declaration" of an "authoritative decision" (Weiss), but that does not settle the matter. The ensuing discussion makes it evident that even the apostle must argue, rather than merely state, his case in order to convince his readers. Though he is convinced that what he is writing to the church in Corinth is "a command of the Lord," he is aware that it must be "acknowledged" as such (1 Cor. 14:37). Authority is only formal until it is actualized through persuasion.[1] The pronouncement of 12:3 ("I make known to you. . . .") thus requires supporting argumentation.

In undertaking this rhetorical task, the apostle "walks into disputed territory."[2] He begins by locating the specific issue of inspired speech in the larger context of the work of the Spirit in the life of the Body of Christ (1 Cor. 12:4-31a). The unity of this first major segment of his discussion is marked by the inclusio created by the use of the term *charismata* in verse 4 ("Now there are varieties of gifts. . . .") and again in verse 31a ("Seek the greater gifts. . . ."). Talbert correctly perceives a chiastic pattern of ABA′ in the passage: "A — the variety of gifts (12:4-11); B — the one body (12:12-27); A′ — the variety of gifts (12:28-30)." Moreover, "12:4-11 . . . is a thought unity held together by an inclusion

---

1. Wire, *Corinthian Women Prophets*, 12-38, emphasizes this point and provides a perceptive analysis of Paul's rhetorical arguments in 1 Corinthians.
2. Georg Eichholz, "Was heisst charismatische Gemeinde?" *TExH* 77 (1960): 8.

(verses 4 and 11, 'the same Spirit')."[3] The term "Spirit," he notes, is not only the "dominant word" in this paragraph but also "the linking word" that ties 12:4-11 to 12:1-3.[4] Likewise, 12:12-27 is "a unit held together by an inclusion (12:12 and 27, body/members/ Christ)."[5] Verses 28-31a conclude the argument from a theological context.

A Theme and Its Thesis

Without prejudice to the theological significance of the term *charisma* (gift) in Paul's vocabulary,[6] it must be asserted that neither the word itself nor the phrase *diaireseis charismatōn* (distributions of gifts) in verse 4 represents the theme of 12:4-11. The parallel, anaphorical structure of verses 4-6 precludes such an emphasis. As the "distributions" *(diaireseis)*[7] listed in 12:8-10 are designated in verse 4 as "gifts" *(charismata)* and attributed to "the same Spirit" *(pneuma)*, so in verses 5 and 6 they are labeled "services" *(diakoniai)* and "workings" *(energēmata)* that have their source respectively in "the same Lord" *(kyrios)* and "the same God" *(theos)*.[8] The topic of 12:4-11 is stated in verse 7, "To each is given the manifestation of the Spirit *(hē phanerōsis*

---

3. Talbert, *Perspectives on the New Testament*, 96.
4. Ibid., 96-97.
5. Ibid., 98.
6. It was Käsemann, *Essays on New Testament Themes*, 63-94, who first called attention to the original and technical use of the term *charisma* in Paul's correspondence, interpreting it as a critical concept over against the conventional understanding of spirituality in the Hellenistic world encountered by the apostle in his missionary ventures. The influence of Käsemann's thesis upon subsequent studies of the term is evident in Joseph Brosch, *Charismen und Ämter in der Urkirche* (1951), 30-32; Brockhaus, *Charisma und Amt*, 37-42; Koenig, *Charismata*, 146 n. 1; Siegfried Schatzmann, *A Pauline Theology of Charismata* (1989), 8.
7. Weiss, *Korintherbrief*, 298, understands the term in this context to denote not merely "difference" or "variety," but the acts of distribution by the one Spirit (cf. 12:11). See also Barrett, *First Corinthians*, 283.
8. Lietzmann, *Korinther I/II*, 61, attributes the interchange of *charismata, diakonia,* and *energēmata* to rhetorical necessity, while Weiss, *Korintherbrief*, 298, sees in the terms *pneuma, kyrios,* and *theos* the influence of a very old triad formula (cf. Ernst von Dobschütz, "Zwei- und dreiliedrige Formeln: Ein Beitrag zur Vorgeschichte der Trinitätsformel," *JBL* 50 (1931): 117-47.

tou pneumatos)[9] for the common good." The sentence may be read either as the heading of verses 8-10,[10] or as a summary of verses 4-6.[11] Conzelmann thinks that the difference is "only one of emphasis."[12] But Fee rightly sees verse 7 as stating Paul's thesis.[13] As such, it serves as the thematic link between verses 4-6 and 8-10. The disclosure of the *Spirit*, then, provides not only the terminological but also the material connection between 12:4-11 and 12:1-3.

The key to interpreting the thesis that "to each is given the manifestation of the Spirit for the common good" is the main verb in the concluding statement of the passage: "The one and the same Spirit works *(energei)* all these things . . ." (v. 11). This statement repeats the thought expressed in verse 6 with reference to God *(theos)*, "who works *(ho energōn)* all things *(ta panta)* in every one *(en pasin)*."[14] The emphasis falls here not upon the different subjects of the verb *energein* (God and the Spirit), but upon the variously designated diverse actions effected by the divine agent. The same admixture of designations of divine agency occurs also in Romans 15:18-19 where Paul speaks of "what Christ has accomplished *(kateirgasato)* through me . . . by the power of the Spirit of God" (NRSV).[15] Yet the clear implication is that the Spirit/Lord/God is manifested in the things *worked*[16] by the divine

---

9. The nature of the genitive in *hē phanerōsis tou pneumatos* is impossible to determine beyond doubt. Robertson and Plummer, *First Corinthians*, 264, defend the objective sense: "the Spirit given by the manifestation." Weiss, *Korintherbrief*, 298-99, argues for a subjective genitive: "the manifestation given by the Spirit." Conzelmann, *1 Corinthians*, 208-9, is undecided. Fee, *First Corinthians*, 589 n. 30, thinks the objective reading is more likely "since the concern is not with the gifts, but with the manifestation of the Spirit through the gifts." Either way, he concludes, the subject of the sentence is the "disclosure of the *Spirit's* activity" in the midst of the congregation.

10. Weiss, *Korintherbrief*, 298.

11. Barrett, *First Corinthians*, 284. See also Robertson and Plummer, *First Corinthians*, 264.

12. Conzelmann, *1 Corinthians*, 208.

13. Fee, *First Corinthians*, 588.

14. The gender of *en pasin* in 12:6 is uncertain, being grammatically either masculine (every one) or neuter (every thing). Since *ta panta* has its antecedents in *charismata, diakonia,* and *energēmata,* it is more likely that *en pasin* refers to the recipients of gifts, ministries, and workings.

15. In Gal. 2:8 the designation is generic: "he who worked *(energēsas)* through Peter making him an apostle to the circumcised also worked *(enērgēsen)* through me in sending me to the Gentiles" (NRSV).

16. Bauer, *Lexicon*, 264, renders the transitive sense of *energein* as *"work, produce,*

unity.[17] The participial phrase that completes verse 11, "distributing *(diairoun)* to each one as it wills *(bouletai),*" qualifies the work of the Spirit as diverse and sovereign.[18] The polemical point could hardly be missed by any in Corinth who conceived of the Spirit's operations stereotypically, and thus understood human spirituality in terms of such a typecast.

A Thesis Illumined

The character of this divine work is illumined in verses 4-6 by the three terms *charismata, diakoniai,* and *energēmata.* Paul here is not classifying the divine activities into discrete and mutually exclusive types. Rather, he is describing the divine activity according to its essential features. Each term sheds its own light on the Spirit's work and interprets the others.[19] The inherent logic of these corresponding expressions is most evident when they are considered in the reverse order of their appearance in the text.

In verse 6 Paul speaks of "distributions of workings" *(diaireseis energēmatōn).* The noun *energēma,* like its synonym *ergon,* derives

---

effect" something, with the accusative of the thing effected, or *"produce someth. in someone,"* with *ti en tini,* citing 1 Cor. 12:6 as an example.

17. Barrett, *First Corinthians,* 284, comments with regard to 1 Cor. 12:4-6, "The Trinitarian formula is the more impressive because it seems to be artless and unconscious." Fee, *First Corinthians,* 588, objects to Barrett's manner of speaking: "It is not in fact a Trinitarian construct as such; that is, Paul's interest is not in the unity of the *Persons* of the Godhead: the relationships are not spoken to at all, nor does he say that the Father, Son, and Spirit are one." This is doubtlessly correct. Yet, as Conzelmann, *1 Corinthians,* 207-8 n. 9, rightly notes: "Verses 4-6 . . . have in view the unity of the originator and mediator of the gifts. The Spirit is nothing other than the manifestation of the Lord, who for his part is the salvation of God."

18. Fee, *First Corinthians,* 599, comments: "The emphasis is less on the Spirit's deliberation in action as on his sovereignty in distributing the gifts, or perhaps in manifesting himself. Thus the gifts, even though they are 'given' to 'each person,' are ultimately expressions of the Spirit's own sovereign action in the life of the believer and the community as a whole. This is the Pauline version of 'the wind/Spirit blows where it/he wills' (John 3:8)."

19. Bert Dominy, "Paul and Spiritual Gifts: Reflections on I Corinthians 12–14," *SWJTh* 26 (1983): 52: "These are not separate categories; rather each term illuminates the others."

from the verb *energein* and occurs in the New Testament only in this passage (12:6, 10). The noun's *-ma* suffix specifies "the result of the action" designated by the verb from which it is derived.[20] Thus the term denotes "that which is done, with possible focus on the energy or effort involved — 'act, deed.'"[21] The latter nuance is evident in the phrase *energēmata dynameōn* (v. 10), which denotes literally "acts or deeds of powers" (*dynameōn* being understood usually as the Greek equivalent of "miracles" in English idiom). As used in this context, therefore, the term *energēma* connotes "power actualized." Further, Paul's attribution of such acts or deeds to God (*theos*) in verse 6 specifies that what he has in mind is "God's power actualized."[22] As a description of divine activity, *energēma* states the obvious: the Spirit "works" (*energein*) in the world and is manifested in its "works" (*energēmata*).

The works of the Spirit are not merely demonstrations of divine power, however. According to verse 5 they are equally and simultaneously *diaireseis diakoniōn* (distributions of services). Louw and Nida emphasize that the noun *diakonia* and the verb from which it derives (*diakonein*) belong to a semantic domain that conveys the idea of rendering assistance or help "by performing certain duties, often of a humble or menial nature."[23] Conzelmann is thus on firm ground in commenting on this text: "*diakonia*, 'service,' is essentially a profane concept. The word must be allowed to keep the general character of its significance."[24] When he infers from this that "the essential point is precisely that everyday acts of service are now set on a par with the recognized, supernatural phenomena of the Spirit," however, the exegetical temperature gauge rises into the danger zone. For not only is the term "supernatural," strictly speaking, anachronistic in this context, but its use blunts the point of Paul's assertion that *all* the works of the Spirit, the menial and mundane as well as the extraordinary and exciting, are equally the *Spirit's* acts of *diakoniai* (services).

20. Funk, *A Greek Grammar of the New Testament*, 59.
21. Louw and Nida, *Greek-English Lexicon* I, par. 42:11.
22. Morris, *First Corinthians*, 166.
23. Louw and Nida, *Greek-English Lexicon* I, par. 35.19. They further note that the concept of "service" conveyed by *diakonein* and *diakonia* sometimes requires a translation that introduces "a specific reference to 'a servant,'" or employs "a phrase such as 'to help in small things' or 'to do the low tasks.'"
24. Conzelmann, *1 Corinthians*, 208.

If verse 5 implies a polemic against a Corinthian understanding of the works of the Spirit, the polemic is two-edged. The term *diakonia* intimates that the activity of the Spirit is "designed for ministry, not for indulgence."[25] Further, in a socially stratified church like that in Corinth,[26] where those of "noble birth" (*eugeneis,* 1:26)[27] customarily received service but never rendered it, Paul's designation of "the same Lord" *(Kyrios)* as the source of such deeds of service could not help but give some of his readers an emotional hernia. For the *Kyrios* who here acts diaconically is none other than the crucified and exalted Jesus, the same one acclaimed in the church's confession "Jesus is Lord" (12:3).[28] Verse 5, therefore, further attests to Paul's conviction that it is the exalted Lord (Jesus) who is both source and norm of authentic Spirit-inspired speech.

In verse 4 Paul designates the actualized, diaconic works of the Spirit as "distributions of gifts" *(charismata).* This is clearly his preferred term for the phenomena under consideration here.[29] Not only does he use it first in this passage, but in Romans 12:6-8 he introduces a list that parallels 1 Corinthians 12:8-10 with the participial phrase: "Having gifts *(charismata)* that differ according to the grace *(charis)* given to us . . ." (v. 6). In both of these texts *charisma* denotes the grace character of the divine actions. The term is formed by the addition of the *-ma* suffix to its virtual synonym *charis* (grace). Again the suffix signals that the word connotes

---

25. Dominy, "Paul and Spiritual Gifts," 52.

26. For the social stratification of the Corinthian community, see Gerd Thiessen, *The Social Setting of Pauline Christianity* (1988), 69-120.

27. Thiessen, *ibid.,* 70-71, notes that the term *eugeneis* in 1:26 designates "a specific sociological category which Paul especially emphasizes." "When repeating the idea in vv. 27-28 he not only contrasts 'noble birth' with 'lower born,' but sharpens the contrast between *eugeneis* and *agenē* by two further designations: *ta exouthenēmena* ('despised') and *ta mē onta* ('things that are not')." The "sociological implications of the concepts cannot be denied."

28. Fee, *First Corinthians,* 587, calls attention to the appropriateness of the correlation of "kinds of service" with "the same Lord" in 12:5, "since this word group is used everywhere in the NT to describe the 'servant' ministry of both Christ and his 'ministers.'"

29. Of the seventeen occurrences of the term *charisma* in the New Testament, all but one (1 Pet. 4:10) are found in the Pauline corpus where it serves both as a general synonym for *charis* (grace), signifying the gift of redemption (Rom. 5:15, 16; 6:23), and as a technical term for (a) one's "condition in life" (1 Cor. 7:7), and (b) the "gifts of grace" imparted by the Spirit (Rom. 12:6; 1 Cor. 1:7; 12:4, 9, 28, 30, 31).

"the result of the action" denoted by its cognate verb, in this case *charizein* (to give, grant, or bestow graciously and generously).[30] Thus *charisma* marks the result or realization of an act of grace. Since Paul in verse 4 attributes the distributions of such gifts to "the same Spirit," it seems warranted to infer that a *charisma* is "a divine gift of grace."

In his seminal essay on Paul's use of the term *charisma*, "Ministry and Community in the New Testament," Käsemann objects that "God's gift of grace" is "a misleading translation of the Greek word because it does not indicate that the gift is inseparable from the gracious power which bestows it, and that it is indeed the manifestation and concretion of this power."[31] This qualification is required, he argues, by 1 Corinthians 12:6 and 11 "where the various charismata are described as *energēmata* from which the *phanerōsis tou pneumatos* follows."[32] His point is that deeds effected by the exercise of power may not be divorced in principle from their source. For this reason the *charismata* may not be separated from the *Pneuma* who works them. A *charisma* is an act of the Spirit, according to Käsemann, "in which the power of grace becomes visible."[33]

As the *charismata* are qualified by their being *energēmata*, so also they are further characterized by being *diakoniai* of the *Kyrios*. Käsemann thinks that Paul goes as far as he can to accommodate Corinthian sensitivities in this passage — agreeing that "*Pneuma* is the power of the Transcendent" and acknowledging that the Spirit is present in its manifestations.[34] Implicit in the terminology of verse 5, however, is the polemical notion that the power and presence of the Spirit at work in human life entails a *claim* upon that life, specifically the claim of the Lord who is equally present in the grace-filled work of the Spirit.[35] We thus possess *charis* (grace: here interchangeable with *pneuma*) only "to the extent to which it seizes hold of us and to which the lordship of Christ acting through it brings us into the captivity of his service." A *charisma* then, as Käsemann defines it more fully, is "the specific part which the individual

---

30. Louw and Nida, *Greek-English Lexicon* I, par. 57.102.
31. Käsemann, *Essays on New Testament Themes*, 64-65.
32. Ibid., 65.
33. Ibid., 66.
34. Ibid., 67.
35. Ibid., 68: The "Spirit invariably *claims us for the Lord* as we are in our corporeality, makes us ready and willing for service in our body and thus draws us in to the Body of Christ as its members" (emphasis added).

has in the lordship and glory of Christ; and this specific part which the individual has in the Lord shows itself in a specific service and a specific vocation. For there is no divine gift which does not bring with it a task, there is no grace which does not move to action."[36]

It is in this sense that the *charismata* are qualified further as *diakoniai*. "Service is not merely the consequence but the outward form and realization of grace," Käsemann contends.[37] The diaconic nature of the *charismata* thus serves as a criterion of the Spirit's work. As he explains:

> For [Paul] the test of a genuine charisma lies not in the fact that something supernatural occurs but in the use which is made of it. No spiritual endowment has value, rights or privileges on its own account. It is validated only by the service it renders.[38]

It is the mark of *diakonia* that distinguishes the *charismata* worked by the Spirit from the conventional pagan conception of spiritual manifestations, which is to say that "they are validated not by the *fascinosum* of the praeternatural but by the edification of the community."[39] Paul's thesis statement in verse 7 bears this out: "To each is given the manifestation of the Spirit for the common good."

In sum the apostle's argument to this point is that the Spirit is manifested in the distributive work of the Spirit, which is defined in terms of its nature as *energēmata* (power), *diakoniai* (service), and *charismata* (grace). Because each of these terms is interpreted by the others, there is no evidence of divine power that is not diaconic and charismatic. Neither is there an act of divine service that is not powerful and grace-filled. Nor may we speak of divine grace in action apart from its serving and dynamic character. From whatever angle of vision the work of the Spirit is perceived, it remains the case that the Lord is present in it, claiming the faith and obedience of the beneficiary of his powerful and serving grace. It is those who acknowledge and submit to his claim who confess "Jesus is Lord" (12:3).

---

36. *Ibid.*, 65.
37. *Ibid.*
38. *Ibid.*, 67.
39. *Ibid.*, 69.

A Thesis Illustrated

As the apostle's thesis statement (1 Cor. 12:7) is illumined generally by verses 4-6, even so it is illustrated specifically by verses 8-10.[40] Nine discrete "distributions" of the Spirit are listed here in order to exemplify the concrete variety of the Spirit's work. Hurd's point that the purpose of the enumeration is to protect the diversity, rather than the unity, of the divine activity against a perceived Corinthian myopia on the subject is now widely conceded.[41] The list itself is variously described as inexhaustive,[42] unsystematic,[43] even *ad hoc* (in light of the Corinthian situation).[44] Of these descriptions, the first is evident from the parallel lists of such phenomena in 1 Corinthians 12:28, 29-30; and Romans 12:6-8 (cf. Eph. 4:11). The second is questionable, depending upon what is meant by *systematic*. The third is the most fruitful for understanding the function of the list in Paul's argument. When it is read as a reflection of the ecclesial situation in Corinth, several of its features take on special significance.

To begin with, it should be noted that clearly five of the nine ways in which the Spirit is said to manifest itself, and probably one more, are related to the issue of divinely inspired utterance broadly conceived. The assured instances include "utterance of wisdom," "utterance of knowledge," "prophecy," "different kinds of tongues," and "interpretation of tongues." Only "discernment of spirits" (*diakriseis pneumatōn*), which follows prophecy and precedes tongues in the list, is uncertain. The debate here centers on the question of whether a general testing of spirits (as in 1 John 4:1) or a specific assessing of prophecy (as in 1 Cor. 14:29 where the cognate verb *diakrinein* occurs in the exhortation to judge the utterances of the prophets) is intended.[45] Fee argues cogently

---

40. Bauer, *Lexicon*, 151, cites 1 Cor. 12:8 as an example of the postpositive *gar* (for) signifying that "the general is confirmed by the specific."

41. Hurd, *Origin of I Corinthians*, 191-92.

42. Karl Maly, *Mündige Gemeinde* (1967), 188.

43. Conzelmann, *1 Corinthians*, 209; Héring, *Corinthiens*, 109; Weiss, *Korintherbrief*, 300.

44. Fee, *First Corinthians*, 585 (see n. 12).

45. Gerhard Dautzenberg, "Zum religionsgeschichtlichen Hintergrund der *diakriseis pneumatōn* (I Kor. 12:10)," *BZ* (1971): 93-104 (cf. his *Urchristliche Prophetie*, 122-48), argues on semantic grounds that the phrase means "interpreting the utterances of the prophets." See Grudem, "A Response to Gerhard Dautzenberg on 1 Cor. 12:10," 253-70, for a refutation of this thesis (cf. Grudem, *The Gift of Prophecy in 1 Corinthians*, 263-88).

that *diakriseis pneumatōn* most likely refers to both activities. In the context of Paul's argument, however, it refers "particularly to the phenomenon of 'discerning, differentiating, or properly judging' prophecies" as evidenced by 14:29.[46] Therefore only three of the works of the Spirit listed in verses 8-10 ("faith," "gifts of healing," and "workings of miracles") fall outside the scope of the category of inspired speech — a remarkable feature of the text that further ties 12:4-11 to the issue addressed in the introductory verses (1-3).

Another characteristic of the list, widely recognized, is the appearance of "tongues" (with its related "interpretation") at the end of this list — as well as at the end of two other lists in 12:28-30. Many read this as a deliberate and emphatic statement, indicating the apostle's polemical intention of subordinating *glossolalia* to the other manifestations as the least of the works of the Spirit.[47] The occasion of this devaluation is then identified as the over-inflated status enjoyed by "tongues" among the enthusiasts within the Corinthian community, who looked upon this particular work of the Spirit as the most assuring confirmation of their pneumatic status.[48] As we have emphasized, however, this interpretation of the reason for devaluing "tongues" assumes that it was a discrete work of the Spirit known as such in Corinth. While the fact that the phenomenon of "tongues" is depreciated in this list and the other two in chapter 12 must be recognized, the question of why this is so should remain open for the moment.

A seldom noticed feature of the list in 12:8-10 is that just as the work of the Spirit that is deemed of least importance is placed at the end of each

---

46. Fee, *First Corinthians*, 596: "There are several reasons for taking this position: (a) Both 1 Thess. 5:20-21 and 1 Cor. 14:29, the two places where Paul mentions the functioning of prophecy in the church, call for a 'testing' or 'discerning' of prophetic utterances; it therefore seems likely, given that the noun used in this passage is the cognate of the verb in 14:29, that the same is true here, since it immediately follows 'prophecy.' (b) That seems all the more likely in this case since these two are followed immediately by 'tongues' and 'interpretation.' This same pattern of tongues plus interpretation and prophecy plus discernment is found again in the instruction on order in 14:26-29."

47. Already noted by Greeven, "Propheten, Lehrer, Vorsteher bei Paulus," 3 n. 6. See also Barrett, *First Corinthians*, 286; Bruce, *1 and 2 Corinthians*, 119; Conzelmann, *1 Corinthians*, 209. Fee, *First Corinthians*, 597 n. 82, thinks such assessments of the significance of the ordering are "purely prejudicial."

48. Thus E. B. Allo, *Première Épitre aux Corinthiens* (1956), 326; Barrett, *First Corinthians*, 286; Conzelmann, *1 Corinthians*, 209; Héring, *Corinthiens*, 129; Wendland, *Korinther* (1948), 95.

catalogue, so also the gift of greatest significance is given at the beginning.[49] The explicit priority ascribed to the apostles, prophets, and teachers in verse 28 and repeated in verses 28-30 suggests that the parallel prominence accorded to the "utterance of wisdom" and the "utterance of knowledge" at the beginning of verses 8-10 is occasioned, even as the subordination of "tongues," by the special status enjoyed by such inspired speech among the Corinthian pneumatics.[50] What the significance of this trait of the text might be requires special consideration.

Utterances of Wisdom and Knowledge

The supposition that the Corinthians were preoccupied with the "utterance of wisdom" *(logos sophias)* is warranted by Paul's sharp criticism of such speech in the first major section of the letter (1:10–4:21), the theme of which is stated in the apostolic claim that Christ sent him to proclaim the gospel "not in wisdom of speech" *(ouk en sophia logou;* 1:17). The subsequent reversal of the enigmatic genitive construction *sophia logou* in such parallel expressions as "not in persuasive words of wisdom" *(ouk en peithois sophias logois)* in 2:4, and "not in words taught by human wisdom" *(ouk en didaktois anthrōpinēs sophias logois)* in 2:13, indicates that in relation to the subject matter there is no essential distinction between "utterance of wisdom" *(logos sophias)* and "wisdom of speech" *(sophia logou).* The former designates the matter that comes to expression in speech, and the latter the manner in which it comes to expression.[51] When Paul reminds the

---

49. Hurd, *Origin of I Corinthians,* 192: "Since 'the utterance of wisdom' heads the first series and 'apostles' the other two, it appears that Paul put first the things most important and put last the things least important."

50. Wilckens, *Weisheit und Torheit,* 46 n. 1, commenting on the relation of *logos, sophia,* and *gnōsis* in 1 Cor. 12:8, characterizes the situation as follows: "*Logos* is clearly charismatic speech that has as its content one time *sophia* and another time *gnōsis.* Paul himself values such charisma, as 1:5 shows; but in Corinth it seems to have gone to 'excess,' i.e. a theological over-evaluation of such charismatic wisdom speech; thus not simply a matter of a too much, but of a too high and too exclusive assessment." Rolf Baumann, *Mitte und Norm des Christlichen* (1968), 75-76, develops this observation into the thesis that the theme of the entire letter is "a unified polemic against the overevaluation of charismatic wisdom speech."

51. Heinrich Schlier, *Die Zeit der Kirche* (1956), 207-8.

Corinthians in 2:1 that at the time of his initial missionary visit he did not preach to them "in lofty speech or wisdom" *(hyperochē logou hē sophias)*, he coordinates the two terms.[52] In the context of 1 Corinthians 1–4, this indicates that whenever Paul focuses his attention solely upon either "wisdom" (1:19, 20, 21, 22; 2:5, 6, 7, 8; 3:19) or "utterance" (4:19, 20) the other expression is not entirely absent from view.[53]

By designating "utterance of wisdom" as a discrete work of the Spirit in 12:8, Paul establishes it formally as an act of inspired speech.[54] Unfortunately, the apostle nowhere in 1:10–4:21 identifies the content of its Corinthian version.[55] This lacuna in our knowledge makes it impossible to identify the "utterance of wisdom" definitively or to distinguish it with any assurance from the related "utterance of knowledge" *(logos gnōseōs)* in 12:8. Add to this the probability that both "wisdom" *(sophia)* and "knowledge" *(gnōsis)* are terms taken over by Paul from the Corinthians and the mystery deepens.[56] C. K. Barrett has suggested, on the basis of usage in 1 Corinthians, that *gnōsis* has to do with practical questions such as the eating of food offered to idols, while *sophia* deals with matters of speculation.[57] The exact opposite conclusion is reached by Jean Héring, who, depending upon Septuagint usage of the terms, associates *sophia* with moral teaching and *gnōsis* with theological knowledge.[58] Bultmann thus concludes that it does not seem possible to make a precise distinction between the two words, "whether in respect of form or of content."[59]

---

52. As in 1 Cor. 14:37, the particle *he* (or) here separates terms that throughout the discussion are related. See Bauer, *Lexicon*, 342.

53. Baumann, *Mitte und Norm*, 67-68.

54. *Ibid.*, 78-79: "*Sophia logou* is to be understood as a *legitimate Christian charisma*, more precisely *as pneumatic-charismatic speech*, as a charisma of 'wisdom speech.' A *formal* element of this wisdom speech is that it shows itself as Spirit-effected and superhuman."

55. Schmithals, *Gnosticism in Corinth*, 141: "Paul's polemic at the beginning of 1 Cor. tells us positively nothing about the content of the wisdom being proclaimed in Corinth." The implicit characterization of Corinthian wisdom speech will be discussed in Chapter Five, "Prophecy and Wisdom."

56. Fee, *First Corinthians*, 591 n. 45. Cf. James D. G. Dunn, *Jesus and the Spirit* (1975), 217-21.

57. C. K. Barrett, "Christianity at Corinth," *BJRL* 46 (1963-64): 276. In his later commentary, *First Corinthians*, 284, he retracts this suggestion by conceding that "attempts to distinguish the phrases are not convincing."

58. Héring, *Corinthiens*, 109.

59. Rudolf Bultmann, "*ginōskō*," *TDNT* I, 708 n. 73.

The argument that "utterance of wisdom" and "utterance of knowledge" cannot be synonymous or interchangeable expressions because the text distinguishes them by assigning the former "to one" *(hō men)* and the latter "to another" *(allō de)*[60] is specious because the grammatical construction differentiates not the works of the Spirit but the recipients of the Spirit's work. While it is always dangerous to make a virtue out of necessity, there is a willingness among some commentators to view the two phrases as at least overlapping in meaning if not actually interchangeable.[61] Conzelmann argues that anything less "is in contradiction to the usage throughout the epistle."[62] Noting that *sophia* does not occur again in the discussion of chapters 12–14, while *gnōsis* appears in 13:2 with "prophecy" and "mysteries," again in 13:8 with "prophecy" and "tongues," and finally in 14:6 with "revelation," "prophecy," and "teaching," Fee argues that because *gnōsis* "has also been taken over from the Corinthians and is so closely tied to the preceding 'utterance of wisdom,' the two should probably be understood as parallel in some way."[63] Consequently, it would appear that Paul has placed two other types of inspired speech highly esteemed in Corinth at the top of his list.

A Crucial Disjunction

One or the other of these last two features of 12:8-10, the placing of "tongues" with its "interpretation" last and the "utterance of wisdom"/"utterance of knowledge" first, could be noted and passed over. In tandem, however, they cry out for an explanation. At a minimum these features dispel the conventional view that the enumeration here is simply a random selection. The pressing question then is *why* Paul concedes to the Corinthians the value of inspired wisdom/knowledge speech by granting it the position of eminence in his own catalogue of the Spirit's works, while depreciating their equally prized tongues by relegating it to the place of least importance. The answer cannot be that

---

60. Wilckens, *Weisheit und Torheit*, 46 n. 1.
61. Lietzmann, *Korinther I/II*, 61: "Paul speaks here as in v. 4-6 *plerophorisch* without strict logical differentiation."
62. Conzelmann, *1 Corinthians*, 209.
63. Fee, *First Corinthians*, 593.

he thinks positively of the former (2:6-16) but negatively of the latter, for in chapter 14 he clearly grants "tongues" a positive if qualified significance (vv. 5, 18, 26-28, 39). A possible solution is that more is involved in these features of the text than the exaltation of one type of inspired speech and the devaluation of another. For the construction of the catalogue also achieves the *separation* of the two types of inspired utterance, signaling perhaps Paul's intention to *disjoin* that which was *conjoined* in Corinthian practice.

Another feature of 12:8-10 encourages such an explanation. It is occasionally noted that the subtle alternation between the pronominal adjectives *allos* (another) and *heteros* (different one) in the enumeration of verses 8-10 may be an indication of an intended threefold structure of the list.[64] Despite his judgment that the text is unsystematic, Conzelmann concedes that "a certain grouping" can be discerned in the alternation between *allos* and *heteros* : "(a) v 8; (b) vv 9-10a; (c) v 10b."[65] Fee also calls attention to the "two idiosyncrasies" of an otherwise standard Hellenistic pattern — the introduction of the third and eighth items (faith and kinds of tongues) by the word *heteros* rather than its synonym *allos*, the usual term in such lists.[66]

The point becomes evident when the list is schematically presented:

> To one *(hō men)* is given . . . the utterance of wisdom,
> > to another *(allō de)* the utterance of knowledge . . . ,
> to a different one *(heteros)* faith . . . ,
> > to another *(allō de)* gifts of healing . . . ,
> > to another *(allō de)* workings of miracles,
> > to another *(allō* [*de*]) prophecy,
> > to another *(allō de)* discernment of spirits,
> to a different one *(heteros)* kinds of tongues.
> > to another *(allō de)* interpretation of tongues.

"This may be variety for variety's sake," Fee acknowledges; "but it is also arguable that this most unusual expression of variety has *some purpose* to it. Very likely this is Paul's own clue . . . as to how the list is to be

---

64. Allo, *Corinthiens*, 324; Weiss, *Korintherbrief*, 299.
65. Conzelmann, *1 Corinthians*, 209.
66. Fee, *First Corinthians*, 584 n. 9.

'grouped.' "[67] The clue is so subtle, however, that he views it as "not terribly significant."[68] This judgment might be allowed to stand were it not for the fact that the alternation of *allos* and *heteros* effectively sets apart from each other the two types of inspired speech known to have been prominent among the Corinthians, a feature of the text that is neither accidental nor insignificant. What then was its purpose?

Paul's description of tongues in chapter 14 encourages us to view the phenomenon as unintelligible, ecstatic utterance.[69] Further, his statement that "tongues are a sign not for believers but for unbelievers" (14:22) reflects the cultural view of the time that such ecstatic speech evidenced divine inspiration (cf. 14:23).[70] "Since bizarre behavior on the part of those regarded as possessed frequently occurred outside the strictures of normal social or religious institutions," Aune explains, "*such behavior functioned as a legitimation of the supernatural nature of the experience* in the absence of built-in institutional guarantees."[71] Against this background, Paul's separation of inspired wisdom/knowledge speech from tongues may be explained as his way of denying an authenticating function to ecstatic utterance. The same point is scored in verse 10 by the parallel separation of tongues from prophecy, and the insertion of the Spirit's work of discernment between the two sharply indicates that that task is differentiated from speaking in tongues. Further, this explanation squares with the evidence of the introduction (12:1-3) where Paul argues that the genuineness of inspired speech must be determined by its material relation to the church's confession and not by evidence of ecstasy. The enumeration of the works of the Spirit in verses 8-10 thus acknowledges both types of inspired speech precious to the Corinthians, but the unique structure of the list effectively denies their being conjoined in a singular event of inspired utterance.

---

67. *Ibid.* (emphasis added).
68. *Ibid.*
69. See Chapter Four below for a full discussion of the issue.
70. The verb *mainesthe* in 1 Cor. 14:22 is almost universally understood as a pejorative statement and thus translated "you are mad." Aune, *Prophecy in Early Christianity*, 35, notes, however, that in common Greek parlance "the word *mantis* ('diviner,' 'seer,' or 'prophet') and the terms *mania* and *mainesthai*, which refer to such states as 'madness,' 'rage,' and 'frenzy,' were cognates." Thus *mainesthe* may also connote "you are possessed."
71. Aune, *Prophecy in Early Christianity*, 34.

A Traditioned List?

If the *ad hoc* character of the catalogue in 12:8-10 is evidenced by the first two items listed in verse 8 ("utterance of wisdom" and "utterance of knowledge") and the last two in verse 10de ("tongues" and its "interpretation"), does that mean the central section of the enumeration (vv. 9-10abc) is *ad hoc* also? There is reason to suspect that the opposite is the case, that Paul has in fact redacted a traditional list by bracketing it with verses 8 and 10de, and by adding to the entire enumeration the pronominal adjectives "to one . . . to another . . . to a different one" which pick up and develop "to each is given" in the thesis statement (v. 7). The incorporated tradition in its simplicity would have been composed of the following five items: "faith, gifts of healing, workings of miracles, prophecy, discernment of spirits." What encourages this supposition is the problematic character of the Spirit's work of "faith" when it is interpreted as the third of the nine items listed. As such it represents a departure from the normative Pauline concept of justifying faith, where it normally ranks first. Although the term *pistis* in this context is an anomaly, commentators respect it as an exception to the apostle's ordinary usage and explain it as a reference to that charismatic faith which moves mountains (1 Cor. 13:2).[72]

As the first item in a traditional list, however, another possibility for interpreting *pistis* in its context in the Corinthian list appears in the light of Romans 12:3-8. For the sake of brevity, a summary of the results rather than a repeat of the argument for the exposition of this passage given in Chapter One above (50-62) will be sufficient. The apostle exhorts the community members in Rome not to think of themselves more highly than they ought to think, but to think with sober judgment (v. 3). This is not a general admonition against false conceit, however, but an appeal to the congregation to honor and exercise their differing gifts *(charismata diaphora)* within the life of the church (v. 6). Judgment in this matter is to be made "according to the measure of faith which God has assigned" (v. 3), meaning "according to the grace which is given to you" (v. 6). The usage of "measure of faith" and "the grace which is given" as parallel expressions in regard to "gifts that differ" has special

---

72. Thus Barrett, *First Corinthians*, 285; Bruce, *1 and 2 Corinthians*, 119; Conzelmann, *1 Corinthians*, 209; Fee, *First Corinthians*, 593; Lietzmann, *Korinther I/II*, 61; Robertson and Plummer, *First Corinthians*, 266.

significance for the connotation of "faith" in the central list given in 1 Corinthians 12:9-10abc. For if each *charisma* is "the concretion and individuation of grace" (Käsemann),[73] then each is also the concrete expression of faith as the new obedience.[74] Of the works of the Spirit as well as justification it may be said therefore, *sola gratia — sola fide.* Thus faith is one, even as grace is one, although in their concretion they effect both justification and a gift of service to the community. In the group of manifestations of the Spirit in 1 Corinthians 12:9-10abc, faith may be understood as the basic work and thus the ground, anthropologically speaking, of all other activities of the Spirit.

Finally, it should be noted that in this central grouping of the works of the Spirit Paul introduces his own preferred term for inspired utterance, "prophecy" *(prophēteia).* His preference for this word and its cognate "prophet" *(prophētēs)* is demonstrated by the fact that this is the only work of the Spirit mentioned by the apostle, by one term or the other, in all three lists given in 1 Corinthians 12 (8-10; 28; 29-30) as well as Romans 12:6-8 (cf. Eph. 4:11). Important too is the observation that prophecy and its discernment alone represent inspired utterance in the centrally listed works of the Spirit. The listing of prophecy in the catalogue indicates that Paul understood it as a community-based phenomenon,[75] and by including the term in the enumeration he introduces the rubric under which he will carry out his criticism of the issue identified in 1 Corinthians 12:3.

To Each . . . for the Common Good

Returning to Paul's thesis statement in verse 7, it remains to be asked how serious he is about each member of the church being a medium of the Spirit's work and what he means by "the common good" *(to sympheron).* Both issues are significant for our understanding of early Christian prophecy. The first raises the question of whether every member of the community was a potential medium of prophesying or whether the phenomenon was restricted to specific individuals who were identified by the church as

---

73. Käsemann, *Essays on New Testament Themes,* 73.
74. *Ibid.,* 75.
75. Müller, *Prophetie und Predigt,* 20.

prophets because they regularly mediated this gift. The second issue entails the apostle's understanding of the purpose of prophetic utterance under the stipulated norm of all works of the Spirit.

It is commonly assumed that by "each" *(hekastos)* Paul means "every" member of the community,[76] which is well within the lexicographical range of the term.[77] Fee demurs, however, arguing that Paul "does not intend by this to stress that every last person in the community has his or her own gift."[78] Were that his intention he would have used his customary expression "every single one" *(heis hekastos).*[79] While Fee does not rule out the possibility of all members mediating a work of the Spirit, "depending on how broadly or narrowly one defines the word *charisma*," he thinks the pronoun in verse 7 is "the distributive (stressing the individualized instances) of the immediately preceding collective ('in all people'), which emphasizes the many who make up the community as a whole."[80]

Such a restriction of the term "each" is difficult to sustain, however, in view of Paul's concluding statement in verse 11 that "the one and the same Spirit works all these things, distributing to each one individually *(idia hekastō)* as it wills." Paul's exhortation in Romans 12:3-8 regarding the *charismata* also argues against restricting the term to those within the congregation (many or few but not all) who are tabbed by the Spirit for special manifestations of its power. That exhortation is directed generally to "every one among you" *(panti tō onti en hymin)* and specifically "to each *(hekastō)* according to the measure of faith which God has assigned him" (Rom. 12:3). Then too the argument from the metaphor of the body in 12:14-26 is predicated upon the fact that each organ has its own special function. Lastly, it was precisely the kind of thinking that defines the works of the Spirit "broadly or narrowly" which had the Corinthians in trouble from Paul's perspective. In view of the apostle's claim that the Spirit effects faith in every Christian, and thus the common confession that "Jesus is Lord" (1 Cor. 12:3), *all* believers are *pneumatikoi* (spirituals). The prob-

---

76. Typical is Barrett, *First Corinthians,* 284: "Each member of the church has a gift; none is excluded." Conzelmann, *1 Corinthians,* 208 n. 17, thinks that the emphasis is not on *hekastos* (each) but on *pros to sympheron* (for the common good), but he acknowledges that "it is in fact presupposed that each Christian has a gift, cf. v. 11; Rom. 12:3ff."
77. Bauer, *Lexicon,* 236: "each, every."
78. Fee, *First Corinthians,* 589.
79. *Ibid.,* 589 n. 28.
80. *Ibid.,* 589.

lematic references in chapter 14 to "all" *(pantas)* speaking in tongues (vv. 5, 23) and prophesying (vv. 24, 31) must be interpreted in the context of this assertion.

What *is* implied by "to each" is the fact that the Spirit works *differently* in the individual members of the church. The Spirit works something in everyone but not everything in anyone. The apostle's rhetorical questions in 12:29-30, each expressed in a manner that expects a negative response, make this explicit: "Are all apostles? Are all prophets? Are all teachers? Do all work miracles? Do all possess gifts of healing? Do all speak with tongues? Do all interpret?" The point of 12:4-11 is that the Spirit distributes its diverse manifestations in accordance with its sovereign will, and no one manifestation is the unique signature of the Spirit's presence in power.

The polemical edge of Paul's argument cuts against the inclination of some of the Corinthians to identify the work of the Spirit with a particular manifestation and to claim special status on this basis. Eichholz speaks of "a pneumatic-elite" in Corinth who distanced themselves as "an aristocracy of Spirit-bearers" from the rest of the community, and argues that the emphatic "to each . . . for the common good" in verse 7 is the primary "contra-accent" of Paul's thesis statement.[81] Fee is convinced, however, that an elitism in Corinth can be read out of the text of 1 Corinthians only if it is first read into it. Not that the community was free of "divisions" (*schismata:* 1:10; 11:18; cf. 12:25), but these were occasioned by issues other than the manifestation of the Spirit.[82] Rather, the Corinthian piety was endemic to the entire community. The controversy over what it means to be spiritual *(pneumatikos)* was thus, according to Fee, not at all intra-mural but between Paul and the congregation as a whole.[83] But is this in fact the case?

Evidence to the contrary is available in the text. The use of the technical term *pneumatikos* in the argument of chapters 1–4 (2:13, 15; 3:1) links that passage with chapters 12–14 where the word also occurs (12:1; 14:37).[84] In 2:6 Paul introduces the term *teleioi* (mature ones)

---

81. Eichholz, "Was heisst charismatische Gemeinde?" 19.

82. Fee, *First Corinthians,* 572: "there is not a single suggestion in Paul's response [to the Corinthians' question] that they were themselves divided on this issue."

83. *Ibid.,* 570 n. 6; 572 n. 16.

84. Brockhaus, *Charisma und Amt,* 153, notes that the same word in the same letter cannot bear two technical senses. The *pneumatikos* in chap. 2 is the same one as the *pneumatikos* in chaps. 12–14.

as a parallel to *pneumatikoi* (spirituals), both of which represent Corinthian parlance.[85] When in 3:1 he plays off the former against *nēpioi* (babes) and the latter against *sarkinoi* (carnal ones), it is reasonable to infer that this terminology is equally Corinthian. For, as Robin Scroggs notes, "Paul cannot be charged with setting up a new division in the church at the same time as he is trying to destroy the ones that exist."[86] The apostle himself is willing to employ this language because he recognizes that such distinctions do in fact exist in the church. His point in 1 Corinthians 3:1 is that all in Corinth, not merely some, are infantile and carnal rather than mature and spiritual because there is "jealousy and quarreling" among them and they are "behaving according to human inclinations" (3:3). Because the claim to spiritual status in chapters 12–14 is clearly predicated upon participation in the Spirit's manifestations, it must be assumed that the distinctions between spiritual and carnal, mature and infantile believers is based upon the same criterion.

To the extent that Paul's development of the body analogy in 12:14-26 is tailored to the Corinthian situation,[87] we may also infer a spiritual elitism in the congregation. Fee himself recognizes that verses 21-26 have "clear implications of alleged superiority."[88] Of verse 21 he writes:

> Both the direction and content of what is said imply a view "from above," where those who consider themselves at the top of the "hierarchy" of persons in the community suggest that they can get along without some others, who do not have their allegedly superior rank.[89]

He further acknowledges that this is "a direct reflection of the divided situation in Corinth," but he dismisses the obvious in favor of the dubious by referring the text to the "social status" of the privileged members of the church.[90] Fee misses the point that social status in a community like that in Corinth could be established by special experiences of the Spirit as well as by wealth and rank. In the context of

---

85. Wilckens, *Weisheit und Torheit*, 99.
86. Robin Scroggs, "Paul: *Sophos* and *Pneumatikos*," *NTS* 14 (1967): 38 n. 4.
87. Martin, *The Spirit and the Congregation*, 20, states boldly: "So Paul in elaborating the body metaphor . . . puts into the mouth of different organs of the human body sentiments, complaints, and claims that assert what the Corinthian readers were saying."
88. Fee, *First Corinthians*, 609.
89. *Ibid.*, 612.
90. *Ibid.*, 609.

chapters 12–14, the "hierarchy" in the Corinthian church to which Paul alludes can only have the evidences of the Spirit as its foundation. The argument in verses 22-24a is that community stratification on this basis is contrary to the nature of the body created by the Spirit. It appears therefore that there was an elitist group in Corinth that claimed special status because of its experiences of the Spirit.

The work of the Spirit prized by the Corinthian elitists is customarily identified with speaking in tongues.[91] That this is a myopic view is evident from the equally high value placed upon inspired wisdom/knowledge speech in Corinth. Given Paul's dramatic separation of these two types of utterances from one another in the enumeration of verses 8-10 because of their integral association in Corinthian practice, it is more likely that the manifestation of the Spirit cherished by the spiritual elitists in the congregation was a speech phenomenon constituted by both intelligible and unintelligible components, with the latter evidencing the authenticity of the former.

Paul's insistence that the Spirit distributes its work "for the common good" *(pros ton sympheron)* stipulates what John Koenig calls "the corporate thrust of the Spirit."[92] The Greek phrase Paul uses to express this regulation is idiomatic and thus susceptible to a variety of English translations such as "with a view to mutual profit,"[93] or "in order to make use of it."[94] If the noun *sympheron* denotes a generic "advantage, benefit," it derives its communal connotation from the primary sense of its cognate verb *sympherein* (to cause to come together).[95] Paul's basic idea here is that the Spirit benefits the church through its diverse works by bringing the individual members together in the one Body of Christ (12:12) where they serve one another in the Spirit.[96] As John Schütz aptly notes, it is "the common life" which is "the goal toward which the

---

91. Of tongues, Conzelmann, *1 Corinthians,* 209, states: "it is the one that is most highly valued in Corinth, precisely because it is unintelligible." See also Fee, *First Corinthians,* 597: "the Corinthians' singular preference for this manifestation is what lies behind this entire argument."
92. Koenig, *Charismata,* 82.
93. Barrett, *First Corinthians,* 284.
94. Conzelmann, *1 Corinthians,* 208.
95. Louw and Nida, *Greek-English Lexicon* I, par. 15.125.
96. Arnold Bittlinger, *Gifts and Graces: A Commentary on 1 Corinthians 12–14* (1967), 25, thinks *sympheron* is a technical term taken from Stoic philosophy where it denotes the restoration (the bringing together again) of the cosmos.

energies of specific gifts are to be directed," the point being that "individuation does not give license to individualism."[97]

In addition to the confession "Jesus is Lord" (12:3), Paul specifies in verse 7 a second criterion for discerning the work of the Spirit. Each manifestation of the Spirit must be ordered clearly to the good of the community if it is genuine. Luke Johnson notes correctly that this second criterion is really "an explication of the first."[98] For the *Pneuma* represents the *Kyrios* in its work, the purpose of which is to establish and develop his lordship in and through the church — the "one body" (12:13) that is "the body of Christ" (12:27). This ecclesial expression of the confessional norm is thus both utilitarian (useful) and teleological (purposeful). The same criterion is polemically operative throughout chapter 14 where the noun *oikodomē* and its cognate verb *(oikodomein)* denote metaphorically the "edification" or "upbuilding" of the church.[99] MacGorman summarizes the bottom line of Paul's thesis statement in verse 7 nicely: "Although *individually* bestowed, the charismatic gifts are *congregationally* intended."[100]

One Spirit — One Body

If 12:8-10 is an exposition of the phrase "to each is given" in verse 7, then 12:12-27 represents a parallel commentary on the concluding phrase of Paul's thesis statement, "for the common good."[101] The ecclesial implications of the latter phrase are now explicitly developed. Paul sets forth the theme of this passage in verse 12, "For just as the body is one and has many members . . . , so it is with Christ." As in 1 Corinthians 1:13 ("Is Christ divided?"), so here Paul uses synecdoche (part for whole or whole for part) to designate the church.[102] The usage is appropriate in that the passage will culminate with the declaration, "Now you are the body of Christ and individually members of it" (12:27). The burden of the theme is to show

---

97. John Howard Schütz, "Charisma and Social Reality in Primitive Christianity," *JR* 54 (1974): 60.
98. Johnson, "Norms for True and False Prophecy in First Corinthians," 36.
99. Brockhaus, *Charisma und Amt*, 162-63.
100. J. W. MacGorman, "Glossolalic Error and Its Correction: I Corinthians 12–14," *RevExp* 80 (1983): 393.
101. Martin, *The Spirit and the Congregation*, 19.
102. G. B. Caird, *The Language and Imagery of the Bible* (1980), 135-36.

that the unity of the church is not compromised by the diversity of the Spirit's work within the one body. Verses 13 and 14 explicate the theme, the first by elaborating on the initial motif, "the body is one," and the second by explaining that the body is by definition composed of "many members."[103] The theme is then illustrated in two parts by the analogy of the body (12:15-26), verses 15-20 exemplifying the diversity of the body's members and verses 21-26 their mutual dependence. Verse 27 concludes the section by identifying the body under consideration as "the body of Christ," which the Corinthians themselves are.

In his essay, "The Theological Problem presented by the Motif of the Body of Christ," Käsemann emphasizes that in 1 Corinthians 12:12 "Paul does not simply establish the fact that the church is a body; the argument is a Christological one, as in Rom. 12:4: it is with Christ himself (to take the most cautious interpretation) as it is with the body; 'in Christ' the church is a body."[104] Because of this christological grounding of the church, he pleads for a nonmetaphorical interpretation of "the body of Christ." "The exalted Christ really has an earthly body," he insists, "and believers with their whole being are actually incorprated into it and have therefore to behave accordingly."[105] As the earthly body of the risen and exalted Lord,[106] the church is "the sphere of his earthly kingdom"[107] or "his present sphere of sovereignty."[108] The conceptual correlation between the body of Christ and the human body in Paul's analogy indicates that the former is profoundly characterized by the nature of the latter. On the basis of Paul's usage of the anthropological term *sōma* (body), Käsemann infers that the apostle conceives of the human body as a being constituted for "membership and participation" and with a capacity for "communication."[109] This qualifies "the body of

---

103. Fee, *First Corinthians,* 600 nn. 3, 5, calls attention to the intensive *kai* (and) with the postpositive *gar* (for) that introduces each sentence: "For indeed."

104. Ernst Käsemann, *Perspectives on Paul* (1971), 103.

105. *Ibid.,* 104. Käsemann's plea for a nonmetaphorical interpretation of "the body of Christ" in Paul's thought was made prior to the current intense philosophical interest in the nature of metaphor. Janet Martin Soskice, *Metaphor and Religious Language* (1985), argues that metaphor has referential power and thus is, or at least can be, "reality depicting" (133). This is the point which Käsemann is seeking to establish.

106. Käsemann, *Perspectives on Paul,* 111.

107. *Ibid.,* 115.

108. *Ibid.,* 117.

109. *Ibid.,* 114.

Christ" as the reality in which "Christ communicates with his people . . . through sacrament, Word and faith."[110] Although it is a universal concept, the "body of Christ" is for Paul "represented by every individual congregation."[111]

It is into this "one body" that believers are baptized by the "one Spirit" (v. 13). Commentators commonly read "we were baptized" *(ebaptisthēmen)* as a reference to the initiatory rite of Christian baptism,[112] although Bruce sees it as the one place in the New Testament apart from the Gospels and Acts where "the baptism of the Spirit" is mentioned.[113] In an extended comment on 1 Corinthians 12:13, Fee argues against both of these referential options.[114] Noting that we are hard pressed to find an equation between the rite of baptism and the reception of the Spirit in Paul's letters, although both are assumed to occur at the beginning of the life of faith, he argues that the verb "baptized" has a metaphorical rather than a technical sense in this text. This is called for by the structure of the sentence into two parallel clauses: "We all were baptized in the one Spirit/We all were caused to drink one Spirit." Reading the text as an instance of Semitic parallelism, where the thought of the first clause is repeated differently in the second, Fee argues that the clear metaphorical character of the verb *potizein* (to give to drink) in the second clause requires a metaphorical rather than a technical interpretation of *baptizein* (to baptize) in the first (cf. 1 Cor. 10:1, "baptized into Moses"). The reference of the text then is not to the *act* of baptism but to the initial *experience* of the Spirit at the time of conversion. This places the emphasis upon the "Spirit" where it properly belongs, as evidenced by the use of the term in both clauses. Paul's argument, therefore, is that the unity of the "one body" is established by the *common* experience of the Spirit among its many members.[115]

110. *Ibid.,* 115.
111. *Ibid.*
112. Thus Barrett, *First Corinthians,* 288; Conzelmann, *1 Corinthians,* 212; Lietzmann, *Korinther I/II,* 63; Robertson and Plummer, *First Corinthians,* 272.
113. Bruce, *1 and 2 Corinthians,* 120.
114. Fee, *First Corinthians,* 603-6.
115. G. J. Cuming, "EPOTISTHEMEN (I Corinthians 12.13)," *NTS* 27 (1980): 283-85, shows that *potizein* includes "giving a drink to plants, or as we say in English, 'watering' them; and it is so used earlier in this epistle: I planted, Apollos *epotisen* (3.6)." On the assumption that *baptizein* in 12:13 designates the act of water baptism, he refers *potizein* to the liturgical action of "a deacon or other minister pouring water over the baptismal candidate from a jar or shell, like a gardener watering a plant. The translation

PROPHECY AND SPIRIT

The connection between this initial experience of the Spirit and the confession effected by the Spirit, "Jesus is Lord" (12:3), should not be overlooked. For by including the believer into "the one body," which is "the body of Christ," the Spirit places the convert in the Lord's "present sphere of sovereignty" (Käsemann).

Paul's ensuing assertion that "the body does not consist of one member but of many" (v. 14) is illustrated by the analogy of the human body, verses 15-20 emphasizing the essential diversity of the bodily parts and verses 21-26 underscoring the mutual dependence of the body's organs. Two explanatory statements in the illustrative analogy require special attention. The first is that "God arranged *(ho theos etheto)* the organs in the body, each one of them, as he chose *(ēthelēsen)*" (v. 18). The second is that "God has composed *(ho theos synekerasen)* the body . . . that there may be no discord *(schisma)* in the body . . ." (vv. 24-25). Both texts attest to the divine ordering of the human body.[116] On the one hand, they pick up on the concluding statement of verses 4-11 that the Spirit "distributes to each one individually as it wills,"[117] and, on the other, they lay the groundwork for the introductory claim of the final segment of Paul's argument in 12:4-31a (vv. 28-31a), "And God has appointed *(etheto ho theos)* in the church. . . ."

In verse 27 Paul departs from the analogy of the body and returns to the theme of verse 12 by summarizing the argument of the entire section in a single sentence: "You are [the] body of Christ and individually members of it."[118] The absence of the definite article in the Greek text indicates that he is thinking here of the church in Corinth neither as the *whole* "body of Christ" nor as *a* "body of Christ" in the sense of merely one among many. Fee thinks the meaning is "something like

---

of 12.13 will then be: We all had the one holy Spirit poured over us." This lexiographical observation applies equally well to Fee's metaphorical interpretation of the term.

116. Louw and Nida, *Greek-English Lexicon* I, par. 37.96, locate *tithēmi* (v. 18) in the semantic domain of "Control, Rule." The verb denotes "to assign someone to a particular task, function or role — 'to appoint, to designate, to assign, to give a task to.'" The verb *synkerannymi* (v. 24) belongs to the semantic domain of "Arrange, Organize," and is defined as "to cause parts to fit together in an overall arrangement: 'to put together, to compose, to structure.'"

117. There is no essential difference between the two verbs *boulein* (12:11) and *thelein* (12:18). Both belong to the semantic domain of "To Intend, To Purpose, To Plan" (Louw and Nida, *Greek-English Lexicon* I, pars. 30.56, 30.58)."

118. Conzelmann, *1 Corinthians*, 214: "Verse 27 sums up."

'Your relationship to Christ (vv. 12-13) is that of being his body,"[119] the implication being that those related to Christ by the Spirit are related to each other. True as this is, it loses the apostle's explicit concept of the "one body" into which all believers are "baptized" by their common experience of the Spirit (v. 13). Käsemann's suggestion that the one body of Christ is "represented by every individual congregation" is thus closer to Paul's point.[120]

God's Ecclesial Order

The significance of verses 12-27 for understanding early Christian prophecy becomes evident in Paul's application of his point in the third and concluding section (vv. 28-31a) of his argument from theological context in 12:4-31a. Though brief by the standard of verses 4-11 and 12-27, it is nonetheless structured: *(a)* a second list of the works of the Spirit which parallels but does not repeat exactly the first occurs (v. 28), *(b)* a third list in the form of rhetorical questions that expect a negative answer follows, and *(c)* a concluding exhortation or statement of fact, depending upon whether the grammatically ambiguous *zēloute* is read as an imperative (be zealous) or an indicative (you are zealous) closes the subsection.

The initial list is introduced by the assertion that "God has appointed *(etheto ho theos)* in the church . . ." (v. 28), the verb reflecting verse 18 (cf. v. 24) and thus reiterating the principle established in verse 12: as it is with the human body, so it is with the body of Christ. Lest his assertion in verse 11 that the Spirit "distributes *(diairein)* to each one individually as it wills" be understood as implying chaos and confusion, Paul makes it plain here that there is "a method to the madness" of the Spirit.

Like the first enumeration (vv. 8-10), the second (v. 28) has important features to be observed. Here, for example, the listing of "first apostles, second prophets, third teachers" introduces into the discussion the novelty of people who bear titles that designate them by the function of the Spirit they individually mediate. Moreover, Paul ranks these titles by the explicit use of the ordinals "first, second, third." On what criterion this prioritizing

---

119. Fee, *First Corinthians*, 617 n. 5.
120. Käsemann, *Perspectives on Paul*, 115.

is made, the text is silent. Given the "common good" *(sympheron)* as the stated purpose of the works of the Spirit (v. 7) and "edification" *(oikodomē)* as the norm of their exercise (chap. 14), we may infer that the titles are ranked on the basis of their relative "usefulness" in building up the church rather than the "dignity" of those who bear them.[121]

Paul's use of titles of people rather than names of the works of the Spirit raises the question of whether or not *offices* are here in view. The problem is a terminological one. Bultmann points out that an office, technically conceived, is a position endowed with its own intrinsic authority, continuing beyond the lifetime of its occupant, and requiring filling when vacated.[122] Obviously the apostles, prophets, and teachers of 1 Corinthians 12:28 may not be considered officers in this sense. Yet, as Bultmann recognizes, the later ecclesiastical offices proper developed out of the *charismata* through the compromise concept that the office bestowed upon its occupant the *charisma* requisite for its fulfillment (cf. 1 Tim. 4:14; 2 Tim. 1:6). If this is so, however, it is legitimate to posit an earlier stage in the development when the work of the Spirit effected in an individual believer a continuing function that warranted the appellation of a title appropriate to the task assigned. A case in point is the title "apostle," which clearly entails both a continuing position and a dependence upon the Spirit's empowerment. Conzelmann distinguishes therefore between a "fixed organization" and "a church order," the former representing a "hierarchy" essential to the nature of the church and the latter "particular activities and positions" that are not sacred but serve a purpose.[123]

In view of Paul's statement that "God has appointed in the church first apostles, second prophets, third teachers," it seems warranted to understand these prioritized titles in terms of a ministerial "church order" in the sense that Conzelmann uses the phrase.[124] The clear in-

---

121. Robertson and Plummer, *First Corinthians*, 279, speak of "an arrangement in order of dignity." Héring, *Corinthiens*, 114, conjectures that the order of priority is based upon an estimate of the "more or less usefulness" of the different functions in relation to the edification of the church.

122. Bultmann, *Theology of the New Testament*, II, 100-111.

123. Conzelmann, *Theology of the New Testament*, 303.

124. Fee, *First Corinthians*, 620, recognizes that the term "apostle" for Paul is "both a 'functional' and 'positional/official' term." But he thinks the other items listed, which designate activities rather than persons, require "apostle" to be understood in 12:28 as "primarily" a functional term. This is a case of the tail wagging the dog. It is Paul himself who makes the distinction between works of the Spirit designated by title

ference is that with the "apostles" there were people in the churches who served the prophetic and didactic functions on a continuing basis and thus were identified as "prophets" and "teachers." Moreover, as Bultmann points out, the apostles, prophets, and teachers in 1 Corinthians 12:28 are *"the proclaimers of the word."*[125] The titles represent, therefore, the apostle's preferred terminology for those who exercise the gifts of inspired utterance. This may be recognized without prejudice to the related question of whether such speech was limited to the title bearers or open potentially to all members of the church. The rhetorical questions of the third list provided in verses 29-30 require acknowledgment that *not all* are apostles or prophets or teachers. But these categorical denials stand in tension with certain statements in chapter 14 that suggest the possibility of *all* prophesying (vv. 5, 24, 31).

Another noteworthy feature of the second list (v. 28) is the fact that the prioritization breaks off at precisely the same point that the titles are dropped in favor of terms that denote activities rather than people: "then deeds of power, then gifts of healing, forms of assistance, forms of leadership, various kinds of tongues" (NRSV).[126] While it is possible to interpret "then . . . then" *(epeita . . . epeita)* as a continuance of the prioritizing of the list in terms of a descending order of importance, this seems unlikely in view of the disappearance of "then" from the list after the fifth item and the reversal of the order between "deeds of power" and "gifts of healing" in 12:9-10.[127] Paul's point seems to be the simple one that these actions of the Spirit come after the first three in importance.[128] What is unambiguous is the location of "tongues" at the bottom of both this list and, in association with its "interpretation," the list that follows (v. 30). Whether or not this is the apostle's way of demeaning the importance of *glossolalia*, he once again separates this type of inspired utterance from the ministries of the word represented by the apostles, prophets, and teachers. Again this cannot be accidental. Paul is twice more disjoining types of Spirit-inspired speech conjoined

---

and those identified by a functional description. The weight of his argument clearly is carried by the prioritized positions.

125. Bultmann, *Theology of the New Testament,* II, 108.

126. The NRSV is here more faithful to the Greek text than the RSV, which interpreted the listed activities in terms of people: "then workers of miracles, then healers, helpers, administrators, speakers in various kinds of tongues."

127. Fee, *First Corinthians,* 619.

128. Robertson and Plummer, *First Corinthians,* 279.

by the Corinthians for the reason stipulated in the discussion of the initial list of the works of the Spirit in 12:8-10.

The argument from theological context concludes with the words *zēloute de ta charismata ta meizona* (v. 31a). The verb is grammatically either imperative or indicative. Most commentators and all standard English translations interpret it as an imperative, expressing the exhortation: "Be zealous of the greater gifts." The criterion by which the "greater" gifts are discernible is commonly identified with the prioritized titles in verse 28, among which tongues is not included. Since apostleship is not a position to which a believer might aspire, the standard argument is that Paul refers here to the two titles listed in ranked order that were in principle open to all church members — the prophet and the teacher. This is allegedly confirmed by the parallel exhortation in 14:1bc that picks up the thread of the argument dropped momentarily in 12:31a in order to present the "more excellent way" (12:31b–14:1a): "be zealous of inspired utterances *(ta pneumatika)*, especially that you may prophesy." Those who view 12:31b–14:1a as a redaction argue that *ta pneumatika* in 14:1b is an editorial seam, the original text reading: "Be zealous of the greater gifts, especially that you may prophesy" (12:31b–14:1c).

Because the concept of "greater gifts" seems to conflict with the emphasis of the apostle's argument in 12:4-30 upon the legitimate variety of the Spirit's work — especially his development of the body analogy in verses 21-26 which stresses mutuality rather than a hierarchy among the various members of the body — some commentators look for an alternative explanation of 12:31a. Baker notes that only in 1 Corinthians 12–14 do we find Paul commanding the exercise of "zeal" *(zēlos)*, inferring that its meaning here is distinctive. Noting further the apostle's claim in 14:12 that the Corinthians are "zealots of spirits" *(zēlōtai pneumatōn)*, he argues that the repeated exhortation, "Be zealous . . ." (12:31a, 14:1b, 39), represents a quotation, explicit or implicit, from the Corinthians. When supplied with quotation marks, verse 31 reads: "'Be zealous of the greater gifts' [you say], but I will show you a more excellent way."[129] The weakness of Baker's proposal is that there are no markers in the text which suggest that a citation is being introduced in 12:31a or, for that matter, anywhere else the injunction occurs.[130] Iber resolves the issue by reading *zēloute* as

---

129. David L. Baker, "The Interpretation of I Corinthians 12–14," *EQ* 45 (1973), 226-28.

130. Fee, *First Corinthians*, 624.

indicative and thus the sentence as a statement: "You are zealous for the greater gifts." The verse simply characterizes the behavior of the Corinthian community and thus pinpoints in a brief formulation the matter at issue between the apostle and the church. The "greater gifts" that were the object of Corinthian zeal, Iber infers, were "the extraordinary ecstatic phenomena" such as *glossolalia*.[131] Verse 31 thus links chapters 12 and 13 by placing "the way" of the Corinthians in antithesis to "the more excellent way" of love *(agapē)*.[132] Attractive as this proposal is, it suffers from the fact that in 14:1 and 39 *zēloute* is unambiguously imperative. It is difficult to believe that the same verb, in the same form, in the same context would represent such a dramatic difference of grammatical mood in this particular instance.[133]

If the priority items of the list given in verse 28 are taken seriously, as Paul obviously intends, then the concluding injunction is perfectly understandable. God has ordered the Spirit's work in the church around those activities that mediate the inspired intelligible word. These *charismata* are "greater" not in the sense of *higher* but in the sense of *essential*. In his development of the analogy of the body, which rightly stresses the variety of its organs (vv. 15-20) and their interdependency (vv. 21-26), the apostle does not mention that some parts of the body are *vital organs*. That fact implicitly comes to expression in the concluding injunction. If this represents a concession to Corinthian conviction, it demonstrates that the debated issue is not whether there *are* "greater gifts" but *what* these gifts are. It is this question that Paul picks up again in chapter 14:1bc, "be zealous of spiritual utterances *(ta pneumatika)*, especially that you may prophesy." Prophecy is the most essential gift to which a believer might aspire because it mediates the gospel to the church in intelligible speech and without benefit of speaking in tongues, as will be demonstrated in the next chapter.

---

131. Gerhard Iber, "Zum Verständnis von I Cor. 12:31," *ZNW* 54 (1963): 49.
132. *Ibid.*, 51.
133. Fee, *First Corinthians*, 624.

Conclusion

What is to be learned about early Christian prophecy from Paul's rhetorical strategy of locating the issue designated in 12:1-3 within the larger context of the Spirit's diverse work in the life of the body of Christ (12:4-31a)? It is evident, to begin with, that the apostle understood prophecy as a discrete manifestation of the Spirit (v. 10). Like the other evidences of the Spirit's diaconic and charismatic power, prophecy is an individuation and concretion of the work of the Spirit intended for the "common good" of the community (v. 7). Because the body of Christ is the locus of the Spirit's activity (vv. 12-13), so the church is the arena of Christian prophecy.[134] By attributing the "distributions" of the Spirit to the same Spirit, Lord, and God (vv. 4-6), Paul intimates that it is the risen and exalted *Kyrios* who is the active agent in prophetic utterances. For this reason, the content of prophecy is subject to the confession of the church effected by the Spirit, "Jesus is Lord" (12:3), which provides the norm for its "discernment" (v. 10). In this regard it is important to note that the apostle expressly assigns this latter task to a special work of the Spirit that is distinguished sharply from speaking in tongues (v. 10).

We learn also that prophecy was so closely associated with certain members of the church that the term "prophet" could be accorded to them as a *nomen agentis* (vv. 28, 29). In this connection the text tells us that the prophets were ranked below the apostles and above the teachers in God's ordering of the church (v. 28). Paul understands these tasks as the "greater gifts" because, as ministries of the word, they are essential to creating and sustaining the body of Christ (v. 31a). Yet his concluding general exhortation to be zealous of the "greater gifts" indicates that prophecy was a manifestation of the Spirit not limited to those titled "prophets." All of this, of course, is Paul's view.

The text of 12:4-31a also reflects the Corinthian understanding of inspired utterance. Their penchant for words of wisdom/knowledge is mirrored here (v. 8) and also in chapters 1–4 of the letter. With this type of intelligible divine communication was intrinsically associated another kind that Paul designates as speaking in tongues and describes in chapter 14 as ecstatic and unintelligible discourse. In the three lists

---

134. Panagopoulos, *Prophetic Vocation in the New Testament and Today*, ed. J. Panagopoulos, 12: For Paul "prophecy is absolutely a theme of ecclesiology and cannot be treated independently."

of the works of the Spirit in chapter 12 (vv. 8-10; 28; 29-30), the apostle not only places tongues at the bottom of each catalogue but also names the gifts of greatest importance at the top. In the initial enumeration the position of prominence is occupied by the "word of wisdom" and the "word of knowledge," acknowledging thereby the importance of these gifts of the Spirit in Corinth. In the second and third enumerations, however, the apostles, prophets, and teachers head the list, indicating Paul's preferred terminology for the mediators of Spirit-inspired speech. What occurs in each list therefore is the effective separation of the first mentioned from the last — intelligible inspired speech from its unintelligible variety. Polemically, this is Paul's way of denying to tongues the function of confirming the authenticity of intelligible utterances ostensibly worked by the Spirit. The apostle carries out this injunction thoroughly in chapter 14, the subject of the next chapter.

CHAPTER FOUR

Prophecy and Tongues

1 Corinthians 14:1-40

RALPH P. Martin reminds us that in 1 Corinthians 14 "we are looking at *the church gathered for and practicing worship in the public assembly.*"[1] Paul states it fully in verse 23, "When the whole church *(hē ekklēsia holē)* gathers *(synelthē)* in the same place *(epi to auto)* . . . ," less so in verse 26, "When you gather *(synerchēsthe)* . . . ," and in verses 19 and 28 by the abbreviation "in church *(en ekklēsia)*." In chapter 14 therefore the apostle returns not only to the point where he interrupted his argument with an interlude on "the more excellent way" (12:31b–14:1a), but to the ecclesial setting out of which the issue of authentic inspired speech emerged (12:1-3). Thus the exhortation that begins chapter 14, "seek the inspired utterances *(ta pneumatika)*, especially that you may prophesy" (v. 1bc), assumes the church at worship as the arena of prophetic actualization. It is in this setting that we must envision the prophets in action.[2]

Theme and Argument

The admonishment of 12:31a, "Seek the greater gifts *(ta charismata ta meizona),*" is repeated with greater precision in 14:1bc. The "greater gifts" are now specified as "spiritual utterances" *(ta pneumatika)*, par-

---

1. Martin, *The Spirit and the Congregation*, 61.
2. Jannes Reiling, *Prophetic Vocation*, 60-61.

ticularly prophesying. In this specification and qualification the theme of chapter 14 is stated. Throughout the passage, however, the foil of prophecy and prophesying is tongues and speaking in tongues. The manner in which Paul places the two phenomena in antithesis to each other in verses 2-5 indicates his intention to enhance prophecy by contrasting it with tongues. The antithetical parallelism becomes evident when the text is presented schematically:

> One who speaks in a tongue speaks . . . to God (v. 2).
> One who prophesies speaks to people . . . (v. 3).
>
> One who speaks in a tongue edifies himself,
> but one who prophesies edifies the church (v. 4).
>
> I want you all to speak in tongues,
> but even more to prophesy (v. 5a).
>
> One who prophesies is greater *(meizōn)*
> than one who speaks in tongues . . . (v. 5b).[3]

The same comparative contrast informs the entire discussion that ensues (see vv. 6, 18-19, 22, 23-25, 27-30, 39).[4]

Paul's judgment that prophecy is "greater" than tongues without interpretation (v. 5) reflects the concept of "the greater gifts" (12:31a) and introduces in the final clause the criterion by which his comparative assessment is made: "so that the church may receive upbuilding *(oikodomēn labē)*." In verse 26 it is stipulated again as a general rule governing all activities of the church at worship: "When you come together, each one has a hymn, a lesson, a revelation, a tongue, or an interpretation. Let all things be done for edification *(pros oikodomēn)*" (cf. v. 12). Prophecy meets this test (vv. 3, 4, 5); tongues without interpretation does not (vv. 4, 17). The reason given for this is that tongues *per se* are unintelligible to the community (v. 2, "no one understands"; cf. vv. 6-12, 13-19, 20-25). Although an oral manifestation of the Spirit, tongues do not communicate meaningful discourse to the congregation.

It is important to notice that by playing off prophecy against tongues in chapter 14, Paul is continuing the separation of *glossolalia*

---

3. Thomas W. Gillespie, "Prophecy and Tongues" (Ph.D. diss., Claremont Graduate School, 1971), 73.

4. Brockhaus, *Charisma und Amt*, 152 n. 53.

from intelligible inspired speech that he began in the three lists of the Spirit's works in chapter 12. In the first he disjoined tongues from words of wisdom/knowledge that were esteemed in Corinth (12:8-10). In the second and third he isolated tongues from apostles, prophets, and teachers (12:28, 29-30). Now it is tongues and prophecy that are separated, each designated as a separate work of the Spirit, each assigned a separate function (14: 2-3, 13-19, 22-25), and each mandated to operate separately in the worshipping assembly (vv. 27-32). By this means the apostle emphatically denies to tongues the value of an authenticating "sign" of prophecy, as verse 22 explicitly states.

"However sharply outlined the *theme* of chap. 14," Conzelmann remarks, "the *argument* is loose."[5] For this reason there is no consensus among commentators on the structure of the passage. Most agree that verses 37-40 represent a conclusion, either of the entire argument of 1 Corinthians 12–14 or at a minimum chapter 14. The disputed issue is whether the major break in the logic occurs at verse 20 or at verse 26. Talbert, for example, argues for the former option on the ground that in 14:20-36 Paul is responding to a pair of Corinthian assertions. The first allegedly appears in verses 21-22 with the citation of Isaiah 28:11-12 (v. 21) and its interpretation (v. 22).[6] The second assertion is said to be cited in verses 34-35 where the injunction against women speaking in the worship assembly occurs.[7] While Talbert's thesis spares Paul the onus of having authored two difficult texts, neither provides a marker that even suggests the introduction of a quotation, much less one originating out of the church in Corinth.

Conzelmann also divides the argument of the passage at verse 20, but on the stylistic ground of the allocution "Brethren *(adelphoi)*."[8] The combination of the formula "What then" *(Ti oun estin)* with the vocative "brethren *(adelphoi)*" at verse 26 is a much stronger signal of a shift in the argument, however.[9] On this ground the chapter is composed of an extended intial segment in which prophecy and tongues are identified terminologically, distinguished phenomenologically, and compared theologically (vv. 1-25); a briefer section in which the preceding argument is applied to the worship life of the church in terms of specific liturgical

---

5. Conzelmann, *1 Corinthians*, 233.
6. Talbert, *Perspectives on the New Testament*, 102.
7. *Ibid.*, 105.
8. Conzelmann, *1 Corinthians*, 240.
9. Fee, *First Corinthians*, 690 (see esp. n. 5).

rubrics (vv. 26-36); and a conclusion (vv. 37-40). The opening section is itself composed of four distinct paragraphs: (1) Verses 1-5 in which the superiority of prophecy to tongues is established on the ground of its intelligibility; (2) verses 6-12 which provide analogies that support the criterion of intelligibility; (3) verses 13-19 which apply the criterion to the believing community; and (4) verses 20-25 which apply the criterion to the situation of the outsider or unbeliever who might be present in the worship assembly.[10]

Lietzmann believes that the essence of both prophecy and tongues is recognizable from the descriptions of these phenomena in 1 Corinthians 14.[11] The development of these portraits is the primary concern of this chapter, beginning with the issue of the terminology involved.

In Terms of a Tradition

Paul denotes the "greater" work of the Spirit here, as elsewhere in his correspondence, by various forms of the verbal stem *phē-* (say, speak) in conjunction with the prefix *pro-* (forth).[12] In chapter 14 the *nomen agentis* prophet *(prophētēs)* occurs in verses 29 and 32 (twice; cf. 12:28, 29); the denominative verb prophesy *(prophēteuein)* in verses 1, 3, 4, 5 (twice), 24, 31, 39; and the *nomen actionis* abstracted from the verb prophecy *(prophēteia)* in verses 6 and 22 (cf. 12:10). Yet the lexicographic limits imposed upon the apostle's consistent use of these terms tell us only that the manifestation of the Spirit designated thereby is related to and identified with an activity of speaking or proclaiming. Paul's understanding of the matter therefore cannot be derived from the dictionary. Neither is the history of religions usage of the terms particularly

---

10. *Ibid.,* 652-88.
11. Lietzmann, *Korinther I/II,* 68.
12. Helmut Krämer, *"prophētēs," TDNT* VI, 783, notes that the difficulty in determining the root meaning is created by the ambiguity of the prefix *pro-*. Because the presupposed verb *prophēmi* may be cited from post-Christian literature only, the significance of the prefix must be discerned from its association with verbs of saying and speaking in earlier references. On this basis it becomes evident that the original sense of *pro-* is "forth," i.e., "speaking out," rather than the temporal "fore-." The root meaning is therefore "*pro*claiming" (forthtelling), although the ancillary concept of "*pre*dicting" (foretelling) is not thereby ruled out.

helpful in this regard. Erich Fascher concludes from his extensive survey of the relevant texts that although in antiquity the phenomenon of prophetic speaking occurs primarily in a religious context, the variety of forms such speaking assumed and the wide range of significance it enjoyed makes it impossible to determine from these sources what the cognate terms meant to Paul or other New Testament authors beyond the common element of belief in divine communications with humans and the consequent commission to carry such messages to others.[13]

Apart from the semantic generality of Paul's language for the phenomenon of prophecy, however, Fascher calls attention to what appears to be a conscious and studious effort on the part of the New Testament writers to avoid the terms popularly associated with the phenomenon of prophecy in the Greco-Roman world.[14] Aune underscores the same point in his more recent examination of the data.[15] But Aune points out that the opposite is equally true. The preferred terms among Christian writers in the apostolic and post-apostolic eras for prophetic activity, agency, and speech *(prophēteuein, prophētēs,* and *prophēteia)* are largely avoided by pagan authors before and during the same time period in favor of *mainesthai* (to be possessed), *mantis* (diviner or seer), and *mania* (inspiration).[16] This striking fact indicates to Aune that the Christian authors' consistent use of the *prophē-* terminology depends upon the language tradition represented by the Septuagint, in which *prophētēs* is the standard translation of the Hebrew *nb',* rather than that afforded by Hellenism. The Christians' habit of speech regarding prophecy is thus "*formally* derived from the Israelite-Jewish prophetic traditions."[17] The question is whether their dependence upon these traditions was merely *formal.*

Aune observes that of the 144 occurrences of the word *prophētēs*

---

13. Fascher, *Prophētēs,* 190.

14. Ibid., 166: The word *mantis* (seer) is never applied to a Christian prophet, nor is the term *chrēsmologos* (oracle) ever used to designate a prophecy. Just as the verb *prophēteuein* is denied to the heathen prophet (with the one exception in Titus 1:12), so the verb *manteuesthai* is avoided as a description of prophesying in the church.

15. Aune, *Prophecy in Early Christianity,* 23f., 28f., 34ff.

16. Ibid., 198-99: "In pagan Greek the verb [*prophēteuein*] is used only rarely and very late in antiquity; the verb most commonly used in Greek sources for the act of prophesying was *mainesthai,* a cognate of the most common Greek designation for a diviner *(mantis).*"

17. Ibid., 199 (emphasis added).

in the New Testament, 86 refer to Old Testament prophets. What made the term applicable to Christian figures, he argues, was *"the prevalent conception of the prophetic role in the OT."*[18] Which is to say that the way in which the early Christians understood the task of the Old Testament prophets determined their view of the function served by corresponding individuals in their own congregations. The significance of this inference can be demonstrated by Paul's own references to the Old Testament prophets. Dunn finds it "somewhat surprising" that the apostle frequently cites the Old Testament prophets in his letters but rarely refers to them by title and only twice in his own words (Rom. 1:2; 3:21).[19] These two texts are invaluable, however, in that they indicate how the apostle understood the role of the scriptural prophets and thereby how he viewed the ministry of their successors in the Christian communities.

Covenant Prophets Old and New

Romans 1:2 speaks of "the gospel of God, which he promised beforehand through his prophets in the holy scriptures." Here the Old Testament prophets (broadly conceived)[20] are presented as mediators of the divine promise of an eschatological event that Paul identifies as the present gospel of God for which he himself has been set apart.[21] The gospel is then defined by the confession in 1:3b-4 in terms of its central content, which is the resurrection of Jesus and his consequent lordship. This is the event promised through the prophets and announced by the gospel. Paul's point is that God's promise is now merged with God's

---

18. *Ibid.*, 195 (emphasis added).

19. James D. G. Dunn, *Romans 1–8* (1988), 165. The other instances occur in Rom. 11:3 (a citation of 1 Kgs. 19:10) and possibly 1 Thess. 2:15 where "the prophets" may refer to either Old or New Testament figures.

20. Cranfield, *Romans* I, 56 n. 4: "By 'prophets' here we should probably understand not just those whom we normally think of as OT prophets nor yet all whose combined legacy makes up the second division of the Hebrew Scriptures, but the inspired men of the OT generally, including such as Moses (cf. Acts 3:22) and David (cf. Acts 2:39f.)."

21. The exposition of Rom. 1:2-4 here follows Käsemann, *Commentary on Romans*, 6-10.

gospel.[22] For this reason Paul can say elsewhere that "the scripture . . . preached the gospel beforehand to Abraham, saying, 'In you shall all the nations be blessed'" (Gal. 3:8). In this instance the giving of the promise (Gen. 12:3; 18:18) is designated not by the verb *proepangellein*, as in Romans 1:2, but by *proeuangelizein*. The prophetic announcement of the promise is thus the equivalent of the pre-proclamation of the gospel. The merging of the promise and the gospel in the resurrection event, which realizes the former and grounds the latter, indicates that the prophets of the Old Testament are distinguished from those who bear the same title in the church not by function but only by their respective temporal locations in relation to this event. Put simply, the prophets of both Testaments meet in the gospel. Thus Käsemann can say of the prophets mentioned in Romans 1:2, "Their task is seen here, not in the explication and application of the gospel through preaching as performed by NT prophets according to 1 Corinthians 14, but in the proclamation of the future eschatological event."[23] Apart from this temporal difference, however, they are united in the proclamation of the promise that is gospel and the gospel that is promise.[24]

The same point is scored differently in Romans 3:21, the other text in which Paul mentions the Old Testament prophets by title. "But now the righteousness of God has been manifested apart from the law," he announces, "although the law and the prophets bear witness to it." By "the law and the prophets" he means the Scriptures as a whole.[25] The claim that the law and the prophets serve a witnessing function is formally a statement about the righteousness of God, but it also says something about the Scriptures themselves.[26] As witnesses they provide

---

22. Käsemann puts it epigrammatically: "As *epangelia* [the Scriptures] participate in the *euangelion*" (*ibid.*, 9). See also Eichholz, *Die Theologie des Paulus im Umriss*, 16: "The gospel has its pre-history *(Vorgeschichte)* in the promissory history *(Verheissungsgeschichte)* of the OT, as one may paraphrase the statement of Paul in Rom. 1:2."

23. Käsemann, *Commentary on Romans*, 9.

24. Beker, *The Triumph of God*, 24, emphasizes that "the promises of the Old Testament have not been 'fulfilled' in the gospel of Christ and should therefore not be spiritualized. Rather they are taken up in the gospel so as to evoke a new expectation and hope for their ultimate 'fulfillment' in the kingdom of God."

25. This rabbinic phrase is found only here in Paul's letters, but it is common in the New Testament (cf. Matt. 11:13//Luke 16:16; Matt. 5:17; 7:12; 22:40; Luke 24:44; John 1:45; Acts 13:15; 24:14; 28:23).

26. Cranfield, *Romans*, I, 202.

binding testimony to the "covenant faithfulness" of God,[27] which is now evidenced eschatologically in the redemptive death of Christ Jesus (Rom. 3:25-26) and revealed, "apart from the law,"[28] in the proclamation of the gospel (Rom. 1:17).[29] If the prophets of the Old Testament are designated in Romans 1:2 as the proclaimers of God's promise that in Jesus Christ becomes God's gospel, so in Romans 3:21 they are depicted, together with the law, as the witnesses to the divine righteousness that in Christ Jesus is now revealed in that gospel. What this means, Hays argues, is that "the dialectical movement of judgment and grace that structures Paul's presentation of the gospel is in fact a recapitulation of the judgment/grace paradigm that undergirds the whole witness of Scripture, especially the prophetic writings of the exilic period. When Paul claims that the Law and the Prophets bear witness to 'the righteousness of God,' which reaches out to save the ungodly, he is calling attention to precisely this fundamental ground structure of Scripture."[30]

This then is what the prophets of the Old Testament do, according to Paul. They proclaim God's promise (realized in the gospel) and bear witness to God's righteousness (revealed in the gospel). We may reasonably infer therefore that those Christians who bore the same title as their Old Testament precursors served a comparable purpose. Käsemann, as noted, thinks this inference is confirmed by the description of the early Christian prophets in 1 Corinthians 14. We will return to this issue following a consideration of Paul's terms for the phenomenon of tongues.

---

27. For a concise summary of the debate over the meaning of "the righteousness of God" in Paul, see Dunn, *Romans 1–8*, 40-42, who argues that righteousness in Hebrew usage is (1) a relational term that, when attributed to God, (2) denotes covenant faithfulness, which (3) entails both the activity and gift of God, and, in its verbal form, (4) signifies an action that both *makes* and *counts* someone righteous.

28. J. Christiaan Beker, *Paul the Apostle* (1985), 81, notes "a double thrust" in Rom. 3:21-31 — "indicated by the phrases 'apart from the law/testified by the law' (v. 21): (1) the exclusion of the works of the law (v. 27) and (2) the affirmation of the law (v. 31)." The law is affirmed, however, by joining it to the prophets and viewing their joint function as the provision of testimony to the righteousness of God.

29. Rom. 3:21 picks up the theme of the revelation of the righteousness of God introduced initially in 1:17. There is no significant difference in the sense of *apokalyptein* in 1:17 and of *phaneroun* in 3:21, both terms belonging to the vocabulary of revelation (Käsemann, *Commentary on Romans*, 93).

30. Richard B. Hays, *Echoes of Scripture in the Letters of Paul* (1989), 47.

In a Manner of Speaking

Compared to the consistent use of the traditioned terms for the phenomenon of prophecy, Paul's language with regard to the phenomenon of tongues lacks precision and discipline. It is noteworthy that there is evidently no denominative verb available to the apostle. In each instance that he expresses this act, it is by means of a verbal phrase such as "speak in tongues" (*lalein glōssais*, 12:30; 13:1; 14:5, 6, 18, 23, 39; cf. *en glōssē*, 14:19) or "pray in a tongue" (*proseuchein glōssē*, 14:14), or "sing [in a tongue]" (*psalein*, 14:15).[31] Nor is there a term available to denote the agent of the designated action. For this purpose Paul falls back upon the participial phrase "one who speaks in a tongue" (*ho lalōn glōssē*, 14:2, 4, 5, 6, 13). To name the action he enlists the common term "tongue" (*glōssa*), which denotes the organ of speech and thus a language, and assigns it the technical task of designating the phenomenon he has in mind. The noun occurs both in the singular (14:2, 4, 13, 14, 26, 27) and in the plural (12:10 [twice], 28, 30; 13:1, 8; 14:5 [twice], 6, 18, 22, 39). The singular alone denominates the phenomenon only once, in 14:26: "each one has a tongue" (*glōssan*); the same is true of the plural, "tongues are a sign" (*hai glōssai*, 14:22). The plural is in keeping with the phrase "different kinds of tongues" (*heterō genē glōssōn*, 12:20; cf. 12:28) and implies a variety of types, suggesting perhaps that the singular designates a particular instance of the diversity and the plural the phenomenon itself.[32] Yet even here there is ambiguity evidenced by such contrasting phrases as "one who speaks in tongues" (14:5; cf. 12:30; 14:6, 18, 23) and "one who speaks in a tongue" (14:2, 4, 13). Clearly Paul intends to express a singular concept by this disparate terminology. But is it possible to identify a technical term or phrase from his usage?

In his lexicographic study of the New Testament evidence, Roy Harrisville provides a synopsis of the scholarly endeavors to answer this question in the affirmative.[33] The suggestions range from the simple *glōssa lalein* (to speak in a tongue) to the more complex *heterais glōssais lalein* (to speak in different tongues), with *glōssais lalein* (to speak in tongues) viewed as the abbreviated formula. His own preference is the simple

---

31. In 14:15 *psalō tō pneumati* (I will sing in the Spirit) parallels the preceding *proseuxomai tō pneumati* (I will pray in the Spirit), the latter being the equivalent of *proseuxōmai glōssē* (I will pray in a tongue) in v. 14.

32. Weiss, *Korintherbrief*, 335; cf. Engelsen, "Glossolalia and Other Forms of Inspired Speech According to I Corinthians 12–14," 183.

33. Roy A. Harrisville, "Speaking in Tongues," *CBQ* 38 (1976): 36-38.

version, although he allows for the possibility of some flexibility (and thus less precision) in the formula: *glōssa (en glōssē or glōssais) lalein*. The Septuagint, profane Greek sources, and the literature of Qumran are then scoured in search of linguistic parallels to, and thus the possible origin of, one or more of the various Pauline formulations. The results are meager. Harrisville concludes that "the Septuagint translator appears to have known nothing of a technical term for speaking in tongues."[34] Likewise, "profane or non-ecclesiastical Greek knew of no technical term of speaking in tongues."[35] With regard to the Qumran sources, however, matters are otherwise. On the basis of a similarity between the translations of Isaiah 28:11-13a by the Septuagint, Aquila, and the Qumran community, he argues that prior to Paul the phrase *glōssa lalein* (to speak a tongue) had become "more or less fixed," and that this usage is reflected in Paul's own version of the Isaiah text in 1 Corinthians 14:21.[36] The question is whether the fixed formula referred to the phenomenon intended by the apostle. Harrisville answers with the hypothesis that "if something akin to glossolalia was practiced in Jewish circles, particularly among those who nourished apocalyptic hopes, the community at Qumran furnished an atmosphere congenial to the emergence of the technical terms under discussion."[37] But as Christopher Forbes observes wryly, "that 'if' is a large one indeed."[38]

Apart from the New Testament itself, therefore, it is not possible to attribute the tongues terminology of 1 Corinthians 12–14 to a particular language tradition. Even if this language usage is *sui generis* to the early Christian communities, however, the issue of its origin remains unresolved. Of the thirty-one New Testament texts in which *glōssa* (a tongue) refers to speech inspired by the Spirit, only four occur outside of 1 Corinthians 12–14 (Mark 16:17; Acts 2:4; 10:46; 19:6). Because of the spurious and late character of the Markan text, it is to Acts that some look for evidence of an early tradition regarding the phenomenon of tongues and its attendant terminology.

Engelsen contends that Luke uses *glōssais lalein* (to speak in tongues) with "a wider and more diffuse meaning" than Paul. Whereas

34. *Ibid.*, 39.
35. *Ibid.*, 41.
36. *Ibid.*, 44.
37. *Ibid.*, 45.
38. Christopher Forbes, "Prophecy and Inspired Speech in Early Christianity and its Hellenistic Environment," Ph.D. diss., Macquarrie University (1987): 59.

the apostle uses the phrase to distinguish unintelligible inspired speech from prophecy, Luke views it as an aspect of the prophetic word. The inference is that "Paul's attempt to separate this speech phenomenon from prophecy points to an earlier stage where such a separation had not taken place." From this Engelsen concludes that "Luke's use of the term in Acts belongs to this pre-Pauline stage."[39] In all likelihood Engelsen's is a correct assessment at the phenomenological level; but such an assessment does not entail the terminological implications he derives from it. For it is not at all clear how Luke understands the phrase "speaking in tongues." In Acts 19:6 it is explicitly associated with prophesying, but in 10:46 it is connected with "extolling God." As for the Pentecost account in Acts 2, Luke interprets the apostle's speaking "in other tongues" (*heterais glōssais*, 2:4) as a "language miracle"[40] in which the apostles were heard speaking by the linguistically pluralistic diaspora crowd in the native dialect (*dialektos*, 2:6, 8) of each one. In this passage, in other words, the phrase "in other tongues" is the equivalent of "in our own language" (*hēmeterais glōssais*, 2:11).[41] The ambiguity of the meager evidence afforded by Acts therefore makes it impossible to identify a pre-Pauline language tradition regarding speaking in tongues, unless one is prepared to argue that the original reference of the terminology is to speaking in unlearned human languages.[42] Such a thesis, however, makes no sense at all of the relevant data in 1 Corinthians 14.

The nonexistence of clear parallels outside of the New Testament to Paul's language for inspired unintelligible speech, together with the paucity and ambiguity of such within the canonical literature, warrants the inference that it is Paul who coined the terminology.[43] Poythress

---

39. Engelsen, "Glossolalia and Other Forms of Inspired Speech According to I Corinthians 12–14," 100.

40. Johannes Behm, "*glōssa*," TDNT I, 725.

41. This does not account, however, for the accusation of intoxication leveled against the disciples in response to this demonstration (2:13). Luke has either conflated a tongues tradition with another concerning a language miracle, or has himself reinterpreted the original report of mass ecstasy by means of such a concept. See Hans Conzelmann, *Die Apostelgeschichte* (1963), 27, who distinguishes between "*Glossolalie*" and "*Sprachenwunder*," the latter designating speech in an unlearned human language.

42. Robert H. Gundry, "'Ecstatic Utterance' (N.E.B.)?" JTS 17 (1966): 299-307, defends this interpretation, as does Forbes, "Prophecy and Inspired Speech," 228.

43. Aune, *Prophecy in Early Christianity*, 199: "It must be recognized . . . that unintelligible utterances were often part of prophetic speech in the ancient world, and that Paul was probably the first to separate glossolalia out as a distinctive category."

notes that if Paul had once before mentioned to the Corinthians this linguistic distinction, he does not bring it up in 1 Corinthians. Even without such a prior differentiation, he continues, "the Corinthian reader would be bound to assimilate quickly the meaning of *lalein glōssē* to something he could grasp phenomenally. Hence, for the Corinthians, anything that *sounded like* speaking in tongues and *functioned* like speaking in tongues *was* speaking in tongues."[44] If Harrisville is correct about the fixed terms in the Qumran and Greek textual traditions of Isaiah 28:11-13a, it is possible that the apostle took his linguistic cue from this text which he cites in 14:21. The variety and imprecision of his terminology in this passage, however, gives the impression that he is writing on an *ad hoc* basis. This in no way detracts from Engelsen's insight that the apostle's intent was to provide a terminological foundation for his separation of intelligible and unintelligible forms of inspired utterance, which in Corinth were conjoined. Meaning "a manner of speech,"[45] in addition to organ and language, the word *glōssa* afforded Paul a suitable vehicle for expressing himself. If there is a formulation in 1 Corinthians 12–14 that approaches a technical sense, the most likely candidate is "tongues" in the absolute sense (*hai glōssai*, 14:22).

What Prophets Speak

In the initial instance of the antithetical parallelism that characterizes 14:1-5, tongues and prophecy are contrasted on three grounds (vv. 2-3): (1) the one who speaks in tongues speaks not to humans but to God, while the one who prophesies speaks to people; (2) the former is unintelligible to human auditors ("no one understands"), but[46] (by implication) the latter is comprehensible to the audience; and (3) the tongues speaker utters "mysteries in the spirit," while the one who prophesies speaks "edification (*oikodomē*) and exhortation (*paraklēsis*) and comfort (*paramythia*)." The first two of these contrasts establishes the *formal* character of early Christian prophecy according to Paul. It is intelligible

---

44. Vern S. Poythress, "The Nature of Corinthian Glossolalia," *WTJ* 40 (1977-78): 134.
45. Behm, "*glōssa*," *TDNT* I, 720.
46. The *de* introducing v. 3 is adversative.

speech directed by the Spirit through the prophetic medium to the congregation. A number of commentators see in the third contrast a clue to the *functional* purpose of prophecy.

With regard to "edification and exhortation and comfort," Hill claims that the three terms when taken together "provide the nearest approach in Paul's letters to a definition of the prophetic function."[47] Arguing that these terms do not coordinate in 14:3, the latter two defining the nature of the first,[48] Hill emphasizes the important role that "exhortation" *(paraklēsis/parakalein)* plays in Paul's letters and infers from this that Christian prophecy is "exhortatory preaching" which "constantly refers back to the work of salvation as its presupposition and basis."[49] He concludes, "The proclamation of the prophet is *pastoral preaching* which, by its very nature, offers guidance and instruction to the community."[50]

Others recognize that the three terms in 14:3 designate the "purpose or result" of prophecy,[51] or fix the "objectives" of prophetic discourse,[52] but they are less sanguine than Hill about the significance of this observation for defining the function of the phenomenon. Reiling agrees that 14:3 "sounds like a functional definition of prophecy" and acknowledges that "there is no other statement in the New Testament which comes closer to a definition than this." But he thinks this is "deceptive."[53] The reason is that none of the terms is limited to prophecy. With regard to *oikodomē* (edification), for example, Paul states that tongues accompanied by interpretation "edifies *(oikodomein)* the church" (14:5). So does *agapē* (1 Cor. 8:1), the exercise of apostolic authority (2 Cor. 10:8; 13:10), and mutual service (Rom. 15:2).[54] Thus Crone concludes that "the notion of *oikodomē* is too wide an application to aid in defining the prophet's role."[55] *Mutatis mutandis*, the same applies to "exhortation" and "comfort."

---

47. Hill, *Prophetic Vocation*, 111 n. 11 (cf. his *New Testament Prophecy*, 123).
48. *Ibid.*, 111 n. 10.
49. *Ibid.*, 115. Cf. Müller, *Prophetie und Predigt*, 24-26, who thinks "exhortation" is the catchword that designates the task of prophecy, which is fulfilled in *Bussrede* (repentance speech) and *Mahnrede* (exhortation speech).
50. Hill, *Prophetic Vocation*, 114.
51. Crone, *Early Christian Prophecy*, 213.
52. Edouard Cothenet, *Prophetic Vocation*, 79.
53. Reiling, *Prophetic Vocation*, 69.
54. Grudem, *The Gift of Prophecy*, 182.
55. Crone, *Early Christian Prophecy*, 213.

The sceptics miss the point, however. At issue is not whether prophecy *alone* builds up the church, which is manifestly not the case. The question is *how* prophecy as the inspired word of the Spirit contributes to this end. Brockhaus observes that the term *oikodomē* in this context is "a *nomen actionis,* denoting (as the verb) the process of building rather than the result."[56] Paul's usage of these cognate terms in relation to proclamation acts is therefore worthy of special attention.

Prophetic Edification

The noun *oikodomē* (edification) signifies the process of building (construction) and the result of that process (edifice). From this literal sense are derived the figurative meanings of edification, upbuilding, and spiritual strengthening, which Paul associates with his apostolic authority (2 Cor. 10:8; 13:10). Vielhauer infers from these texts that *oikodomē* is a technical designation of the apostolic task, which entails the activity of God in grace that is *fulfilled by preaching* in the grounding, preserving, and promoting of the Christian community.[57] Schütz concurs, commenting:

> Paul does not think of authority as anything other than the authority granted him in his commission to preach the gospel. . . . "Building" is simply a metaphor Paul uses to express his sustained interest in and responsibility for the gospel understood in its durative dimension, with reference to the community. . . . When, therefore, Paul says his *exousia* is *oikodomein,* he is claiming for himself the same authority which inheres in his commission to preach the gospel. The center of gravity of this figure is the activity of God, continuous and continuing in the life of the community.[58]

Essential is the notion that *oikodomē* and the proclamation of the gospel are both *functionally* and *materially* related.

Paul exploits the figurative possibilities of the terms in "the great

---

56. Brockhaus, *Charisma und Amt,* 187.
57. Philipp Vielhauer, *Oikodome* (1940), 77-78.
58. John Howard Schütz, *Paul and the Anatomy of Apostolic Authority* (1975), 224-25.

allegory" of 1 Corinthians 3:10-15.[59] Here the metaphor of the church as God's *oikodomē* (building, 3:9)[60] is allegorized along the lines of *foundation* and *superstructure*. In 3:10 he claims that in founding the church in Corinth he laid the one foundation *(themelion tithenai)* that another is now building upon *(epoikodomein)*. What this implies is explicated in Romans 15:20 where the phrases "laying a foundation" and "building upon it" refer to the preaching of the gospel. The express ambition of the apostle to proclaim the gospel "not where Christ has already been named," lest he build on another's foundation, indicates that laying foundations and preaching the gospel in virgin territory are synonymous concepts. Conversely, building *(oikodomein)* on another's foundation is equivalent to preaching the gospel "where Christ has already been named." Thus in spite of his personal rule of missionary strategy, Paul acknowledges his longing to preach the gospel in Rome (Rom. 1:15), which means to build upon the foundation already laid there. The point is that the verbs *oikodomein* (to build) and *euangelizesthai* (to preach the gospel) are interchangeable in Romans 15:20 (cf. Rom. 1:15).[61]

It is in this sense that the role of Apollos in Corinth is to be understood. He is one who "builds upon" *(epoikomein,* 1 Cor. 3:10) the foundation laid by Paul the "wise architect." In a word, Apollos proclaimed the gospel in Corinth where Christ had already been named in the missionary preaching of Paul. The result was not only new converts (3:5) but the general upbuilding of the entire community (3:6-9).[62] Both the laying of a foundation and building upon it are

---

59. Otto Michel, *"oikodomein," TDNT* V, 140.

60. Ernst Käsemann, *Leib und Leib Christi* (1933), 171-73, derives this concept in Paul from the aeon terminology of Gnosticism. Vielhauer, *Oikodome,* 121-22, attributes it to the Old Testament concept of the building up of the house of Israel (Jer. 12:15-16). Michel, *"oikodomein," TDNT* V, 140, assuming from the context that the image of a spiritual temple is in the apostle's mind (1 Cor. 3:16), proposes a source in Jewish Hellenism.

61. Vielhauer, *Oikodome,* 86-87.

62. Barrett, *First Corinthians,* 84, observes that in designating himself and Apollos to the Corinthians as "servants through whom you believed *(episteusate),*" Paul implies by the use of the aorist that Apollos also had engaged in evangelism in Corinth, and with success. But the metaphor of the church as "God's field," with Paul and Apollos serving as "fellow workmen," one planting and the other watering for the sake of the growth that God gives, makes it clear that the apostle has in mind here not merely the creation of faith but its nurture as well.

therefore metaphors for the key term *euangelizesthai* (preach the gospel), the difference between the two being merely temporal.[63] For foundation and superstructure are materially one. The church receives upbuilding through the continuing proclamation of the word that initially called it into existence. The terms *oikodomein/oikodomē* thus designate the *creatio continua*[64] of the church through the preaching of the gospel to the church.

In 1 Corinthians 14:26 Paul lays down the liturgical law to the Corinthians, "Let all things be done for building up *(oikodomein)*." Prophesying, as a cultic event, is subject to this norm. It meets the test because, as an act of proclamation, it effects *oikodomē* (v. 3) through an articulation of the one gospel that alone creates and builds up the church. Like the gospel itself, prophecy is the product of revelation (*apokalyptein*, v. 30; cf. Gal. 1:12, 16) and the medium of revelation (*apokalypsis*, vv. 6 and 26; cf. Rom. 1:17; 3:21; 2 Cor. 4:2-6). The question of the way in which prophesying entails revelation may be left open for the moment. The point here is that prophesying is functionally and materially determined by the gospel. Through this cultic event "in church" the gospel is heard afresh and the community is constituted anew.[65]

Prophetic Exhortation

According to 1 Corinthians 14:3, the one who prophesies also "speaks exhortation" *(paraklēsis)*. Together with its cognate verb *(parakalein)* this term signifies in Pauline usage the comprehensive concept of "exhortation," the context determining the exact nuance.[66] In verse 3 *paraklēsis* serves not as an exposition of *oikodomē*, as Hill maintains, but as a coordinate term with its own contribution to make in designating the function and content of prophesying. Distinguished from ordinary discourse by its appealing, pleading, urging manner, the verb *parakalein* appears in association with similar terms that connote pressing speech,

---

63. Vielhauer, *Oikodome*, 84.
64. *Ibid.*, 92.
65. *Ibid.*
66. Anton Grabner-Haider, *Paraklese und Eschatologie bei Paulus* (1967), 5.

such as *martyresthai* (implore, 1 Thess. 2:11), *nouthetein* (admonish, 1 Cor. 4:14, 16), and *paramytheisthai* (encourage, 1 Thess. 2:11; 5:14).[67] Similarly it occurs with expressions like *stērizein* (strengthen, 1 Thess. 3:2; cf. 2 Thess. 2:17) and *oikodomein* (upbuild, 1 Thess. 5:11).

Paul's use of *parakalein* and *oikodomein* in 1 Thessalonians 5:11 as terminological equivalents[68] suggests that exhortation connotes a sense parallel with gospel proclamation. Evidence of this is provided by 1 Thessalonians 2:2-3, where Paul reminds the community of his initial missionary preaching.[69] The original "statement of the gospel of God" (v. 2) is designated in retrospect as "our exhortation" (*hē paraklēsis hēmōn*, v. 3).[70] Here missionary preaching is designated without qualification as *paraklēsis*.[71] That this is not a fortuitous association of terms is attested by 2:9-12 where the verb *parakalein* also refers to the initial proclamation in Thessalonica. The statement in verse 9 that "we preached *(ekēruxamen)* to you the gospel of God" is the antecedent of the "exhorting and encouraging and charging *(parakalountes kai paramythoumenoi kai martyromenoi)*" mentioned in verse 11. The terms *paraklēsis/parakalein* in these texts designate the preaching of the gospel.[72]

According to 1 Thessalonians 3:1-3, the subsequent proclamation of the word to the community is also designated *paraklēsis*. Here the return of Timothy to Thessalonica is recalled. Paul pointedly designates his emissary as "God's co-worker in the gospel of Christ" (v. 3), implying that Timothy participates in the work of proclamation.[73] The purpose of the visit is expressly stated, "to establish and exhort you *(eis to stērizai kai parakalesai)* in your faith" (v. 2). Timothy's ministry in Thessalonica

---

67. Schlier, *Die Zeit der Kirche*, 77.

68. Michel, "*oikodomein*," *TDNT* V, 141.

69. Anton Vögtle, *Die Tugend- und Lasterkataloge im Neuen Testament* (1936), 19, distinguishes between the "missionary preaching" that founded churches and the ensuing "community preaching" that sustained them.

70. Funk, *Grammar*, par. 452, treats the postpositive *gar* as a causal-coordinating conjunction that connects vv. 2 and 3.

71. Grabner-Haider, *Paraklese und Eschatologie bei Paulus*, 33. The reference in 1 Thess. 2:2 to declaring the gospel "in the face of great opposition" indicates clearly that the public preaching to nonbelievers is in Paul's mind when in 2:3 he refers to this activity as "our exhortation."

72. Carl J. Bjerkelund, *Parakalō* (1967), 26.

73. Henneken, *Verkündigung und Prophetie*, 23.

has its parallel in the work of Apollos in Corinth (1 Cor. 3:5-15).[74] What is termed "building upon the foundation" in 1 Corinthians 3:10 is designated "strengthening and exhorting" the church in 1 Thessalonians 3:2. The language varies, but the activity denoted is the same. Both Timothy and Apollos preached the gospel to churches founded by Paul, and this community preaching is *paraklēsis* (exhortation) even as the missionary proclamation.

Under the influence of the form-critical investigation of the New Testament letters, *paraklēsis* has become a synonym for the literary genre of paraenesis — those hortatory sections which contain general "rules and directions" that regulate the life of faith (see Rom. 12–13; Gal. 5:13–6:12; 1 Thess. 4:1-12; 5:1-11, 12-22).[75] Into the orbit of this genre have also been drawn the *parakalō*-formulas (Rom. 12:1; 15:30; 16:17; 1 Cor. 4:16; 16:15; 1 Thess. 4:10b-12; 5:14) and their equivalents (1 Thess. 4:1; 5:2; cf. 2 Thess. 2:1-2), which often introduce such hortatory passages.[76] The association of the hortatory with the ethical is evidenced by 1 Thessalonians 2:9-12, "we exhorted each one of you and encouraged you and charged you to lead a life worthy of God, who calls you into his own kingdom and glory." Likewise in 1 Thessalonians 4:1-8 the exhortation has as its explicit goal the "sanctification" of the community (v. 3). Similarly, the instructions in 1 Thessalonians 5:12-22 are identified as exhortation (5:14; cf. 5:12). It is exegetically certain therefore that the term *paraklēsis* is used on occasion by Paul to designate discourse with an ethical content.

Discussions of the theological problem of the relation of the imperative to the indicative in Paul's ethic have underscored the intrinsic connection between the kerygma as salvation message and the paraenesis as human response.[77] The latter is therefore conceptualized as the ethical unfolding of the divine mercy that is announced in the gospel. Edmund Schlink speaks of it as "the [ethical] exposition of the accom-

---

74. Henneken, *ibid.*, 21, calls attention to the fact that apart from 1 Thess. 3:2 Paul uses the expression "co-worker with God" only in 1 Cor. 3:9, and there with reference to himself and Apollos. Timothy returns to Thessalonica to do there what Apollos does in Corinth, build upon the foundation laid by Paul.

75. Martin Dibelius, *Die Formgeschichte des Evangeliums* (3rd ed. 1959), 239-42.

76. Bjerkelund, *Parakalō*, 13-23.

77. Schlier, *Die Zeit der Kirche*, 78; Wilfred Joest, *Gesetz und Freiheit* (2nd ed. 1956), 151; Edmund Schlink, "Gesetz und Paraklese," in *Antwort: Karl Barth* (1956), 326.

plished salvation act."[78] It is this understanding of New Testament paraenesis that informs Hill's designation of prophecy in early Christianity as "pastoral exhortation" or "exhortatory preaching" that "constantly refers back to the work of salvation as its presupposition and basis."[79] The deficiency in such a proposal is its limitation of prophesying to "guiding Christians towards conduct more worthy of the Gospel by the communication of the *paraklēsis* that upbuilds."[80]

That Paul does not restrict *paraklēsis* to issues of ethical conduct is clear from 1 Thessalonians 4:13-18, where he addresses the question "concerning those who are asleep" in death (v. 13). The passage presupposes a lack of instruction in Thessalonica on the hope of the resurrection of the dead (v. 13). However this lacuna is explained,[81] the purpose of the text is to fill in a theological blank in the church's understanding. The "word of the Lord" (vv. 15-17) represents *a theological exposition of the confession* "we believe 'Jesus died and rose again'" (v. 14). No mere rational inference deduced from the confessional statement, verses 15-17 articulates "a special revelation" that unfolds the implications of the gospel confession in relation to the issue of the dead.[82] "Therefore exhort *(parakaleite)* one another with these words" (v. 18), the exposition concludes, indicating thereby that *paraklēsis* is equally applicable to the unfolding of theological issues implicit in the gospel.

While the Thessalonians have no need for instruction "concerning love of the brethren" (an ethical subject, 4:9) or "concerning the times and the seasons" (a theological matter, 5:1), such gaps as there are represent the occasion of Paul's express desire to return personally to Thessalonica "in order to complete that which is lacking in [their] faith"

---

78. Schlink, *Antwort: Karl Barth*, 327.
79. Hill, *New Testament Prophecy*, 128.
80. *Ibid.*, 129.
81. Henneken, *Verkündigung und Prophetie*, 76-77, attributes it to the omission of the hope of the general resurrection of the dead in Paul's missionary proclamation due to his expectation of the imminent return of the Lord (see 76 n. 12 for references to the literature on the question).
82. Henneken, *ibid.*, 81-98, addresses the issue of whether *en logō kyriou* (by a word of the Lord) is to be understood as *(a)* an apocalyptic stylistic expression, *(b)* a claim to the inspiration of the Spirit, *(c)* a community tradition, or *(d)* an agraphon of the earthly Jesus, and makes a convincing case for reading vv. 15-17 as an inspired prophetic word. The fact that it comes by revelation in no way compromises its character as exposition of the content of the faith.

(3:10).⁸³ No doubt this is the purpose of subsequent apostolic visits to established churches, and it serves as a commentary on Timothy's return to Thessalonica "to strengthen and to exhort *(parakalesai)* [them] concerning [their] faith" (3:2). Through exhortation as theological and ethical exposition of the confessed gospel, faith is strengthened. The prophet who "speaks exhortation" exercises this task.

Prophetic Encouragement

The "one who prophesies," according to 1 Corinthians 14:3, also "speaks encouragement" *(paramythia)*. The textual evidence for the third of Paul's descriptive terms for the act of prophesying is meager. The substantive occurs in his letters only here and in Philippians 2:1, while the cognate verb *(paramytheisthai)* appears in 1 Thessalonians 2:12 (in association with *parakalein* and *martyrein* [plead]) and 1 Thessalonians 5:14 (in connection with *parakalein* and *nouthetein* [warn]). The basic sense of the verb is "to speak" to someone, with the connotation of "in a friendly way."⁸⁴ Louw and Nida locate it with *parakalein* in the semantic sub-domain of encouragement and consolation: "to cause someone to become consoled — 'to console, to comfort, to encourage.'"⁸⁵ Because the nuances of *paramythia* are so subtle in distinction from related terms, the commentators tend to read it in 1 Corinthians 14:3 as a synonym for *paraklēsis*.⁸⁶

A. J. Malherbe suggests, however, that Paul's utilization of the various hortatory terms in 1 Thessalonians reflects his awareness of "methods and traditions" derived from the moral philosophers "who for centuries had been engaged in the moral reformation of people."⁸⁷ The theory and practice of ancient psychagogy stressed the necessity of match-

---

83. Grabner-Haider, *Paraklese und Eschatologie bei Paulus*, 12, comments with reference to 1 Thess. 3:10 that the task of paraklesis is to explore the deficiencies of faith and to fill them.

84. Gustav Stählin, *"paramytheomai,"* TDNT V, 817.

85. Louw and Nida, *Greek-English Lexicon* I, par. 25.153.

86. Conzelmann, *1 Corinthians*, 235: "The two terms are here practically synonymous."

87. A. J. Malherbe, "'Pastoral Care' in the Thessalonian Church," NTS 36 (1990): 372-91.

ing moral utterance to the human condition of those addressed. Sensitivity to personal qualities and psychological states of the intended audience was included. Moral exhortation also required familiarity with the particular circumstances of the listeners. Given this personal and social context, the challenge was to address the person or group in a style that would effect the desired result. Prominent among the hortatory terms at the speaker's disposal was *paramythia*. Malherbe writes: "That Paul always uses *paramytheisthai* or its cognates in conjunction with some form of *paraklēsis* ([1 Thess] 5.14; 1 Cor 14.3; Phil 2.1) has obscured the fact that it also describes a very particular kind of exhortation, namely consolation or condolence."[88] The moral philosophers recognized that not only the bereaved required consoling, but also those who suffered such distresses as poverty, social criticism, or scorn. Malherbe concludes, "The point is that Paul's *paramythia* did not have in view bereavement caused by death; rather other conditions which required comfort appear to have existed in Thessalonica from the earliest days of the church's existence."[89]

These astute observations emphasize that in speaking *paramythia* (as well as *paraklēsis*) the one who prophesies is engaged in *contextual proclamation* of a pastoral kind. That Paul was aware of and utilized the psychagogic traditions of his time is a statement about the style of his rhetoric, however, not the source of the exhortation and encouragement he proclaimed. It is plain from Philippians 2:1 that for the apostle *paraklēsis* is "in Christ *(en Christō),*" *paramythia* is "of love *(agapēs),*" and *koinonia* is "of the Spirit *(pneumatos).*" Exhortation, comfort, and communion are the effects of the love of God that is revealed in Christ and shed abroad in human hearts by the Spirit (Rom. 5:5-8). Stählin thus concludes: "All the comfort which the apostle (1 Th. 2:12), the prophets (1 C. 14:3) and Christians themselves (1 Th. 5:14; Phil. 2:1) give is drawn from the Gospel."[90] Prophetic words of *paramythia* draw upon this source.

Paul's claim that "one who prophesies speaks edification, exhortation, and encouragement to people" (1 Cor. 14:3) is thus a statement about *the function and the content* of early Christian prophecy.[91] Allowing for the various nuances of the three terms that together form the

---

88. *Ibid.*, 387.
89. *Ibid.*, 388.
90. Stählin, *"paramytheomai," TDNT* V, 823.
91. *Contra* Engelsen, "Glossolalia," 145, and Dautzenberg, *Prophetic Vocation,* 137, who deny explicitly that anything about the content of prophetic speech may be gleaned from 1 Cor. 14:3.

direct object of this inspired speaking *(lalein)*, each names the action of the Spirit that is grounded materially in the gospel and mediated through its proclamation.

Ecstasy and Inspiration

By contrast, "the one who speaks in a tongue, speaks not to people but to God; for no one understands, but he speaks mysteries *(mysteria)* in the Spirit" (1 Cor. 14:2). Since there is no record (literary or otherwise) of an instance of speaking in tongues from the New Testament period, what can be known of the phenomenon depends upon Paul's characterization of its main features.[92] Included are the (1) nature, (2) function, (3) content, and (4) inspiration of tongues. Of these, the third and fourth present the greatest difficulties. Nonetheless, if taken at face value, the apostle's claim that "I speak in tongues more than you all" (v. 18) indicates that his description derives from personal and empirical experience. This is to say that Paul knows the phenomenon from within and without, and he writes about it as both advocate and critic.

The most obvious characteristic of tongues is its *unintelligibility* to human auditors. Paul states flatly that "no one understands" the one who speaks in a tongue (v. 2). Evidently this includes the tongue speaker, for it is further stipulated that "the one who speaks in a tongue should pray for the power to interpret" (v. 13). The incomprehensibility of

---

92. Conzelmann, *1 Corinthians*, 234, claims: "If we would explain [tongues], then we must set out from comparable material in the history of religion...." This assumes, however, that (1) there is "comparable material" in the history of religion texts, and (2) it is more clearly presented therein. On the basis of the criterion of unintelligibility, and arguing that tongues was an ecstatic phenomenon, Engelsen, "Glossolalia," 4-61, concludes that the phenomenon is well attested in ancient Greek and Hebrew sources as well as those outside the New Testament dating from the pre-Christian and early Christian period. Forbes, "Prophecy and Inspired Speech," 126-227, limits the relevant evidence to "the immediate environment" of the New Testament (50 B.C.–A.D. 150) and comes to the conclusion that "nowhere in the world of pre-Christian Hellenism has a substantial parallel for early Christian glossolalia been found" (206). The same is true, he argues, for the evidence available from the intertestamental Jewish literature (228). It should be noted, however, that for Forbes tongues is (1) nonecstatic, and (2) designates speaking in unlearned human languages. The results of such investigations thus depend entirely upon the assumptions that guide them and the criteria employed.

tongues to the ordinary listener is underscored by the two comparative examples provided in verses 7-11. The first is an analogy between musical instruments that play no recognizable tune because their "sound" (*phōnē*) lacks "distinction" (*diastolē/adēlos*, vv. 7-8),[93] and the human instrument (*glōssa*)[94] that fails to communicate in that it speaks no intelligible word (*mē eusēmon logon*, v. 9).[95]

The second illustration builds upon the speech character of the *logos* in verse 9 by comparing tongues with human languages that are inherently meaningful but fail to communicate to those who do not understand them (vv. 10-11). Here it is "the meaning of the language (*hē dynamis tēs phōnēs*)" that is obscure to those who do not speak it. Conzelmann cautions that verse 11 is a comparison, not a description of tongues.[96] Yet the logic of the analogies, which moves from inarticulate sounds to unknown languages, does suggest that tongues is more like an unknown language than an inarticulate vocalization.[97] Rather than being a series of nonsense syllables, tongues seems to have its own inner logic.[98] It is this feature that makes possible the "translation of tongues" (12:10; cf. 12:30; 14:5, 13, 27, 28).[99]

---

93. Brosch, *Charismen und Ämter in der Urkirche*, 61: "The meaning of a piece of music depends upon the distinction of the tones, which must stand in a measured relationship to one another according to their height and depth, their duration and intensity, if they wish to form a melody."

94. Lietzmann, *Korinther I/II*, 71, holds *tēs glōssēs* to be a reference to tongues in the technical sense. This is improbable in view of the genitive construction with *dia* and the definite article rather than *en* with the indefinite substantive, which is the common formulation of tongues in the technical sense, as noted by Weiss, *Korintherbrief*, 325. The comparison is between the musical instruments, on the one hand, and the instrument of human speech on the other. Cf. Bauer, *Lexicon*, 161.

95. Stuart D. Currie, "Speaking in Tongues," *Int.* 19 (1965): 290, notes that this analogy is the basis of the hypothesis that tongues is something akin to musical cadence effected by certain vocalizations, a kind of "lalling" as it is sometimes called.

96. Conzelmann, *1 Corinthians*, 236.

97. With reference to 1 Cor. 14:9-11, Frank W. Beare, "Speaking With Tongues," *JBL* 83 (1964): 243, concludes: "This does not suggest a formless babble, or 'lalling,' but a succession of words which give the impression of language, but are unintelligible to the hearers."

98. Brosch, *Charismen und Ämter in der Urkirche*, 63, calls attention to the fact that although a tongue is not a *logos eusēmos* (14:9), it is still a *logos*.

99. Anthony C. Thiselton, "The 'Interpretation' of Tongues," *JTS* 30 (1979): 15-36, argues on the basis of the lexicographical evidence from Philo and Josephus that *diermēneuein* often means neither to translate nor to interpret but simply "to put into

In his attempt to distinguish intelligible from unintelligible inspired speech conceptually and to separate them from each other practically, Paul avers that the one who speaks in a tongue speaks "not to people but to God" (14:2; cf. v. 28). That this is more than a euphemism is clear from verse 14 where he speaks of praying in a tongue. The designation of tongues as prayer here may not be attributed to the catchword influence of the verb *proseuchesthai* (pray) in verse 13, since the exhortation to the tongue speaker to pray that the utterance might be interpreted requires a prayer "in the mind" *(en noi)* and not "in a tongue" *(glōssē)*.[100] Rather, verse 14 indicates that Paul assigns to tongues the function of prayer and praise.[101] In view of the common assumption in both early Judaism and primitive Christianity that prayer serves a preaching function and therefore is not intended exclusively for God,[102] Paul faults prayer in a tongue because its unintelligibility precludes the building up of the worshipping community. Thus a prayer of blessing (v. 16) or thanksgiving (v. 17) in a tongue excludes the *idiōtēs* (outsider, v. 16).[103] Unable to comprehend what is being said, such a person is unable to participate in the prayer through the liturgical acclamation "Amen" (v. 17).[104] Accordingly, the phrase "not to people" in verse 2 is both descriptive and polemical.[105]

---

words" or "to produce articulate speech." Even if this is the intended sense of the verb and its cognate nouns in 1 Cor. 12–14, as Thiselton contends, the fact remains that tongues represents at a minimum ecstatic sounds that entail material content (cf. the "blessing/thanksgiving" of 14:16). It is difficult to see much difference therefore between articulating and interpreting such sounds.

100. Robinson, *Apophoreta*, 221.

101. Fee, *First Corinthians*, 670; Lietzmann, *Korinther I/II*, 68; Weiss, *Korintherbrief*, 322.

102. Robinson, *Apophoreta*, 221 n. 54.

103. Lietzmann, *Korinther I/II*, 72, designates the *idiōtai* as nonecstatics, whether Christian or non-Christian, within the community. Bauer, *Lexicon*, 370, thinks the *idiōtai* and *apistoi* (14:23) stand in contrast to the congregation, the former being "a kind of proselytes or catechumens" in distinction from the unbelievers. Conzelmann, *1 Corinthians*, 239, is undecided, although he believes the simplest solution is to identify such people as "nonecstatics." Fee, *First Corinthians*, 672-73, concludes that the term refers to anyone who is an "outsider" to the meaning of the prayer in a tongue.

104. Heinrich Schlier, *"amēn,"* *TDNT* I, 335-38, defines the "Amen" as the answer to the prayer or praise of another, which in the tradition of Judaism permitted the congregation to make the prayer or praise of the leader its own.

105. Bauer, *Lexicon*, 151, notes that *gar* (for) occurs twice in 14:2 to allow the second clause ("for no one understands") to confirm the first ("for the one who speaks in a tongue speaks not to people but to God").

The apostle designates the content of prayer and praise in a tongue as "mysteries" (*mysteria*, v. 2), thereby bequeathing to posterity an exegetical conundrum. The problematic issue is whether this term bears the technical sense of the eschatological secrets grounded in God's pretemporal counsel and revealed now by the Spirit, as elsewhere in 1 Corinthians (2:1, 7; 4:1; 13:2; 15:51), or merely indicates the unintelligibility of the unknown tongue in which such speaking occurs. Those who favor the second option do so because the mysteries represented by the first, as Fee puts it, "would scarcely need to be spoken back to God."[106] On the basis of the antithetical parallelism of verses 2 and 3, however, Dautzenberg argues that "mysteries" must be accorded the same substantive sense as "edification, exhortation and encouragement."[107] Further, the assertion that these "mysteries" are spoken "in the Spirit" must be taken seriously and understood in the light of verses 14-16 where such inspiration is defined as an act of the Spirit which bypasses the human mind *(nous)*. This does not imply, however, that tongues are without content. Indeed, Dautzenberg contends that the basic assertion of verse 2 is that the one who speaks in a tongue "speaks mysteries," which Paul critiques not because of the content of such speech but because they are uttered only "in the Spirit" (i.e., unintelligibly).[108] Were the same mysteries expressed "with the Spirit . . . and with the mind also" (v. 15), they would be prophetic utterances. Thus Dautzenberg concludes that the content of prophecy and tongues is the same, namely, the mysteries of God's eschatological purpose as revealed by the Spirit.[109] Unfortunately, Dautzenberg does not see the connection that Paul makes between the pretemporal counsel of God and God's counsel as it is realized in the cross of the "Lord of Glory" (1 Cor. 2:7) and proclaimed in the gospel (1 Cor. 2:1).[110]

The crucial question is whether tongues as unintelligible prayer and praise may be understood from the evidence provided by Paul's description as an *ecstatic* phenomenon. It must be noted that the apostle does not use the term *ekstasis* (ecstasy) either in 1 Corinthians 14 or anywhere else in his preserved correspondence. In asking this question,

106. Fee, *First Corinthians*, 656.
107. Dautzenberg, *Urchristliche Prophetie*, 234.
108. Ibid., 235.
109. Ibid., 237.
110. Günther Bornkamm, *"mystērion," TDNT* IV, 819: "In the Pauline corpus the term *mystērion* is firmly connected with the *kerygma* of Christ."

therefore, we are not only imposing an alien term upon the data but are also imposing upon it the technical sense enjoyed by that word in the religious world of first-century Hellenism. In that context *ekstasis* designated at a minimum an altered state of consciousness under the influence of divine power, as Aune has emphasized.[111] According to Pfister, the term connotes a state of being different from the ordinary mental condition. The implication is not that the human mind has left the body but that the person so inspired has been separated temporarily from the mind.[112] If this is ecstasy, then the question is whether Paul conceived of the work of the Spirit that effected either prophetic utterance or speaking in tongues in such a manner.

1 Corinthians 14:14 indicates that he did: "For if I pray in a tongue, my spirit *(to pneuma mou)* prays but my mind *(ho nous mou)* is unfruitful *(akarpos)*." The parallelism between "my spirit" and "my mind" confirms that Paul is speaking anthropologically in both instances.[113] Yet the context requires a close association between "my spirit prays" and speaking "in the Spirit" (v. 2). Fee expresses the intrinsic connection between the human and the Holy Spirit in the moment of inspiration by the awkward but apt phrase "my S/spirit prays."[114] However this is conceived, Paul clearly states that his mind *(nous)* is fruitless (uninvolved) if he prays in a tongue. In his classical study of the apostle's anthropological terms, Bultmann shows that the mind represents to Paul not a special faculty but "the knowing, understanding, and judging" which belong to humanity *per se*.[115] In other words, the term designates self-awareness or consciousness. If the mind in this sense is bypassed by the Spirit in the act of speaking in tongues, as Paul says it is, we can only conclude that the state described represents ecstasy as defined. The argument that this cannot be the case because the apostle assumes the speaker in a tongue can control the inspiration if there is no interpreter on hand in the assembly (v. 28) ignores the fact that ecstasy can be

---

111. Aune, *Prophecy in Early Christianity*, 33.
112. Friedrich Pfister, "Ekstase," *RAC* IV, 944-54.
113. Barrett, *First Corinthians*, 319-20, acknowledges that the parallelism between *to pneuma mou* and *ho nous mou* speaks for the anthropological character of both phrases, but argues that this is not supported by Paul's usage elsewhere. The evidence is to the contrary, however. Paul speaks of "my spirit" in the human sense in 1 Cor. 16:18; 2 Cor. 2:13 (cf. 7:13); and Rom. 1:9.
114. Fee, *First Corinthians*, 671.
115. Bultmann, *Theology of the New Testament*, I, 211.

controlled or uncontrolled.[116] Tongues then is in fact a type of unintelligible ecstatic speech. This is not to say, however, that it is merely the Christian equivalent of all unintelligible types of inspired utterance known in the ancient world. It is simply to say that tongues shared with those phenomena the formal characteristic of unintelligibility and thereby would have been associated with them in the pagan mind.

Aune claims that the experience designated by ecstasy or its equivalent terms "underlies all ancient oracular speech, whether Greco-Roman, Jewish, or early Christian."[117] Paul does not bear him out. In 1 Corinthians 14:15 the apostle asks, "What am I to do?" (the question assuming human decision). His answer is, "I will pray in the spirit and I will pray in the mind also; I will sing in the spirit and I will sing in the mind also." Again the parallelism indicates the use of anthropological terminology. It is not his intention here to distinguish between inspiration and rationalism but between inspiration and inspiration. If there is a type of Spirit-inspiration that avoids the mind, there is also an inspiration of the Spirit that includes both the human spirit and the mind. 1 Corinthians 2:16 attests that Paul, under the influence of a Greek version of Isaiah 40:13, can speak of the divine *pneuma* in terms of "mind" *(nous Christou)*. Moreover, he affirms in the same passage that the Spirit works to create human understanding of the gracious gifts given by God (2:12), an understanding that is communicated in "words not taught by human wisdom but taught by the Spirit. . . ." (2:13). In view of the antithetical parallelism between prophecy and tongues throughout chapter 14, it would seem that in verse 15 Paul is contrasting the respective kinds of inspiration that effect each. The burden of his polemic is to establish the fact that the understanding of the prophet is not circumvented under the influence of the Spirit, resulting in intelligible speech that is no less an inspired utterance than the unintelligible speech of tongues even though it does not entail ecstasy.[118]

---

116. Aune, *Prophecy in Early Christianity*, 34.
117. *Ibid.*, 21.
118. Terrance Callan, "Prophecy and Ecstasy in Greco-Roman Religion and in 1 Corinthians," *NovT* 27 (1985): 125-40, argues "that in 1 Cor 14 Paul denies that Christian prophecy is accompanied by trance" (128).

Tongues as a Sign

An important source of information about both the Pauline and Corinthian understanding of inspired utterance is 14:20-25. Following the discussion of the effect of tongues upon believers in the congregation at worship (vv. 7-19), Paul returns to the explicit contrasting of prophecy to tongues with which he began the discussion (vv. 2-5). The literary structure of the new passage is evident: an opening exhortation (v. 20), a citation of Isaiah 28:11-12 (v. 21), two antithetical assertions (v. 22), and a concluding pair of illustrations (vv. 23, 24-25).[119] The flow of the argument, however, is less evident. Problematic is the logical relationship of the assertions to the scriptural quotation, on the one hand, and to the two illustrations on the other. Fee suggests that verse 22, the crux of the difficulty, is best understood from what follows rather than what precedes in the text.[120] We will follow his lead in this regard.

The imagined setting of the two hypothetical situations depicted in verses 23-25 is the whole church assembled in one place for worship (v. 23a). In the second illustration (vv. 24-25), Paul envisions a scene in which "all prophesy." The question is what effect such intelligible inspired speech would have upon the outsider or unbeliever who might be present. The answer corresponds materially to the initial statement of the effects of prophesying (v. 3). With regard to believers, "the one who prophesies speaks edification and exhortation and encouragement." Through prophesying the outsider or unbeliever is "convicted *(elenchetai),*"[121] "called to account *(anakrinetai),*" and has the secrets of his or her heart "manifested *(phanera ginetai).*"[122] What occurs through prophetic proclamation is the proleptic judgment of the eschatological Day, an intrinsic theme of Paul's gospel (Rom. 2:16; 1 Cor. 4:3-5), which issues in the acclamation of the converted: "God is really among you"

---

119. B. C. Johanson, "Tongues, a Sign for Unbelievers?" *NTS* 25 (1979): 186-90, provides a detailed analysis of the literary structure of 1 Cor. 14:20-25.
120. Fee, *First Corinthians,* 681.
121. Barrett, *First Corinthians,* 326, identifies the term by its usage among the Greek moralists, who employed it for the work of the conscience.
122. Lietzmann, *Korinther I/II,* 73, and Héring, *Corinthiens,* 128, interpret this as the gift of "mind reading." Conzelmann, *1 Corinthians,* 243, however, correctly views it as the consequence of the illuminating power of Christian preaching (2 Cor. 4:2): "This unveiling is a gift of the God who sees into the inward parts, who is *kardiognōstēs,* a 'knower of the heart,' Rom. 8:27; 1 Th. 2:4" (n. 31).

PROPHECY AND THE GOSPEL

(v. 25).[123] Conversion is effected because God is encountered in judgment and grace through the prophetic word, which for Paul can only be the gospel (2 Cor. 4:4-6).[124] Hill rightly infers that here "Paul demonstrates his desire to affirm the missionary function of the word, even of the inspired prophetic word spoken in worship."[125]

With regard to the first illustration, however, matters are quite different (v. 23). If "all speak in tongues, and outsiders or unbelievers enter, will they not say *'mainesthe'?*" The untranslated Greek verb in this quotation is commonly read as a pejorative statement and rendered "You are mad," thereby betraying modern estimates of ecstatic states. Aune points out that "the verb most commonly used in Greek sources for the act of prophesying was *mainesthai*,"[126] which suggests that the Greek-speaking Corinthians would have understood the statement as an affirmation of divine inspiration, "You are possessed."[127] In other words, outsiders and unbelievers present in an assembly of Christians in which they all spoke in tongues would recognize this as evidence of ecstatic inspiration but would not be led thereby to an encounter with God. Paul's polemical point is that tongues elicits the response, "*You* are possessed," but prophecy effects the confession, "*God* is really among you."[128]

The object of these two comparative illustrations is the statement in verse 22 which is composed of parallel assertions:

---

123. Fee, *First Corinthians*, 687: "That Paul intends this to mean conversion is indicated by the final exclamation, which is a conscious reflection of Isa. 45:14 (cf. Zech. 8:23): God, speaking through the prophet, says that the Egyptians will come over to you, and 'will worship' before you, and say, 'Surely God is with you.'"

124. Hill, *New Testament Prophecy*, 126: "Prophecy by its inspiration *and* content reveals that God is present in the midst of the assembly — even the unbeliever confesses this (vv. 24f.)."

125. *Ibid.*, 124.

126. Aune, *Prophecy in Early Christianity*, 198.

127. Johnson, "Norms for True and False Prophecy in First Corinthians," 41: "Actually, the word used here, *mainesthe*, should not be understood as meaning merely 'mad' or 'raving,' but should be understood in that context of the Hellenistic world in which *mania* was the technical expression for ecstatic pagan prophecy. In other words, Paul has the unbeliever mistake the Christian prayer meeting as just one more enthusiastic Hellenistic cult. The scandal here, in the strict sense, is that the distinctive word of the Gospel is not heard."

128. See Peter Roberts, "A Sign — Christian or Pagan?" *ExpTim* 90 (1978-79), 199-203, for a similar conclusion.

Thus,
tongues [are] a sign not to believers but to unbelievers,
but
prophecy [is a sign] not to unbelievers but to believers.[129]

Verse 23 illustrates the first clause, and verses 24-25 explain the second. That mass speaking in tongues would lead outsiders and unbelievers to exclaim, "You are possessed," indicates that to the pagan mind of the first-century Greek-speaking world such a display of unintelligible speech was a *sēmeion* (sign) of divine inspiration. Not so for believers, however, who know from their experience that the "sign" of God's presence is the intelligible word of prophetic gospel proclamation which effected their own conversion and continues to edify, exhort, and encourage them in the life of faith. Because of its intelligible and nonecstatic character, prophecy is not an ostensible "sign" of inspiration to outsiders and unbelievers, but becomes so when they are converted by its gospel proclamation.

How then do the two assertions (v. 22) and their respective illustrations (vv. 23-25) relate to the scriptural citation in verse 21? The crucial point here is neither that Paul quotes a source other than the Masoretic or Septuagint texts, nor that he modifies the text in minor ways.[130] The crux lies in what he omits altogether, namely, the intelligible prophetic word which God has spoken to Israel according to Isaiah 28:11-12. When the elision is bracketed into Paul's citation and modified to conform to his version of the main verb, it reads:

---

129. The sentence lacks a main verb in both clauses, which is commonly corrected by supplying the appropriate form of "to be." Funk, *Grammar,* par. 145 (1), renders [*einai*] *eis* as "to serve for." Thus "tongues [serve for] a sign not to believers but to unbelievers, but prophecy [serves for a sign] not to unbelievers but to believers." The dative of "believers" and "unbelievers" is one of respect. The parallel structure of the sentence suggests that the absence of both *eis* and *sēmeion* in the second clause is an ellipsis.

130. Origen attributed Paul's quotation in 14:21 to Aquila and other Greek versions apart from the LXX (*Philocalia,* IX, 2). The most that can be said is that Paul and Aquila (second century) were working from a common source (thus Harrisville, "Speaking in Tongues," 42-45). Fee, *First Corinthians,* 679 n. 20, notes that both Paul and Aquila use the combined form *heteroglōssos,* invert the order of "tongues" and "lips," and include the phrase *en cheilesin heterōn.* Pauline innovations include "I will speak" rather than "the Lord will speak" (MT) and "they will speak" (LXX), and the addition of "says the Lord."

> By people of strange tongues
>   and by the lips of foreigners
> I will speak to this people,
>   [to whom I have said,
>   'This is rest;
>   give rest to the weary;
>   and this is repose';]
>   yet even then they will not listen to me,
> says the Lord.

Johanson observes that "the omission of the intelligible message has the effect of making the object of the hearer's refusal to listen, not the intelligible message as in the MT and LXX, but the unintelligible speech of 'foreigners' through whom God says he will speak."[131] But is the absence of the intelligible word of God in Paul's citation to be construed as a convenient omission that allows him to turn the Isaiah text to his own purposes? Or is it rather an instance of the apostle's characteristic use of *metalepsis* or *allusive echo* in citing scripture, as Hays argues? Hays explains that an allusive echo suggests to the reader "that text B should be understood in light of a broad interplay with text A, *encompassing aspects of A beyond those explicitly echoed.*"[132] Read in this light, Paul's point in verse 21 is that "strange tongues" (*heteroglōssai*), whether of the Assyrian or ecstatic type, do not confirm the prophetic word and thereby effect obedience. The succeeding assertions state his case (v. 22) and the illustrations demonstrate it (vv. 23-25).

That Paul was compelled to make this case indicates that it was not the view of the Corinthians.[133] The opening exhortation is therefore replete with irony if not sarcasm: "Brethren, do not be children (*paidia*) in your understanding (*phrēn*) . . . , but in understanding be mature (*teleiois*)" (v. 20).[134] What separates the children from the adults in this instance is their respective attitudes toward the value of ecstatic speech.

---

131. Johanson, "Tongues, a Sign for Unbelievers?" 182.

132. Hays, *Echoes of Scripture in the Letters of Paul*, 20 (emphasis added).

133. Conzelmann, *1 Corinthians*, 241: "In regard to this passage it is permissible to read between the lines that Paul is indirectly characterizing the activities in Corinth as childish."

134. *Paidion* (child, infant) occurs only here in Paul (cf. *nēpios* in 1 Cor. 3:1-2; 13:11). *Phrēn* (thinking, understanding, discernment) is a *hapax legomenon* in the New Testament.

Those who are spiritual infants view it as the *sine qua non* of the work of the Spirit, indeed, as the confirming "sign" of prophetic utterance. Since Paul coined the technical term "tongues" *ad hoc* in order to deal with the situation in Corinth, the phrase "tongues are a sign" may not be identified as a Corinthian slogan that Paul is repeating back to them.[135] That does not imply, however, that the term *sēmeion* (sign) was not Corinthian parlance for the value assigned by them to the phenomenon of ecstatic speech. Given Paul's sparing and usually negative use of the word "sign,"[136] such a conjecture is warranted.[137] As Johanson observes, "this claim for the apologetic value of tongues clearly becomes *the* bone of contention in I Cor. xiv.20-25."[138]

A God of Peace and Not Disorder

The discussion moves from analysis to application in 14:26-36 as indicated by the introductory question, "What should be done then, my friends?" (NRSV). The scene now shifts from the hypothetical "if you come together" (v. 23) to the actual "when you gather" (v. 26). Yet the picture is somewhat ideal: "each one has a hymn, a lesson, a revelation, a tongue, an interpretation." For while it is true that "the manifestation of the Spirit is given to each for the common good" (1 Cor. 12:7), the enumerations of the various works of the Spirit make it plain that everyone does not receive a liturgical gift (12:8-10, 28, 29-30).[139] The list of the works of the Spirit in verse 26 adds nothing new. Paul has already

---

135. Contra J. P. M. Sweet, "A Sign for Unbelievers," *NTS* 13 (1967): 241.
136. Krister Stendahl, *Paul Among Jews and Gentiles* (1976), 115 n. 8.
137. Christopher Forbes, "Early Christian Inspired Speech and Hellenistic Popular Religion," *NovT* 27 (1986): 269, rejects the view here presented on the ground that if the Corinthians had conjoined prophecy and tongues, the latter authenticating the former, "Paul would not have suggested (in I Cor. 14) that the Corinthians ought to prophecy [sic] *rather than* speak in tongues with outsiders present, because prophecy would normally have accompanied glossolalia anyway." Indeed, but Paul's point is that tongues calls attention to itself and thus away from the prophetic word, which then is unable to fulfill its missionary purpose. The assumption underlying the apostle's citation of Isa. 28:11-12 is that unintelligible speech functioned among the Corinthians as the "sign" that validated intelligible prophetic utterance.
138. Johanson, "Tongues, a Sign for Unbelievers?" 194.
139. Conzelmann, *1 Corinthians*, 244 n. 38.

PROPHECY AND THE GOSPEL

mentioned inspired hymning (v. 15), teaching and revelation (v. 6), and tongues with its interpretation (12:10, 30; 14:5, 13). What is odd about this list is the absence of the term *prophecy*, especially in view of the succeeding regulations for the tongue speaker (vv. 27-28) and the prophets (vv. 29-32). The equally unexpected list in verse 6 is illuminating.

Here Paul contrasts speaking in tongues not only with prophecy (as expected from vv. 2-5) but also with speaking in the form of a knowledge *(gnōsis)*, a revelation *(apokalypsis)*, and a teaching *(didache)*.[140] Attempts to distinguish meaningfully between these terms have proven fruitless.[141] Fee finds their common denominator in inspired intelligibility.[142] The apostle would no doubt agree, but he probably would explain that the various terms of the list in verse 6 represent various types of prophesying. The connection between revelation and prophetic speech is made in verse 30, and the relation of teaching to prophecy is established by verse 31 (cf. v. 19). In 12:8 Paul speaks of an inspired "word of knowledge," and in 14:15 he mentions singing "in the spirit and in the mind." Evidently the intended references of these terms transcend the limits of our historical knowledge, but that is not cause for inferring that "there is a general lack of precision in Paul with regard to these various items."[143]

The regulation of tongues (vv. 27-28) and of prophecy (vv. 29-32) has the effect, as Käsemann notes, of setting limits to the Spirit which indwells the community and its worship.[144] For Paul, however, matters

---

140. Lietzmann, *Korinther I/II*, 71, interprets *en* with the dative of manner as analogous to *en parabolais elegen* (Mark 3:23), indicating the form in which the speech comes to expression. Wilckens, *Weisheit und Torheit*, 64 n. 1, views *lalein en apokalypsei* (14:6) as a parallel expression to *lalein en mystēriō* (1 Cor. 2:7), and emphasizes that the term *mystērion* has a material as well as a formal sense.

141. Barrett, *First Corinthians*, 317, concludes that these terms "shade too finely into one another for rigid distinctions."

142. Fee, *First Corinthians*, 662. He overstates his case, however, when he infers from the location of *prophēteia* third in the list that "the real issue is not tongues and prophecy as such but tongues and intelligibility, for which prophecy serves as the representative example." The *Anathema Iēsous* (12:3) did not lack intelligibility. As established by Paul in 12:1-3, the issue is how to discern authentic prophetic utterance apart from evidences of ecstasy. Intelligibility is an issue because it is required for the testing of prophecy in terms of its content. Prophecy, however, is "the real issue" of 1 Cor. 12–14.

143. *Ibid.*, 663.

144. Käsemann, *Essays on New Testament Themes*, 82.

of liturgical order and ecclesiastical authority are grounded in the nature of God. He does not hesitate therefore to declare that the God who ordered the ministry of the church (12:28) also regulates its worship: "For God is not a God of confusion *(akatastasia)* but of peace *(eirēnē)*, as in all the churches of the saints" (v. 33). The Spirit may be spontaneous, even arbitrary in its distributive work (12:11), but it is true to the nature of God and therefore not capricious. In worship this is particularly the case. Käsemann writes, "Liturgy is the most ancient form of confession; as such, it is therefore for Paul the criterion of the proclamation of the Gospel...."[145] In a word, the worship of the community is ordered because it is in the liturgy that the gospel is heard and confessed ever anew.

Under the general rubric that all things should be done "decently and in order" (v. 40), Paul issues regulations for the exercise of tongues and prophecy that are virtually parallel in their formulation. Instances of tongues are limited to two or "at most" three, "one at a time," and they are to be interpreted. Instances of prophecy are limited to two or three (suggesting sustained discourse of some length),[146] and they are to be evaluated *(diakrinein)*. This last injunction, according to Käsemann, is "a terrifying pronouncement" in view of its implication that the voice of the Spirit is subjected to theological judgment.[147] But this is the summary point of the entire discussion that began at 12:1-3 with the issue of how to discern authentic prophetic speech apart from the evidence of ecstasy. The context in which theological discernment is exercised transcends the limits of the local church, as the concluding admonition of this section intimates: "What! Did the word of God originate with you, or are you the only ones it has reached?"[148] The "going out" *(exēlthein)* and the "reaching to" *(katantein)* of the word of

---

145. *Ibid.*, 79.
146. Hill, *New Testament Prophecy,* 123. The argument of Fee, *First Corinthians,* 691-93, that "two or three" in both vv. 27 and 29 mean "in sequence" (prior to being interpreted or judged) rather than "at one service" is unconvincing, relying as it does too heavily upon the scene depicted in v. 24, which is strictly hypothetical.
147. Käsemann, *Essays on New Testament Themes,* 67.
148. Fee, *First Corinthians,* 699-705, argues persuasively that vv. 34-35 "simply lack any genuine correspondence with either the overall arguments of chaps. 12–14 or the immediate argument of vv. 26-40" (702) and therefore should be viewed as an interpolation. Accordingly, v. 36 completes the thought of v. 33, which explains the basis of the regulations of vv. 27-32.

God refers to a proclamation tradition that is temporally prior to and materially normative of prophetic inspiration.[149] Paul's own appeal to an authoritative gospel tradition in 1 Corinthians 15:1-5, in order to test the prophetic word that "there is no resurrection of the dead" (15:12), affords a concrete example of such discernment.

Who "the others" are who "weigh what is said" by prophets is unclear from the text (v. 29), however. Grammatically, they could be either the other prophets or the others in the congregation as a whole. Given the pairing of prophecy with discernment and tongues with interpretation in 12:10, the parallel structure of the two regulations in 14:27-32 suggests that as tongues is to be interpreted by one who has that gift, so also prophecy is to be evaluated by those empowered by the Spirit to exercise such a task. Also ambiguous is the scope of the term "all" *(pantas)* in verse 31, "For you can all prophesy one by one, so that all may learn and all be encouraged." Fee argues that it is "gratuitous" to refer the first "all" to the prophets and the next two to the whole community.[150] That would be so were there no evidence in chapters 12–14 to warrant limiting the first "all" to prophets. Paul does speak hypothetically of "all prophesying" in 14:24, but his rhetorical question "Are all prophets?" in 12:29 expects a negative answer with respect to actual practice. Because the actual takes precedence over the hypothetical, there is reason to limit "you may all prophesy" to those inspired by the Spirit to do so. Fee recognizes this, but the inference he draws from it is that the noun "prophets" is "functional language" that denotes "the one who is prophesying," as in 14:3. In order to make this stick, however, it would be necessary to read the corresponding term "apostle" (12:28) in the same way, which is impossible. At most it can be said only that in principle prophesying was not limited to those people in the church who exercised this work of the Spirit on a continual basis and were named "prophets" for this reason.

---

149. The point may be made and defended without pushing it as far as does Birger Gerhardsson, *Memory and Manuscript* (1961), with his thesis that Paul recognized the principle that the word of God would proceed from Jerusalem in the last days, and accordingly "accepted the twelve Apostles and the first Christian congregation as guardians of that logos which proceeded from Jerusalem" (274). At a minimum, the apostle is concerned in Gal. 2:1-10 to demonstrate that his gospel enjoys the imprimatur of the Jerusalem authorities, and in 1 Cor. 15:11 he appears equally desirous of claiming unity in preaching with the other apostles.

150. Fee, *First Corinthians*, 694.

Conclusion

It is now possible to return to 1 Corinthians 12:1-3 and view it in the light of Paul's discussion in chapter 14 of the issue identified there. The ecstatic state which the Corinthians knew from their pagan religious experience and continued to value as a "sign" of prophetic inspiration is now clearly identified as the phenomenon which Paul designates for the first time as speaking in tongues. The apostle's description of the phenomenon locates it in the category of ecstasy, and its unintelligibility relates it *formally* to the ecstatic utterances common in the temples at Corinth and elsewhere in the first-century religious world. Yet his positive attitude toward tongues, which he neither condemns outright nor damns by faint praise,[151] indicates that *materially* it qualifies as an authentic work of the Spirit (12:10). To deprive tongues of its "sign" value, Paul creates a new language for denoting the phenomenon and defines it as a discrete charisma of prayer and praise in sharp distinction from prophecy.

In the process of separating tongues from prophecy, the apostle's own understanding of the latter work of the Spirit is stated. With regard to believers, prophesying effects edification, exhortation, and encouragement through the gospel that creates and continues to create the church (14:3). With regard to unbelievers, it effects conviction of sin and confession of faith by means of gospel proclamation (14:24-25). The content of prophecy as nonecstatic intelligible preaching is subject to testing by the church's confession (12:3) in the context of its proclamation tradition (14:36). Specifically, prophecy is the theological and ethical exposition of the gospel (1 Thess. 4:13-18). The validity of this claim is confirmed by 1 Corinthians 2:6-16 in the context of chapters 1–4. To this passage we now turn.

---

151. William Richardson, "Liturgical Order and Glossolalia in 1 Corinthians 14.26c-33a," *NTS* 32 (1986): 145.

CHAPTER FIVE

Prophecy and Wisdom

1 Corinthians 2:6-16

DAVID Hill asks, "Is the phenomenon of 'prophecy/prophet' always and necessarily absent when the word *prophētes* is not found?" An affirmative answer, he concedes, enjoys the strength of relying upon the sources to "label" their own subject matter. Yet he warns that "to assume that the phenomenon of prophecy was *always* bound in a one-to-one correlation to the word or word-group causes this approach to the material to have limited value."[1] The present chapter argues that 1 Corinthians 2:6-16 is a text in which early Christian prophecy is the unlabeled subject matter and that, according to its testimony, the function of such prophecy was the interpretation of the apostolic kerygma.[2] The case for this thesis will be made by demonstrating exegetically the inherent wisdom character of the kerygma as attested in 1 Corinthians 1:18–2:5, the material relation between the kerygma and the wisdom revealed by the Spirit according to 2:6-16, and the identity of prophecy as the medium of this revelatory activity of the Spirit on the basis of the evidence provided in 1 Corinthians 12–14.

---

1. Hill, *New Testament Prophecy*, 3.
2. Dautzenberg, "Botschaft und Bedeutung der urchristlichen Prophetie," 131-61, argues that 1 Cor. 2:6-16 is an example of a prophetic revelation of a mystery, but he dissociates it from the kerygma in principle.

Quarrels and Divisions

1 Corinthians 2:6-16 concludes the polemical attack upon a type of "verbal wisdom" (1:17) initiated by Paul at 1:18, a text that is located in the first major section of the body of the letter (1:10–4:21). In this extended passage, Paul addresses a variety of issues related to the "quarrels" (*erides*, 1:11; cf. "jealousy and strife" [*zēlos kai eris*], 3:3) within the church reported to him by Chloe's people (1:11). Nils Dahl identifies four of these issues: (1) the "divisions" (*schismata*, 1:10; cf. 11:18) in Corinth provoked by misguided loyalties to apostolic and other missionary figures (1:12; 3:4, 5-9, 21-23; 4:6);[3] (2) the connection between these dissensions and wisdom (*sophia*);[4] (3) the references to Corinthian "boasting" (1:29-31; 3:2; 4:7) and being "puffed up" (4:6; cf. 3:18-21); and (4) the need for Paul to defend his apostleship, past and present, before their tribunal (1:16-17; 2:1–3:4; 4:1-21).[5] To this list Schütz rightly adds the issue of baptism (1:14-17), which he views as the "central core" of the problem in Corinth — "a collapsed eschatology and a misplaced sense of freedom."[6]

With his proposal, Schütz addresses the crucial problem of coordinating these several issues in order to explain how they are interrelated. Baptism is a likely thematic candidate because Paul's pointed remarks regarding the limited number of baptisms he performed in Corinth and the absurdity of the notion that he baptized anyone in his own name

---

3. Paul assumes that Cephas (Peter) was known to the church in Corinth (1:12; 3:22; 9:5; 15:5), but whether by face (9:5?), or by tradition (15:5), or both is uncertain. Despite the arguments of C. K. Barrett, "Christianity at Corinth," *BJRL* 46 (1963-64): 269-97, there is nothing in 1 Cor. to suggest that Cephas was a major player in the controversy addressed in 1:10–3:23. The fact that Paul and Apollos are the only names to appear in all four of the relevant texts encourages the inference that they alone, but without their consent, were at the center of the storm in Corinth. The source and significance of "I am of Christ" (1:12) is problematic. (See the summaries of the proposed options in Fee, *First Corinthians*, 58; Conzelmann, *1 Corinthians*, 33-34; Hurd, *The Origin of I Corinthians*, 97-99.)

4. Of the thirty-three instances of the terms *sophia* (wisdom) and *sophos* (wise) in the seven undisputed letters of Paul, twenty-seven occur in 1 Corinthians and twenty-five in chaps. 1–3.

5. N. A. Dahl, "Paul and the Church at Corinth According to 1 Corinthians 1:10–4:21," in William Reuben Farmer, ed., *Christian History and Interpretation* (1967), 313-35.

6. Schütz, *Paul and Apostolic Authority*, 189.

(1:13-16) link the references to "quarreling" over the loyalty claims (1:11-12) with the topic of preaching the gospel "not in verbal wisdom *(ouk en sophia logou)*" (1:17); and this same phrase introduces the theme of 1:18–2:5 where "the word of the cross" (1:18) — the kerygma (1:21) — is played off against Corinthian "words of wisdom" (2:4; cf. 2:1) that are evidently the occasion of "boasting" (1:31; cf. 3:21).

Baptism also provides a material base for discerning the coherence of the issues of 1 Cor. 1:10–4:21 in four illuminating ways. First, Paul's association of the undivided Christ with the event of the crucifixion and the baptismal act in the three rhetorical questions of 1:13 sets forth the themes of his understanding of baptism as presented in Rom. 6:1-11. Käsemann contends that here Paul is correcting the baptismal tradition of the Hellenistic community, which viewed baptism as "a rite of initiation" that "gives a share in Christ's destiny." He explains:

> The liturgical texts Col 2:1ff.; Eph. 2:4ff.; 5:14 show that originally baptism itself was understood as translation into the world of the resurrection out of the sleep of sin, or as participation in the death and resurrection of Christ, or, according to [Rom.] 8:29, his glory. *The Corinthian enthusiasts held a similar view.* A Christianity directed against such enthusiasm, to which Paul belonged, viewed baptism as participation in the death of Christ and a pledge of *future* glorification.[7]

That the "eschatological reservation" (Käsemann) in the apostle's view of baptism had dropped out among the Corinthians is evident from their understanding of Christian existence as attested in 1 Cor. 4:8: "Already you are filled! Already you have become rich! Without us you have become kings! And would that you did reign, so that we might share the rule with you!" Wilckens notes that the emphatic *ēdē* (already) that introduces the first two clauses of this text indicates the chief feature of the Corinthian view, which he characterizes as a "trans-eschatological" mode of life.[8] In other words, the Corinthians affirm that they stand already on the other side of the eschatological judgment and have received the fullness of the end-time blessings. In keeping with this conviction is their confident aphorism, "There is no resurrection of the dead" (1 Cor. 15:12). The *future* resurrection is superfluous, Käsemann

---
7. Käsemann, *Commentary on Romans,* 161-62 (emphasis added).
8. Wilckens, *Weisheit und Torheit,* 17.

observes, "since they imagine that baptism has already set them in an angelic state."[9]

A second way in which baptism provides a unifying ground for the various issues identified in 1:10–4:21 is by its close association with reception of the Spirit (1 Cor. 12:13). Paul himself defines Christian existence in terms of a "radical possession"[10] by the Spirit: "But you are not in the flesh, you are in the Spirit, if the Spirit of God really dwells in you. Any one who does not have the Spirit of Christ does not belong to him" (Rom. 8:9). In this context, "belonging" to Christ (being "of him" [*autou*]) is equivalent to the "indwelling" of "the Spirit of God" (*pneuma theou oikei en hymin*), which also parallels being "in the Spirit" (*en pneumati*). The claim "I am of Christ" (1:12) and the affirmation "You [all] are of Christ" (3:22) both entail these notions of the Spirit's relation to the believer. How this basic Pauline conviction could be misunderstood in the context of a "collapsed eschatology" (Schütz) is not difficult to imagine. Thiselton states flatly that *"an over-realized eschatology leads to an 'enthusiastic' view of the Spirit,"*[11] citing A. D. Nock's description of the situation in Corinth as an apt illustration: "Many of the converts, convinced that they were on a new plane of life, felt that they could do anything: they were kings (4.8), they were in the Spirit, they were dead to the flesh and emancipated — so that their physical conduct might seem to them a matter of indifference; they were altogether superior to the unchanged men around them."[12] Fee coins the expression "spiritualized eschatology" to denote the phenomenon,[13] which would certainly account for the "boasting" in Corinth as well as the Corinthian "verbal wisdom" addressed in 1:18–2:16. For the Spirit, given in association with baptism, is the source of such wisdom utterances (2:10-13; 12:8).

Further, baptism explains the sense in which the claims, "I am of Paul," "I am of Apollos," "I am of Cephas," "I am of Christ" (1:12) may be understood. Assuming that these claims are formulated in "the idiom derived from baptism"[14] (Gal. 3:27-29), a number of commentators

---

9. Käsemann, *Commentary on Romans*, 161.
10. *Ibid.*, 223.
11. Anthony C. Thiselton, "Realized Eschatology at Corinth," *NTS* 24 (1978): 512.
12. A. D. Nock, *St Paul* (1938), 174.
13. Fee, *First Corinthians*, 12.
14. James M. Robinson and Helmut Koester, *Trajectories through Early Christianity* (1971), 32 n. 12.

attribute the divisive loyalties to a view of the Christian missionaries as mystagogues who, through the sacrament, mediated "a spiritual paternity"[15] in the manner of the mystery religions.[16] Paul's depreciation of his role as a baptizer in Corinth (1:14-17) is thus a denunciation of such an exaggerated estimation of the role of the missionary, which he corrects in his extended account of the proper part played by "God's fellow workers" (3:5–4:7).[17] Koester objects to this explanation on the ground of its limited applicability. Because "I am of Christ" parallels the other slogans in 1:12, he argues, it requires an equivalent interpretation. Since an appeal to baptisms performed in Corinth as the basis of a special allegiance to Christ is impossible, the rite is ruled out as the occasion of individualistic loyalties to the apostles.[18] More recently, however, Wire has suggested that the claim "I am of Christ" followed by the question "Is Christ divided?" marks a rhetorical move from reporting to ridicule in the interest of establishing a basis for a common faith.[19] The apostle himself says as much in his summary statement of the issue: "For all things are yours, whether Paul or Apollos or Cephas . . . all are yours; and you are Christ's *(hymeis de Christou),* and Christ is God's" (3:21-23). This positive assessment of being "of Christ" suggests that the corresponding slogan in 1:12 is also positive and is intended rhetorically as a corrective to the others. If this is correct, the ground of Koester's objection is removed and baptism offers the most compelling explanation of the individual expressions of loyalty to Paul, Apollos, and (perhaps) Cephas.

Finally, the Corinthian view of Christian existence as "trans-

---

15. Conzelmann, *1 Corinthians,* 36.

16. Richard Reitzenstein, *Die hellenistischen Mysterienreligionen* (3rd ed. 1937), 40-41; Wilckens, *Weisheit und Torheit,* 11-21; Conzelmann, *1 Corinthians,* 35-36; Robert W. Funk, *Language, Hermeneutic, and Word of God* (1966), 290; Robinson, *Trajectories,* 21-33.

17. Fee, *First Corinthians,* 61: "Paul's reason for this question ['Were you baptized in my name?'] probably flows out of their slogans. To be baptized 'into the name of' someone means that the baptisand has turned over allegiance . . . to the one named in the rite. The Corinthian slogans at least imply such an understanding. . . . It also seems probable, on the basis of Paul's arguments in both 10:1-6 and 15:29, that the Corinthians themselves held a somewhat 'magical' view of baptism. With such a view they perhaps also held in high regard those who had baptized them."

18. Helmut Koester, *Gnomon* 33 (1961): 591.

19. Wire, *The Corinthian Women Prophets,* 51: "by a mocking 'I am Christ's!' and a rebuking 'Is Christ divided?' he [Paul] is appealing to a shared faith in Christ."

eschatological" freedom in the Spirit mediated by special human figures through baptism also accounts for Paul's need to defend his apostolic authority in 4:1-21. That this is no mere addendum to the preceding discussion is emphasized by Schütz, who argues that 1:10–4:21 in its entirety is "an elaborate exposition of apostolic authority in preparation for its application in 5:1."[20] What necessitates Paul's apologetic is the view of the eschatological radicals that the presence of the last days in the power of the Spirit makes all authentic *pneumatikoi* (spirituals) equal and apostles superfluous.[21] This perspective is reflected in the apostle's uncharacteristic remark that "the spiritual one judges all things, but is to be judged by no one" (1 Cor. 2:13). Pearson attributes this statement to Paul but the terminology to the Corinthians.[22] Thiselton takes it as a quote, conveying the Corinthian conviction "that they could all 'discern' which particular teacher could best meet their own needs; and . . . that if need be they could do without teachers altogether, since each could discern spiritual truths for himself."[23] In defending his apostleship against such a view, Schütz recognizes, Paul is "not interested in asserting *his* authority *over against* someone else's, but genuine, apostolic authority toward the Church." This authority, he continues, is "the proper interpretation of power" that is intrinsic to the gospel itself, which is the issue that informs the discussion in 1:18–2:5.

Wisdom/Power and Foolishness/Weakness

The argument of 1 Corinthians 1:18–2:5 is structured by a series of three categorical antitheses. Two of these may be formulated terminologically as wisdom/foolishness (*sophia/mōria*) and power/weakness (*dynamis/astheneia*). Curiously, the antithetical terms of each set are never juxtaposed in the text. In no statement is wisdom played off against foolishness or power against weakness.[24] Rather, foolishness is

20. Schütz, *Paul and Apostolic Authority*, 190.
21. Thiselton, "Realized Eschatology at Corinth," 513.
22. Pearson, *The Pneumatikos-Psychikos Terminology in I Corinthians*, 38.
23. Thiselton, "Realized Eschatology at Corinth," 513.
24. An exception is 1 Cor. 3:19, where "the wisdom of this world" is declared to be "foolishness to God." But this does not invalidate the observation with regard to 1:18–2:5.

opposed to power in 1:18, and wisdom to power (twice) in 2:4-5. Such formulations convey not a lack of logical precision but rather the coordinate character of the terms wisdom/power and foolishness/weakness. Through this coordination, the two logical sets of antitheses are reduced to one. The assumption shared by all parties to the dispute is that wisdom without power is weakness and hence foolishness. Authentic wisdom is thereby characterized by a certain (for the moment unspecified) power. At issue, therefore, is what counts as power/wisdom, on the one hand, and as weakness/foolishness on the other.

The question is located within the context of the third antithesis between "those who are perishing" and "those who are being saved" (1:18, also designated as "those who believe" [1:21] and "those who are called" [1:24]). What counts as wisdom/power and foolishness/weakness is assessed differently in each of these circles. Among "those who are being saved," the *kērygma* (1:21 = "the word of the cross" [1:18]) or "Christ crucified" (1:23, cf. 2:2) is recognized as both wisdom and power. As the paradigmatic believer, Paul argues that "the power of God and the wisdom of God" are inherent in "Christ" (1:24) — the one crucified. The precedence of power over wisdom in this formulation is not fortuitous. For it is the divine power at work in the weakness of "Christ crucified" that constitutes this event as the divine foolishness that is wisdom. Apart from this power, the message of the cross qualifies only as human folly.

The nature of the power that establishes the wisdom of the kerygma is stipulated in 1:30. In an awkward sentence, Paul explains to the church in Corinth that it is "out of [God]" that it has its existence "in Christ, who has been made wisdom to us from God, [that is] righteousness and holiness and redemption."[25] Wisdom here is not one of four christological appelations, but rather is defined in terms of its power to effect the salvation depicted by the final three terms.[26] For Paul the power which establishes the wisdom character of the kerygma is "strictly soteriological."[27] The "word of the cross" (1:18) counts as wisdom because God is pleased "to save those who believe" by means

25. Fee, *First Corinthians*, 85-86.
26. Conzelmann, *1 Corinthians*, 52 n. 27, denies that the last three terms of v. 30 are an exegesis of *sophia*. But Fee, *First Corinthians*, 85-86, notes that the sentence structure indicates the interpretation of wisdom by the "historical-soteriological terms" that follow.
27. Conzelmann, *1 Corinthians*, 51.

of the message of that event (1:21). "Christ crucified," in a word, is "the power of God and the wisdom of God" (1:24).

From the perspective of "those who are perishing," the "word of the cross" is a scandal to Jews and foolishness to Greeks (1:22). This is so, Paul explains, because the former require "signs" and the latter (as representative Gentiles) seek "wisdom" (1:23). By signs *(sēmeia)* he means, of course, the evidences of power that confirm claims of divine authority.[28] By such a standard the message of "Christ crucified" is as much an oxymoron as is "fried ice."[29] It is scandalous to the typical Jewish auditor because it claims power for an event of ultimate weakness. Greeks deem "the word of the cross" foolishness for the same reason. Their wisdom criterion shares with the Jewish standard the assumption that weakness cannot be the medium of divinely revealed wisdom. Paul pejoratively designates their wisdom as "human wisdom" (2:5; cf. 2:13), "wisdom of the world" (1:20; cf. 3:19), wisdom "of this age" (2:6), thereby identifying its actual rather than alleged origin and thus denying its claim to a source in divine power.

Both the Jewish demand of signs and the Greek quest for wisdom are based upon criteria of power. Neither permits a perception of wisdom in the apostolic kerygma because each is incapable of entertaining the possibility of divine power being manifested in human weakness. It does not occur to "those who are perishing" that "the foolishness of God is wiser than [the wisdom] of humans, and the weakness of God is stronger than [the power] of humans" (1:25). So long as the criteria of what counts as wisdom/power and foolishness/weakness remain in force, there is an impasse. That people are not necessarily prisoners of their assumptions, however, is demonstrated by the Corinthian believers who no longer belong to "those who are perishing" but to "those who are being saved." To this transition and how it occurred Paul turns in 1:26–2:5.

Paul presses the point of the paradoxical relationship between wisdom/power and foolishness/weakness in the kerygma by appealing

---

28. Karl Heinrich Rengstorf, *"sēmeion," TDNT* VII, 235, 258-59. That Paul understood *sēmeion* as authenticating evidence of divine power is clear from 2 Cor. 12:12, where "the signs of an apostle" are designated as "wonders and mighty works" *(terata kai dynameis)*, and Rom. 15:19, where he speaks of Christ working through him "by the power of signs and wonders, by the power of the Spirit" *(en dynamei sēmeiōn kai teratōn, en dynamei pneumatos)*.

29. Fee, *First Corinthians,* 75.

to its correspondence with the social composition of the Corinthian congregation (1:26-31). In the fact that at their calling "not many" were "wise according to the flesh" or "powerful" or "well-born" (1:26) he perceives that "God has chosen the foolish things of the world to shame the wise, the weak things of the world to shame the strong, the base and despised things of the world, even things that are not, to nullify the things that are, so that no flesh may boast in the presence of God" (1:29). Thiessen observes that the point of this text is often missed because it is read as confirmation of "the romantic idea of a proletarian Christian community, a religious movement of the lower classes."[30] Noting that the term *oudeneia* (things that are nothing) is "a *topos* derived from the realm of philosophical ridicule," he concludes:

> Thus when Paul writes that those whom society and the world (*kosmos*, 1 Cor. 1:28) regard as nothing are in reality representatives of that wisdom which is contained in Christ, his Greek diction reveals how others perceive the social status of those whom he is addressing.[31]

The sociological reality of the church, in other words, attests to the same weakness/foolishness that characterizes the redemptive message of Christ crucified. At the same time it testifies to the power/wisdom of the gospel to effect salvation, although it excludes boasting of this status.[32]

In 2:1-5 Paul reminds the Corinthians of how this occurred in their own experience. He recalls that on his initial visit to Corinth his proclamation of "the mystery of God" *(to mystērion tou theou)*[33] did not meet the rhetorical standards of "excellence of speech or of wisdom"

---

30. Thiessen, *The Social Setting of Pauline Christianity*, 70-71.
31. Ibid., 71.
32. Richard W. Horsley, "Wisdom of Word and Words of Wisdom in Corinth," *CBQ* 39 (1977): 233-34, demonstrates that the terminology of "powerful," "noble birth," "wealthy," and "reigning like kings" (1:26; 4:8) is "standard language for Philo who used it to make the same distinctions in religious status" and thus to refer to "a spiritual elite (Sob. 55–57; Sac. 43–44)."
33. The manuscript evidence in favor of reading *mystērion* rather than *martyrion* is impressive although not conclusive, thus accounting for the strong differences of opinion among scholars. Bruce M. Metzger, *A Textual Commentary* (1971), 545, argues persuasively that the issue can only be resolved on internal grounds, and that the term *mystērion* is to be preferred on the basis that it "here prepares for its usage in ver. 7." For a contrary view, see Fee, *First Corinthians*, 88 n. 1.

(hyperochēn logou ē sophias) which they, being at the time among "those who are perishing," had every cultural reason to expect (2:1).[34] As he previously correlated the terms speech *(logos)* and wisdom *(sophia)* in the phrase "not in verbal wisdom" (1:17), so now he relates them under the rubric of "excellence" *(hyperochēn)*, a term connoting superiority and authority, and thus power. By contrast, he came to them "in weakness" *(en astheneia)* and "in fear" *(en phobō)* and "in much trembling" *(en tromō pollō;* 2:3). Neither his "speech" *(logos)* nor his "message" *(kērygma)*[35] evidenced the power of "persuasive wisdom" *(ouk en peithoi sophias;* 2:4a).[36] This reflected his decision "not to know anything among [them] except Jesus Christ, and that one crucified" (2:2). The point is that his ministry conforms to his message in the same way that the social composition of the church in Corinth corresponds to the kerygma that brought it into being.

Surprisingly, given what he has conceded, Paul claims power for his own proclamation. His speech and his message may not meet the worldly standards of "persuasive words of wisdom," but they do combine "in demonstration of the Spirit and of power" (2:4b).[37] In the ostensible weakness of both his public presence and proclamation, the power of the Spirit is at work. Yet, and this is the paradox, it is demonstrated in and through the weakness of the ministry and message of the apostle. By the proclamation of the kerygma through such evident human weakness, the Spirit convinces hearers of the reality of God's redemptive power at work in the weakness of "Christ crucified." The validity of this claim is confirmed by the incontrovertible fact that the

---

34. L. Hartman, "Some Remarks on 1 Cor. 2:1-5," *SEÅ* 34 (1974): 109-20, demonstrates that the rejected terms throughout this text derive from Greek rhetoric.

35. The distinction intended here between *logos* and *kērygma* is difficult to determine. Many commentators read the terms as a differentiation between the content (*logos* = "message") and the act (*kērygma* = "preaching") of Paul's proclamation. Krister Stendahl, "Kerygma und Kerygmatish," *ThLZ* 77 (1952): 715-20, demonstrates that *kērygma* is a content term in the apostle's vocabulary. Apart from being a redundancy, *logos* must mean "speech" in the context.

36. Timothy H. Lim, " 'Not in Persuasive Words of Wisdom, but in the Demonstration of the Spirit and Power,'" *NovT* 29 (1987): 146, argues that in 1 Cor. 2:4 Paul "appears to be rejecting not human communication in general, but that specific, studied art of persuasive speech as was practiced by orators and rhetoricians of the Graeco-Roman world and by at least some of the Corinthian preachers."

37. Fee, *First Corinthians*, 95: "The combination here is probably very close to a hendiadys (the use of two words to express the same reality: 'the Spirit, that is, Power')."

members of the church in Corinth have themselves come to faith through the weakness of Paul's ministry and message. Faith is itself the "sign" they seek, for it has its foundation "not in human wisdom but in the power of God" (2:5).

The conflict reflected in 1:18–2:5 therefore is not between the apostolic kerygma and inspired "verbal wisdom" *per se*, but between the power/wisdom demonstrated in the kerygma and the alternative power/wisdom of inspired speech claimed by the Corinthians. At issue, in other words, is the basic question of authentic divine inspiration. What distinguishes these two versions of Spirit-inspired discourse is the grounding of the apostolic kerygma in "Christ crucified." Its competition in Corinth is either not grounded or no longer grounded in "the word of the cross."[38] The nature and function of the "verbal wisdom" prized, advocated, and practiced in Corinth therefore merits closer examination.

Corinthian Verbal Wisdom

Traditional exegesis, following the lead of such terminological clues as the "debater of this age" (1:20), "superiority of speech or wisdom" (2:1), and "persuasive words of wisdom" (2:4), characterizes the wisdom speech against which Paul directs his critical remarks in 1:18–2:5 as the formal rhetorical techniques of disputation and argumentation generally associated with Greek philosophical wisdom.[39] Two distinguishable issues are here related, the nature of the wisdom in view (philosophical) and the form of its articulation (rhetoric).

More recent assessments of the Corinthian scene reflected in 1 Corinthians 1:18–2:16, however, challenge the traditional view of both the nature and form of Corinthian verbal wisdom. Käsemann paves the

---

38. Funk, *Language*, 290-91, correlates the nature of the Corinthians' wisdom with the trans-historical mode of existence to which they believe sophia entitles them (1 Cor. 4:8).

39. Weiss, *Korintherbrief*, 23; Lietzmann, *Korinther I/II*, 9. More recently, Schlier, *Die Zeit der Kirche*, 207, argues that Paul's polemic is directed at those who present the gospel in a rationally convincing rhetoric, which, because of the intrinsic relationship between form and content, inevitably involves a distortion of the kerygma by forcing it into the unhistorical and impersonal categories of philosophy.

way for an alternative interpretation of the nature of Corinthian wisdom by calling attention to the religious character of *sophia* in the popular philosophies, mysteries, and magic of Hellenism that promised salvation and redemption.[40] Herbert Braun, working from the text, notes that Paul's polemic against Corinthian wisdom closely parallels his criticism of the Law as a way of salvation and concludes that wisdom functioned redemptively among the Corinthians.[41] The soteriological function of the Corinthian wisdom is implicit in Paul's rhetorical question, "Has not God made foolish the wisdom of the world?" (1:20),[42] and is explicit in the ensuing explanation: "For since in the wisdom of God the world did not know God through wisdom, it pleased God to save those who believe through the foolishness of the kerygma" (1:21). Here the knowledge of God is designated as redemptive and the event by which God "*befooled* wisdom" (Godet)[43] is identified as that proclaimed in the apostolic message of "Christ crucified." He makes the same point in his insistence that the power of the kerygma is evident in "Christ Jesus, whom God made our wisdom, [that is] our righteousness and sanctification and redemption" (1:30). His argument in each instance is that the salvation announced in the kerygma denies to "the wisdom of the world" that saving knowledge of God which it claims to afford. According to Paul, such wisdom deceives people into thinking that they are "wise in this age" (3:18), seduces them into believing that they already participate fully in the end-time blessings (4:8), tempts them to boast before God (1:29; cf. 3:21), and empties the cross of its eschatological, critical power (1:17).[44]

Noting that Paul's own positive claim to speak wisdom (2:6-16) formally parallels that of the Corinthians, Baumann emphasizes the Spirit-inspired character of the *logos* (speech) in which the Corinthian

---

40. Ernst Käsemann, *Exegetische Versuche und Besinnungen* (1960), I, 268.

41. Herbert Braun, *Gesammelte Studien zum Neuen Testament und seiner Umwelt* (1967), 181.

42. Conzelmann, *1 Corinthians*, 43, notes that the judgment on "the wisdom of the world" is stated "in the form of a question, not by reasoning, but by asserting an act of God."

43. Cited by Fee, *First Corinthians*, 72 n. 22.

44. Schütz, *Paul and Apostolic Authority*, 192, notes that the cross "has an eschatological, critical function which, while it does not usurp God's final judgment in irrevocable fashion, anticipates and perhaps even determines it. It is this critical function, this 'power' of the word of the cross, which is in danger of being vitiated, according to v. 17."

sophia (wisdom) comes to expression.[45] His inference is confirmed by the inclusion of the "word of wisdom" *(logos sophias)*/"word of knowledge" *(logos gnōseōs)* among the works of the Spirit listed in 12:8-10. This "manifestation of the Spirit" is the same "verbal wisdom" that is mentioned in 1:17 and discussed in 1:18–2:16. The resultant problem, however, is how to square the inspired character of such utterances with the clear references to Greek rhetoric in 2:1-5. Horsley warns that an anomaly occurs when *sophia* — with its background in Jewish Wisdom speculation or a Gnostic Sophia-myth — is identified as "the means and content of salvation," and *logos* as the eloquence characteristic of "popular Hellenistic philosophy." He resolves the anomaly by locating the source of Corinthian "verbal wisdom" in "the Hellenistic Jewish tradition represented by Philo and the Wisdom of Solomon" where eloquence is not only "an important religious possession," but is "closely connected with *sophia* as the means of salvation as well."[46] Accordingly, in this tradition divine inspiration and human rhetoric are not mutually exclusive. For "eloquence is clearly an effect and an important expression of the soul's intimate relationship with Sophia, which is both the means and the content (or goal) of salvation."[47]

At issue is not the validity of such inspired utterances in principle, which Paul explicitly concedes (12:8), but their content. Of the character of Corinthian wisdom, Wire writes:

> Paul's argument here suggests that the Corinthians speak not only in invocation and confession but discursively, reflecting on words and meanings, proposing to each other distinctions that clarify usage and can be supported by mutual experience. Maxims, definitions, and short quotations may become slogans to summarize their stand and opportunities to demonstrate common commitment.[48]

Her comment, although conjectural of necessity, does bring to mind such Corinthians aphorisms as "All things are lawful for me" (6:12), "Food is meant for the stomach and the stomach for food" (6:13), "It

---

45. Baumann, *Mitte und Norm*, 78-79.
46. Horsley, "Wisdom of Word and Words of Wisdom in Corinth," 225.
47. *Ibid.*, 229. The possible connection between this tradition and Apollos — a native of Alexandria who was an "eloquent man" and "fervent in spirit" (Acts 18:24-25) — is evident.
48. Wire, *The Corinthian Women Prophets*, 49-50.

is well for a man not to touch a woman" (7:1), "All of us possess knowledge" (8:1), "All things are lawful" (10:23), "There is no resurrection of the dead" (15:12), and perhaps even "Jesus be damned" (12:3). If these texts represent the "verbal wisdom" against which Paul inveighs, and if they were accompanied by speaking in tongues, as we have argued, then they would have been authenticated by that evidence of power which served as the "sign" of the Spirit's "manifestation" in Corinth.[49]

The antithesis which the apostle sets up between "verbal wisdom" (1:17) and "the word of the cross" (1:18) is therefore not an opposition between philosophical speculation evinced in the style of Greek rhetoric and a religious message manifest "in demonstration of the Spirit and power" (2:4), but a contrast of two competing religious proclamations, both of which claim the inspiration of the Spirit and liberating import. The focus of Paul's polemic is the content of Corinthian wisdom, which in his judgment has lost its grounding in the kerygma that alone offers a valid criterion for discerning the authenticity of inspiration. It is on this ground that he makes his own claim to speak wisdom that is subject to the message of Christ crucified.

Wisdom and the Mystery of Christ Crucified

It is important to note that what changes in the transition from 1:18–2:5 to 2:6-16 is not the subject matter itself but the manner in which it is articulated.[50] The emphasis falls upon the first term in the power/wisdom

---

49. Horsley, "Wisdom of Word and Words of Wisdom in Corinth," 235 n. 26, calls attention to "the close relation between eloquent expression of words of *sophia* and the experience of prophetic ecstasy or inspiration by the Divine Spirit. . . . The discussion of *parrēsia* in *Her.* 4:14-15, described as eloquence of the soul heard by God and not by any mortal, is also strikingly similar to Philo's portrayal of prophetic inspiration, and cannot help but remind one of Paul's cautionary discussion of glossolalia in 1 Cor. 14:2-5."

50. Peter Stuhlmacher, "The Hermeneutical Significance of 1 Cor 2:6-16," in Gerald F. Hawthorne, ed., *Tradition and Interpretation* (1987), 330-32, chronicles the remarkable reversal of scholarly opinion on the history-of-religions background of 1 Cor. 2:6-16 and the relation of the pericope to its immediate context. In the exegetical line that begins with Bousset and extends through Bultmann to Käsemann and Wilckens,

duality as it is related to the kerygma in 1:18–2:5, but at 2:6 it shifts to the second term. The wisdom implicit in the message of "Christ crucified" now comes to explicit expression in Paul's claim that "we speak wisdom among the mature" (2:6).[51] Although this wisdom is contrasted to the "human wisdom" of 2:5 by the Greek particle *de* in its adversative sense (but), it remains "wisdom" nonetheless. As Thiessen explains, "The term 'wisdom' always contains a cognitive element," including knowledge, reflection, even "theory." In the present context "wisdom" enables people "to understand" (*eidenai*, 2:12), "to interpret" (*sygkrinein*, 2:13), and "to judge" (*anakrinesthai*, 2:14, 15). In sum, "All these cognitive verbs indicate a process of understanding, conceiving, and interpreting."[52] Wisdom as such is thus not alien to the apostolic kerygma. The latter is foolishness to "those who are perishing" not because it is unintelligible but because it all too clearly calls for a reversal of the human standard of power that determines what counts as wisdom.[53]

---

a consensus developed that viewed the thematic shift from "the word of the cross" (1:18–2:5) to "wisdom among the mature" (2:6-16) as a loss of the subject matter intended in 1:18-25. Paul loses his grip on the critique of wisdom conducted in the previous section and capitulates in 2:6-16 to the vocabulary and conceptuality of the mystery religions or incipient gnosticism. Stuhlmacher marks the beginning of the reversal of this interpretation with the 1968 publication of *Paul* by Günther Bornkamm (163-64), followed by Wilckens in *Theologia Crucis—Signum Crucis*, C. Andresen and G. Klein eds. (1979), 513; Gerd Thiessen, *Psychological Aspects of Pauline Theology* (1987), 345-94; G. Sellin, "Das 'Geheimnis' der Weisheit," *ZNW* 73 (1982): 69-96; Friedrich Lang, *Die Brief an die Korinther* (1986), 41; Ellis, *Prophecy and Hermeneutic*, 47-50; and himself (*op. cit.*, 334). According to the new consensus, Jewish wisdom traditions provide the history-of-religions background to 2:6-16 and allow its material continuity with 1:18–2:5 to be recognized. Cf. also Schlier, *Die Zeit der Kirche*, 206-32; Kurt Niederwimmer, "Erkennen und Lieben," *KD* 11 (1965): 75-102; Funk, *Language*, 275-305; and Otto Betz, "Der gekreuzigte Christus: unsere Weisheit und Gerechtigkeit," in *Tradition and Interpretation*, 195-215.

51. The often noted shift from the first person singular in 2:1-5 to the first person plural in 2:6-16 should not be pressed too hard. Paul often expresses himself by the editorial "we," as Fee, *First Corinthians*, 101 n. 13, correctly observes. In 2:1-5 the apostle refers to his own ministry at the time of his initial missionary visit to Corinth, requiring the first person singular. In any case, *laloumen* ("we speak") in 2:6 resumes *kēryssomen* ("we preach") in 1:23, as Funk, *Language*, 279 n. 12, points out.

52. Thiessen, *Psychological Aspects*, 386.

53. Niederwimmer, "Erkennen und Lieben," 85, asks, "Wherein consists the 'foolishness' of the kerygma? Not in the sense that the kerygma is absurd — it is stated in meaningful statements — but in this, that it is paradoxical. It does not fit into the value world of man. It calls for a 'reversal of value.'"

The wisdom which Paul claims to speak "among the mature" is differentiated from "human wisdom" (2:5) and "the wisdom of this age and of the rulers of this age" (2:6) by both its source and its content. As "God's wisdom" (*theou sophian,* 2:7), it belongs to God and thereby has its source in God.[54] For this reason it is qualified as "hidden" (*tēn apokekrymmenēn,* 2:7), meaning unknown and implying unknowability unless made known by God. With regard to content, it is the "wisdom of God [consisting] in a mystery" (*theou sophian en mystēriō,* 2:7).[55] All attempts to interpret *mystērion* in a purely formal sense fail because it is fundamentally a substantive term.[56] Here it picks up the mystery mentioned in 2:1, where it designates the content of apostolic proclamation.[57] The "wisdom of God," accordingly, consists in the mystery of "Christ crucified" as attested in "the word of the cross."[58]

The two relative clauses which qualify the opening statement of 2:7a regarding "God's hidden wisdom" affirm respectively its soteriological and hidden character. The first clause designates God's wisdom as a wisdom "which God foreordained before the ages unto our glory" (2:7b), indicating that it is a pre-temporal salvation plan that is directed toward an eschatological salvation blessing. The second describes it as a wisdom "which none of the rulers of this age knew, for if they had known, they would not have crucified the Lord of Glory" (2:8).[59] This

---

54. Fee, *First Corinthians,* 104 n. 26: "The *theou* is emphatic, *theou sophian;* the genitive is probably possessive in this case, although it may also lean toward source, i.e., wisdom that not only belongs to God, but also comes from God."

55. Bauer, *Lexicon,* 260, lists "consisting in" among the legitimate senses which the Greek preposition *en* can bear. In agreement is Dautzenberg, "Botschaft und Bedeutung der urchristlichen Prophetie," 142: "We speak wisdom, which is the mystery."

56. Bornkamm, "*mystērion,*" *TDNT,* IV, 820: "The mystery is not itself revelation; it is the object of revelation. This belongs constitutively to the term."

57. Funk, *Language,* 295.

58. Robin Scroggs, "Paul: *Sophos* and *Pneumatikos,*" *NTS* 14 (1967): 35, argues that "Paul must have had an esoteric wisdom teaching entirely separate from his kerygma" on the ground that the kerygma is the *martyrion tou theou* (testimony of God, 2:1) and wisdom is the eschatological *mystērion* (mystery, 2:7). It is thus clear that the textual decision regarding the proper reading of 2:1, either *martyrion* or *mystērion,* is important. Yet it is not crucial, for it can be demonstrated that the primary textual antecedent of *sophia* in 2:6-8 is "Christ our wisdom, that is our righteousness and sanctification and redemption" (1:30).

59. The issue of the intended reference of the phrase *tōn archontōn tou aiōnos touto* in 2:6 and 8 continues to vex New Testament scholarship, the alternatives being

epistemic lack on the part of the rulers of this age implies that "God's wisdom" was "hidden" in the crucifixion of Jesus, here titled "the Lord of Glory" *(ton kyrion tēs doxēs)*.[60] Not only does "God's hidden wisdom" consist in the mystery of "Christ crucified," but it provides that event with its cognitive value. It is precisely this *meaning* of the cross which Paul claims to articulate in the wisdom spoken among the mature.

The ignorance of "God's hidden wisdom" represented by the rulers is sharply contrasted in 2:9 with the knowledge of this wisdom among believers. By an appeal to the testimony of Scripture,[61] Paul links his discussion of the wisdom that is hidden (2:6-8) with the ensuing topic of the wisdom that is revealed (2:10-13).[62] Of the possible solutions to the problem created by the anacoluthic character of the citation (caused by the lack of a main verb), that proposed by Bo Judd illuminates the text most convincingly.[63] The four relative clauses that compose the citation itself are viewed as an ellipsis, the reader being invited to supply the unexpressed verb. What verb is warranted, Judd argues, is suggested by the opposition of verse 9 to verse 8 established by the introductory strong adversative *alla* (but). Because what is opposed in verse 8 by verse 9 is the ignorance of the rulers (*oudeis egnōken*, "none knew"), the elliptical sentence may be completed by adding the required counterclaim to knowledge (*egnōkamen*, "we do know").[64] What is known is specified by the two relative pronouns (*ha*, "the things") which intro-

---

the "historical rulers" responsible for the crucifixion of Jesus and the "demonic powers." Fee, *First Corinthians*, 103f., contends that the latter possibility "needs finally to be laid to rest since the linguistic evidence, the context, and Pauline theology all argue against it" (citing the decisive linguistic evidence in n. 24). Thiessen, *Psychological Aspects*, 369-70, agrees that "civil officials" are meant, but argues that these "are not merely the concrete rulers of Palestine, Pilate and Antipas, but earthly rulers in general, in Corinth and Judea. He observes, however, that these historical rulers "are heightened symbolically to demonic powers" (378).

60. Lang, *Korinther*, 43-44, notes that "'Lord of Glory' in Judaism is a divine title (Ethiopic Enoch 22:14; 63:2 and often)." Funk, *Language*, 294, emphasizes that "it is clear that the Pauline assumption underlying 2:8b is that the Lord of Glory was crucified."

61. The source of the quotation is unknown. Although similar phrases can be found in Isa. 64:4; 52:15 (cf. Sir. 1:10), the text as cited can be found neither in the Old Testament nor in Jewish apocryphal literature.

62. Barrett, *First Corinthians*, 72.

63. Bo Judd, "1 Corinthians 2:9," *NTS* 31 (1988): 603-9.

64. *Ibid.*, 607-8.

duce the four clauses of the citation. Each has as its textual antecedent the "hidden wisdom of God" (2:7). The first three clauses ("The things that eye has not seen and ear has not heard and the human heart has not conceived") emphasize the hidden nature of God's wisdom, while the fourth ("the things that God has prepared for those who love him") underscores the soteriological character of the divine wisdom. Further, the phrase *hētoimasen ho theos* ("God has prepared") is coordinate with *proōrisen ho theos* ("God has foreordained") in 2:7.

The basis of the believer's knowing what the rulers of this age did not know is stated in the succeeding explanatory statement, "For to us God has revealed *(apokalyptein)* [it] by the Spirit" (v. 10a).[65] Stuhlmacher aptly identifies this statement as "the primary hermeneutical thesis of the apostle."[66] That this is the case is confirmed by the turn of the discussion at this point from the character and content of "God's wisdom" to its medium, "God's Spirit" (*to pneuma tou theou*, 2:11). The way has been prepared for this shift by the apostle's earlier claim that his speech and kerygma at Corinth were "in demonstration of the Spirit and power" (2:4). From the coordination of authentic wisdom with effective power throughout 1 Corinthians 1:18–2:5, together with the identification of the Spirit as the agent of such power, it is clear that the Spirit is the implicit coordinate of wisdom in 2:6-8 as well. As the Spirit is the agent that effects faith through the kerygma (2:5), so also it is the medium of the wisdom that unfolds the kerygma.

Being the one who "searches all things, even the depths of God" (2:10b), the Spirit is privy to "the things of God" (*ta tou theou*, 2:11). Based as the latter phrase is upon its analogy in "the things of a human" (*ta tou anthrōpou*), the neuter plural definite article *ta* (the things) denotes something like "the mind" or "the thoughts" of a human and of God respectively. Yet in the context of Paul's argument, the definite article has its antecedent in the indefinite pronoun *ha* (the things) of

---

65. Reading *gar* (for) rather than *de* (but). Fee, *First Corinthians*, 109-10, comments: "The contrast, therefore, despite the emphatic position of 'to us,' lies not so much between 'us' and 'them' as on the reason they could not, but we can, understand the things that God has prepared for his people. That is, as vv. 10b-13 make clear, the emphasis lies on the *means* of revelation, the Spirit, not on the recipients themselves, although the latter of course are always in view, an emphasis that will be picked up again in vv. 14-16."

66. Stuhlmacher, "The Hermeneutical Significance of 1 Cor 2:6-16," 337.

2:9, and thus in "the hidden wisdom of God" of 2:7. Accordingly, the Spirit is enabled to make that wisdom known.

That the Spirit does make "God's wisdom" known to humans is implied by the giving of the Spirit itself. "We have received not the spirit of the world but the Spirit which is of God," Paul declares, "in order that we may understand the gracious things which have been bestowed upon us by God" (*hina eidōmen ta hypo tou theou charisthenta hēmin*, 2:12).[67] The participial phrase in this clause picks up and interprets *ha hētoimasen ho theos* ("the things which God has prepared") in 2:9,[68] a phrase which has its own antecedent in *hen proōrisen ho theos* ("which God foreordained") and thus in the *theou sophia* ("God's wisdom") of 2:7. But the ultimate antecedent of "the gracious things bestowed by God" in the context of 1:18–2:16 is located in 1:30, where the apostle specifies the content of the wisdom which Christ has been made to us from God in terms of "righteousness, sanctification, and redemption."[69]

Speaking Wisdom by the Spirit

The wisdom that is given and received "through the Spirit" (2:10) is also articulated in human speech by the Spirit. Paul thus states in 2:13 that "the things which we speak [we speak] not in words taught by human wisdom but [in words] taught by the Spirit" (*ha kai laloumen ouk en didaktois anthrōpinēs sophias logois all' en didaktois pneumatos*). In the

---

67. Baumann, *Mitte und Norm*, 241, argues rightly that the larger context indicates that *ta charisthenta* refers to the cross as the completed act of God. Eduard Schweizer, "pneuma," *TDNT* VI, 426 n. 617, overstates the point: "The *bathē tou theou* are the *ta tou theou* of v. 11 and the *ta charisthenta hēmin* (aor.) of v. 12, so that the ref. is to the gracious action which God has already accomplished, not to something special or future." The redemption grounded in the mystery of God's foreordained purpose is established historically by the cross of Christ and has clear eschatological significance.

68. Barrett, *First Corinthians*, 75, identifies "the things that God has freely given us" with "the undefinable and undescribable things of verse 9." Cf. Fee, *First Corinthians*, 113; Conzelmann, *1 Corinthians*, 67 n. 108.

69. Stuhlmacher, "The Hermeneutical Significance of 1 Cor 2:6-16," 338, comments: "What Christians gain with the gift of the Spirit as the power of illumination is insight into the mysteries of revelation, but above all the understanding of the gracious gifts bestowed by God in Christ in the form of justification, sanctification and redemption (cf. 2:12 with 1:30)."

opening phrase *ha kai laloumen* ("what things also we speak"), the relative pronoun refers to *ta charisthenta* ("the things given") in 2:12 and the verb reaffirms the claim made initially in 2:6 and repeated in 2:7. What is new in verse 13 is the transition from knowing to speaking.[70]

The participial phrase which concludes 2:13, *pneumatikois pneumatika synkrinontes,* is ambiguous due to the uncertainty of (1) the gender of *pneumatikois* (being either masculine or neuter) and (2) the intended sense of the verb. The latter can mean "to compare" (as in 2 Cor. 10:12), or "to combine" (as in classical Greek), or "to interpret" (as in the LXX often). Although used by Paul in the sense of "to compare" in 2 Corinthians 10–12, this sense seems inappropriate in the present context. Given the known influence of the Septuagint upon the apostle, the classical sense ("to combine") may also be discarded. The verb *synkrinein* thus means "to interpret," and what is interpreted is *pneumatika* (spiritual things), which has as its immediate antecedent *ta charisthenta* (the gracious gifts bestowed, v. 12). The verb has as its indirect object *pneumatikois,* which, if neuter in gender, would have the sense of "interpreting spiritual things in spiritual words,"[71] or, if masculine, "interpreting spiritual things to spiritual people."[72]

The forward flow of the argument in 2:6-16 favors a masculine reading of *pneumatikois.*[73] For the apostle immediately proceeds to comment on what he says in verse 13 by contrasting the *psychikos* (natural person) in verse 14 with the *pneumatikos* (spiritual person) in verse 15. The former, representing "those who are perishing," does not receive "the things of the Spirit of God" *(ta tou pneumatos theou)* because they are "foolishness" *(mōria)* according to the criterion of power/wisdom operative among such people. Because the neuter plural

---

70. Conzelmann, *1 Corinthians,* 67.

71. Thus Barrett, *First Corinthians,* 76; Conzelmann, *1 Corinthians,* 67; and Fee, *First Corinthians,* 115.

72. Lietzmann, *Korinther I/II,* 13; Robertson and Plummer, *First Corinthians,* 46-48; Stuhlmacher, "The Hermeneutical Significance of 1 Cor 2:6-16," 338.

73. Friedrich Büchsel, "*krinō,*" *TDNT* III, 954, adds to this argument a stylistic observation: "*pneumatikois* is best taken personally as a dat. of remoter obj.: 'for spiritual men.' This interpretation has the advantage of fitting in with v. 14: 'The non-spiritual man does not receive the things of the Spirit.' On the other hand, the instrumental understanding of *pneumatikois* is contrary to Paul's preceding use, not of an instrumental dat., but of a construction with *en (en . . . logois).*"

article *ta* ("the things") has its antecedent in the *pneumatika* ("spiritual things") of verse 13, Paul is here designating the type of person who is unable to benefit from the work of the Spirit designated just previously as "interpreting spiritual things to spiritual people," namely, the unbeliever.[74] In contrast to the *psychikos*, the *pneumatikos* is said in 2:15 to judge "all things" (*panta* = *ta tou pneumatos tou theou*, "the things of the Spirit of God," 2:13). This distinction is then applied to the Corinthian situation in 3:1-3, where the *psychikos* (natural person) is replaced by the *sarkinoi* (carnal people) who are *nēpioi en Christō* (infants in Christ).

Paul's language in 2:6-16 has encouraged the view that when he claims in verse 6 to speak wisdom "among the mature" *(en tois teleiois)* he is limiting the wisdom of God to the circle of the *pneumatikoi* (spiritual people) and intimating that it is an esoteric knowledge restricted to a select few within the larger congregation.[75] His distinction between the *pneumatikos* and the *psychikos*, however, clearly identifies the believer and the unbeliever respectively. This absolute distinction is paralleled by his relative differentiation between the *pneumatikos* and the *sarkinos*. That the latter term is not equivalent to *psychikos* is evident from the apostle's express statement that "carnal people" are "infants in Christ" (3:1). This differentiation between the *sarkinos* and the *psychikos* requires that their common antonym *(pneumatikos)* be understood in a double sense. In relation to "unbeliever" *(psychikos)*, "spiritual one" denotes the "believer." In relation to "immature believer" *(sarkinos = nēpios)*, it has the sense of "mature believer" (and is thus equivalent to *teleios*). In restricting his wisdom speech to the "mature" (2:6), and in decrying his inability to address the Corinthians as "spiritual people" (3:1), Paul makes the point that they are "immature."[76] That is to say, they are not among "the ethically and intellectually disciplined" believers

---

74. Scroggs, "Paul: *Sophos* and *Pneumatikos*," 52, comments: "The *psychikos* is the one who has not been restored to his intended relationship with God and thus does not live a life by the spirit."

75. Wilckens, *Weisheit und Torheit*, 52-53.

76. Conzelmann, *1 Corinthians*, 59-60: "The division between believers of a lower and a higher order arises from the fact that the addressees do not conform to the true status conferred upon them (3:1ff). In order to bring this out, he takes up the two-order schema. . . . Thus Paul declares that as yet he had been unable to impart wisdom to the Corinthians. He does not uphold any secret discipline, however, but explains his silence as merely a matter of pedagogy."

who are "obedient to the kerygma" and thus "able to receive the sophia Paul can impart."[77] Since *pneumatikos* is the self-designation of the prophets in Corinth, his distinction between the "mature" and the "immature" believer, together with his restriction of the deeper wisdom of God to the former, effectively discredits their claim to an elite status within the community.

What is interpreted to "mature believers" is specified in 2:6-16 by a variety of terms and phrases which have a common reference: "the things of the Spirit of God" (2:14); "what things also we speak" (2:13); "the things which God has given to us" (2:12); "all things" investigated by the Spirit (2:10); "what things eye has not seen and ear has not heard and the human mind has not conceived, what things God has prepared for those who love him" (2:9); "the hidden wisdom of God in a mystery, which God foreordained before the ages for our glory, which none of the rulers of this age knew, for if they had known, they would not have crucified the Lord of God" (2:7). It is this grounding of the wisdom that Paul speaks to the mature in the one crucified which establishes its material connection to the kerygma on the basis of a common subject matter. Thus "We speak wisdom" (2:6, 7, 13) has its literary and theological antecedent in "We preach Christ crucified . . . the power of God and the wisdom of God" (1:23, 24). The proclamation of this wisdom is therefore the interpretation of the kerygma in terms of its inherent theological and ethical implications. For God has made Christ crucified "wisdom for us," which entails "righteousness and holiness and redemption." As Stuhlmacher puts it, the discussion in 1 Cor. 2:6-16 "has the practical aim of leading the Corinthians . . . into complete insight into the gospel."[78]

---

77. Scroggs, "Paul: *Sophos* and *Pneumatikos*," 38.

78. Stuhlmacher, "The Hermeneutical Significance of 1 Cor 2:6-16," 334. So also Niederwimmer, "Erkenen und Lieben," 86, who holds that the wisdom Paul affirms in 2:6-16 "is precisely the kerygma" in the sense that it is the "explication of the *logos tou staurou* [word of the cross] in direct continuation of the antithetical theme of the previous argument." Conzelmann, *1 Corinthians*, 57, while keeping open the possibility of "a positive, undialectical wisdom" in 2:6-16, concedes that in the apostle's argument here it "cannot be a supplementary factor alongside the word of the cross, but can only be the understanding of this word, which includes in particular the understanding of its foolishness." So conceived, "Wisdom would then be theology as a clarification of the proclamation."

A Prophetic Wisdom?

The crucial question, of course, is whether the wisdom spoken in "words taught by the Spirit" (2:13) can be identified legitimately as prophetic speech despite the fact that the terms *prophētes* (prophet), *prophēteia* (prophecy), and *prophēteuein* (to prophesy) do not appear in 2:6-16. A *prima facie* case for such an identification can be made by noting the number of key terms from 2:6-16 that reappear in the apostle's discussion of prophecy in 1 Corinthians 12–14. These include: (1) *apokalyptein* (to reveal, 2:10; 14:30); (2) *pneumatikoi* (spiritual ones, 2:13; 12:1) and *pneumatikos* (spiritual one, 2:15; 14:37); (3) *pneuma* (Spirit, 2:10 [twice], 13; 12:4, 7, 8 [twice], 9, 11) and *pneuma theou* (Spirit of God, 2:11, 12, 14; 12:3); (4) *sophia* (wisdom, 2:6 [twice], 7; 12:8); (5) *teleioi* (mature, 2:6; 14:20); (6) *anakrinein* (judge, 2:14; 14:24); and (7) *mystērion* (mystery, 2:1, 7; 13:2; 14:2).[79] Such a clustering of common terms in these two passages addressed to the same congregation and focused upon the same topic of speech inspired by the Spirit surely warrants the assumption of a common subject matter identified explicitly in chapter 14 as prophecy.

In addition, Funk calls the preference for the verb *lalein* (to speak) in 2:6-16 (vv. 6, 7, 13) over *kēryssein* (to preach, 1:23) or *katangellein* (to proclaim, 2:1) "striking," suggesting "that Paul may have certain charismatic gifts in mind (cf. the characteristic use of *lalein* in 1 Corinthians 12:3, 30; 13:7; 14:2ff.), the profusion of which in Corinth he has already indicated (1:5ff.)."[80] Significantly, the apostle uses *lalein* to designate prophetic utterance in chapter 14 (vv. 3, 6, 29). The fact that this verb is also used extensively in 1 Corinthians 12–14 with reference to "tongue speaking" (*glōssa lalein,* 12:30; 13:1; 14:2, 4, 5, 6, 13, 18, 19, 23, 27, 39) does not detract from but rather enhances the value of his observation. For the phenomenon of tongues was identified in Corinth as the authenticating "sign" of intelligible prophecy. The terminology alone therefore ties 1 Corinthians 2:6-16 and 12–14 together by reflecting a common situation in the Corinthian congregation.[81]

The connection between these two passages, however, is material as well as terminological. The issue in 1 Corinthians 1:18–2:5 is wisdom speech that claims God's redemptive power. Paul critiques the Corinthians'

---

79. It should also be noted that *sēmeion* (sign) occurs in 1:22 and 14:22.
80. Funk, *Language,* 285 n. 42.
81. Jacques Dupont, *Gnosis* (1960), 249.

wisdom discourse — venerated among them as inspired utterance — for having lost its substantive relationship to the kerygma. In 2:6-16 he counters their claim by advocating a wisdom that is grounded in the kerygma of Christ crucified (2:8), revealed through the Spirit of God (2:10), and articulated in words taught by the Spirit (2:13). The question, in other words, concerns what counts as genuine inspired utterance — the same problem that dominates the discussion in chapters 12–14.[82] The substance of the matter addressed in both passages comes to expression in five common interrelated themes: (1) revelation *(apokalypsis)* of (2) God's mystery *(mystērion)* through (3) human agents *(pneumatikoi = prophētēs)* who (4) speak in the Spirit *(lalein pneumati)* and whose utterances (5) must be judged *(anakrinein/diakrinein)* on the basis of their content.

If the content of the Spirit's revelatory activity attested in 1 Corinthians 2:10 is specified as wisdom that makes God's gracious gifts in Christ crucified understandable (v. 12), the revelation associated with prophecy in chapter 14 is materially ambiguous (vv. 6, 26, 30).[83] Convinced that "the possession and public declaration of a revelation was the characteristic, if not exclusive contribution of a prophet to the assembly's worship," Hill delineates the range of possible interpretations of this prophetic enterprise:

> In the light of the list of spiritual gifts in 12.8f. it may be related to 'the utterance of wisdom' mentioned there, i.e. mature, insightful, practical instruction and exhortation: but it could go further and include the intelligible communication of some supernatural disclosure of God's purpose, or even of some ecstatic auditory experience (2 Cor 12.7).[84]

The scope of this suggestion is predicated upon the assumption that Paul's use of the terms *apokalypsis/apokalyptein* (revelation/reveal) lacks a unifying concept. Because of its extensive implications, this conjecture requires examination.

---

82. Why the same subject is taken up twice in one letter may be explained by noting that Paul responds in 1:10–4:21 to an oral report from Chloe's people (1:11) whereas in chaps. 12–14 he is replying to a question addressed to him in a letter from the congregation in Corinth (12:1).

83. Fee, *First Corinthians*, 662, notes that "revelation" in this context is formally intelligible speech and functionally "some kind of utterance given by the Spirit for the benefit of the gathered community."

84. Hill, *New Testament Prophecy*, 126.

Revelation of the Gospel

Just as prophecy and gospel converge in Paul's usage of the terms *oikodomē* (edification) and *paraklēsis* (exhortation) with their cognate verbs, so they also meet in his employment of the words *apokalypsis* (revelation) and *apokalyptein* (reveal).[85] In defending before the Galatians the authority of both his gospel and his apostolate, Paul appeals to revelation. With regard to his gospel, he claims that his proclaimed message is "not of human origin" (*kata anthrōpon*, Gal. 1:11), in that he did not receive it "from a human source" (*para anthrōpou*, 1:12a) but "through a revelation of Jesus Christ" (*di' apokalypseōs Iēsou Christou*, 1:12b). As for his apostleship to the Gentiles, he declares that it was the pleasure of God "to reveal his Son to me *(apokalypsai ton huion autou en emoi)*, in order that I might preach him *(euangelizōmai auton)* among the nations" (Gal. 1:16).

Stuhlmacher locates the origin of the terms *apokalypsis* and *apokalyptein* as Paul uses them here in the conceptual world represented by Jewish apocalyptic literature.[86] Foundational to apocalypticism is the conviction that the events of the end of time — the eschatological "secrets" or "mysteries" — have been revealed by God to special agents who, in turn, declare to the world the God who is coming at the close of this age. Within apocalyptic thought there is a crucial dialectic between hiddenness and disclosure. What is disclosed by revelation, however, will be *verified* only at its ultimate manifestation at the end of the present age. The messenger of such "revelations" is thus highly vulnerable to disbelief and misunderstanding. As Schütz aptly observes, "The message may be ultimate, but it is not transparent."[87]

Stuhlmacher argues that Paul operated within the framework of this understanding of revelation, and that he viewed "revelations" as proleptic disclosures of the reality awaiting eschatological manifestation. Clearly the apostle's understanding of revelation unfolds against a hori-

---

85. Hannelis Schulte, *Der Begriff der Offenbarung im Neuen Testament* (1949), 9 (cf. 21), warns that the concept of revelation in the New Testament generally and in Paul particularly must be related to several word groups rather than to a single term and its cognates. Our focus upon *apokalypsis/apokalyptein* aims at establishing a terminological bridge between gospel and prophecy, the assumption being that the investigation of concepts must at least begin with the terms in which the concepts are expressed, and that the consistent use of terms may well indicate a unified concept.

86. Peter Stuhlmacher, *Das paulinische Evangelium* (1968), I, 76-82.

87. Schütz, *Paul and Apostolic Authority*, 133.

zon of future expectation. The parousia of Christ is denoted as "a revelation" (*apokalypsis*, 1 Cor. 1:7). He speaks also of the revelation of the eschatological "glory" (*doxa*, Rom. 8:18) and of "the children of God" (*hoi huioi tou theou*, Rom. 8:19) as an outstanding future event. The present work of the Spirit is only the "first fruits" (*hē aparchē*) of the future redemption (Rom. 8:23). The coming of Christ will entail a revelation of the judgment of God (Rom. 2:5; 1 Cor. 3:13; 4:5; cf. 2 Cor. 5:10). These texts clearly attest to a decidedly eschatological dimension in Paul's understanding of revelation. What is noteworthy is the connection between the present and future revelation established by a common subject. It is Jesus Christ the judge/redeemer who is disclosed now to some and will be disclosed to all in the eschaton. It is against the horizon of this expectation that Paul's claim to a gospel grounded in "a revelation of Jesus Christ" (Gal. 1:12b) must be understood.

Paul's appeal to revelation as the source of his gospel is necessitated by the attack mounted against it by intruders into the Galatian churches who accuse him of the same perversion of the gospel that he charges them with perpetrating (Gal. 1:7). Within the context of the letter to the Galatians, the perceived offense of Paul's message can only be its law-free character.[88] In his refusal to require either circumcision (2:3; 5:1-12; 6:12-15) or Torah observance (2:14-18) of his Gentile converts, his opponents rightly recognize the displacement of the redemptive significance of the Law in favor of Christ alone (2:16-21; 3:13-14, 21; 4:4-7). In the final analysis, what is at issue in the Galatian controversy is the soteriological adequacy of the apostle's gospel. As H. D. Betz formulates it, "The problem . . . is the 'truth of the gospel,' that is, *the legitimate interpretation of the kerygma* and of the 'revelation of Jesus Christ.' It is the legitimate *theological interpretation* of this 'Jesus Christ' which is in dispute between Paul and his opponents."[89]

Within the context of this dispute, what does the appeal to revelation entail? Lührmann finds the answer in the personal commentary Paul provides that God was pleased "to reveal his son to me" (1:16a). The verb here makes explicit the object of the revelation ("God's son" = "Jesus

---

88. Stuhlmacher, *Das paulinische Evangelium*, I, 67, notes that this explains (*a*) the accusation that Paul preaches an easy gospel, (*b*) the attack upon the authority of his apostleship, and (*c*) Paul's attempt to maintain both his independence from and fellowship with Jerusalem.

89. Hans Dieter Betz, "Orthodoxy and Heresy in Primitive Christianity," *Int* 19 (1965): 309 (emphasis added).

Christ"), thus establishing the objective genitive construction in 1:12.[90] The apostle does not say that the source of his gospel was a self-revelation of Jesus Christ, even though Galatians 1:12 and 16 seem to identify the incident in question with the appearance of the risen Christ to Paul before Damascus which he denotes elsewhere by the phrase *ōphthē kamoi* ("he appeared even to me," 1 Cor. 15:8; cf. 9:1). The visual character of this event,[91] however, does not warrant the inference that "revelation" and "vision" are coterminous in Paul's vocabulary.[92] The difference between them emerges when it is recognized that Galatians 1:16 is not merely a repetition of the claim of verse 12 that Jesus Christ has been revealed to Paul, but that he has been revealed *as the Son of God*.[93]

While he frequently uses the term "Son" as an honorific title for Jesus in his unique relation to God,[94] Paul employs it also in a more technical sense to connote the redemptive significance of the "coming" or "sending" of the Son into the world when viewed in its totality.[95] This is particularly evident in Galatians 4:4-5, a Pauline instance of the New Testament "sending" formulas which couple a statement about the commission of the Son with a clause that explains the redemptive character of his mission:[96]

---

90. Dieter Lührmann, *Das Offenbarungsverständnis bei Paulus* (1968), 76.

91. Wilhelm Michaelis, *Die Erscheinungen des Auferstandenen* (1944), 104-9, argues from the LXX usage of *ophthēnai*, in connection with divine activity, that the question of the manner of perception is completely neutralized by the controlling Old Testament emphasis upon the word-revelation communicated in the divine appearance. Karl Heinrich Rengstorf, *Die Auferstehung Jesu* (1967), 117-28, recognizes that the term designates not only the revelatory character of the resurrection appearances, but primarily the way in which this revelation occurred, i.e., by "becoming visible." It may be asked, however, whether the distinction Michaelis is concerned to make was not in fact made by Paul himself through the respective uses of the terms *apokalyptein* and *ophthēnai*.

92. The apostle does claim "visions and revelations of the Lord" (*optasias kai apokalypseis kyriou*; 2 Cor. 12:1), but this does not confirm the interchangeability of the terms. Paul's assertion is made in a spirit of concession that reflects its polemical intention. Dieter Georgi, *Die Gegner des Paulus im 2. Korintherbrief* (1964), 296-97, cites the absence of the definite articles and the plural number as evidence that Paul here deals with a theme of his opponents.

93. Lührmann, *Das Offenbarungsverständnis bei Paulus*, 77, makes this exegetical insight the point of departure for his interpretation of the center of gravity in Paul's understanding of revelation.

94. Kramer, *Christ, Lord, Son of God*, 185.

95. Ibid., 122; cf. also Conzelmann, *Theology of the New Testament*, 200; Reginald H. Fuller, *The Foundations of New Testament Christology* (1965), 231.

96. Kramer, *Christ, Lord, Son of God*, 113, cites John 3:16; 1 John 4:9, 10, 14; Gal.

> God sent forth his son,
>> born of a woman,
>> born under the law,
> in order to redeem those who were under the law,
> so that we might receive adoption.

When compared with the formula in its simple state, lines 2-4 are recognizable as embellishments that reflect Paul's understanding of the law, the original formulation being: "God sent forth his Son *(ho huios)*, in order that we might receive adoption *(huiothesia)*." In a similar way Paul relates the title to the saving work of Christ in Galatians 2:20, faith finding its true object in "the Son of God, who loved me and gave himself for me." Here the self-giving is identified by the context ("I have been crucified with Christ") as his death upon the cross. The soteriological character of the title "Son" in Galatians is important for the interpretation of "a revelation of Jesus Christ" (1:12) as the revealing of his Sonship (1:16), because this is precisely what is at stake in the Galatian conflict.

Paul's antagonists rebuke him for preaching a law-free gospel in which the soteriological role of the Torah is displaced by the redeeming mission of the Son of God. They do not dispute the death and resurrection of Jesus, but rather the implications which Paul draws from that event. Pannenberg argues that the resurrection of Jesus as an event within the context of Jewish apocalyptic expectations was self-interpreting,[97] but it was not self-evident on this basis to Paul's Galatian opponents that Christ is the end of the law (Rom. 10:4).[98] At this point, rather, Paul's gospel springs the apocalyptic tradition and develops in a new direction altogether.[99] It is in defense of his theological innovation

---

4:4-5; Rom. 8:3-4 as examples. See also Eduard Schweizer, "Zum religionsgeschichtlichen Hintergrund der 'Sendungsformel,'" *ZNW* 57 (1966): 199-210.

97. Wolfhart Pannenberg, *Jesus — God and Man* (1968), 67: "For Jesus' Jewish contemporaries, insofar as they shared the apocalyptic expectation, the occurrence of the resurrection did not first need to be interpreted, but for them it spoke meaningfully in itself: If such a thing had happened, one could no longer doubt what it meant."

98. In Pannenberg's summary of "the most important elements that characterize the immediate inherent significance of Jesus' resurrection" (*ibid.*, 67-73), the question of the continuing role of the law in the new situation appears only in connection with the Gentile mission, in regard to which "the significance of the resurrection of Jesus . . . was less clear" than in other matters.

99. Ulrich Wilckens, "Der Ursprung der Überlieferung der Erscheinungen des Auferstandenen," in Wilfried Joest and Wolfhart Pannenberg eds., *Dogma und Denkstrukturen* (1963), 89-90.

that Paul has recourse to "revelation" — which is to say that what is revealed to Paul is not simply the risen One, but the Son in his eschatological significance as redeemer. In other words, revelation is *a hermeneutical event* that discloses the redemptive meaning of the crucified and risen Jesus. Beside the completed mission of the Son, Lührmann contends, revelation is "a parallel action of God which interprets the meaning of the sending."[100]

The respective interpretations of Paul's basic revelation terminology by Stuhlmacher and Lührmann are not mutually exclusive, of course, but simply correspond to the future and present dimensions entailed by the concept.[101] Lührmann focuses upon the hermeneutical aspect of present revelation, while Stuhlmacher places present revelation in an eschatological context. Who or what is presently revealed in a meaningful manner is the reality that will be revealed universally in the eschaton. When Paul speaks of "a revelation of Jesus Christ" as the source of his gospel (Gal. 1:12), the one revealed to him in that event is the same "Lord Jesus Christ" whose eschatological "revelation" the Corinthians are said to "await" (1 Cor. 1:7) "in the Day of our Lord Jesus Christ" (1:8). The point is that Paul's gospel has its source in a hermeneutical event that he terms "revelation" and is itself a prophetic interpretation of the identity and significance of Jesus the crucified.

Paul's Prophetic Gospel

That Paul understood his apostleship in terms of prophetic ministry is clear from his interpretation of his call to preach, which is consciously formulated according to the model of the call of the Old Testament prophets.[102] The dependence of the phrase "he who set me apart *from my mother's womb* and *called* me through his grace" (Gal. 1:15) upon "*from my mother's womb he called* my name" (Isa. 49:1 [LXX]) is generally recognized.[103] As the exilic prophet understood the role assigned to

---

100. Lührmann, *Das Offenbarungsverständnis bei Paulus*, 78-79, distinguishes sharply between the Christ event as such and the revelation of his significance for human life which God mediates as a separate act of grace (see 79 n. 3).

101. Schütz, *Paul and Apostolic Authority*, 133.

102. Stuhlmacher, *Das paulinische Evangelium*, I, 72.

103. Heinrich Schlier, *Der Brief an die Galater* (1962), 53, suggests that a typological dependence upon Isa. 41:9 may also be implicit.

him by God's call as that of a "servant" (*doulos*, Isa. 49:3, 5 [LXX]), so also Paul identifies himself as "a servant *(doulos)* of Christ" (Gal. 1:10; cf. Rom. 1:1; Phil. 1:1).[104] Comparison is invited also of Paul's call from the womb with that of Jeremiah (Jer. 1:5) — a parallel that may include a common awareness of being appointed a prophet to the nations (Gal. 1:16; Rom. 15:15-16).[105] Further, Paul's express identification of his gospel with the preaching of good news promised by Deutero-Isaiah (Rom. 10:15 = Isa. 52:7) should be recognized.[106] These parallels not only demonstrate that the apostle saw himself as a descendant of the Old Testament prophets, but exhibit the eschatological, prophetic character of his gospel.[107] Thus in Galatians 1:15-16 Paul seeks to defend his gospel on the ground of its source in "a revelation of Jesus Christ," and his apostleship on the basis of his call as a prophet of God.[108]

It is not surprising therefore that the apostle speaks of revelation *occurring* in his proclamation of the gospel. In Romans 1:16-17 he declares:

> For I am not ashamed of the gospel; it is the power of God for salvation to everyone who has faith, to the Jew first and also to the Greek. For in it the righteousness of God is revealed *(apokalyptetai)*.

---

104. Käsemann, *Commentary on Romans*, 5, understands Paul's self-designation *(doulos)* as a personal appropriation of "the honorific title of the OT men of God which had also been adopted at Qumran. . . . This title expresses (as in Revelation) election as well as the submission of an instrument to the will of God." Dunn, *Romans 1–8*, 8, calling attention to the influence of the other Isaianic "Servant" passages upon Paul (Isa. 49:8 — 2 Cor. 6:1-2; Isa. 52:15 — Rom. 15:21; Isa. 49:4 — Phil. 2:16), thinks it likely that the apostle's understanding of his call and status was shaped by Isa. 49:1-8. Otto Michel, "Evangelium," *RAC* VI, 1117, contends that Paul viewed himself as the Servant of God attested by Deutero-Isaiah. The general designation of the Old Testament prophet as "servant *(doulos)* of the Lord" (2 Kgs. 9:7; 17:13, 23; 21:10; 24:2; Ezra 9:11; Jer. 7:25; 25:4; 29:19) is also relevant for Paul's prophetic self-consciousness.

105. Ragnar Bring, "The Message to the Gentiles," *ST* 19 (1965): 33-34.

106. Gerhard Friedrich, *"euangelion," TDNT* II, 719, notes that in Rom. 10:15 the prophecy of Isa. 52:7 is identified with the messengers of the gospel. The plural reading of the participle, which is attested neither in the LXX nor the Masoretic text (cf. Acts 10:36 and Eph. 2:17, which cite Isa. 52:7 in the singular), is explained by Friedrich as Paul's following a Palestinian Jewish tradition in which the watchers on the walls (Isa. 52:8), the witnesses of Yahweh's coming, become his evangelists.

107. Traugott Holtz, "Zum Selbstverständnis des Apostels Paulus," *TLZ* 91 (1966): 325-26.

108. Stuhlmacher, *Das paulinische Evangelium*, I, 72. See also Jacob M. Myers and Edwin D. Freed, "Is Paul Also Among the Prophets?" *Int* 20 (1966): 40-53.

The striking use of the present perfect indicates *(a)* that the righteousness of God is now being revealed in the preaching of the gospel,[109] and *(b)* that the visual character of the revelation accorded to Paul is not normative for his understanding of the phenomenon. What is consistent here with Gal. 1:12, 16 is the hermeneutical character of God's revelatory activity in gospel proclamation. The content of such revelation, as Paul designates it in this text, is an interpretation of the mission of the Son in terms of "the righteousness of God," a "fixed formula" according to Käsemann, for God's redemptive activity which Paul inherited from the Old Testament by way of early Judaism and early Christianity.[110] So interpreted, the gospel in its proclamation becomes the revelatory medium of "the power of God for salvation to everyone who has faith" (Rom. 1:16). Accordingly, "the righteousness of God" revealed in the proclamation of the gospel is of one piece with "the revelation of Jesus Christ" (Gal. 1:12) that Paul received in his encounter with the risen Son of God (Gal. 1:16). Both ways of speaking represent positive formulations of the soteriological meaning of "Christ crucified" (1 Cor. 1:23; 2:2), the difference being that the former is couched in terms derived from the church's scriptural tradition. That Paul views this interpretation of his encounter as grounded in revelation is evident from Philippians 3:2-16 where he develops the gift character of the divine righteousness within the context of his own experience. His concluding exhortation to the "mature" *(teleioi)* to be "thus minded" is issued in the confidence that "if in anything you are otherwise minded, God will reveal *(apokalypsei)* that also to you" (3:15).[111] Once again Paul places his gospel, his interpretation of the saving significance of Jesus, under the criterion of a revelation of God.[112] The understanding given in revelation is proclaimed as the gospel, and in that proclamation revelation continues to occur.

---

109. Otto Michel, *Der Brief an die Römer* (1955), 176.

110. Ernst Käsemann, "God's Righteousness in Paul," *JTC*, I, 102-3, emphasizes the importance of recognizing the pre-Pauline origin of the phrase, citing Deut. 33:21 for the Old Testament; Matt. 6:33 and James 1:20 for the New; *T. Dan* 6:10 and 1QS 11:12 for early Judaism.

111. Frank W. Beare, *Philippians* (1969), 131: "He is ready to wait until God opens the minds of the others to the truth as he has expounded it."

112. Lührmann, *Das Offenbarungsverständnis bei Paulus*, 43.

A Commentary on Prophecy

Clearly Paul's concept of "revelation" as a hermeneutical event that discloses proleptically the *meaning* of the reality of God's eschatological salvation, which has been secured in the cross and resurrection of Jesus, is materially parallel to the revelatory work of the Spirit depicted in 1 Corinthians 2:6-16. In the language of this passage, such revelation is designated "the wisdom of God, hidden in a mystery, which God decreed before the ages for our glorification" (2:7), the wisdom now revealed to us by the Spirit (2:10) in order that we may "understand the gifts bestowed on us by God" (2:12) in Christ crucified, the wisdom that Paul and other agents of revelation articulate "in words not taught by human wisdom but taught by the Spirit, interpreting *pneumatika* (spiritual things = *ta charisthenta*, God's gracious gifts) to the *pneumatikoi* (those who have received the Spirit = *teleioi*, mature believers). Materially grounded in the apostolic kerygma of Christ crucified — "the mystery of God" (2:1) — such revelatory utterances represent the continuing interpretation of the theological and ethical substance of the gospel. Given by the Spirit, these utterances are "spiritually discerned (*pneumatikōs anakrineta*, 2:14). Yet they fall into the category of "all things" which are subject to substantive "criticism" (*anakrinein*, 2:15).

Can the same correlation be made between Paul's remarkably consistent concept of revelation as an interpretative event and the "revelation" attributed to prophecy in 1 Corinthians 14? Yes, beyond any reasonable doubt.[113] The material and terminological parallels between 2:6-16 and chapters 12–14 are much too striking to be ignored. Both passages focus on the topic of speech inspired by the Spirit, and both illumine it from different angles — the first by insisting upon the material connection between such utterances and the apostolic kerygma, and the second by distinguishing them from speaking in tongues, requiring the utterances to be judged on the basis of the gospel confession, and regulating them as a liturgical act. Surely it is legitimate to infer that 2:6-16 is a commentary on the prophetic activity discussed in chapter 14. If so, then the revelation associated with prophecy in 14:6, 26, and

---

113. Wire, *The Corinthian Women Prophets*, 48: "There are definite links between Paul's digression on wisdom (1:18–2:16) and his later argument on spiritual gifts (12:1–14:40). . . . Paul rejects any consistent nomenclature or demarcation of gifts that supports a sharp distinction between some who seek wisdom and others who prophesy."

30 denotes the same activity of the Spirit attested in 2:10-13. Prophetic revelation is thereby defined as the work of the Spirit in unfolding the implications of the gospel that is itself grounded in "a revelation of Jesus Christ" (Gal. 1:12, 16). It is in this sense that "the one who prophesies speaks edification and exhortation and encouragement" (14:3).

In the same sense, the prophetic interpretation of the gospel in the act of proclamation is an occurrence of revelation that convicts, calls to account, and exposes the inner secrets of the outsider or unbeliever in the worshipping congregation and effects thereby that person's conversion (14:24-25). The parallel between 1 Corinthians 2:1-5 and 14:25-26 is undeniable. It is the hermeneutical proclamation of the "mystery of God" (2:1), "in demonstration of the Spirit and power" (2:4), that grounds faith "in the power of God" (2:5) and effects the acclamation of the converted, "God is truly among you" (14:25).

Conclusion

The function of early Christian prophecy, at least as advocated by Paul, is the continual creation of the church through the proclamation of the gospel, and the interpretation of the mystery of God's eschatological redemption established in Jesus Christ, attested by the kerygma, and revealed by the Spirit. Prophecy builds up the church by adding new converts to its number (1 Cor. 14:24-25) and by edifying, exhorting, and encouraging believers in the context of their lived faith. Prophecy explicates the gospel in terms of its theological and ethical implications within the life-situation of the congregation. Paul is willing and able to call the yield of prophetic revelation "wisdom" or "knowledge" because it does in fact effect human understanding of the whole matrix of interrelated issues implicit in the kerygma — issues concerning the significance of the gospel, its consequences, and the relation of Christ crucified to God, the world, and humanity.[114] According to Niederwimmer, "In this apocalyptic wisdom lies the origin of Christian theology."[115] In view of the formal and material connection which Paul makes between the source of his gospel in revelation and the revelation that

---

114. Niederwimmer, "Erkennen und Lieben," 88.
115. *Ibid.*, 88 n. 36.

occurs through his gospel, Niederwimmer's claim requires qualification. If this wisdom is embryonic theology, it is "theology as clarification of the proclamation" (Conzelmann)[116] that is itself theologically grounded and formulated.

What distinguishes Paul's understanding of this work of the Spirit from the revelatory "verbal wisdom" advocated and practiced by the prophets in Corinth is his insistence that all authentic inspired utterance has the kerygma of Christ crucified as its ground and subject. For Paul wisdom is not the ground of Christ but Christ is the ground of wisdom (1 Cor. 1:24, 30), and as such he is the "foundation" that is "laid" (1 Cor. 3:11).[117] The prophets who build upon *(epoikodomein)* this foundation do so against the horizon of the eschatological testing of their work: "each one's work will become manifest; for the Day will disclose it, because it will be revealed *(apokalyptetai)* with fire, and the fire will test what sort of work each one has done" (3:13). What this means is that the "discernment of spirits" (1 Cor. 12:10) carried out in the "judging" of prophetic utterance (14:29) is itself a proleptic instance of the eschatological judgment upon prophesying.

---

116. Conzelmann, *1 Corinthians*, 56.
117. Niederwimmer, "Erkennen und Lieben," 87.

CHAPTER SIX

Prophecy and Kerygma

1 Corinthians 15:1-51

WHAT were the early Christian prophets doing when they were prophesying? The argument of the previous chapters is that, according to Paul, they were interpreting the apostolic kerygma in sustained discourse under the revelatory inspiration of the Spirit. In Paul's understanding, the prophets appointed by God in the church (1 Cor. 12:28) were, together with the apostles, the hermeneuts of the foundational message of Christ crucified and raised from the dead. A sample of such prophetic discourse, this chapter will argue, is found in 1 Corinthians 15. This claim is evidenced by (1) the intertextual connections between chapter 15 and the immediately preceding discussion of prophecy in chapter 14, (2) the explicit citation of the kerygma in 15:3ff., and (3) the interpretation of its eschatological implications in terms of the revealed "mystery" attested in verses 51-55.

The present chapter will argue further that 1 Corinthians 15 illustrates the injunction of 14:29 that the material content of all prophecy be "judged" *(diakrinein)*. The text shows the apostle engaged in an extensive critique of another prophetic interpretation of the kerygma, advocated by "some" in Corinth, that declared "There is no resurrection of the dead" (v. 12). While this is admittedly a novel reading of 1 Corinthians 15, and the supporting argument is necessarily inferential and cumulative, it will be shown that the text itself invites the interpretation now presented.

Resurrection and Prophecy

According to Conzelmann, 1 Corinthians 15 "is a self-contained treatise on the resurrection of the dead." Yet he also notes that "Paul introduces the new theme without a transition."[1] It is this anomaly which causes Antoinette Wire to wonder "why Paul does not begin this section in his usual way with 'But concerning resurrection . . .' (cf. 7:1, 25; 8:1; 12:1; 16:1, 12) or 'I have heard . . .' (cf. 1:11; 11:18) and then counter their letter or voice with his view of resurrection."[2] In the absence of an explicit reference to the source of the apostle's information that some in Corinth are denying the resurrection of the dead (v. 12), the evident occasion of this passage, commentators commonly attribute Paul's knowledge of this matter to an oral report.[3] What prompts such educated guessing is the assumption, expressed by Lietzmann and Kümmel, that the resurrection theme of chapter 15 is "without inner or outer connection" with the preceding chapter.[4] This is obviously true at the thematic level. But the picture changes when chapter 15 is recognized as an instance of the prophetic speech that is the subject of chapter 14. The material issue in chapter 15 is indeed the resurrection of the dead, but the formal issue is the prophetic utterance of verse 12 that occasions and requires Paul's prophetic response.

Moreover, there *are* "inner connections" between chapters 15 and 14 that too easily escape notice. "Although this chapter [15] constitutes an abrupt change of subject matter," Fee writes, "it is nonetheless significantly related both to the immediately preceding concern of chaps. 12–14 and to many other matters in the letter as a whole."[5] The relation of Paul's treatment of the Corinthian denial of the resurrection of the dead in chapter 15 to the rest of the letter is commonly acknowledged. In fact it is these "other matters" that shed light upon the rationale of the position Paul here opposes. What needs specification are the ways in which chapter 15 is "significantly related" to chapters 12–14.

Fee himself calls attention to the connections between the two

---

1. Conzelmann, *1 Corinthians*, 249.
2. Wire, *The Corinthian Women Prophets*, 159.
3. Thus Barrett, *First Corinthians*, 335; Conzelmann, *1 Corinthians*, 249; Robertson-Plummer, *First Corinthians*, 329; Lietzmann/Kümmel, *Korinther I/II*, 77, however, identify the source as "the lost letter of the Corinthians."
4. Lietzmann/Kümmel, *Korinther I/II*, 76.
5. Fee, *First Corinthians*, 713.

passages located in 15:1-11, which take up two themes from 14:33-38. The first is that all who believe in Christ are dependent upon the kerygmatic tradition (15:3ff.) which provides the common ground of apostolic preaching (15:11). Paul here answers his previous rhetorical question, "Did the word of God originate with you? Or are you the only ones it has reached?" (14:38). The second theme repeated in 15:1-11 from 14:36-38 is that of Paul's own apostolic ministry as the source of the Corinthians' life in Christ. Fee sees Paul's unexpected defense of his apostolic ministry in 15:9-10 as a reflection of the conflict between him and the Corinthians last addressed in the pronouncements of 14:37 and 38: "If anyone thinks he is a prophet or a spiritual, let him acknowledge that what I write to you is a command of the Lord. Anyone who does not recognize *(agnoei)* this is not recognized *(agnoeite)*."[6]

Fee further senses "a nice piece of irony" in the double use of the verb in 14:38 (*agnoein* literally = "to be ignorant") and the opening verb of 15:1, "I make known to you" *(gnōrizō)*, a stylistic touch that "ties what follows to what has immediately preceded." He comments:

> To those who think of themselves as "spiritual" over against Paul, he pronounces the judgment that their "ignorance" of his word as the commandment of the Lord meant they would be "ignored" by God himself. Now he "makes known" to them what they already know, but seem to have forgotten.[7]

The same combination of terms is found in 1 Corinthians 12:1 and 3, "where the lack of a chapter break makes the connection more visible."[8] On the basis of these connections, Fee also reads the postpositive conjunction *de* in 15:1 as "probably consecutive" ("and") rather than adversative ("but").[9]

These intertextual connections between chapters 14 and 15 suggest a more intrinsic relationship between the two passages than is commonly recognized. By themselves, however, they are insufficient warrant for claiming that the epistolary unit which begins in 1 Corinthians 12:1 ("Now concerning the spirituals [or the prophets]") actually extends through chapter 15. The main obstacle to such an inference is the evident

---

6. *Ibid.*, 714; cf. 718, 719.
7. *Ibid.*, 719.
8. *Ibid.*, 719 n. 25.
9. *Ibid.*, 720 n. 28.

change of theme from prophecy and tongues in chapter 14 to the resurrection of the dead in chapter 15. Because it is unclear how this new subject can be subsumed under the topic announced in 12:1, commentators infer that a break in the thematic development of the letter occurs at 15:1 — a break that is unmarked stylistically by an introductory transition.

This obstacle disappears, however, if the denial of the resurrection of the dead by some in Corinth has its source in an alleged instance of prophetic speech. When 15:12b is understood as a quote from a Corinthian prophet ("There is no resurrection of the dead"), the subject of chapter 15 is clearly apropros to the discussion of Spirit-inspired speech initiated at 12:1. On this supposition, chapter 15 represents Paul's exercise of "the discernment of spirits" (12:10) required in judging the material content of all ostensible prophetic utterance (14:29) by the criterion of the apostolic kerygma (15:1-11). The key issue is whether there are textual warrants for identifying 15:12b as a citation of a prophetic pronouncement accepted as authoritative by some in Corinth.

The first question is whether the Corinthian denial of the resurrection of the dead (v. 12b) should be read as direct or indirect discourse. Although the NRSV does not place the statement within quotation marks, as it does other declarations in the letter suspected of being Corinthian "slogans" or "watchwords" (6:12, 13; 7:1; 8:1, 4, 8; 10:23; 12:3), there is greater grammatical reason for viewing 15:12b as a quotation than there is for any of the other verses so identified by the translators. Of these, only the two in 12:3 ("Let Jesus be cursed" and "Jesus is Lord") are introduced by a verb of speaking *(legein)*. All the others appear in the text without benefit of a stylistic marker that would signal the presence of direct discourse. What then is the basis of the committee's decision to present these phrases or statements as quotations? The answer is the growing scholarly awareness of the contours of the position advocated by those in the church at Corinth whom Paul opposes on a variety of fronts in 1 Corinthians. Such awareness is achieved by inferring from the apostle's arguments throughout the letter what the theological profile is of the position he argues against, which is similar to reconstructing an unknown question from its known answer. Often called "mirror reading" the text, this method is exemplified by Wire's study of the women prophets in Corinth:

> A rhetorical analysis of 1 Corinthians can give us accurate information about the Corinthian women prophets as Paul knew them by

reading Paul's letter as an attempt to persuade in a particular argumentative situation in which they play some role. . . . This rhetorical or argumentative situation includes both the goals of the speaker and the counter-arguments that are anticipated as the speaking progresses.[10]

Aided by such reconstructions of the Corinthian situation, the NRSV committee has placed these phrases and statements within quotation marks because they seem more appropriate as expressions of Paul's opponents than as convictions of the apostle.[11]

It is perplexing then why the statement of the position of some in Corinth that occasions chapter 15 is presented in the NRSV as indirect discourse. The denial of the resurrection of the dead is explicitly attributed to the Corinthians in 15:12b, "How can *some of you say* that *(hoti)*. . . ." Moreover, the verb of saying *(legein)* in conjunction with *hoti* ("that") grammatically signals that the ensuing statement represents *direct discourse (hoti recitativum)*.[12] Martinus de Boer notes that Paul modifies the simple "[Christ] was raised" *(egēgertai)* of the kerygmatic tradition in verse 4 to read *"from the dead* [Christ] has been raised" *(ek nekrōn egēgertai)* in verse 12a, apparently in order "to highlight the point of contact" between the tradition and the denial of the "resurrection *of the dead*" in Corinth (v. 12b).[13] This suggests that one quotation (15:4b) is being amplified in verse 12a under the influence of another (15:12b). Thus if the above cited texts from 1 Corinthians warrant quotation marks, as they do, then surely 15:12b all the more. Both grammatical and contextual considerations legitimate verse 12b being translated, "Now if Christ is preached as raised from the dead, how can some of you say 'There is no resurrection of the dead'?"

Can this citation of a Corinthian statement be identified further

---

10. Wire, *The Corinthian Women Prophets*, 3.

11. A sampling of the standard commentaries documents the development of scholarly sensitivities to this matter. Thus Robertson/Plummer identify only 8:4 as a citation (6:12 and 8:1 are considered possibilities). Lietzmann/Kümmel list 6:12; 8:1, 4; 10:23; and 12:3 as quotations. Barrett and Bruce each treat all of the suggested quotations as such. Fee demurs only on 8:1, 4, and 8. It may be noted in this connection that 1 Cor. 6:13; 7:1; and 8:8 do not appear among the phrases presented as quotations in the RSV.

12. Funk, *Grammar*, par. 397(5): "By far the most common form of complement with verbs of saying is *direct* discourse which can be introduced by *hoti (recitativum)*."

13. Martinus C. de Boer, *The Defeat of Death* (1988), 211 n. 10.

as a *prophetic* utterance? Among the Corinthian quotations recognized as such in the NRSV translation of this letter, it is important to note that the two found in 12:3 clearly claim the inspiration of the Spirit. Arguments for reading "Jesus be cursed" as a real rather than hypothetical declaration have been adduced in Chapter Two and will be assumed here. The point is that the utterance attributed its source to divine inspiration, a claim allegedly confirmed by the attending prophetic ecstasy identified among the Corinthians as speaking in tongues. Paul is compelled to declare flatly that "no one speaking by the Spirit of God" ever utters such a statement because it is antithetical to the confession "Jesus is Lord," which *is* effected by the work of the Spirit. Here then a quotation originating in Corinthian piety and practice is identified as an instance of prophetic utterance attributed by them to the Spirit.

Whether this same attribution qualifies the other words of the Corinthians cited in the letter — "All things are lawful to me" (6:12); "It is good for a man not to touch a woman" (7:1); or "All of us possess knowledge" (8:1) — cannot be determined with any certainty. Observing that these texts are all "brief, self-legitimating assertions," Wire postulates that they "could have arisen as *prophetic legitimation oracles* justifying certain conduct or claims."[14] Brox's suggestion that the two confessional formulas in 12:3 entailed commentary, if applicable to the other Corinthian "slogans," commends the possibility that they all are abbreviated themes of extended prophetic discourse.[15] Perhaps the most that can, and the least that must be said is that it would be surprising indeed if these utterances were not instances of the Corinthian preoccupation with prophecy (1 Cor. 12–14) or inspired "words of wisdom" (12:8; cf. 1:18–2:8).

But a further clue to the prophetic character of 15:12b is given in the way the quotation is introduced by a verb of saying *(legein)*. This has its parallel in 12:3, where the same verb introduces two other citations in a context determined by the phrase "speaking in the Spirit of God" *(en pneumati theou lalōn)*. If the speech cited in 12:3 is clearly attributed to inspired utterance, then it may be inferred that the same is true of 15:12b. An argument may not, of course, claim confirmation by such a small exegetical detail. But the connection of 12:3 and 15:12 by the common theme of "speaking in the Spirit of God" is sufficiently suggestive and illuminating to merit the hypothesis that the Corinthian

---

14. Wire, *The Corinthian Women Prophets*, 14 (emphasis added).
15. Brox, "ANATHEMA IĒSOUS," 109.

pronouncement "There is no resurrection of the dead" is a prophetic word that required critical evaluation in accordance with the injunction of 14:29. Chapter 15 conducts this assessment and thus completes the discussion of Spirit-inspired speech begun at 12:1. There is no marked transition between chapters 14 and 15 because the new theme of the resurrection of the dead belongs *formally* to the previous treatment of prophecy. The only actual transitions that occur in the thematic development of the letter after 12:1 are found in 16:1 and 16:12.

Deniers of the Resurrection of the Dead

The identification of the Corinthian denial of the resurrection of the dead as an instance of local prophetic discourse intensifies the issue of its meaning within a Christian context. This issue, as de Boer points out, includes "not only what they were actually denying but also what, by implication, they seemed to be affirming."[16] A variety of solutions have been proposed,[17] but only the two identified by Bultmann remain live options. In a rather brief remark, he surmises that the Corinthians "were contending against the realistic teaching of the resurrection as contained in the Jewish and primitive-Christian tradition" or they had "spiritualized" the doctrine, meaning that the denial of the resurrection of the dead in 1 Corinthians 15:12b implied that "the resurrection has already occurred."[18] The two possibilities may be formulated as follows: (1) "There is no (bodily) resurrection of the dead (because immortality is a-somatic)"; and (2) "There is no (future) resurrection of the dead (because believers are raised with Christ already in the Spirit by baptism)."[19]

---

16. De Boer, *Defeat of Death*, 96.

17. For a helpful survey of the discussion up to 1968, see Jack H. Wilson, "The Corinthians Who Say There Is No Resurrection of the Dead," *ZNW* 59 (1968): 90-107. The report is updated to 1981 by Karl A. Plank, "Resurrection Theology: The Corinthian Controversy Reexamined," *PRS* (1981): 41-54.

18. Bultmann, *Theology*, I, 169.

19. A third possible explanation, "There is no (such thing as) the resurrection of the dead (because death is the end of life)," is suggested by Karl Barth, *The Resurrection of the Dead* (1933), 167-71. On the basis of 15:19 and 32, Barth infers that the Corinthian view is one in which the Christian hope is "limited to life, conceived without the divine horizon, without the certainty of resurrection. . . ." This is impossible, however, in view

The first explanation, which focuses upon the denial of a *bodily* resurrection in Corinth predicated upon a belief in immortality, takes its textual point of departure from the evident Corinthian disdain of the human body (1 Cor. 6:12-20; cf. 15:35). Fueled by an anthropological dualism, this body pessimism is evident in the antithetical terms so dear to the Corinthians — "spiritual"/"natural" (*pneumatikos/psychikos*; 1 Cor. 2:14-15; 15:46) and "spiritual"/"carnal" (*pneumatikos/sarkinos*; 3:1-2). But it is particularly evident in the terminology of Paul's argument in 15:44-54:

"physical body"/"spiritual body"
(*sōma psychikon/sōma pneumatikon*, v. 44);

"living soul"/"life-giving spirit"
(*psychē zōsan/pneuma zōopoioun*, v. 45);

"the first human"/"the second human"
(*ho prōtos anthrōpos/ho deuteros anthrōpos*, v. 47);

"human of dust"/"human of heaven"
(*anthrōpos ek choikos/anthrōpos ex ouranou*, vv. 47, 48);

"image of the [one] of dust"/"image of the [one] of heaven"
(*eikōn tou choikou/eikōn tou epouranou*, v. 47);

"corruption"/"incorruption"
(*phthora/aphtharsian*, v. 50);

"perishable"/"imperishable"
(*phtharton/aphtharsian*, v. 53);

"mortal"/"immortal"
(*thēton/aphtharsian*, v. 54).

The use of contrasting pairs of terms is, of course, not unusual for Paul. But these antithetical terms are peculiar to this polemical discussion of

---

of the Corinthian practice of proxy-baptism on behalf of the dead (15:28). The same applies to the modification of Barth's proposal by Albert Schweitzer, *The Mysticism of Paul* (1968), who attributes the Corinthian denial to the ultraconservative belief of Jewish Christians that only believers still alive at the return of the Messiah would be delivered from death.

the resurrection of the dead, an oddity that gives Richard Horsley "reason to believe that we have here further language of the Corinthians whom Paul is addressing."[20]

Various assessments of the source of this terminology, the nature of its implied dualism, and thus its basis for a hope of immortality, have been offered. The traditional version is that the Corinthians were influenced by the ontological dualisms of *Greek philosophy* regarding human nature, and thus denied the resurrection of the body in favor of a positive belief in the immortality of the soul or spirit.[21] The fortunes of this once popular explanation have suffered decline, however, because of the increasing recognition that the Hellenistic background of the New Testament is more religious in nature than philosophical. Consequently, *Gnosticism* replaced Greek philosophy as the likely source of the Corinthian dualistic terminology. Thus Bultmann interprets 1 Corinthians 15:12 in the light of 2 Corinthians 5:1-5, where "a better informed" Paul "combats the Gnostic view that man's self at death will be released from the body (and from the 'soul') and will soar in the state of 'nakedness' into the heavenly world."[22] Schmithals, identifying this view as "nothing other than the general doctrine of immortality,"[23] explains:

> The motivation for the Gnostic's denial of the resurrection is the Gnostic dualism.... Man, so far as he is *sarx*, is for the Gnostic not only perishable but also despicable. The flesh, which is buried, is the largely anti-godly, but at best — in the Jewish sphere — worthless, dwelling of the human self. The idea that this lifeless prison must first be awakened to life before the man himself attains genuine life appears to the Gnostic self-consciousness as blasphemy.[24]

The initial influence of the idea of a Gnostic background to the situation at Corinth has waned as subsequent research into Gnosticism has made

20. Richard A. Horsley, "'How Can Some of You Say That There is No Resurrection of the Dead?' Spiritual Elitism in Corinth," *NovT* 20 (1978): 206.
21. Typical is the comment by Robertson and Plummer, *First Corinthians*, 356, that the deniers in Corinth were Gentiles, "brought up under the influence of Greek philosophy," for whom "it was incredible that a soul, once set free by death, would return to its unclean prison."
22. Bultmann, *Theology*, I, 169 n. *.
23. Schmithals, *Gnosticism in Corinth*, 157.
24. *Ibid.*, 158.

it impossible to speak any longer of a pre-Christian Gnosis; such research has also made it improbable that Paul's Corinthian opponents were even of a proto-Gnostic persuasion.

More recently, Birger Pearson and Richard Horsley have revived the view that the Corinthians denied the resurrection of the dead because they believed in immortality by locating the source of this belief in what Pearson calls "Hellenistic Jewish wisdom speculation [or mysticism]"[25] and Horsley "Hellenistic Jewish theology [or religiosity]."[26] The argument turns on the postulate that in 15:45-54 Paul is both using and correcting a Corinthian understanding of Genesis 2:7 derived from an exegetical tradition typified by Philo of Alexandria. Pearson comments that the Corinthians not only rejected the resurrection of the dead in favor of an immortality doctrine, but "they held to this doctrine on the basis of Scripture!"[27]

According to Horsley's exposition of the Philonic texts,[28] Philo interprets Genesis 2:7 (in connection with Gen. 1:27) to teach that there are two *anthrōpoi*, two kinds of human beings, the one "heavenly" and the other "earthly." The former is "made after the image of God" and the latter is "moulded" out of "earth."[29] The heavenly human is by nature "incorruptible" (*aphthartos*), while the earthly, composed of matter, is "mortal" (*thētos*; *Leg. all.* 1.31). Horsley notes:

> In comparison with I Cor. xv 45-54 we find in these Philonic discussions of the two types of mankind all of the principal terminology paralleled, with the exception of the antithesis of "spiritual" and "psychic" — that is, all of the other pairs of antithesis (corruptible vs. incorruptible, mortal vs. immortal, earthly vs. heavenly) as well as the "image" motif.[30]

Philo further contends, contrary to Paul (1 Cor. 15:46), that the heavenly human is temporally "earlier" (*proteron*; *Op. mund.* 134) than the earthly, who is thus "the second human" (*ho deuteros anthrōpos*; *Leg. all.* 2.4-5). For Philo, according to Horsley, this connotes an ontological priority as

---

25. Pearson, *The Pneumatikos-Psychikos Terminology in 1 Corinthians*, 82.
26. Horsley, "Spiritual Elitism in Corinth," 207, 224.
27. Pearson, *The Pneumatikos-Psychikos Terminology in 1 Corinthians*, 17.
28. Horsley, "Spiritual Elitism in Corinth," 217-23.
29. *Ibid.*, 217; see n. 29 for the extensive references to the relevant Philonic texts.
30. *Ibid.*, 217-18.

well.³¹ Inferior in being and caught in bodily circumstances, the earthly human would be hopelessly "corruptible" *(phthartos)* were it not for "God's inbreathing" (Gen. 2:7b) of the divine Spirit (*Leg. all.* 1.32).³²

It is precisely this immortalizing of the "soul" by the divine Spirit that gives hope to the earthly human in the face of death. Philo's anthropology, Horsley observes, "is governed by the dualism of the naked and the dead, that is, the immortal soul and the mortal body."³³ Accordingly, to Philo "dead" and "body" are virtually synonymous terms. What occurs at death is the final separation of the Spirit-immortalized soul from the body (*Leg. all.* 1.105). Put otherwise, the Spirit-immortalized soul is represented as departing rather than dying (*Rer. div. her.* 276). "The ideal state of the soul in its immortality is to be *naked* of the body and earthly matters," Horsley concludes, adding astutely that Paul's formulation in 1 Corinthians 15:53-54 of the mortal "putting on" immortality "can be seen to be a direct contrast with or reversal of this ideal state of the soul according to the kind of Hellenistic Jewish religiosity represented by Philo."³⁴

Pearson summarizes this reconstruction of the situation which occasioned the Corinthian denial of the resurrection of the dead and Paul's response to it as follows:

> His opponents in Corinth, under the influence of teachers who had grown up in Diaspora Judaism, were espousing a doctrine of a-somatic immortality, and denying the bodily resurrection. In stating their case, they were using a current exegesis of Genesis 2.7 to show from scripture that their view was the correct one. This exegetical tradition stressed the divine "inbreathing" in man, by which the earthly man participated in the spiritual *eikōn tou theou* (Gen 1.27).³⁵

For this reconstruction to work convincingly, however, it is necessary to show that the Corinthian use of the antithetical terms *pneumatikos* and *psychikos* also derives from this exegetical tradition.

The fly in the ointment, as De Boer points out, is that Philo does not use these terms "in the sense of the Corinthian pneumatics whom

---

31. *Ibid.*, 218.
32. *Ibid.*, 219.
33. *Ibid.*, 223.
34. *Ibid.*, 224.
35. Pearson, *The Pneumatikos-Psychikos Terminology in 1 Corinthians*, 24.

Paul addresses in 2.14-15 or 15.45-49."[36] The point is expressly conceded by Horsley,[37] who counters: "Since the *pneumatikos-psychikos* contrast does not occur in Philo and other contemporary Hellenistic Jewish literature, the argument must be couched in terms of a similarity of thought-patterns and not in terms of a derivation of these particular words."[38] The absence of the specific terminology, however, leaves De Boer unpersuaded. Finding what he is looking for in the tractate *Poimandres* (*Corp. Herm.* 1), De Boer concludes that despite the temporal priority of 1 Corinthians over the tractate, the latter "provides the only clear parallels to the *psychikos/pneumatikos* dualism and it indicates that the Corinthian pneumatics whom Paul takes to task in 1 Cor. 15.35ff. (and 2.14ff.) employed Gen. 2:7 to support an anthropology that . . . was dualistic in a gnostic sense." What De Boer means by "a gnostic sense" is that the Corinthians "probably believed that they were pneumatic *by nature.*"[39]

Not only is it unwarranted methodologically to appeal to a later document in order to interpret an earlier text, it is in this case also unnecessary. For standing between the Hellenistic Jewish tradition represented by Philo and the Corinthian Christians is the Pentecost event and the continuing outpouring of the Spirit upon believers. What characterizes the Corinthian situation, as A. J. M. Wedderburn points out, is a keen awareness of being specially endowed with the Spirit of God. It is this, he suggests, "which in part explains the difference between Paul's terminology [in 1 Cor. 6:13 and 15:23-28] and that of the usual Hellenistic distinction of mortal body and immortal soul: for the Corinthians that which they treasure as divine and life-giving is the *pneuma* specially granted to them and not the *psychē* which is in every man."[40] Wedderburn acknowledges that while the Corinthians' negative attitude toward the body may have been influenced by typical Hellenistic views, these were not the source of their positive beliefs: "that which is important and divine and lasting was not a natural endowment of all men; it was bestowed on some only as an eschato-

---

36. De Boer, *The Defeat of Death*, 101.
37. Horsley, "Spiritual Elitism in Corinth," 207, 212.
38. *Ibid.,* 221 n. 41.
39. De Boer, *The Defeat of Death*, 102 (emphasis added).
40. A. J. M. Wedderburn, "The Problem of the Denial of the Resurrection in I Corinthians XV," *NovT* 23 (1981): 238.

logical endowment of men by God, the outpouring of the divine Spirit."[41] Noting further that new experiences require new language, he proposes that the terms *pneumatikos/psychikos* arose among the Corinthians out of "a desire to find language to describe their sense of supernatural endowment so as to differentiate it from the (merely) natural endowment of others who advanced competing claims to wisdom."[42] The compatibility of such a view with Philo's contention that the "soul" receives its immortality from the "in-breathing" of the divine Spirit should not be overlooked.

Belief in a Realized Resurrection

The second explanation of the negative occasion and the positive meaning of the denial of the resurrection of the dead in Corinth picks up on Bultmann's alternative suggestion that some in the church had "spiritualized" the traditional Christian hope by claiming the resurrection had occurred already in their experience of the Spirit's transforming power received in baptism. First posited by Hans von Soden,[43] followed by Schniewind and Käsemann,[44] the option of accounting for the Corinthian denial on the basis of a "realized resurrection" belief has achieved something of a majority status among New Testament scholars. Hence, as James Robinson views it, "when Paul criticizes 'some of you' for asserting that 'there is no resurrection of the dead' (15:12), one *now* assumes he is alluding to a position that is not to be taken as the enlightened rationalism of the Greek philosophic mind but rather as the turgid fanaticism of those who have already risen and are living it up in glory."[45]

Such matters of exegetical importance, however, must be decided on the basis of the textual evidence rather than that of scholarly opinion. The presence in the early church of a belief in a "realized resurrection" is attested by 2 Timothy 2:18. According to the Deutero-Paulinist, a

41. *Ibid.*, 238-39.
42. *Ibid.*, 238 n. 37.
43. Hans von Soden, "Sakrament und Ethik bei Paulus," in *MTS* I (1931): 1-40.
44. Julius Schniewind, "Die Leugnung der Auferstehung in Korinth," *Nachgelassene Reden und Aufsätze* (1952), 110-39; Käsemann, *New Testament Questions*, 108-37.
45. Robinson, *Trajectories*, 33 (emphasis added).

certain Hymenaeus and Philetus "have gone astray with regard to the truth, by affirming: 'The resurrection has taken place already [!],' and they are upsetting the faith of some."[46] But this testimony is from a time one or two generations after Paul and, like the tractate *Poimandres,* may not legitimately be used to explain what was going on in first-century Corinth. It does demonstrate, however, that the resurrection was susceptible to a "realized" interpretation. Whether or not this was the implicit view of the Corinthian deniers can be determined only by the data afforded by the primary source, 1 Corinthians itself. Even there the evidence is contextual and inferential. It is not for this reason negligible, however, because any interpretation of 15:12 must seek confirmation by demonstrating its compatibility with what is otherwise known from Paul's letter of the situation at Corinth. For a reconstruction to be convincing, the evidence must be construed both comprehensively and coherently.

A promising point of departure from within chapter 15 is provided by verse 19. The opening conditional clause literally reads, "If in this life in Christ we are hopers only...."[47] The crucial translation issue is whether the adjective "only" *(monon)* modifies the participle "hopers" *(ēlpikotes)* or the clause as a whole. If the former, the sense is "If in this life in Christ we are *only hopers,*" implying that believers have hope and nothing else in this life. If the latter is preferred, the meaning is "If *only in this life* we are hopers in Christ," suggesting that the believer's hope is limited to this life. According to Plank, either reading may be understood as a reference to belief in a "realized resurrection."[48] By limiting hope to "this life only" (the translation preference of most commentators)[49] Paul may be understood as criticizing a one-sided emphasis upon "this life" in Corinth. Plank infers that such an emphasis intimates that they "deny the resurrection of the dead by disguising it as a resurrection of the living."[50] Alternatively, by challenging the view that in this life

---

46. *Ibid.,* 32.

47. The Greek phrase *ēlpikotes esmen* may be understood either as a periphrastic perfect ("we have hope") or as a copula with a participle functioning as a substantive ("we are people who have hoped" or "we are hopers"); cf. Fee, *First Corinthians,* 744 n. 32.

48. Plank, "The Corinthian Controversy Reexamined," 48-49.

49. See Barrett, *First Corinthians,* 349-50; Conzelmann, *1 Corinthians,* 263, 267; Fee, *First Corinthians,* 744-45.

50. Plank, "The Corinthian Controversy Reexamined," 48.

believers are "only hopers" the apostle himself seems to advocate a "realized resurrection." On this reading of verse 19, according to Plank, Paul "understands the position of the Corinthians to entail a denial of the power of the resurrection in this life."[51] Given the apostle's apparent awareness of the Corinthian preoccupation with the power of the Spirit (1 Cor. 12–14) and its effects (4:8), however, this is not a permissible reading of verse 19.

What Plank misses here is the possibility that verse 19 articulates not Paul's position but that of the Corinthians, as Schütz posits. Together with 1 Corinthians 4:8, he contends, the claim that believers are pitiable if in this life they have "only hope" represents the "epitome of the Corinthian position."

> The Corinthians have far more than mere hope, they have a radically collapsed eschatology. Already they 'are filled', already they have 'become rich', *they* already reign (I, 4:8) regardless of the status of the *regnum Christi*.[52]

Moreover, Schütz notes that in verses 13-19 "Paul's 'argument' does not actually look very Pauline."[53] Calling attention to (1) the "at best singular mode of reasoning for Paul" in verses 13-18, which "argues from a general theory of the resurrection to Christ's,"[54] (2) the term *pseudomartyres* (false witnesses) in verse 15, a Pauline *hapax legomenon*,[55] and (3) the unusual phrase "you are still in your sins *(harmartiais)*" in verse 17, which speaks uncharacteristically of people "being in" their sins and departs from Paul's customary generic sin-

---

51. *Ibid.*, 49.
52. Schütz, *Paul and Apostolic Authority*, 90.
53. *Ibid.*, 89.
54. *Ibid.*, 88: "it appears that the truth or falsity of all propositions in vv. 13-17 (and v. 18, too, as we shall see) is derived from the truth or falsity of the general claim that the dead are not raised. That is the logic of the passage."
55. *Ibid.*, 91-92: "In fact, the whole concept of preaching or proclamation as *martyrein* seems more Corinthian than Pauline. Only in 15:16 *[sic]* is the verb used for this activity *(kata tou theou)*. This is all the more striking in the face of the noun *martyrion* in 1:6. Far from setting any precedent for the Pauline use of the verb, *martyrion* there reflects the characteristic usage of *the Corinthian community itself*, embedded as it is in the midst of Paul's sarcastic reflection of the Corinthians' self-understanding as 'enriched in all speech and knowledge . . . not lacking any spiritual gift.' Thus the equation of preaching with *martyrein* and what is preached with *martyrion* appears to be part of the customary Corinthian vocabulary."

gular *harmartia* (sin),[56] Schütz infers that here "Paul is rehearsing a Corinthian argument designed to reduce to absurdity any *denial* that the resurrection from the dead has already taken place."[57]

Further, verses 13-19 represent an interpretation of the kerygma itself. "Point for point it is a *negative* appeal to the older tradition," Schütz observes, "designed to legitimate the view that there is now a 'resurrection.'"[58] As he explains the Corinthian reading of the argument, "If there is no resurrection from the dead (*on and in their terms*, i.e., 'resurrection' as deliverance from the 'death' of sin and transferral to the realm of the spirit), then Christ is not raised, preaching and faith are in vain, and Christians are 'still in their sins.'"[59]

Schütz's novel thesis gains plausibility from the fact that a vulnerability of the language of resurrection in the kerygma to a spiritualized interpretation can be demonstrated. Consider the pertinent line of the cited tradition: "[Christ] was raised on the third day in accordance with the scriptures" (v. 4b). The formula does not state expressly that Christ was raised "from the dead," although this is implied by the preceding affirmations that he "died" and "was buried" (vv. 3b-4a). In the absence of such an express statement, it is easy to see how the implications of the context could be cancelled by a Corinthian understanding of the qualifying stipulation that Jesus was raised "on the third day."

It is widely recognized that the third line of the cited tradition parallels the first stylistically:

Christ died for our sins
                    according to the scriptures; (v. 3b)
he was raised on the third day
                    according to the scriptures. (v. 4b)

The phrase "for our sins" in the first line is rightly identified as an interpretation of Christ's death as a sacrificial event in Old Testament

---

56. *Ibid.*, 92. Schütz notes that the plural "sins" occurs also in 15:3 ("Christ died for our sins"), a usage which he rightly attributes to the cited tradition. "Is [Paul] then in v. 17 influenced by that earlier paradosis? Such seems unlikely in the face of v. 56 where he reverts to his more usual style."
57. *Ibid.*, 92.
58. *Ibid.*, 93.
59. *Ibid.*

terms,[60] and thus in this sense "according to the scriptures." Its formal parallel "on the third day," however, is commonly viewed as a reference to either (1) the historical date of the resurrection event (and thus related to the verb "he was raised"),[61] or (2) an unspecified prophecy (and thus related to the prepositional phrase "according to the scriptures"),[62] or (3) general prophecies fulfilled by the resurrection event (and thus related to both the verb and the prepositional phrase).[63] None of these explanations is satisfying, however, because all of them ignore the fact that "on the third day" interprets the phrase "he was raised" *theologically* in the same manner that "for our sins" interprets "he died."

Somewhat surprisingly, the point is overlooked that the day of the resurrection, "the third day" following the death of Christ, is *the first day* of the week — the day of creation and thus of the new creation. This point is not likely to have been lost on Corinthians who, as the discussion in 15:45-54 assumes, were familiar with the Genesis creation texts. Moreover, Paul himself declares elsewhere in his Corinthian correspondence: "If anyone is in Christ, there is a new creation: everything old has passed away; see, everything has become new!" (2 Cor. 5:17; cf. Gal. 6:15). This view of the present state of the believer, apart from the control of the apostle's so-called "eschatological reservation," could present itself, not as a denial of the kerygma, but as its authentic interpretation.[64]

---

60. Conzelmann, *1 Corinthians*, 255: "The death of Jesus is interpreted by [the phrase] as an atonement sacrifice or as a vicarious sacrifice."

61. Ronald J. Sider, "St. Paul's Understanding of the Nature and Significance of the Resurrection in I Corinthians XV 1-19," *NovT* 19 (1977): 139: "the most likely hypothesis is that 'on the third day' appears in this early statement because of unusual events on the third day after Jesus' death."

62. Barrett, *First Corinthians*, 340: "The order of words in the Greek suggests, though it does not require, that *according to the Scriptures* should be taken with *on the third day*." But he acknowledges: "It is not easy to produce Old Testament documentation for *the third day*. Hos. vi.2 is not very convincing; Jonah ii.1f. is used in Matt. xii.40, but no other New Testament writer shows a similar interest in Jonah and the whale; 2 Kings xx.5; Lev. xxiii.11 are not more helpful."

63. Fee, *First Corinthians*, 726-27, contends (*a*) that "on the third day" most likely "came into the creed primarily because this was in fact the day of the discovery of the empty tomb and of the first resurrection appearances," and (*b*) that "according to the scriptures" has the same force here (line 3) that it did in line 1, asserting that the OT as a whole bears witness to the resurrection on the third day."

64. Robinson, *Trajectories*, 34: "It would seem to be this heretical interpretation of the kerygma in terms of an already consummated eschaton for the initiated that is behind the various Corinthian excesses to which Paul addresses himself in 1 Corinthi-

The connection between such an interpretation of Christ's resurrection and the rite of Christian baptism is rather obvious. Paul himself interprets baptism kerygmatically as effecting union with Christ in his death and resurrection (Rom. 6:3-5). If this represents standard teaching among his churches, then it would have been known in Corinth. Minus Paul's eschatological proviso that "we *will* certainly be united with him in a resurrection like his" (Rom. 6:5), however, his own understanding of baptism would encourage the belief that resurrection has occurred already in the sacramental event. That the Corinthians had a special interest in and a novel understanding of baptism is evident from the way Paul deemphasizes both his role as a baptizer in Corinth (1:13-16) and the strange practice of vicarious baptism on behalf of the dead in Corinth (15:29). Although it is not possible to know with certainty what understanding of baptism informed this custom,[65] De Boer cannot be too wide of the mark when he writes: "Such baptism, a practice associated with the claims of the deniers, was assumed to effect the liberation of the 'spirit' of the deceased."[66] The alleged effects of baptism with regard to the *living* are found in 4:8 and hinted at in Paul's criticism of a Corinthian sacramentalism in 10:1-22. Fee comments: "Perhaps they believed that along with the gift of the Spirit baptism was their 'magical' point of entrance into the new pneumatism that seems to have characterized them at every turn."[67] Käsemann is more definite: From the perspective of their sacramental realism, the Corinthians see a "complete redemption to have already been effected, in that by baptism a heavenly spiritual body has been conferred and the earthly body has been degraded to an insubstantial, transitory veil." It is on this ground and for this reason that they deny "the corporeal resurrection yet to come."[68] Such a hope is, in their view, superfluous.[69]

---

ans." That the Corinthian interpretation is "heretical" is Paul's view, of course, not the Corinthians'.

65. Fee, *First Corinthians*, 764-67, following a lengthy survey of efforts to explain (or explain away) the difficulties of this text, concludes: "But finally we must admit that we simply do not know."

66. De Boer, *The Defeat of Death*, 104.

67. Fee, *First Corinthians*, 767.

68. Käsemann, *New Testament Questions*, 126.

69. Beker, *The Triumph of God*, 72: "a resurrection of the dead (that is, a resurrection of dead bodies) is both disgusting (because the body is inimical to salvation) and superfluous, and unnecessary (because our present spiritual union with Christ constitutes the redemption of our true self)."

Martinus de Boer acknowledges that a Corinthian belief in "realized resurrection" would explain Paul's chiding his readers for being "boastful" (1:29, 31; 4:7; 5:6) and "puffed up" (4:6, 18, 19; 5:2; 8:1; 13:4) as well as their claim to "wisdom" (1:19–2:7; 3:18-23) and "knowledge" (8:1-3, 7; 15:34). It would also account for their boast of "authority" (8:9; 9:4f.) and "freedom" (9:1; 10:20), encapsulated in the slogan "all things are lawful to me" (6:12). Yet De Boer remains unconvinced. His reservation is that Paul does not argue in chapter 15 "*against* the presumed sacramental or spiritual resurrection of *living* Christians" but rather "*for* a resurrection of the *dead (nekrōn),*" that is, "of those who are dead and buried as the now resurrected Christ once was (15.4)." Accordingly, it is inappropriate to reinterpret the Corinthian denial in terms of a positive belief in a "realized resurrection." The plain sense of 1 Corinthians 15:12 is clear enough, he concludes:

> Paul reports that some in Corinth were saying that 'there is no resurrection *of the dead*'. And it is against this claim, and thus *for* a resurrection of the dead, that Paul argues. *The fundamental issue is thus death itself.*[70]

But it is not clear why the recognition of death as the "fundamental issue" of the text is incompatible with a Corinthian belief in "realized resurrection." Schütz, for example, affirms both the Corinthian spiritualism and the Pauline realism. "From the whole of ch. 15 we see that it is the definition of death and the role assigned to it which most fundamentally separates Paul from the Corinthians' position," he writes; "the issue of resurrection is never divorced from this basic problem."[71] Death is indeed the "fundamental issue" of Paul's prophetic speech, but it is couched in a context of Corinthian denial which, as De Boer himself points out, entails both negative and positive meaning.

Wedderburn's recognition of the possible role played by the Corinthians' experience of the Spirit in establishing among them a belief in immortality warns against viewing the options of an "immortality" doctrine and a "realized resurrection" belief as being mutually exclusive in an attempt to understand all that is implied by the Corinthian denial of the resurrection of the dead. It seems most likely that Corinthian religious sensibilities were offended by both the *bodily* and *future* fea-

---

70. De Boer, *The Defeat of Death*, 105.
71. Schütz, *Paul and Apostolic Authority*, 92.

tures of the traditional view, the former because it violated their dualistic anthropological assumptions and the latter because it cast the shadow of "eschatological reservation" upon the "already" *(ēdē)* character of their presumed status as "spirituals" *(pneumatikoi)*. It is on the basis of these dual convictions that the Corinthian prophets interpreted the implications of the apostolic kerygma. And it is this interpretation that Paul calls to account in his own prophetic exposition of the basic Christian message in 1 Corinthians 15.

Paul's Prophetic Discourse

What Conzelmann says of 1 Corinthians 13, which he also views as "a self-contained unity,"[72] is equally appropriate to chapter 15: "At all events the passage must be expounded in the first instance on its own. We must set out from the *form*."[73] In this regard, the question of internal structure or arrangement is crucial. George Kennedy's comment on the nature of discourse has heuristic value:

> A speech is *linear and cumulative,* and any context in it can only be perceived in contrast to what has gone before, especially what has immediately gone before, though a very able speaker lays the ground for what he intends to say later and has *a total unity* in mind when he first begins to speak.[74]

The linear development of the argument in chapter 15 is discernible in the grammatical and stylistic devices Paul uses to mark transitions in his thought. The following transitional markings appear in the text: "And I make known to you, brethren" (*Gnōrizō de hymin, adelphoi;* v. 1); "But if" (*Ei de;* v. 12); "But, as a matter of fact" (*Nyni de;* v. 20); "But someone will ask" (*Alla erei tis;* v. 35); "This I say, brethren" (*Touto de phēmi, adelphoi;* v. 50); and "Therefore, brethren" (*Hōste, adelphoi;* v. 58). Chapter 15 is thus formally arranged into six sections or units of thought which may be presented schematically in terms of their individual themes:

72. Conzelmann, *1 Corinthians,* 217.
73. *Ibid.,* 218.
74. George A. Kennedy, *New Testament Interpretation through Rhetorical Criticism* (1984), 5 (emphasis added).

1. "The gospel I preached to you" (vv. 1-11).
2. "There is no resurrection of the dead" (vv. 12-19).
3. "Christ, the first fruits of the dead" (vv. 20-34).
4. "How are the dead raised?" (vv. 35-49).
5. "Lo, I tell you a mystery" (vv. 50-57).
6. "Therefore, be steadfast" (v. 58).

Recent efforts to organize the argument more precisely in terms of the arrangements specified by the species of Greek rhetoric are unconvincing.[75]

A striking feature of the text's inherent form is that the argument of verses 12-49 is bracketed by an appeal to the common apostolic message in the first major section (vv. 1-11) and to a prophetic revelation in the last (vv. 50-57).[76] The intervening argument is structured by the apostle's responses to (1) "some" in Corinth who say "There is no resurrection of the dead" (vv. 12-19, 20-34),[77] and (2) "someone" who asks "How are the dead raised? With what kind of body do they come?" (vv. 35-49). With regard to Paul's rhetorical strategy, the question is how the appeal to the revelation (vv. 50-57) functions in relation to (1) the cited kerygmatic tradition (vv. 1-11) and (2) the intervening argument as a whole (vv. 12-49).

Helmut Merklein identifies verses 50-58 as an instance of Pauline

---

75. Burton L. Mack, *Rhetoric and the New Testament* (1990), 56-59, views chap. 15 as "a perfect example of rhetorical argumentation." The perceived perfection is marred, however, by Mack's acknowledgment that here "strategies from *judicial* modes of argumentation are interwoven into an essentially *deliberative* declaration" (emphasis added). Once it is conceded that a text is an admixture of species the genre identification is compromised and any attempt to use a hybrid model gives the impression that a procrustean bed is being prepared. Mack does this when he identifies v. 20 as the thesis statement of the argument that *concludes* the so-called narration section of the speech, which allegedly begins at v. 3. V. 20, however, signals a logical shift in the argument by its introductory "but, as a matter of fact" *(nyni de)*, which prepares the way for the new theme of Christ "the first fruits of the dead" that is developed in vv. 21-22. See Fee, *First Corinthians,* 748, esp. n. 10.

76. Aune, *Prophecy in Early Christianity,* 250: "Modern scholarship widely regards 1 Cor. 15:51-52 as a prophetic revelation received by Paul."

77. Vv. 12-19 and 20-34 are structured in parallel fashion: *(a)* affirmation (vv. 12//20); *(b)* implications (vv. 13-18//21-28); *(c)* consequence(s) (v. 19//29-34). In the logic of the second set, the negative consequences (vv. 29-34) pertain if the situation is otherwise *(epei)* than that stated in the affirmation (v. 20) and its positive implications (vv. 21-28).

prophetic speech and rightly observes that the apostle's conclusion in these verses is an independent saying rather than the speculative product of the preceding argument.[78] He argues, however, that while the concluding prophetic saying is formally connected with the kerygmatic tradition in verses 1-11 by the argument of verses 12-49, it is materially unrelated to both the kerygma and the intervening argumentation.[79] Merklein's judgment on this point is determined by his view that prophecy expresses something not contained in the kerygma, meaning its content may not be deduced logically by reflection on the kerygma. Prophecy functions to close the "empty places" (*Leerstelle*) not closed by the kerygma.[80] Merklein does not, however, explain why prophecy may not be understood as filling "empty places" with content *implicit* in the kerygma. Nor does he consider how Paul's appeal to the revelation at the conclusion of the argument functions in his rhetorical strategy.

Now, according to Kennedy, "an able speaker . . . has a total unity in mind when he first begins to speak." If Paul qualifies for such acclaim, he develops his argument from the beginning in the knowledge that it will climax with his appeal to the mystery that has been revealed to him regarding the defeat of death in God's final victory over all his enemies (cf. vv. 24-28). The point has its parallel in the way the evangelists narrate the gospel story in the knowledge of its culmination in the event of the resurrection of Jesus. The outcome of the story is withheld to the last, but it controls the narration as a whole from the beginning. The same is true of the composition of 1 Corinthians 15. In this prophetic critique of the Corinthian interpretation of the resurrection of Christ as attested by the kerygma, and in his own exposition of the cited tradition, the apostle is guided from the outset by the revelation mediated to him by the Spirit (vv. 51-55). Moreover, this revelation not only interprets the implications of the kerygmatic assertion that Christ "was raised on the third day according to the scriptures" but controls the argument of verses 12-49 at each of its crucial points. Because the kerygma is here interpreted by revelation, chapter 15 may be identified as an instance of prophetic discourse.[81]

---

78. Helmut Merklein, "Der Theologe als Prophet: Zur Funktion prophetischen Redens im theologischen Diskurs des Paulus," *NTS* 38 (1992): 423.

79. *Ibid.*, 420.

80. *Ibid.*, 422.

81. Whether it can be designated further form-critically as a *sermon* (or homily) is an open question. The issue of orality is not the problem. Paul probably dictated his

Creed or Kerygma?

Paul begins his prophetic discourse in chapter 15 with an implicit appeal to revelation: "I make known (or reveal) to you, brethren" (*Gnōrizō de hymin, adelphoi;* v. 1). While recognizing that the verb *gnōrizein* can signify a common communication, Weiss notes that in the New Testament it is often used in the technical sense of making known a revelation.[82] That the Corinthians know already what is announced here seems to soften the sense of the verb to a mere "I remind you."[83] According to Bauer, however, it is warranted to give the verb its strong meaning because "the doctrinal instruction" which follows introduces something new.[84] What is new to the Corinthians is precisely the argument for a future bodily resurrection of the dead in the light of the divine mystery revealed to Paul and announced at the conclusion of this speech (vv. 50-57).

The apostle's opening claim to prophetic authority serves initially, however, to remind the church of "the gospel which I proclaimed to you, which also you received, in which also you stand, through which also you are being saved" (vv. 1-2a). In Paul's parlance, "the gospel" (*to euangelion*) connotes the *act* of proclaiming the Christian message and the *content* of the message proclaimed. Both nuances are at work in verse 1. Schütz points out, however, that Paul's manner of speaking in verses 1 and 2 introduces a "limiting factor" in the objective or content character of the gospel. He writes:

---

correspondence, and his letters were doubtlessly read aloud in the congregations. As Wilder, *Early Christian Rhetoric*, 14, explains: "The voice of the writer is the voice of the speaker to a remarkable degree." The problem is the absence of comparable samples which would allow for genre identification. Given the sparsity of direct evidence of Jewish or Christian congregational preaching before the middle of the second century A.D., it is not possible to speak with any assurance of the formal character of homiletical discourse in the first century, much less of a prophetic *sermon* (see Lawrence Wills, "The Form of the Sermon in Hellenistic Judaism and Early Christianity," *HTR* 77 [1984]: 277-99; also C. Clifton Black II, "The Rhetorical Form of the Hellenistic Jewish and Early Christian Sermon: A Response to Lawrence Wills," *HTR* 81 [1988]: 1-18). The argument that 1 Cor. 15 represents prophetic discourse does not rely upon a genre identification but upon the definition of such speech as interpretation of the kerygma under the influence of a revelation.

82. Weiss, *Korintherbrief*, 295 (citing Col. 1:27 and often in Eph.; Rom. 16:26; John 15:15; 17:26; Luke 2:15, 17).

83. Fee, *First Corinthians*, 719.

84. Bauer, *Lexicon*, 162.

The gospel which Paul preached is thought of here as a present reality in which the Corinthians can be said to 'stand' and 'through which' they *are being* saved. The focus is less on the gospel as *what* they *believed* than on the gospel as *where* they *are*.[85]

From this he concludes that the term *euangelion* (gospel) has three senses, not two, in the apostle's usage: "One is this fixed object of preaching, one is the act of preaching, and one is something rather more elusive, the gospel as an on-going entity 'in' which one can 'be' or 'stand.'" Following Schniewind, Schütz dubs this third nuance the "pregnant" sense, meaning "that use of the noun which exhibits its significance as an 'effective force.'"[86]

The importance of these distinctions becomes evident when the issue of the gospel's relation to tradition is raised, as it is by Paul's reminder of "in what word" *(tini logō)* he preached the gospel in Corinth (v. 2).[87] The phrase functions as the antecedent of the *tradition* introduced in verse 3 by the technical terms for its transmission, "deliver" *(paradounai)* and "receive" *(paralambanein)*.[88] Paul is evidently citing a particular formulation, delivered to and received by the Corinthians, which serves as the basis of his proclamation of, and their status in, the gospel. The question of the *extent* of the citation that clearly begins in verse 3b may be postponed momentarily for the sake of addressing first the problematic issue of its *genre*.

Since Conzelmann's seminal study,[89] the confessional or creedal character of the tradition introduced at verse 3b has attained virtual canonical status among New Testament scholars. Yet in an earlier work Vernon Neufeld observed that confessional formulas in Paul's writings are characterized by four identifying features: (1) an introductory verb of confessing (*homologeō* or a synonym); (2) a grammatical device indicating indirect discourse (*hoti* or its equivalent); (3) the use of participles, relative clauses, or parallelism to create a rhythmic cadence; and

---

85. Schütz, *Paul and Apostolic Authority,* 42.
86. Ibid., 43.
87. Fee, *First Corinthians,* 720-21, unscrambles the convoluted sentence in vv. 1-2 by reading "in what word I preached to you" as a resumption of the opening clause following the intervening digression. The line of thought is thus: "I make known to you the gospel I preached to you, that is, with what word I preached to you."
88. W. D. Davies, *Paul and Rabbinic Judaism* (1955), 249.
89. Hans Conzelmann, "On the Analysis of the Confessional Formula in I Corinthians 15:3-5," trans. Mathias Rissi, *Int* 20 (1966): 15-25.

(4) a confessional theme articulated in a dual or antithetical way.[90] The tradition cited in 1 Corinthians 15 clearly meets the second criterion, but not the first. Further, it only meets the third (parallelism) and fourth (dual theme) criteria if the citation is limited to verses 3b-5a. Thus the identification of the genre of the tradition quoted as a confession or a creed is less certain than presently recognized.

A viable alternative appears when it is recognized that the tradition, however delimited, is bracketed by the standard terminology of early Christian proclamation. Preceded by the noun *euangelion* (gospel) and its verbal cognate *euangelizein* (to proclaim; vv. 1-2), the citation is followed by *kēryssein* (to preach; vv. 11-12) and *kērygma* (message; v. 14). It is unclear whether these sets represent semantic equivalents or are differentiated in some sense. Bultmann insists that they are synonymous, stressing that the nouns are to be understood as *nomen actionis*.[91] Käsemann thinks the substantives are "indissolubly related, but must be distinguished." In distinction from kerygma, which he takes with Bultmann as the name of an act of preaching, the term "gospel" connotes also "the central content" of the proclamation (as in Rom. 1:3-4 and 1 Cor. 15:1-5) and the "power that determines life and destiny."[92] Käsemann, in other words, agrees with Schütz in identifying three nuances of the word "gospel." The question is whether he and Bultmann have correctly defined the sense of the term "kerygma" in the usage of Paul.

Schütz sees an implied distinction in chapter 15 between *euangelizein* and *kēryssein*, observing that Paul does not use the latter verb (vv. 11-12) "until after he has finished the *paradosis*."[93] If this terminological shift is other than a stylistic variation, the material difference may be represented by the substitution of "*in what word* I preached to you" in verse 2 for "*the gospel* I preached to you" in verse 1. In that the "word" *(logos)* in verse 2 refers to and designates the cited tradition, the implication would be that, following the citation, the tradition is identified by the term *kērygma* (v. 14). That kerygma is a content term in verse 14 is evident from its intrinsic relation to faith: "But if Christ is not raised, empty then our message *(kērygma)*, empty also your faith

---

90. Neufeld, *The Earliest Christian Confessions*, 42-68.
91. Bultmann, *Theology*, I, 87-89.
92. Käsemann, *Commentary on Romans*, 8-9.
93. Schütz, *Paul and Apostolic Authority*, 69.

(pistis)" (cf. 15:11, "thus we preached [*kēryssein*] and thus you believed [*pisteuein*]"). Faith is elicited by an act of preaching, but its object is the content of the preaching. Kerygma is also a content word in 1 Corinthians 1:21 where it is designated as "foolishness" not because it is an act of proclamation but because it is "the word of the cross" (1:18). Similarly Paul refers in 1 Corinthians 2:4 to his "speech" (*logos:* the act of speaking) and his "message" (*kērygma:* the content of his speaking).[94]

The conclusion is warranted, therefore, that kerygma is the apostle's term for the substantive tradition that undergirds and unites all apostolic preaching. For this reason the formula should be identified as the apostolic kerygma rather than as an early Christian confession or creed.

Where the traditioned formula concludes in the text is a matter of considerable speculation. Murphy-O'Connor summarizes the state of the discussion:

> In the literary analysis of 1 Cor 15:1-11 only two points command complete agreement: (1) Paul introduces a quotation in v. 3b, and (2) he is speaking personally from v. 8 on. There is a wide consensus on a third point, viz., that the quotation introduced in v. 3b terminates in v. 5, both because the grammatical structure changes in v. 6 and because vv. 3b-5 contains a very high proportion of non-Pauline terms.[95]

Greater clarification would be achieved, however, if the question of the pre-Pauline origin and development of verses 3b-5 and 6-7 were treated separately from the issue of where in the text *the Corinthians* would have recognized the conclusion of the citation. After all, this was a tradition Paul had "delivered" and they had "received." The credibility of the apostle's appeal to common ground in the kerygmatic tradition would be compromised in direct proportion to any alterations or additions the citation might include. It is dangerous, therefore, to infer from the change in construction occurring in verses 6-7 that this text represents "a free composition of Paul who supplements the quotation in vv. 3b-5 by information drawn from his own personal knowledge."[96]

---

94. Although the Pauline authorship of Rom. 16:25 is open to question, it uses kerygma in the same sense as in 1 Corinthians.

95. Jerome Murphy-O'Connor, O.P., "Tradition and Redaction in 1 Cor 15:3-7," *CBQ* 43 (1981): 582.

96. *Ibid.*, 585. See also Barrett, *First Corinthians*, 343; and Conzelmann, *1 Corinthians*, 257.

Another point seemingly overlooked in the literature on this passage is that the tradition cited is controlled not by stylistic concerns but by the events attested. Important to note, therefore, is the simple observation that the verbs "he died," "he was buried," and "he was raised" refer to *singular* events. By contrast, "he appeared" refers to *multiple* occurrences. John Kloppenborg further notes that in the Septuagint and the New Testament *ōphthē* (appeared) "is regularly followed by a reference to witnesses (in the dative)" when used of persons or of God.[97] Semantic custom, therefore, requires the completion of the verbal statement by the phrase "to Cephas, then to the twelve" (v. 5). This not only breaks the strict parallelism that is evident when the formulation is restricted to verses 3b-5a, but it opens the door to the other appearances of the risen Christ attested in verses 6-7. In view of Paul's having become a legend in his own time because of his conversion (Gal. 1:23), the possibility of the appearance to him being included in the apostolic preaching tradition cannot be ruled out. The formula could have concluded with the statement, "Last of all, he appeared also to Paul" (v. 8). On this reading of the tradition, the apostle's editorial hand is visible in the parenthetical comment of verse 6 ("most of whom are still alive, although some have died") and in the way he personalizes verse 8 ("Last of all, as to one abnormally born [*hōperei tō ektrōmati*], he appeared also to me [*kamoi*]").

Of special interest is the apostle's editorial assertion that he is "the one born abnormally" *(to ektrōma)*, a term that denotes literally any kind of premature birth (abortion, still-birth, or miscarriage) and connotes figuratively something or someone horrible or "freakish."[98] This pejorative appellation is commonly attributed to the Corinthians, who allegedly viewed Paul as physically weak or small of stature. A more compelling case is made by Peter von der Osten-Saken for understanding the term as Paul's self-designation.[99] Arguing that the phrase "as to one abnormally born" stands in apposition to *kamoi* (even to me), he argues that it is an interpretation of "the least *(elachistos)* of the apostles" (v. 9) rather than "last *(eschaton)* of all" (v. 8). The self-designation is

---

97. John Kloppenborg, "An Analysis of the Pre-Pauline Formula 1 Cor 15:3b-5 in Light of Some Recent Literature," *CBQ* 40 (1978): 358.

98. Fee, *First Corinthians*, 733.

99. Peter von der Osten-Saken, "Die Apologie des paulinischen Apostolats in 1 Kor 15:1-11," *ZNW* 64 (1973): 245-62.

grounded in Paul's conviction that he is "unworthy to be called an apostle, because he persecuted the church of God" (v. 9; cf. Gal. 1-13; Phil. 3:6). Paul's point is that he is not disqualified from apostleship because he was once "the horrible one." "By the grace of God I am what I am" (v. 10). According to Osten-Saken, it is not fortuitous that the defense of his apostleship occurs *after* the citation of the tradition and *before* the exposition of the tradition which begins at verse 12. The apology, in other words, is the bridge between the kerygmatic tradition and its binding interpretation. What is at stake, he concludes, is nothing less than Paul's authority as an expositor of the kerygma.[100]

Wire points out, however, that Paul's claim to authority is correlated in his letters with the exercise of that claim in the form of rhetorical arguments. That is to say, the apostle is not able merely to assert his position; he must argue for it. As Wire puts it:

> Paul claims a hearing on the basis of insistent arguments from God's calling, from revelation, from hard work, and from modeling Christ. The letters do not claim to be authoritative in their own right or this argument would be redundant.[101]

With regard to 1 Corinthians 15, the claim is based not only upon his apostolic calling (vv. 9-10), which identifies him with the foundational tradition (vv. 3b-8), but also upon a revelation by which the kerygmatic formula is interpreted (vv. 50-58). It is this revelation, characteristic of early Christian prophecy, that informs the argument of chapter 15 as a whole.

A Revelation of a Mystery

The argument of chapter 15 concludes with verses 50-57. The opening statement that "flesh and blood cannot inherit the kingdom of God, nor does the perishable inherit the imperishable" (v. 50), summarizes the preceding discussion of the "spiritual body" that attends the resurrection of the dead and introduces the new thought that those who are alive "at the last trumpet" will also "be transformed" (v. 52). In support

---

100. *Ibid.*, 260.
101. Wire, *The Corinthian Women Prophets*, 10.

PROPHECY AND KERYGMA

of this claim, Paul appeals to a revelation. At issue are the extent and the structure of the revealed mystery.

Merklein argues that the prophetic revelation saying is composed of verses 50-58 and structured according to four parts: (1) the introduction (vv. 50-51a); (2) the prophetic word (vv. 51b-52a); (3) the interpretation of the prophecy (vv. 52b-57); and (4) the concluding exhortation (v. 58).[102] His analysis is predicated, however, upon Dautzenberg's untenable view that *diakriseis pneumatōn* (1 Cor. 12:10) means interpretation of dark prophetic utterances. Thus the distinction between the prophetic word proper (vv. 51b-52a) and its interpretation (vv. 52b-57) has no support. Further, Merklein includes the prophetic texts cited in verses 54b-55 (Isa. 25:8; Hos. 13:14) within the interpretation section but neither mentions them specifically nor suggests what role they play in the explanation of the prophetic word.

Aune limits the prophetic oracle regarding the divinely concealed "mystery" to verses 51-52, which is introduced by the demonstrative particle *idou* ("behold" or "lo") and structured chiastically (a b c c′ a′ b′):[103]

> Behold! I tell you a mystery:
> a All shall not sleep,
> b but all shall be changed.
> c In a moment, in the twinkling of an eye, at the last trumpet.
> c′ For the trumpet shall sound,
> a′ and the dead shall be raised imperishable,
> b′ and all shall be transformed.

Aune argues that the problem of the conclusion of the oracle is solved by the chiastic structure of verses 51-52. But the impure chiasm compromises Aune's claim, as does his further observation that "Paul continues to use poetic parallelism in vv. 53ff."[104] It is significant that Aune, like Merklein, ignores the function of the cited prophetic texts in the concluding section of Paul's argument, and this in spite of his explicit recognition of the fact that the divine mysteries are commonly "concealed in dreams, *in texts such as the OT*, and in aspects of physical reality such as the stars and planets."[105]

---

102. Merklein, "Der Theologe als Prophet," 416-18.
103. Aune, *Prophecy in Early Christianity*, 250-51.
104. Ibid., 251.
105. *Ibid.* (emphasis added).

Fee attributes the source of this revelation to Paul's encounter with the risen Christ: "The heavenly existence of Christ in a *pneumatikon sōma* ('supernatural body') means that yet another 'mystery' is now revealed to God's people."[106] But the apostle locates the origin of this insight in a revelation mediated by the Scriptures. When all this occurs, Paul explains,

> then the saying that is written will come true:
>
> "Death has been swallowed up in victory" (Isa. 25:8).
> "Where, O death, is your victory?
> Where, O death, is your sting?" (Hos. 13:14)

As the only place where the apostle cites unfulfilled prophecy, this is a remarkable text.[107] It implies that the source of the revealed mystery is the promised victory.

Walter Harrelson, noting that Paul quotes neither of these texts in the form found in the Masoretic or Septuagint versions, examines each in the Hebrew and concludes that Paul's rendition faithfully represents the sense of both.[108] The point of Isaiah's prophecy that "[God] will swallow up death completely," according to Harrelson, is that God will triumph over "all the powers and forces of the creation that stand in opposition to the deity." In its context, Isaiah 25:8 "portrays the day of victory, the day of *God's* triumph, the season of blessedness that awaits the world."[109] Hosea's rhetorical questions, "Where are your plagues, O death? Where is your destruction, O Sheol?" are predicated upon the divine promise, "I will ransom them from the hand of Sheol; I will redeem them from death." Here the divine voice is heard again in the prophetic indictment of Ephraim for its idolatry and apostasy from God, Harrelson explains, only this time the divine wrath is redirected away from Ephraim against the destructive powers.[110] Hosea's vision is less cosmic than that of Isaiah, but it "affirms . . . outspokenly that God will not fail to engage death and

---

106. Fee, *First Corinthians*, 800.
107. Noted by Fee, *ibid.*, 803.
108. Walter Harrelson, "Death and Victory in 1 Corinthians 15:51-57: The Transformation of a Prophetic Theme," in *Faith and History: Essays in Honor of Paul W. Meyer*, in John T. Carroll, Charles H. Cosgrove, E. Elizabeth Johnson, eds. (1990), 149-59.
109. *Ibid.*, 153 (emphasis added).
110. *Ibid.*, 156.

plague in mortal combat."[111] Harrelson thus concludes that Paul has "ingeniously linked" these two texts "to support the recently developed doctrine of resurrection."[112]

It would be more accurate to say that Paul links these texts not to support but to *interpret* the resurrection in the light of such prophetic promises of God's eschatological victory over the powerful reality of death. Thus the resurrection is, strictly speaking, neither an anthropological nor a christological but a theological issue in which nothing less than the sovereignty of God over the creation is at stake. It is for this reason that the apostle exhorts the Corinthians to sober up and come to a right mind, "for some people have *no knowledge of God*" (v. 34). The hermeneutical context for the interpretation of the implications of the kerygmatic claim "[Christ] was raised on the third day in accordance with the scriptures" is the witness of the sacred writings to who God is and what God will do. How this revelation of the mystery of God's redemptive purpose informs the developing argument of chapter 15 may now be demonstrated.

An Argument from Revelation

The argument of verses 12-19 is structured by a deductive form of logic which T. G. Bucher identifies as the *modus tollens* developed by the Stoics.[113] The key examples are: "If there is no resurrection of the dead, then Christ has not been raised" (v. 13); and "If the dead are not raised, then Christ has not been raised" (v. 16). The logic of both of these texts works on the basis of *implication* ("If . . . then . . .").[114] If either the

---

111. *Ibid.*, 158.
112. *Ibid.*, 157.
113. Theodor G. Bucher, "Die logische Argumentation in 1. Korinther 15,12-20," *Bib* 55 (1974): 465-86; cf. his subsequent essays: "Auferstehung Christi und Auferstehung der Toten," *MTZ* 27 (1976): 1-32; "Nochmals zur Beweisführung in 1. Korinther 15,12-20," *TZ* 36 (1980): 129-52; "Allgemeine Überlegungen zur Logik im Zusammenhang mit 1 Kor 15,12-20," *LB* 53 (1983): 70-98. See also the rejoinders by Michael Bachmann, "Zur Gedankenführung in 1. Kor. 15,12ff.," *TZ* 34 (1978): 265-76; "Rezeption von 1. Kor. 15 (V. 12ff.) unter logischem und unter philologischem Aspekt," *LB* 51 (1982): 79-103.
114. Bucher, "Die logische Argumentation," 466.

protasis or the apodosis is demonstrable, the other is thereby affirmed; that is to say, the truth of the assertion entails the validity of the inference and the reverse. Because Paul affirms categorically the reality of Christ's resurrection in verse 20, Bucher reasons that the resurrection of the dead is established irrefutably.[115] It is not, however. For the necessary *connection* between the two events is not yet even identified, much less demonstrated, by the apostle's argumentation. As J. C. Beker observes:

> The circular nature of Paul's argument in 1 Cor. 15:12-19 is obvious because for him there is a logical interaction between the two foci of the resurrection of Christ and the final apocalyptic resurrection. The cogency of the argument is based on a premise that is seemingly not open to discussion. But this premise is for the Corinthians probably the questionable postulate that determines everything else. In other words, Paul's circular argument is not convincing, because it lacks a sufficient warrant. What needs to be argued is actually taken for granted.[116]

Beker's impatience with Paul, however, is premature. For not everything can be said at once. The premise of the argument is here unexpressed, but it is discussed in verses 20-28 and identified in verses 50-55 as the victory of God over death. There also its warrant is provided by the revelation of this "mystery." The point is that the content of that revelation is the implicit assumption of the argument in verses 12-19.

The first explicit mention of the necessary connection between the resurrection of Christ and the resurrection of the dead is found in the introduction of the second major section of the argument (vv. 20-34). Not only is the resurrection of Christ affirmed in verse 20, but the risen one is identified as "the first fruits *(aparchē)* of those who sleep [in death]." The implications of this identification are drawn out in verses 21-28, and the consequences, if in fact Christ is not the "first fruits" of the dead, are specified in verses 29-34.[117] The apostle's rhetorical strategy here is to remove the resurrection of Christ from any possible

---

115. Ibid., 470-71, 486.
116. Beker, *The Triumph of God*, 74.
117. Vv. 29-34 represent not a separate *ad hominem* argument, as Fee, *First Corinthians*, 76-75, argues, but the consequences if Christ is not the "first fruits" of the resurrection harvest. Rhetorically, vv. 29-34 parallel the consequence of the denial of the resurrection of the dead stipulated in v. 19.

isolation as an event *sui generis* and locate it in the context of the resurrection of the dead.

Paul explains the significance of Christ being the "first fruits" of the dead in verses 21-22, introducing each verse with an explanatory *gar* (for). In verse 21 he takes up the motif of the two *anthrōpoi* (humans), which was attributed in the discussion of verses 45-49 above to Corinthian anthropological speculations.[118] The one is the agent of "death" *(thanatos);* the other the agent of "resurrection of the dead" *(anastasis nekrōn).* In verse 22 these figures are identified respectively as Adam, in whom "all die," and "the Christ" *(ho Christos),* in whom "all shall be made alive." While the origins of the Adam-Christ typology remain obscure,[119] they are predicated upon intertestamental Jewish beliefs which, according to N. T. Wright, identified Israel with Adam as "God's true humanity" and the Messiah as the representative of Israel.[120] As Wright interprets Paul:

> The Messiah has now been installed as the one through whom God is doing what he intended to do, first through humanity and then through Israel. Paul's Adam-christology is basically an Israel-christology, and is predicated on the identification of Jesus as Messiah, in virtue of his resurrection.[121]

Thus the connection between his resurrection and that of the dead is established on messianic grounds.

Yet, as De Boer points out, the claim that Christ is the first fruits of those who have fallen asleep still "*presupposes* the inextricable connection between his resurrection and the resurrection of the dead (vv. 12-19)." That the former includes the latter and cannot be divorced from it is the point of the metaphor of Christ the "first fruits." But De Boer argues that the claim "contains an inherent weakness, one that the

---

118. See pages 205-11.

119. Käsemann, *Commentary on Romans,* 142: "In spite of strenuous efforts, no adequate explanation in the history of religions has been found for the rise of the Adam-Christ typology." De Boer, *The Defeat of Death,* 110, thinks Paul created it himself.

120. N. T. Wright, *The Climax of the Covenant: Christ and the Law in Pauline Theology* (1991), 18-40. Thus "when Paul aligns Christ in some way with Adam the role he is thereby assigning to the former is that which, *mutatis mutandis,* his Jewish contemporaries would give to Israel, or perhaps to Israel's anointed king (27)."

121. *Ibid.,* 29.

deniers of the resurrection of the dead would immediately have pressed, and it is this: If the risen Christ is indeed the first-fruits of those who have fallen asleep, *where is the resurrection of the dead?*"[122]

Paul's answer to such a question is that the two events are related in terms of a temporal "order" *(tagma):* "Christ the first fruits, then at his coming *(parousia)* those who belong to Christ" (v. 23). The reason for the delay of the resurrection of the dead *until* the coming of the risen Messiah[123] is that "he must reign until he has put all his enemies under his feet" (v. 25, alluding to Ps. 110:1; cf. vv. 27-28, citing Ps. 8:6). But De Boer pushes the Corinthian perspective still further by observing that these two texts from the Psalms are related also in Ephesians (1:21), 1 Peter (3:21b-22), and Hebrews (2:8) "in explicit connection with *Christ's exaltation over principalities, power, or angels.*" From this he infers that in 1 Corinthians 15:20-28 "*Paul is adapting and reinterpreting christological traditions known to the Corinthians, traditions in which Ps 110.1 and Ps 8.7b [sic] had in fact already come to play a fixed role in connection with Christ's resurrection which was understood to entail his exaltation over the principalities and powers.*"[124] If so, the Corinthians would have heard verse 27a ("[God] has put all things in subjection under [Christ's] feet") as a support of their position rather than Paul's.

All that can be said with confidence, however, is that 15:23-28 is the earliest witness to this messianic reading of Psalm 110:1 in connection with Psalm 8:6,[125] and that the apostle is thus the first known to have identified the messianic enemies as "every ruler and every authority and power" *(pasan archēn kai pasan exousian kai dynamin;* v. 24) and to have specified "death" *(thanatos)* as "the last enemy to be destroyed" (v. 26). It may be noted in this connection that neither of the Psalms which inform Paul's vision of "the end" *(to telos),* when the Messiah "delivers the kingdom to God the Father" (v. 24), identifies death as one of his enemies. But Isaiah 25:8 and Hosea 13:14 do designate death as a cosmic power that will be defeated by God. It

---

122. De Boer, *The Defeat of Death,* 124 (emphasis added).

123. Wright, *Climax of the Covenant,* 41-55, convincingly challenges the common assumption that *Christos* (Christ) was primarily a proper name rather than a messianic title for Jesus in Paul's letters and among his Gentile churches. Note the definite article with the noun *(ho Christos)* in 1 Cor. 15:22, 23.

124. De Boer, *The Defeat of Death,* 117-18.

125. Donald Juel, *Messianic Exegesis* (1988), 141, thinks it was Paul who first made the connection by reading "subjection" in Ps. 110:1 in terms of Ps. 8:6.

would appear, therefore, that the apostle is here interpreting the Psalm texts in the light of the prophetic citations reserved for the climax of the argument (vv. 54-55).

A triumphalist interpretation of the resurrection of the Christ in terms of the Psalm texts is precluded by the apostle's insistence that the "subjection" of the messianic enemies entails their "destruction" (*katargein*; vv. 24, 26). The risen Christ is not merely exalted above the cosmic powers; he is destined to waste them. Where the Psalm texts used in the argument speak of a subordination, Paul specifies eradication. On what basis? A warrant for this interpretation is again found in Isaiah 25:8, which stipulates in the Hebrew text that "[God] will swallow up death completely." Harrelson comments:

> Death too will be swallowed up! Why this verb, used elsewhere in the Hebrew Bible to depict the devouring of wild animals or especially to picture the earth and Sheol and death opening up to swallow the rebellious (Num 16:31) or those under the power of the enemy's curse? Death will be swallowed up on this day, just as death has regularly swallowed up those who fell under its power.[126]

Paul's Greek captures the radical sense of the Hebrew verb by the translational equivalent *katapinein* (v. 54), which connotes in its figurative sense "total extinction as a result" of being "swallowed up."[127] Because death abides as an empirical reality in human experience, the apostle insists that the "until" of Psalm 110:1 remains in force (v. 26). By virtue of his resurrection from the dead, Christ indeed "reigns" (*basileuein*). But the continuing power of death over human life demonstrates that his sovereignty is "not yet" fully realized.

That it is God's teleological intentions that connect the resurrection of Christ in the past with that of the dead in the future is confirmed by the proviso of verses 27b-28:

> But when it says, 'All things are put in subjection,' it is plain that this does not include the one who put all things in subjection under him. When all things are subject to him, then the Son himself will also be subjected to the one who put all things in subjection under him, so that God may be all in all.

---

126. Harrelson, "Death and Victory in 1 Corinthians 15:51-57," 153.
127. Bauer, *Lexicon*, 417.

Essentially, this is the same vision that informs the affirmation of God's triumph over death in verses 54b-55. The common themes of verses 20-28 and 50-58 are (1) *the sovereignty of God*, expressed in verse 24 as "the kingdom" *(hē basileia)* which Christ will deliver to God (cf. v. 25) and in verse 50 as "the kingdom of God" *(basileia theou)*, and (2) *the reality of death* (*thanatos;* vv. 21, 26, 54 [Isa. 25:8], 55 [twice: Hos. 13:14], 56). God will be "all in all" when his sovereignty over the creation is fully established by the eschatological defeat of death. This is the implicit premise of Paul's argument for the *future* resurrection of the dead in verses 20-28, a premise that is warranted by the revelation of the "mystery" explicitly attested in verses 50-58.

Fee contends that the apostle's argument in verses 35-49 is controlled by the appearance of the risen Christ to him, in which it was evident that "Christ's resurrection was not the resuscitation of a corpse, but the transformation of his physical body into a 'glorified body' (Phil. 3:21) adapted to his present heavenly existence."[128] Indeed, this seems to be the import of the list of witnesses to the appearances of the risen Christ in the kerygmatic tradition (vv. 5-8). The implied narrative of the witnesses thus concerns not only the reality of Christ's resurrection but also its bodily nature. The one who "appeared" after he was "raised" is identifiable as the one who "died" and was "buried." Thus to the questions of the skeptic "How are the dead raised? With what kind of body do they come?" Paul answers "As with Christ, the same yet not the same; this body, but adapted to the new conditions of heavenly existence."[129]

Yet the argument of verses 35-49 focuses precisely upon the necessity of the "new conditions" of resurrection life, and in this regard it is controlled not by a report on the nature of the body of the risen Christ but by the principle that "flesh and blood cannot inherit the kingdom of God, nor does the perishable inherit the imperishable" (v. 50). This text summarizes the argument in verses 35-49 and introduces the concluding appeal to the revelation of the "mystery" that grounds the stated principle. Expressed in the form of synonymous parallelism, the principle identifies "flesh and blood" with the "perishable" *(phthora)* and "the kingdom of God" with the "imperishable" *(aphtharsia)*. It is this principle that explains the nature of the body in

128. Fee, *First Corinthians*, 777.
129. *Ibid.*

the resurrection of the dead (vv. 42-44). Under the hegemony of death, the present body is subject to conditions that are characterized by such terms as "perishable" *(phthora)*, "dishonor" *(atimia)*, "weakness" *(astheneia)*, and "physical" *(psychikos)*. The future conditions of resurrection life, by contrast, are designated as "imperishable" *(aphtharsia)*, "glory" *(doxa)*, "power" *(dynamis)*, and "spiritual" *(pneumatikos)*. Thus both the resurrection of the dead and the transformation of the living "at the last trumpet" will entail the perishable body "putting on" *(endysasthai)* imperishability and the mortal body "putting on" immortality (v. 53). What will effect this change in the conditions of human existence is the eschatological defeat of death as prophesied by Isaiah and Hosea (vv. 54b-55). This is the implicit premise of the argument throughout 1 Corinthians 15, a premise explicitly stated in and warranted by the appeal to the revelation attested in its concluding section (vv. 51-55).

Conclusion

The case for regarding 1 Corinthians 15 as an instance of prophetic discourse rests on three considerations: (1) it is an interpretation of the apostolic kerygma (vv. 3b-8) in the light of a revelation (vv. 50-58), the chief characteristic of early Christian prophecy; (2) it carries out a critique of the Corinthians' prophetic word, "There is no resurrection of the dead" (v. 12b); and (3) it is located by its epistolary context and its intertextual links with chapter 14 within the discussion of "the spirituals [or prophets]" (12:1), the theme of chapters 12–15. It must be concluded, therefore, that 1 Corinthians 15 exemplifies a prophetic utterance of the kind Paul knew and advocated.

Conclusion

THE historical question of what the early Christian prophets were doing when they were prophesying evokes an answer that has theological significance. This book's investigation of Paul's understanding and practice of Christian prophecy has led to the conclusion that it was (1) an exposition of the kerygma in terms of its intrinsic divine wisdom, (2) effected by the revelatory activity of the Spirit within an ecclesial context, (3) expressed in extended discourse that included exposition of Scripture and logical argumentation, and (4) subjected to material criticism. The remaining question is whether these results validate Ernst Käsemann's thesis that such prophecy represents the beginning of Christian theology. If so, theology at this nascent stage of its development would be understood as a hermeneutical task.

Theology as Prophetic Interpretation

When Käsemann published his essay "The Beginnings of Christian Theology," contending that the genesis of theological thought is historically discernible in the post-Easter and post-Pentecost preaching of the prophets,[1] the proposal evoked prompt critical responses from Ernst Fuchs and Gerhard Ebeling.[2] Much of the exchange centers on the

---

1. Käsemann, *New Testament Questions*, 82-107.
2. Gerhard Ebeling, "The Ground of Christian Theology"; Ernst Fuchs, "On the Task of a Christian Theology," *JTC* 6 (1969): 47-68 and 69-98, respectively.

validity and value of Käsemann's provocative thesis that "apocalyptic is the mother of all Christian theology," but two other issues raised by Ebeling bear upon the propriety of identifying the prophets as theologians.

Recognizing that the question of historical beginnings includes the issue of the ground of Christian theology, Ebeling addresses the dogmatic problems inherent in Käsemann's thesis. One such is the concept of theology itself, and the legitimacy of applying the term to the early prophetic proclamation. The word "theology" may not be used to designate a historical phenomenon, Ebeling argues, without regard to the history of its meaning — "that is, it cannot be indiscriminately applied to any and every talk of God."[3] Ebeling thinks that theology in the sense of "responsible reflection on what our proclamation says of God" occurs historically in the encounter between the biblical and Greek traditions. In Christian proclamation, "where the nearness of God is asserted with self-evident authority," this kind of reflection is unnecessary because proclamation and theology are "completely interwoven." It is "the problem of a difference between word and God," according to Ebeling, that necessitates "reflection on the controversial language of faith."[4] Thus "with reservations" he accepts the application of the concept theology to the earliest phase of Christian proclamation, adding that "with the primitive Christian kerygma theology [in the sense of 'responsible reflection'] at once becomes a necessary task."[5] Within Ebeling's paradigm of two modes of discourse, accordingly, there appears to be no intermediary place for the notion of a *responsible interpretation* of the kerygma as carried out by the early Christian prophets.

Working with the language theories of the philosophers Husserl and Heidegger, Robert Funk identifies *three* cardinal modes of discourse that may be plotted on a spectrum.[6] At the end closest to primordial discourse, "language is characterized by directness, immediacy, spontaneity, nondiscursiveness. . . ." Here "language re-flects, without reflecting upon, the world." Funk terms this the "re-flective" mode of discourse. The point on the spectrum furthest removed from primordial discourse is identified as "secondary reflectivity." Here language itself,

---

3. *Ibid.*, 48.
4. *Ibid.*, 48-49.
5. *Ibid.*, 49.
6. Funk, *Language, Hermeneutic, and Word of God*, 231-34.

in the form of linguistic formulations, is the object of reflection. Linguistic analysis and theological discourse (in many of its periods) represent this mode of secondary reflectivity, according to Funk. In between these poles falls a mode of discourse that may be called "primary reflectivity," in which "language does not reflect upon language as such, but upon the fate of re-flective language in the face of a concrete but competitive *Lebenswelt*." In other words, as Funk explains, "it holds reflective language up to that which it *intends* (its object in the phenomenological sense), in view of the way in which it is heard, by the speaker and others." The reason language requires these distinctions, he concludes, is that "secondary reflectivity [Ebeling's "responsible reflection"] feeds on primary reflectivity and not on re-flective language [Ebeling's "primitive Christian kerygma"]."

Funk goes on to characterize the Pauline letter as language in the mode of primary reflectivity. He writes:

> The letters presuppose the proclamation (kerygma) — whether Paul's own or that which came to him out of the tradition — and refer to it, in that Paul is reflecting upon the fate of that proclamation among his readers. In this mode of reflection he moves between two poles: (a) what the proclamation intends, i.e., the focal actuality it holds in view or ... the "subject matter" of the proclamation; and (b) the way in which that proclamation is being heard, i.e., its fate among his hearers in view of their situation, their expectations.[7]

The prophetic discourse of 1 Corinthians 15 exemplifies primary reflectivity upon the fate of the re-flective language of the kerygma in the concrete and competitive "life world" of the Corinthians. It holds the kerygma up to its subject matter — the reality of the risen Christ who reigns as the agent of God's sovereign promise to destroy death and reclaim the creation on conditions that exclude mortality. Early Christian prophecy as interpretation of the kerygma may be located with primary reflectivity on the spectrum of Funk's paradigm.

Käsemann himself, in his exposition of 1 Corinthians 2:6-16, gropes for some distinction like Funk's between primary and secondary reflectivity. "The discussion here concerns what we call theology," he writes, "and sophia in our text is best translated by theology if one remains conscious of the fact that what is meant is not a science in the

---

7. *Ibid.*, 238.

modern sense but salvation teaching *(Heilslehre)*."[8] In the Corinthians passage Paul speaks of "God's wisdom, hidden in a mystery" (2:7), which, when revealed by the Spirit (2:10), effects understanding of "the gifts bestowed on us by God" (2:12). When Paul adds that "we speak of these things in words not taught by human wisdom but taught by the Spirit, interpreting spiritual things to spiritual people," the mode of discourse in view may be designated primary reflectivity. For this speech is concerned about the fate of "the word of the cross" (1:18 = 15:3b, "Christ died for our sins according to the scriptures"). So also the revealed "mystery" attested in 1 Corinthians 15:51-55 addresses the way the Corinthians are hearing the kerygmatic word that Christ "was raised on the third day according to the scriptures" (15:4b).

Thus in his response to Ebeling's critique of his thesis, Käsemann acknowledges that the use of the term *theology* requires diachronic distinctions. But he thinks it dangerous to identify the beginnings of theology with the encounter of the biblical tradition with Greek thought. "Are the early Fathers therefore the first theologians? Is classical Greece the godparent of Christian theology?" he asks rhetorically. "The New Testament scholar may be permitted to ask what price we should have to pay and what gamble we should embark upon if, as theologians, we were to become heirs of Greek thinking in our systematics."[9]

Although the role assigned by Käsemann to the prophets in early Jewish Christianity cannot be sustained because the sayings attributed to them from the gospel tradition are not identifiable as prophetic utterances,[10] his thesis that the prophets were the first theologians receives support from Paul's understanding and practice of prophetic speech. A qualifying difference is that for Käsemann the utterances he identifies as prophetic represent the earliest formulations of the kerygma rather than expositions of the formulated kerygma. Paul's view is that the kerygmatic tradition is a given, the common ground of all who preach the gospel (1 Cor. 15:11). In this regard, it must be recognized that the tradition cited by Paul includes interpretation of the events attested: "Christ died *for our sins* according to the scriptures"; "he was raised *on the third day* according to the scriptures" (15:3b, 4b). It is arguable that this statement of the kerygma represents the mode of

---

8. Ernst Käsemann, *Exegetische Versuche und Besinnungen* (1960), I, 268.
9. Käsemann, *New Testament Questions,* 115 n. 8.
10. See the discussion in the Introduction, pages 11-17 above.

CONCLUSION

discourse that Funk terms "re-flective" discourse or "primordial interpretation." As he explains (depending upon Heidegger):

> Primordial interpretation, according to Heidegger, grasps things in a totality of reference-relations, it reaches out into a totality of involvements, without fragmenting that totality in discrete or isolable points. Things understood in this structure are understood *as* something only in relation to this circumspective totality.[11]

On these terms the cited kerygmatic tradition grasps the death, burial, resurrection, and appearances of Christ in that "totality of reference-relations," that "totality of involvements," located in the Scriptures. Christ is understood in this structure *as* the atoning sacrifice, *as* the new creation, in Scriptural terms.

If Paul's claim that he received his gospel "not from a human source" but "through a revelation of Jesus Christ" (Gal. 1:12) represents an event of primordial interpretation, then the kerygma itself is the result of revelation. This would explain why the apostle is able to say without contradiction that he was not "taught" his message and that he "delivered" to the Corinthians what he also "received" in the form of tradition (1 Cor. 15:3a). His point is that he, as an apostle, received his primordial interpretation of Christ directly from Christ, and is thus at one with all the apostles in the received tradition that "re-flects" the reality attested. It seems appropriate, however, not to designate this primordial interpretation as theology. For theology entails reflection, first as primary reflectivity upon the fate of the re-flective language of the kerygma, and then as secondary reflectivity upon the prophetic interpretations of the kerygma. With these distinctions and qualifications, the early Christian prophets may be identified as the first theologians of the church.

Criteria of the Spirit

The second issue raised by Ebeling in his criticism of Käsemann's proposal is the dogmatic problem of the discernment of legitimate interpretation. Käsemann himself focused the issue early in his essay when he wrote:

11. Funk, *Language*, 231.

> I propose to illustrate by the help of a few examples the way in which the history lying behind our Gospels was filled with very severe theological tensions; how it contains the experience of something very like a confessional controversy; and how the opposing camps both boasted of their own possession of the Spirit and also measured the adversary (and found him wanting) by certain criteria of the Spirit.[12]

In Käsemann's reconstruction of the internecine conflict he sees reflected in Matthew's Gospel, prophetic word is pitted against prophetic word, inspiration against inspiration, spirit against spirit.[13] Moreover, the divisive issue is theological. "It is not enthusiasm as such, but the stamp of different theologies, which is already dividing primitive Christianity into opposing confessional camps with a degree of sharpness that is not to be minimized. Both groups are fundamentally and totally determined by their theology, they stand and fall with it."[14]

Even if Käsemann's reconstruction of early Jewish Christianity from the Matthean Gospel is purely hypothetical, his description of the perceived conflict is directly applicable to the situation reflected in 1 Corinthians. What separates the apostle from the Corinthian enthusiasts is fundamentally the issue of eschatology, as Käsemann notes elsewhere.[15] In their position is reflected Hellenistic enthusiasm's radical interpretation of the baptismal statement that the redeemed are risen with Christ and enthroned with him in the heavenly state.

> Expectation of an imminent Parousia thus ceases to be meaningful because everything which apocalyptic still hopes for has already been realized.[16]

Although Paul's own theological posture is "a compromise" between present and future eschatology, he remains "unable to adopt their basic premise that the Christian participates not only in the Cross, but also in the Resurrection of his Lord." Viewed through the eyes of his Corinthian adversaries, Paul's theology appears as "a retarding, more, a reactionary stage of development."[17]

---

12. Käsemann, *New Testament Questions*, 83.
13. *Ibid.*, 87.
14. *Ibid.*, 89.
15. *Ibid.*, 130-37.
16. *Ibid.*, 130-31.
17. *Ibid.*, 132.

CONCLUSION

Ebeling wants to know how the theological task is to be conducted amidst such controversy. An appeal to the kerygma is fruitless because it is a manifold interpretation from the start and therefore in need of interpretation. Even if *the* kerygma could be discovered, which Ebeling rules out in principle rather than as an historical accident, it would yet be "a controversial linguistic event wide open to confessional debate."[18] Käsemann, in his reply, agrees "that this one kerygma beyond all interpretations never identifiably existed and never can."

> But we are also agreed that nevertheless there is this one kerygma, which I should call the Gospel, at once the heart and criterion of all the variations of preaching and interpretation; thus certain forms of preaching and theological statement can be shown to be particularly adequate, others to be thoroughly inappropriate.[19]

How it can be affirmed that "there is this one kerygma" and that it "never identifiably existed and never can," Käsemann does not explain. Yet, whether or not the tradition cited by Paul in 1 Corinthians 15:3-8 is *the* kerygma in the sense denied by Ebeling and Käsemann, it is evident from chapter 15 that the formula is capable of a Corinthian and a Pauline interpretation. Ebeling's point is thereby scored. The question, however, is whether the kerygma alone is the only possible criterion of the legitimacy of prophetic discourse.

In making the case for his interpretation of "[Christ] was raised on the third day according to the scriptures," Paul cites the kerygma under the assumption that its authority is not questioned in Corinth. At the same time he grounds his argument elsewhere. His hermeneutical appeal is founded fundamentally upon the revelation of the "mystery" given by the Spirit through insight into the eschatological implications of Isaiah 25:8 and Hosea 13:14 (vv. 51-55). Moreover, these two texts illumine not only the kerygmatic formula (v. 4b) but equally the messianic promises heard in Psalms 110:1 and 8:6 (vv. 25, 27). More than any other passage, Käsemann contends, 15:20-28 lays bare "the dominant motif of Paul's theology of the Resurrection." He continues:

---

18. Ebeling, "The Ground of Christian Theology," 49 n. 4: "*The* kerygma, in the sense of the true original form of the kerygma in comparison to which all traditional kerygmatic formulations would only be secondary interpretations, never existed."

19. Käsemann, *New Testament Questions*, 115 n. 8.

The apostle is here proclaiming the certainty of our resurrection, but he does it noticeably in such a way as to set the anthropological hope from the beginning in a wider context. The content of the Resurrection is primarily not anthropological at all, but christological. It is the work of the Second Adam and therefore its meaning is not immediately and primarily our re-animation, but the lordship of Christ. "Christ must reign": that is the nerve centre of the design and the firm ground which gives us confidence concerning our own destiny.[20]

Clearly, Paul is here interpreting not the *kerygma* as such but the *confession* of the church that "Jesus is Lord" (1 Cor. 12:3).

Psalm 110:1 spells out the meaning of the confession: "The Lord says to my Lord, 'Sit at my right hand, till I make your enemies your footstool." Reading "enemies" in terms of the subjection of "all things" in Psalm 8:6, Paul infers that "Jesus is Lord" entails his reigning "until" *(achri)* he has put all his enemies under his feet (v. 25). The inclusion of death as "the last enemy" is based upon the eschatological vision of Isaiah 25:8 and Hosea 13:14 (vv. 51-55). Thus the inaugurated but as yet unfulfilled messianic reign is of divine necessity *(dei)* and thus mandated by scripture. But the horizon of the passage is not christological but *theological*. For at "the end," having destroyed "every rule, and every authority and power" (v. 24), Christ the Lord will deliver the kingdom to God the Father (v. 24) so that "God may be all in all" (v. 28). As J. Lambrecht puts it, "The end is decidedly theocentric."[21]

Paul's interpretation of the kerygma is thus grounded upon a revelation, derived mediately from Scripture (Isa. 25:8; Hos. 13:14), that interprets Scripture (Pss. 110:1; 8:6) and thereby illumines the confession (1 Cor. 12:3). Conversely, the confession makes possible the application of the Psalm texts to Jesus. Their vision of the subjection of the Messiah's "enemies" invites the inclusion of God's eschatological defeat of death as attested by Isaiah and Hosea. The revelation of the "mystery" of God's victory interprets the significance of the kerygma in its affirmation that "[Christ] was raised on the third day according to the scriptures." The apostle's appeal to revelation entails, therefore, three interacting and mutually interpreting criteria: the kerygma, the Scriptures, and the confession. These three perspectives give Paul a "fix" on

---

20. *Ibid.*, 133.
21. J. Lambrecht, "Paul's Christological Use of Scripture in 1 Cor. 15.20-28," *NTS* 28 (1982): 511.

the *reality* proclaimed by the kerygma, attested by the Scriptures, and confessed by the church, namely, the crucified and risen Christ himself who reigns by God, for God, and to God. The distinction between this reality and its linguistic attestation in kerygma, Scripture, and confession must now be clarified by way of further consideration of Paul's understanding of the gospel.

A Rhetoric of Glory

Paul speaks frequently in his letters of "the gospel of Christ" (*to euangelion tou Christou*; Rom. 15:19; 1 Cor. 9:12; 2 Cor. 2:12; 9:13; 10:14; Gal. 1:7; Phil. 1:27; 1 Thess. 3:2; cf. Rom. 1:9; 2 Cor. 4:4). The ambiguity of the genitive construction, which grammatically can be objective (the gospel about Christ) or subjective (Christ's gospel), cannot be overcome on purely formal grounds. Exegetical decisions on this point thus commonly serve dogmatic interests.[22] In view of Paul's apparent usage of both nuances, however, it is best to leave the tension unresolved and to recognize in the ambiguous phrase an inherent dialectic in the apostle's conception of the gospel.

An instance of both emphases in the same context is found in 2 Corinthians 4:4-6. Paul's explicit statement in verse 5 that "we preach not ourselves but Jesus Christ [as] Lord" makes it clear that the gospel has both an objective and specifiable content (cf. 1 Cor. 1:22; Gal. 1:16; Rom. 1, 3).[23] Here it may be noted that the objective content of the kerygma and of the confession (1 Cor. 12:3) coalesce linguistically. But what is meant by their *objective content*?

Paul Ricoeur's analysis of human discourse provides an answer to the question. To begin with, his claim that "discourse is *the* event of language" may be restated as "the gospel is the event in its proclamation." The basic unit of discourse is the sentence, according to Ricoeur, which

---

22. Stuhlmacher, *Das paulinische Evangelium*, I, 207-8, provides a brief sketch of the exegetical line by which the subjective genitive option has come into prominence, largely out of a dogmatic interest in preserving the continuity between the earthly Jesus who came preaching and the exalted Christ who still speaks through the message of his apostles as the active subject.

23. Gerhard Friedrich, *"euangelion," TDNT* II, 731, concludes: "If we were to sum up the content of the Gospel in a single word, it would be Jesus the Christ."

is identified as "the propositional content, the 'said as such.'"[24] What is asserted in Paul's brief summary of his preaching is that "Jesus [the] Christ [is] Lord." Such a proposition is conceived by Ricoeur as "the object of the speech event."[25] Also called the *meaning* of discourse, it has a *noetic* (psychic) source in the intellectual intention of the speaker or author and a *noematic* (mental or ideal) status as the objective expression of that intention.[26] For Ricoeur, however, the meaning of discourse is constituted by its *sense* and its *reference,* expressed as the "what" and "about what" of the "said as such." His explanation of this distinction may be stated with reference to the kerygma and confession:

> Whereas the sense is immanent to the discourse, and objective in the sense of ideal, the reference expresses the movement in which language transcends itself. In other words, the sense correlates the identification function [Jesus] and the predicative function [is Lord] within the sentence [kerygma or confession], and the reference relates language to the world [the reality of the Lord Jesus]. It is another name for discourse's claim to be true.[27]

This distinction between the sense and reference of discourse is entailed in the objective sense of Paul's phrase "the gospel of Christ." It characterizes also the discourse represented by the kerygma, the Scriptures, and the confession. It is in fact their respective references to a common object that establishes their criteriological value in judging the legitimacy of the preaching of the gospel and prophetic utterance. Thus Schütz is correct when he insists that the gospel has "*its point of gravity . . . somewhere outside the sum total of its content.*"[28]

For Paul the referential object of gospel proclamation (Jesus Christ) is also the active subject in the preaching that refers to him. It is this point that is scored by the subjective sense of "the gospel of Christ" in the expanded version of this phrase in 2 Corinthians 4:4. When Paul speaks here of "the light of the gospel of the glory of Christ," he attests that the object of the gospel is a transcendent reality present *in* the

---

24. Paul Ricoeur, *Interpretation Theory: Discourse and the Surplus of Meaning* (1976), 9.
25. Ibid., 11.
26. Ibid., 12.
27. Ibid., 20.
28. Schütz, *Paul and Apostolic Authority,* 42-43 (emphasis added).

proclamation rather than merely an immanent ideality *of* the message. The concatenation of genitives in the phrase may be rendered either as "the light emanating from the gospel which is characterized by 'glory' and 'Christ'" or "the light emanating from the gospel which consists in 'glory' that *is* 'Christ,'" who is the "image *(eikōn)* of God."[29] The second reading properly identifies "Christ's glory" as the gospel's *content*,[30] and for this reason is preferable. The preaching of the gospel is thus designated as the locus of a Christophany.

Within the argument of 2 Corinthians 3:3–4:6, the phrase also relates "Christ's glory" to the theophanic manifestations of glory narrated in the scriptures by contrasting it with the glory revealed to Moses in the giving of the Law (3:7). Reflected for a time in the face of Moses, the appearance of that glory ceased *(katargein;* 3:7, 11, 13) while the glory of Christ "endures" *(menein;* 3:11). The glory revealed to Moses attended the giving of the "old covenant" (3:14), which inaugurated "the ministry of death, chiseled in letters on stone tablets" (3:7), or "the ministry of condemnation" (3:9). Christ's glory accompanies the giving of a "new covenant" (3:6) that is characterized as "the ministry of the Spirit" (3:8) or "the ministry of righteousness" (3:9). By contrasting the two covenants, Paul demonstrates the superiority of Christ's glory to that revealed to Moses *and* its connection with the scriptural narrative of God's past revelatory activity. As Newman puts it, "Paul not only employs Glory to tether analeptically his foundational story to the long Jewish narrative of salvation, he also employs Glory as an important 'sign' *within* the foundational story itself."[31]

Paul's emphasis upon the active presence of Christ's glory manifesting itself in the proclamation of the gospel thus signals that the grammatical dialectic in the objective and subjective nuances of "the gospel of Christ" reflects an ontological dialectic of the *being* of Jesus Christ and the *language* of the proclamation in and through which he manifests himself.[32] Only when this point is fully considered is it appropriate to speak of the *content* of Paul's gospel at all. What is required,

---

29. Carey C. Newman, *Paul's Glory-Christology: Tradition and Rhetoric* (1992), 220.

30. Funk, *Grammar,* par. 168 (2).

31. Newman, *Paul's Glory-Christology,* 218.

32. Stuhlmacher, *Das paulinische Evangelium,* I, 80, designates Paul's gospel as the spatial, temporal "word room" *(Wort-Raum)* in which Christ is present to humans.

in Gadamerian terms, is recognition of the priority of the *Sache* (subject matter) over the *Sprache* (language) in their dialectical relationship.[33] What is said in the proclamation of the gospel, in other words, is called forth by the reality of Jesus Christ, conforms to his reality, and thus re-flects his glory. How this dialectic impacts the issue of legitimizing prophetic speech may now be considered.

How It Played in Corinth

The criteriological issue in early Christian prophecy may be illustrated by Wire's exposition of 1 Corinthians 15,[34] in which she reads the text in terms of an imagined Corinthian response to it from their *realized* resurrection perspective. Because her own sympathies lie with the apostle's opponents in Corinth, who are identified primarily but not exclusively as the *women* prophets, it is unimportant that Wire's views and those of the Corinthians are not always distinguishable. For our purposes, the discussion may be limited to the role played by the kerygma, confession, and Scripture as criteria of prophetic utterance in her hypothetical and provocative reconstruction.

With regard to the *kerygmatic tradition* cited in verses 3b-8,[35] Wire thinks it cannot represent a "fixed creed" because Paul feels free to adapt it to his own purpose. That purpose is to "validate past events," particularly the appearances of Christ, in order to establish Paul's experience "not as one among other evidences of the spirit but as the closing event in a resurrection canon." It is "probable," Wire argues, that the women prophets would not honor Paul's claim to be the *last* of the resurrection

---

33. Hans-Georg Gadamer, *Truth and Method* (1975), 386, argues that this priority begins with the formation of the word. Following with approval Thomas Aquinas, he explains: "In thinking, a person does not move forward from the one thing to the other, from thinking to speaking to himself. The word does not emerge in a sphere of the mind that is still free of thought *(in aliquo sui nudo)*. Hence the appearance is created that the formation of the word arises from the movement of the mind towards itself. In fact no reflective process operates when the word is formed, for the word is not expressing the mind, but the intended object *(Sache)*. The starting-point for the formation of the word is the intelligible object . . . that fills the mind."

34. Wire, *The Corinthian Women Prophets*, 159-76.

35. Ibid., 160-63.

CONCLUSION

witnesses because "they themselves know the living Christ in the spirit." Indeed, his claim would have been heard "as a denial that Corinthian spiritual experience can be a primary source for knowledge of the risen Christ." At issue is what counts as a resurrection appearance. Wire concedes that the prophets "may not think of their experiences as resurrection appearances strictly in Paul's sense," but this is immaterial because "it is Paul's interest, not theirs, to make resurrection appearances function as a list to validate past events." Wire explains:

> They expect to see Christ themselves, or to hear Christ in their own speaking, to know Christ is alive because they are living a new identity in Christ that they have not lived before. If they do not say that "he appeared" to them, it would only be because their experience of Christ's rising is broader than this term Paul chooses from apocalyptic and Christian tradition to establish these validating past events.[36]

Thus the cited kerygma "means that their present experience and communication of the risen Christ are being challenged by another gospel based strictly on the witness of certain male apostles and a single large group." This other gospel, Wire concludes, "is restricted to the claim that Jesus was once alive in the early days — or in Paul's case, years — after his resurrection."[37]

The topic of *confessional* formulas and their role in the Corinthian response to Paul's argument in chapter 15 is evident in Wire's reconstruction of their view of baptism.[38] There are three discernible baptism traditions at work in Corinth, one of which associates baptism with water and the receiving of the Spirit. It is thus the experience of the Spirit that connects baptism and confession among the Corinthian prophets. As Wire explains the relation of the Spirit to the confession in an earlier comment on 1 Corinthians 12:3, Paul "presents 'Jesus is Lord,' not as a required formula, but as an acclamation of the spirit." This "tight identification" of the phrase with the Spirit of God "suggests that the Corinthians' attention is on the freedom and creativity of the spirit in them, not this lowest common denominator — in which the spirit is confined to words of uniformity and subordination."[39] This

36. *Ibid.*, 161.
37. *Ibid.*, 163.
38. *Ibid.*, 167-68.
39. *Ibid.*, 136.

reduction of a christological statement about Jesus to an anthropological account of spiritual experience typifies the Corinthian attitude toward confessional traditions.

Wire argues that "there is considerable indirect evidence that the Corinthians take their baptism to be a death and resurrection with Christ,"[40] another of the baptism traditions which shape Corinthian sacramental sensibilities. Thus in response to Paul's argument in verses 20-28, the Corinthian prophets "would probably not" accept the designation of Christ as "first fruit" of the dead (v. 20). "Their confession about Christ's dying and rising might be spoken in terms of his impact on the living, in images signifying not an outstanding promise but some kind of present fulfillment, not first fruit but harvest."[41] Similarly Paul's statement "as in Adam all die, so in Christ all will be made alive" (v. 22) places a temporal restriction upon Christ's power to make alive and possibly explains "why the Corinthians might deny the resurrection of the dead."

> Here [the restriction] functions to make death . . . the entry to life in Christ and meanwhile leaves them as good as dead in Adam, dependent on the indirect word of certain early witnesses that Jesus was once raised and therefore has become the first fruit assuring resurrection of the dead. They will not give up their claim that the decisive transformation has already [!] taken place in Christ and that they are fully alive.[42]

For the Corinthian prophets, the event of being made alive occurs in baptism and they *now* "confess Christ or speak in the Spirit, not after death."[43] The question is whether the Corinthians are here drawing upon a particular baptismal tradition and confession as a basis or a warrant for their *spiritual experience*.[44] Wire's comment on the confession "Jesus is Lord" (12:3) suggests that the latter is the case.

Wire also recognizes that the *Scriptures* play a role in the position of the prophets in Corinth. This issue is addressed in her discussion of

---

40. *Ibid.*, 168.
41. *Ibid.*, 165.
42. *Ibid.*
43. *Ibid.*, 166.
44. Wire, *ibid.*, 167-68, identifies the third tradition of baptism present in Corinth as that which interprets baptism as a "putting off of the old humanity" and "putting on Christ."

Paul's argument in verses 45-47, which turns on Genesis 2:7. With Pearson and others, she perceives that Paul is here "seeking to reverse a Platonizing exegesis of Genesis in Corinth, one developed under the influence of Hellenistic-Jewish wisdom" as represented by Philo Judaeus and the Wisdom of Solomon.[45] The active presence of such an exegetical tradition in Corinth creates the expectation that the apostle's other scriptural arguments in chapter 15 might be dealt with seriously in Wire's imagined scenario. For this reason her treatment of the Psalm texts (vv. 25, 27) and the prophetic texts (vv. 54-55) is disappointing. Paul's reference to Psalms 110:1 and 8:6 in support of his claim that Christ is the first fruit of the dead (v. 20) is passed over as an appeal to "the authority of two psalms" for the "military" description of Christ's victory over all his enemies.[46] Similarly the significance of Paul's citation of Isaiah 25:8 (v. 54) is reduced to the notation that "the cry of victory over death, spoken by Isaiah in the future tense and apparently claimed by believers as an accomplished fact in the past, is again thrown into the future by Paul's introduction."[47] The remark does suggest that despite the exegetical tradition in Corinth, it is Wire's view that the prophets were accustomed to reading Scripture in the light of their own spiritual experience.

In Wire's bold reconstruction of the Corinthian response to the apostolic argument of chapter 15, therefore, the clash of experience with tradition is sharply presented. The prophets in Corinth view the *kerygma* as a relic that validates past events in the interest of grounding hope for the future. The *confession* of Jesus as Lord is assessed as a "lowest common denominator" which confines the Spirit "to words of uniformity and subordination." And the *Scriptures,* though read, receive their meaning from the experience of the Spirit that the Corinthians bring to them. It could be argued, accordingly, that for Wire's Corinthian prophets the only criterion of the Spirit is the experience of the Spirit itself (speaking in tongues?). If such is the case, then it is "the pneumatic who becomes the subject of theology" in Corinth, as Conzelmann puts it.[48]

---

45. *Ibid.,* 171.
46. *Ibid.,* 165.
47. *Ibid.,* 173.
48. Conzelmann, *Theology of the New Testament,* 259.

Resurrection and Death

Wire's imagined response of the Corinthian pneumatics to the argument of 1 Corinthians 15 is clearly tendentious. For not even a Corinthian prophet could be aware of what Paul says about the Spirit's work in chapter 12 and claim with a straight face that the apostle denies the validity and value of the community's experience of the Spirit or that he restricts the renewing power of Christ to the future beyond death. Discernment and discipline of the Spirit's activity in the congregation is equivalent to its denial only to a fanatic. To suggest that "Paul reduces the gospel to proof that Jesus was alive shortly after his death, which guarantees resurrection beyond the grave and vindication of sacrificial work," as Wire does,[49] is to obfuscate the issue that divides Paul and the prophets in Corinth. That issue is whether experiences of the Spirit may be equated with the "appearances" of Christ, and whether the renewal of human life effected by the Spirit and associated with baptism is equivalent to the resurrection of the dead. Paul's answer to both questions is No.

The criteriological significance of Paul's rhetoric of glory for this dispute is that the reality of the risen Christ determines our understanding of both his past resurrection and the future resurrection of the dead. The apostle connects the motifs of resurrection and glory in Romans 6:4, which stipulates that "Christ was raised from the dead by the glory of the Father." More to the point of the dispute, Paul asserts in Philippians 3:21 that, in the eschatological transformation, our bodies will be "conformed to the body of his glory" *(tō sōmati tēs doxēs autou)*. The basis of this claim is Christ himself who "appeared" to Paul and other witnesses in the immediate post-resurrection period (1 Cor. 15:5-8). The apostle is compelled to speak of the resurrection in terms of a "glorious body" or a "spiritual body" (15:44) because that language is required by the reality manifested to him. The purpose of his citing witnesses to these resurrection "appearances" is not to prove "that Jesus was alive shortly after his death" but to attest to the *result* of that event and thus ground the discussion of the resurrection in the given nature of Christ's "glorified" or "spiritual body."

If the Corinthian prophets identified or equated their experiences of the Spirit with the appearances of the risen Christ, as Wire suggests, then

---

49. Wire, *The Corinthian Women Prophets*, 175.

CONCLUSION

they would indeed have heard the appeal to the tradition as a challenge to their position. It is not the tradition *per se* that calls into question their understanding, however, but the *reality* witnessed in the appearances and attested by the tradition. That the risen Christ is present to believers in the Spirit is explicitly affirmed by Paul, as Goppelt points out:

> "The Spirit of God" is in you, "the Spirit of Christ" is in you, "Christ" is in you; these words were written side by side in Rom. 8:9-11 as synonyms. The Spirit was the "Spirit of the Son" (Gal. 4:6) and the "Spirit of the Lord" (II Cor. 3:18) not simply because it was his gift (Acts 2:33) but because this One offered himself in the Spirit. . . .[50]

But Goppelt immediately emphasizes that even the statement "the Lord is the Spirit" (2 Cor. 3:17) "does not wish to equate the exalted One with the Spirit but to interpret the work of the Spirit christologically; the exalted One was at work through the Spirit and therefore was at work as the Spirit within man."[51] It is thus possible for the apostle to attribute authentic prophetic words to the Spirit (1 Cor. 12:10) and to declare that the "glory of Christ" is manifest in the proclamation of the gospel (2 Cor. 4:4). But the *mode* of christological presence in these instances is not that of the appearances, and it is the latter rather than the former which determines the nature of Christ's resurrection from the dead as well as "those who belong to Christ" (15:23).

That resurrection entails the dead rather than the living is also certified by the kerygmatic tradition cited by Paul. He who "was raised" is the same one who "died" and "was buried." It may be that the Corinthians lacked "preoccupation" with death, as Wire suggests,[52] and that they believed "life in Christ is generative and creative so that death is not defeated by capture and destruction of an evil life-force but death's weakness and pain are overpowered with health and life."[53] Paul's answer to such naivete is that death is not weak and its pain is universal. For "in Adam all die" (v. 22). That means, as Conzelmann points up, that death "affects *us*" in that it "annihilates us."[54] The focal issue in

---

50. Leonhard Goppelt, *Theology of the New Testament,* trans. John E. Alsup, ed. Jürgen Roloff, 2 vols. (Grand Rapids: Wm. B. Eerdmans, 1981-1982), II, 121.
51. *Ibid.,* 121-22.
52. Wire, *The Corinthian Women Prophets,* 164.
53. *Ibid.,* 176.
54. Conzelmann, *Theology of the New Testament,* 281.

1 Corinthians is death itself, De Boer insists, because for Paul it is "not merely a medical or empirical fact without any theological import, but the dualistic antithesis of the eschatological *zōē* [life] promised in the gospel." He explains:

> Death has this meaning for Paul precisely in the light of the fact that the exalted Christ embraced by both him and the Corinthians *has been raised from the dead*. In short, Paul makes physical death into a 'problem' for the Corinthians, a cosmic problem that can and must be perceived as such in view of the cosmic 'solution', the resurrected Christ who is the first-fruits of those who have fallen asleep.[55]

Thus it is the objective reality of the risen Christ and of death, both attested in the kerygma, that compels Paul to interpret the church's confession "Jesus is Lord" in the light of Psalms 110:1 and 8:6 as a christological interregnum. Likewise, the promised victory of the Messiah over "all his enemies" includes death on the basis of its eschatological destruction foretold by Isaiah and Hosea. When death is vanquished at "the end" (vv. 24-26), then "the kingdom of God" is established under conditions of immortality (v. 50).

A "Corinthian theology" ensues, Beker observes, whenever "the Spirit is fused with the kingdom of God." He means that the Corinthian pneumatics understood their experience of the Spirit as "the complete presence of the kingdom of God," thus compelling Paul to interpret the Spirit in a way that distinguishes it from God's kingdom without "relaxing" or "fusing" their dynamic relationship.[56] The apostle achieves this by locating the Spirit's activity temporally between Christ's resurrection and the defeat of death. This temporal qualification allows him to speak of the "first fruit" *(aparchē)* of the Spirit (Rom. 8:23) and to see in such gifts the "guarantee" *(arrabōn)* of the eschatological swallowing up of mortality by life (2 Cor. 5:5).

On these terms the apostle would not deny that "spiritual experience can be a primary source for knowledge of the risen Christ," only that such experience can define the nature of the resurrection. Neither would Paul claim that the kerygmatic tradition "validates" the past events it attests, only that the confirming witness of the Spirit is tethered to those attested events. Nor would he think of the church's confession

---

55. De Boer, *The Defeat of Death*, 114.
56. Beker, *The Triumph of God*, 94.

"Jesus is Lord" as "a required formula" that confines the Spirit "to words of uniformity," although he would "subordinate" the Spirit to the lordship of Jesus as interpreted by the Scriptures. Because the Spirit is for Paul the source of the church's kerygma, confession, and Scriptures, it may be discerned and validated by the joint testimony of these three criteria to the reality of the risen Christ who transcends their interacting witness to him. On the basis of these criteria, Paul denies that the experience of the Spirit is the equivalent of Christ's resurrection appearances and that baptismal renewal effects the resurrection of the living. The question is whether the validity of his argument depends, as Beker phrases it, "on making an apocalyptic worldview essential to the truth of the gospel."[57]

An Apocalyptic Theology

Käsemann contends that in Corinth "the anti-enthusiastic battle is waged by the apostle under the sign of apocalyptic."[58] More specifically, "I Cor. 15 shows that what is at stake is a fundamentally different theological conception which enables Paul to remain true at this point to the apocalyptic tradition."[59] In these two statements are focused issues that continue to resist convincing resolution. What is "the sign of apocalyptic"? What constitutes "the apocalyptic tradition"? And, more importantly, what is the "theological conception" generated by this apocalyptic tradition which is "fundamentally different" from that represented by the enthusiasm of the Corinthian prophets? Addressing these issues is like approaching a black hole in which all light is swallowed up by the density of the matter.[60]

John Collins marks out the limited areas of consensus on apocalypticism among scholars: (1) "widespread agreement" that "a distinction should be made between the literary genre apocalypse and the

57. Ibid., 78.
58. Käsemann, *New Testament Questions*, 132.
59. Ibid., 133.
60. For a survey of the research up to 1972, see Klaus Koch, *The Rediscovery of Apocalyptic* (1972). The discussion is updated by Richard E. Sturm, "Defining the Word 'Apocalyptic': A Problem in Biblical Criticism," *Apocalyptic and the New Testament*, Joel Marcus and Marion L. Soards, eds. (1989), 17-48.

wider, looser categories of 'apocalyptic' or 'apocalypticism'"; (2) "general agreement" on the relevant literary corpus; and (3) accord that the "primary distinguishing feature" of the genre is its material dependence upon revelation.[61] The basic problem, as Collins sees it, "lies in the propensity of scholars to select some feature of an apocalyptic writing that happens to interest them, and arbitrarily declare it to be the essence of 'apocalyptic' or apocalypticism."[62] In this regard Collins is particularly critical of those who, like Käsemann, have focused on apocalyptic as a *theological concept* without regard to genre issues.[63] The advantage of this point of view, he sardonically concedes, is that it is "not constrained by the evidence of the ancient apocalyptic literature" and allows the theologian to define apocalyptic "in whatever way is most convenient for the explication of Jesus or Paul." Collins's criticism is valid so far as the methodological issue is concerned: "There can be no consensus in the definition of a term such as 'apocalyptic' unless we accept the constraints of a specific body of evidence." But it loses much of its constraining force when he refers the term "first and foremost to *the kind of material* found in apocalypses."[64] For the inference seems warranted that theological themes and concepts found in some of the apocalypses need not be characteristic of them all in order to qualify as apocalyptic in origin and nature.

Now in fairness to Käsemann, it must be acknowledged that his interest in apocalyptic focuses upon a few theological themes that do appear in certain apocalypses and the New Testament. In "The Beginnings of Christian Theology," for example, he speaks of "one or two characteristic apocalyptic themes as forming the real beginning of primitive Christian theology."[65] And in the sequel, "Primitive Christian Apocalyptic," his concern is once again for "a first Christian theology constructed with distinctively apocalyptic themes."[66] The two themes of particular importance that Käsemann identifies are the near expec-

---

61. John H. Collins, "Genre, Ideology and Social Movements in Jewish Apocalypticism," in *Mysteries and Revelations: Apocalyptic Studies since the Uppsala Colloquium*, John J. Collins and James H. Charlesworth, eds. (1991), 11-32.
62. *Ibid.*, 12.
63. *Ibid.*, 12-13, citing the advocacy of this approach by Sturm, "Defining the Word 'Apocalyptic,'" 37.
64. *Ibid.*, 13 (emphasis added).
65. Käsemann, *New Testament Questions*, 102.
66. *Ibid.*, 120.

CONCLUSION

tation of Christ's return[67] and God's sovereignty. Although the first collapsed under the weight of its non-fulfillment, the second is perennial and thus foundational. As Käsemann formulates it, "The heart of primitive Christian apocalyptic . . . is the ascension to the throne of heaven by God and by his Christ as the eschatological Son of Man — an event which can also be characterized as proof of the righteousness of God."[68]

That this represents a Christian version of a Jewish apocalyptic theme is attested by Klaus Koch, who writes:

> The transition from disaster to final redemption is expected to take place by means of an act issuing from *the throne of God*. For this purpose God will solemnly ascend his throne or even permit that throne to be ascended by the Son of man. . . . This final ascent of the throne is a relatively old idea, which can already be demonstrated at the pre-apocalyptic stage in Isaiah 24.23; it can be explained by the fact that the throne is viewed as the indispensable foundation of sovereignty.[69]

Käsemann recognizes this theme of divine sovereignty as the issue addressed by Paul in 1 Corinthians 15:20-28. Here the realized eschatology of the Corinthian enthusiasts is picked up by Paul, but "apocalyptically anchored and delimited as it is not with them" by "the *basileia Christi*."[70] From this Käsemann concludes, "The apocalyptic question 'To whom does the sovereignty of the world belong?' stands behind the Resurrection theology of the apostle."[71] The "fundamentally different theological conception" that divides the apostle and the Corinthian prophets turns out to be a theological issue of *pre-apocalyptic* origin and, it must be added, *post-apocalyptic* significance. The abiding apocalyptic theme is the theological question, Who is God in relation to the world?

Wire perceptively recognizes that it is the identity of God that is at issue in Paul's Corinthian controversy. For her it centers on the theme of "subordination." With reference to 1 Corinthians 14:34, Wire comments:

---

67. *Ibid.*, 109 n. *: "I speak of primitive Christian apocalyptic to denote the expectation of an imminent Parousia."
68. *Ibid.*, 105.
69. Koch, *The Rediscovery of Apocalyptic*, 31.
70. Käsemann, *New Testament Questions*, 133.
71. *Ibid.*, 135-36.

There Paul also appeals to God's nature to justify subordination among the prophets, 'for God is not a God of disruption but of peace' (14:32-33). A God of disruption in this context seems to imply a God who fosters the tensions involved in broad communal participation, a God of zeal (12:31; 14:1, 12, 39). In contrast, Paul stresses a communal life of 'decency and order' (14:40) and a future with each event 'in its order' (15:23). In Corinth, Paul's God might be described as a God of peace and order.[72]

The God of the Corinthians, conversely, "would not be reserving and assigning at all, but would give all gifts immediately and across every boundary to the joyful disruption of their common life."[73] Again, the God of the women prophets in Corinth "is not identified with peace and order, withholding life until some proper sequence of events occurs, but God is identified with disruption that overwhelms the structures that ossify life."[74] Most objectionable of all for Wire, however, is that Paul's argument in verses 20-28 "envisions the consummation of Christ's 'making alive' as Christ's own subjection to God, thereby exalting such subordination as the highest possible act for a human being, and defining God in terms of exclusive and isolated power over all things."[75] Thus if the God whom Paul serves is the God of peace and order, the God of the Corinthians is the egalitarian God who shares his sovereignty with all. To paraphrase Mary Daly's well-known aphorism, "If God is a human, then the human is God." The divisive issue in Corinth is thus fundamentally neither anthropological nor pneumatological nor christological but *theological* in the basic sense of the term.

Israel's Resurrection God

When the kerygma declares of Christ that "he was raised" (1 Cor. 15:4), the "divine passive" of the verb implies God as the acting subject,[76] and the prepositional phrase "according to the scriptures" identifies the God

---

72. Wire, *Women Prophets*, 166.
73. *Ibid.*, 174.
74. *Ibid.*, 176.
75. *Ibid.*, 165-66.
76. Fee, *First Corinthians*, 726 n. 64.

CONCLUSION

implied. Thus the God whom Paul serves is the God of Israel's Scriptures, who is the God of the church's kerygma.

In his essay "Paul the Theologian," Ulrich Mauser states that when Paul reads Scripture he hears "the voice of the living God of Israel understood from the position given by the gospel of Jesus Christ."[77] Picking up on Jon Levenson's statement that "Talmud and Midrash do not present themselves as the teleological consummation of the Tanakh,"[78] Mauser suggests that Paul links the gospel of the new covenant with the Scriptures of the old precisely by this concept of "teleological consummation."[79] "All Old Testament theologies within the New Testament stand in awe of an event which upholds, completes, and surpasses the former words of God to Israel," he observes, but Paul is the first witness to this "teleological systematic of Scripture."[80] Thus, in his use of Scripture, "a powerful teleological drive is discernible" in such claims as the new covenant surpasses the old in splendor (2 Cor. 3:6-11), Christ is the end of the law (Rom. 10:4), and the gospel of God was promised beforehand by the prophets in the holy Scriptures (Rom. 1:2).

Mauser demonstrates that Paul's teleological reading of Scripture is particularly evident in his theological treatment of Adam, Abraham, and Moses. In regard to this, he observes, it is "striking how the teleological reading of those basic figures in the Old Testament is connected with the issues of God's singleness and universality," even though this is true in the case of Moses "in a significantly broken fashion." Thus "the oneness of God" is identified by Mauser as "the dominating center of Paul's understanding of Scripture."[81] This "monocracy of God" (1) entails "the distinct and separate personhood of an individual who is not to be confused with anybody else," and (2) "denotes at the same time the divine person whose rule embraces all of creation, and most particularly the totality of human history which, in the power of the one God, is one single history." The God of Paul, Mauser concludes, is the "person whose being is unique so that it cannot, and must not be confused with any other, but this single God is also in command of the

---

77. Ulrich Mauser, "Paul the Theologian," *HBT* 11 (1989): 92.

78. Jon D. Levenson, "Why Jews Are Not Interested in Biblical Theology," *Judaic Perspectives on Ancient Israel*, J. Neusner, B. A. Levine, and E. D. Fredrichs, eds. (1987), 286.

79. Mauser, "Paul the Theologian," 82-83.

80. *Ibid.*, 96.

81. *Ibid.*, 97.

totality of all creation, especially of human history from its inception to its destiny."[82]

The apocalyptic theme of divine sovereignty viewed from an eschatological perspective, therefore, is clearly rooted in the scriptural witness to the one God who orients the creation teleologically to the realization of his lordship. Thus the apocalyptic question "To whom does the sovereignty of the world belong?" stands behind not only the resurrection theology of Paul in 1 Corinthians 15, as Käsemann rightly claims, but also the apostle's scripturally dependent knowledge of God. The theme of God's eschatological victory over death as the last enemy in the establishment of his sovereignty over the creation may be rooted mediately in Jewish apocalyptic, but it is ultimately grounded in the God of Israel's Scriptures. God's sovereignty in relation to the creation is thus a genuine theological issue whether or not it is articulated in the language and conceptuality associated with apocalypticism. That is why Käsemann has reason to wonder "whether Christian theology can ever survive in any legitimate form without this theme."[83]

If Paul's understanding of who God is accords with the Scriptures (*kata tas graphas;* 1 Cor. 15:3b-4), then it is equally true that it is informed by that event "which upholds, completes, and surpasses the former words of God to Israel" — the one event of Jesus Christ attested by the kerygma. God is identified in the kerygma as the implied subject of "[Christ] was raised." The God of Israel's Scriptures is here denoted as the One who raised Jesus from the dead. Paul thus believes in the God of Abraham, but since the resurrection of Jesus the God of Abraham is known as the One "who gives life to the dead and calls into existence the things that do not exist" (Rom. 4:17).

Just as the reality of the risen Christ has ontological priority over the language of the gospel in Paul's rhetoric of glory, so also the knowledge of God is grounded in the being of God as mediated by Christ through the gospel. Paul states this explicitly in 2 Corinthians 4:6, "For it is the God who said, 'Let light shine *(phōs lampsei)* out of darkness,' who has shone in our hearts to give the light of the knowledge of the glory of God in the face of Jesus Christ" (4:6). The apostle here spells out the anthropological *result* of the kerygmatically mediated christophanies designated in verse 4. Only now "the light" which has its

---

82. *Ibid.*
83. Käsemann, *New Testament Questions,* 107.

CONCLUSION

medium in "the gospel" and its source in "Christ's glory" is designated "the knowledge of God's glory in the face of Jesus Christ."[84] The ultimate ground of the christophanic activity in the preaching of the gospel is thus the God whose image Jesus is.

Hays notes that the "apparent quotation in this passage is actually not a direct quotation from Scripture at all" but "a discursive supposition posited by Paul out of the intertextual matrix of Israel's Scripture."[85] Thus echoes of two foundational texts are evoked by the citation. One is "Let there be light" (Gen. 1:3a), which is suggested when Paul's verb *lampsei* is read as a third person imperative, "Let light shine." The other text comes to mind when the verb is translated as a future indicative, "Light will shine," thus echoing the prophetic promise of Isaiah:

> O people who walk in darkness,
>   behold a great light.
> You who dwell in a land and shadow of death,
>   light will shine *(phōs lampsei)* upon you." (9:1 LXX)

Hays concludes that "Paul's words, quoting neither of these texts but echoing both, fuse Israel's confession of God as creator with Israel's hope of a messianic deliverer, thereby implicitly declaring the present illumination of Paul's faith community to be the action of the God who is both creator and redeemer."[86]

The creator and redeemer God of Israel's Scriptures is the God whom Paul serves in the gospel of Jesus Christ. This teleological God orients creation sovereignly to its "end" (the kingdom of God). This resurrection God exercises sovereignty over death by raising Jesus from the dead to a life free from the conditions of mortality, thereby promising the same for all who belong to Jesus in the resurrection of the dead. Who God is and who is God are known through the preaching of the gospel. God's identity and sovereignty are respectively revealed and evidenced by the resurrection of Jesus, "according to the scriptures."

Beker's argument that "Jewish apocalyptic constitutes the sub-

---

84. Newman, *Paul's Glory-Christology*, 223: "Glory fits Jesus into a long line of God's appearances; Glory is now revealed in a person or a preached message about that person (rather than in tabernacle or temple); and like the apocalyptic writers, Paul affirms that a relationship with God can be established through 'knowing' Glory."
85. Hays, *Echoes of Scripture*, 152.
86. Ibid., 153.

stratum and master symbolism of Paul's thought" because "it constituted the language world of Paul the Pharisee" and therefore "forms the indispensable filter, context, and grammar by which Paul appropriated and interpreted the Christ-event" is both valid and misleading.[87] At the level of "substratum," it is an accurate historical description of the apocalyptic language and grammar Paul used to appropriate and interpret "the revelation of Jesus Christ" given to him. But the apocalyptic "language world" of the apostle is not constitutive of the reality "appropriated and interpreted" by Paul in his gospel. On the contrary, it is the reality of the God who raised Jesus from the dead that calls forth an interpretative response that requires the modification of the language and grammar of Jewish apocalyptic. Ebeling notes that neither the giving of the Spirit nor a single eschatological resurrection (Jesus) is typical of Jewish apocalyptic, and thus represent "an essential change" in its near expectation.[88] Thus it is evident that Paul was compelled to adapt his apocalyptic language and grammar to the reality revealed to him rather than the reverse, in accordance with his rhetoric of glory in which being has priority over saying. That Paul's "language world" was "indispensable" for *him* may be conceded, provided that historical and logical necessity are not confused. Alternative languages and grammars may be employed, with required modifications, in the interpretation of the reality attested in the kerygma.

Summation

Viewed through the window provided by 1 Corinthians, the conflict between the apostle and his opponents in Corinth over the issue of Spirit-inspired speech evidences a Pauline vision of Christian prophecy that is complex and sophisticated. The task of the prophets, as Paul understands it, is to explicate through divine revelation the implications, theological and behaviorial, of the apostolic kerygma (15:3b-8). This hermeneutical endeavor results in human understanding of "the gifts bestowed upon us by God" in Christ crucified and risen, as the Spirit reveals (2:10) "God's wisdom" (2:7) in "words taught by the Spirit,

---

87. Beker, *The Triumph of God*, 66.
88. Ebeling, "Ground of Christian Theology," 55.

interpreting spiritual things to those who are spiritual" (2:13). An example of such prophetic discourse is provided by chapter 15, in which Paul interprets the eschatological implications of the kerygmatic claim that Christ "was raised on the third day according to the scriptures" (v. 4). The source of his interpretation is the revelation of the "mystery" mediated by the Spirit through Isaiah 25:8 and Hosea 14:14 (vv. 54-55), prophetic texts that promise God's eschatological victory over death. Although mentioned only at the conclusion of this extended prophetic discourse, the revelation controls the apostle's argument throughout verses 12-49. Thus Paul's prophetic word is not restricted to verses 50-58 but extends from the beginning of the chapter to its conclusion.

As speech in the mode of "primary reflectivity," early Christian prophecy, as Paul exercises it, qualifies as theological discourse and may thus be identified historically as the beginning of Christian theology. Although effected by the Spirit, prophecy is subject to material criticism (14:29) on the basis of criteria other than behavioral evidences of the Spirit such as speaking in tongues (14:2-5; cf. 12:1-3). The criteria evident in Paul's discussion of inspired utterances in chapters 12–15 are the church's confession (12:3), kerygma (15:3b-8), and Scriptures (15:25, 27, 45-49, 54-55). As "re-flective" modes of discourse, these three criteria have criteriological authority not in themselves but in their referential power to show forth the reality of Israel's God who raised Jesus from the dead. It is the "fix" on the common subject of these criteria that makes theological criticism of prophetic speech possible. Theology at this nascent stage of its development is both a hermeneutical and a critical task. What the early Christian prophets were doing when they were prophesying is theology, and for this reason they may be identified as the first theologians of the church.

Bibliography

Allo, Ernest B. *Saint Paul: Première Épître aux Corinthiens.* Paris: J. Gabalda, 1956.
Aune, David E. *Prophecy in Early Christianity and the Ancient Mediterranean World.* Grand Rapids: Wm. B. Eerdmans, 1983.
Bachmann, Michael. "Rezeption von 1. Kor. 15 (V. 12ff.) unter logischem und unter philologischem Aspekt," *LB* 51 (1982): 79-103.
―――. "Zur Gedankenführung in 1. Kor. 15,12ff.," *TZ* 34 (1978): 265-76.
Bachmann, Philipp. *Der Erste Brief des Paulus an die Korinther.* Kommentar zum Neuen Testament 7. 3rd ed. Leipzig: A. Deichert, 1921.
Baker, David L. "The Interpretation of I Corinthians 12–14," *EvQ* 45 (1973): 224-34.
Barrett, Charles K. "Christianity at Corinth," *BJRL* 46 (1963-64): 269-97.
―――. *A Commentary on the Epistle to the Romans.* New York: Harper & Row, 1957.
―――. *A Commentary on the First Epistle to the Corinthians.* New York: Harper & Row, 1968.
Barth, Karl. *The Epistle to the Philippians.* London: SCM Press, 1962.
―――. *The Resurrection of the Dead.* Translated by H. J. Stenning. London: Hodder and Stoughton, 1933.
Bartling, Walter J. "The Congregation of Christ — A Charismatic Body: An Exegetical Study of 1 Corinthians 12," *CTM* 40 (1969): 67-80.
Bassler, Jouette M. "1 Cor 12:3 — Curse and Confession in Context," *JBL* 101 (1982): 415-21.
Bauer, Walter. *A Greek-English Lexicon of the New Testament and Other Early Christian Literature.* 4th ed. Edited and augmented by Wil-

liam F. Arndt and F. Wilbur Gingrich. Chicago: University of Chicago Press, 1952.

Baumann, Rolf. *Mitte und Norm des Christlichen.* Neutestamentliche Abhandlungen 5. Münster: Aschendorff, 1968.

Beare, Frank W. *A Commenatry on the Epistle to the Philippians.* 2nd ed. London: A. & C. Black, 1969.

———. "Speaking with Tongues," *JBL* 83 (1964): 229-46.

Behm, Johannes. "glōssa," *TDNT* I, 719-27.

Beker, J. Christiaan. *Paul the Apostle: The Triumph of God in Life and Thought.* Philadelphia: Fortress Press, 1985.

———. *The Triumph of God: The Essence of Paul's Thought.* Minneapolis: Fortress Press, 1990.

Berger, Klaus. "Die sog. 'Sätze heiligen Rechts' im N.T.: Ihre Funktion und ihr Sitz im Leben," *TZ* 28 (1972): 305-30.

———. "Zu den sogenannten Sätzen heiligen Rechts," *NTS* 17 (1970-71): 10-40.

Best, Ernest. *A Commentary on the First and Second Epistles to the Thessalonians.* New York: Harper & Row, 1972.

Betz, Hans D. *Galatians: A Commentary on Paul's Letter to the Churches in Galatia.* Philadelphia: Fortress Press, 1979.

———. "Orthodoxy and Heresy in Primitive Christianity," *Int* 19 (1965): 299-311.

Betz, Otto. "Der gekreuzigte Christus: unsere Weisheit und Gerechtigkeit," in *Tradition and Interpretation in the New Testament: Essays in Honor of E. Earle Ellis for his 60th Birthday.* 195-215. Edited by Otto Betz and Gerald F. Hawthorne. Grand Rapids: Wm. B. Eerdmans; Tübingen: J. C. B. Mohr (Paul Siebeck), 1987.

Bittlinger, Arnold. *Gifts and Graces: A Commentary on I Corinthians 12–14.* Grand Rapids: Wm. B. Eerdmans, 1967.

Bjerkelund, Carl J. *Parakalō: Form, Funktion und Sinn der Parakalō-Sätze in den Paulinischen Briefen.* Oslo: Universitetsforlaget, 1967.

Black, Carl Clifton II. "The Rhetorical Form of the Hellenistic Jewish and Early Christian Sermon: A Response to Lawrence Wills," *HTR* 81 (1988): 1-18.

Bonwetsch, N. "Die Prophetie im apostolischen und nachapostolischen Zeitalter," *ZkWkL* 5 (1884): 408-24; 460-77.

Boring, M. Eugene. "Christian Prophecy and the Sayings of Jesus: The State of the Question," *NTS* 29 (1983): 104-12.

———. *The Continuing Voice of Jesus: Christian Prophecy and the Gospel Tradition*. Louisville, KY: Westminster/ John Knox Press, 1991.

———. "How May We Identify Oracles of Christian Prophets in the Synoptic Tradition? Mark 3:28-29 as a Test Case," *JBL* 91 (1972): 501-21.

———. *Sayings of the Risen Jesus: Christian Prophecy in the Synoptic Tradition*. Society for New Testament Studies: Monograph Series 46. Cambridge: Cambridge University Press, 1982.

Bornkamm, Günther. *Early Christian Experience*. New York: Harper & Row, 1969.

———. "mysterion," *TDNT* IV, 802-28.

———. *Paul*. New York: Harper & Row, 1968.

Bousset, Wilhelm. "Der erste Brief an die Korinther," in *Die Schriften des Neuen Testament*, vol. 2, 3rd ed. 74-167. Edited by W. Bousset and W. Heitmüller. Göttingen: Vandenhoeck & Ruprecht, 1917.

Braun, Herbert. *Gesammelte Studien zum Neuen Testament und seiner Umwelt*. 2nd ed. Tübingen: J. C. B. Mohr (Paul Siebeck), 1967.

Bring, Ragnar. "The Message to the Gentiles: A Study of the Theology of Paul the Apostle," *ST* 19 (1965): 30-46.

Brockhaus, Ulrich. *Charisma und Amt*. Wuppertal: Theologischer Verlag Brockhaus, 1972.

Brosch, Joseph. *Charismen und Ämter in der Urkirche*. Bonn: P. Hanstein, 1951.

Brox, Norbert. "ANATHEMA IHSOYS (1 Kor 12,3)," *BZ* 12 (1968): 103-11.

Bruce. Frederick F. *1 and 2 Corinthians*. The New Century Bible Commentary 46. Grand Rapids: Wm. B. Eerdmans, 1971.

———. *1 and 2 Thessalonians*. Word Biblical Commentary 45. Waco, TX: Word Books Publisher, 1982.

Bucher, Theodor G. "Allegemeine Überlegungen zur Logik im Zusammenhang mit 1 Kor. 15,12-20," *LB* 53 (1983): 70-98.

———. "Auferstehung Christi und Auferstehung der Toten," *MTZ* 27 (1976): 1-32.

———. "Die logische Argumentation in 1. Korinther 15,12-20," *Bib* 55 (1974): 465-86.

———. "Nochmals zur Beweisführung in 1. Korinther 15,12-20," *TZ* 36 (1980): 129-52.

Bultmann, Rudolf. "ginōskō," *TDNT* I, 689-719.

———. *The History of the Synoptic Tradition.* New York: Harper & Row, 1963.

———. "pisteuō," *TDNT* VI, 174-228.

———. *Theology of the New Testament.* 2 vols. Translated by Kendrick Grobel. New York: Charles Scribner's Sons, 1951-1955.

Büchsel, Friedrich. "krinō," *TDNT* III, 921-54.

Caird, George B. *The Language and Imagery of the Bible.* London: Duckworth, 1980.

Callan, Terrance. "Prophecy and Ecstasy in Greco-Roman Religion and in 1 Corinthians," *NovT* 27 (1985): 125-40.

Campenhausen, Hans Freiherr von. *Ecclesiastical Authority and Spiritual Power in the Church of the First Three Centuries.* Stanford, CA: Stanford University Press, 1969.

Collins, John H. "Genre, Ideology and Social Movements in Jewish Apocalypticism," in *Mysteries and Revelations: Apocalyptic Studies since the Uppsala Colloquium.* Journal for the Study of the Pseudepigrapha Supplement Series 9, 13-32. Edited by John J. Collins and James H. Charlesworth. Sheffield: Sheffield Academic Press, 1991.

Conzelmann, Hans. *Die Apostelgeschichte.* Tübingen: J. C. B. Mohr (Paul Siebeck), 1963.

———. *Der Erste Brief an die Korinther.* Göttingen: Vandenhoeck & Ruprecht, 1969. (ET) *1 Corinthians: A Commentary on the First Epistle to the Corinthians.* Hermeneia 46. Philadelphia: Fortress Press, 1975.

———. "On the Analysis of the Confessional Formula in I Corinthians 15:3-5," translated by Mathias Rissi, *Int* 20 (1966): 15-25.

———. *An Outline of the Theology of the New Testament.* New York: Harper & Row, 1969.

———. "Was glaubte die frühe Christenheit?" *STU* 25 (1955): 61-74.

Cothenet, Edouard. "Les prophètes chrétiens comme exégètes charismatiques de L'Écriture," in *Prophetic Vocation in the New Testament and Today,* 77-107. Edited by J. Panagopulos. Leiden: E. J. Brill, 1977.

———. "Prophetisme dans le Nouveau Testament," *DBSup* VIII, 1222-1337.

Cranfield, Charles B. E. *A Critical and Exegetical Commentary on the Epistle to the Romans.* The International Critical Commentary 45. 2 vols. Edinburgh: T. & T. Clark, 1975-1979.

———. "*Metron Pisteōs* in Romans XII.3," *NTS* 8 (1961-62): 345-51.
Crone, Theodore M. *Early Christian Prophecy: A Study of Its Origin and Function*. Baltimore: St. Mary's University Press, 1973.
Cullmann, Oscar. *The Christology of the New Testament*. Rev. ed. Philadelphia: Westminster Press, 1963.
Cuming, G. J. "*EPOTISTHEMEN* (I Corinthians 12.13)," *NTS* 27 (1980): 283-85.
Currie, Stuart D. "Speaking in Tongues," *Int* 19 (1965): 274-94.
Dahl, Nils A. "Paul and the Church at Corinth According to I Corinthians 1:10–4:21," in *Christian History and Interpretation: Studies Presented to John Knox*, 313-35. Edited by W. R. Farmer, C. F. D. Moule, and R. R. Niebuhr. Cambridge: Cambridge University Press, 1967.
Dana, Harvey E., and Julius R. Mantey. *A Manual of the Greek New Testament*. New York: Macmillan Co., 1928.
Daube, David. "Participle and Imperative in I Peter," in *The First Epistle of St. Peter: The Greek Text with Introduction, Notes and Essays*. Edited by Edward G. Selwyn. London: Macmillan Co., 1949.
Dautzenberg, Gerhard. "Botschaft und Bedeutung der urchristlichen Prophetie nach dem ersten Korintherbrief (2:6-16; 12-14)," in *Prophetic Vocation in the New Testament and Today*, 131-61. Edited by J. Panagopoulos.
———. *Urchristliche Prophetie: Ihre Erforschung, ihre Voraussetzungen im Judentum und ihre Struktur im ersten Korintherbrief*. Beiträge zur Wissenschaft von Alten und Neuen Testament 104. Stuttgart: W. Kohlhammer, 1975.
———. "Zum religionsgeschichtlichen Hintergrund der *diakriseis pneumatōn* (I Kor. 12:10)," *BZ* 15 (1971): 93-104.
Davies, William D. *Paul and Rabbinic Judaism: Some Rabbinic Elements in Pauline Theology*. New York: Harper & Row, 1955.
de Boer, Martinus C. *The Defeat of Death: Apocalyptic Eschatology in 1 Corinthians 15 and Romans 5*. Sheffield: Sheffield Academic Press, 1988.
Derrett, J. Duncan M. "Cursing Jesus (1 Corinthians XII.3): The Jews as Religious 'Persecutors,'" *NTS* 21 (1974): 544-54.
Dibelius, Martin. *Die Formgeschichte des Evangeliums*. 3rd ed. Tübingen: J. C. B. Mohr (Paul Siebeck), 1959.
Dobschütz, Ernst von. *Die Thessalonicher-Briefe*. Göttingen: Vandenhoeck & Ruprecht, 1974.

———. "Zwei- und dreiliedrige Formeln: Ein Beitrag zur Vorgeschichte der Trinitätsformel," *JBL* 50 (1931): 117-47.

Dodd, Charles H. *The Apostolic Preaching and Its Development.* New York: Harper & Brothers, 1962.

Dominy, Bert. "Paul and Spiritual Gifts: Reflections on I Corinthians 12–14," *SWJTh* 26 (1983): 46-68.

Dunn, James D. G. *Baptism in the Holy Spirit.* Philadelphia: Westminster Press, 1970.

———. *Christology in the Making.* Philadelphia: Westminster Press, 1980.

———. *Jesus and the Spirit.* Philadelphia: Westminster Press, 1975.

———. "Prophetic 'I'-Sayings and the Jesus Tradition: The Importance of Testing Prophetic Utterances Within Early Christianity," *NTS* 24 (1977-78): 175-98.

———. *Romans 1–8.* Word Biblical Commentary 38A. Dallas: Word Books Publisher, 1988.

———. *Romans 9–16.* Word Biblical Commentary 38B. Dallas: Word Books Publisher, 1988.

———. *Unity and Diversity in the New Testament.* Philadelphia: Westminster Press, 1977.

Dupont, Jacques. *Gnosis: La Connaissance religieuse dans les Épîtres de Saint Paul.* Louvain: E. Nauwelaerts, 1960.

Ebeling, Gerhard. "The Ground of Christian Theology," *JTC* 6 (1969): 47-68.

Edwards, Richard A. "The Eschatological Correlative as a *Gattung* in the New Testament," *ZNW* 60 (1969): 9-20.

———. *The Sign of Jonah in the Theology of the Evangelists and Q.* Studies in Biblical Theology 18. London: SCM Press, 1971.

Eichholz, Georg. *Die Theologie des Paulus im Umriß.* 2nd ed. Neukirchen-Vluyn: Neukirchener Verlag, 1977.

———. "Was heißt charismatische Gemeinde?: 1. Korinther 12," *TExH* 77 (1960): 4-27.

Ellis, Edward Earle. *Prophecy and Hermeneutic in Early Christianity.* Tübingen: J. C. B. Mohr (Paul Siebeck), 1978.

Engelsen, Nils I. J. "Glossolalia and Other Forms of Inspired Speech According to I Corinthians 12–14." Ph.D. diss., Yale University, 1970.

Fascher, Erich. *Prophētēs, eine Sprach- und religionsgeschichtliche Untersuchung.* Gießen: A. Töpelmann, 1927.

Fee, Gordon D. *The First Epistle to the Corinthians.* Grand Rapids: Wm. B. Eerdmans, 1987.
Forbes, Christopher. "Early Christian Inspired Speech and Hellenistic Popular Religion," *NovT* 28 (1986): 257-70.
———. "Prophecy and Inspired Speech in Early Christianity and its Hellenistic Environment." Ph.D. diss., Macquarie University, 1987.
Frid, Bo. "The Enigmatic *alla* in 1 Corinthians 2:9," *NTS* 31 (1985): 603-11.
Friedrich, Gerhard. "euangelion," *TDNT* II, 707-37.
———. "prophētēs," *TDNT* VI, 828-61.
Fuchs, Ernst. "On the Task of a Christian Theology," *JTC* 6 (1969): 69-98.
Fuller, Reginald H. *The Foundations of New Testament Christology.* New York: Charles Scribner's Sons, 1965.
Funk, Robert W. *Language, Hermeneutic, and Word of God.* New York: Harper & Row, 1966.
Funk, Robert, Friedrich W. Blass, and Albert Debrunner. *A Greek Grammar of the New Testament and Other Early Christian Literature.* Chicago: University of Chicago Press, 1961.
Gadamer, Hans-Georg. *Truth and Method.* New York: Crossroads, 1975.
Georgi, Dieter. *Die Gegner des Paulus im 2. Korintherbrief: Studien zur religiösen Propaganda in der Spätantike.* Wissenschaftliche Monographien zum Alten und Neuen Testament 11. Neukirchen-Vluyn: Neukirchener Verlag, 1964. English translation, *The Opponents of Paul in Second Corinthians.* Philadelphia: Fortress Press, 1986.
Gerhardsson, Birger. *Memory and Manuscript: Oral and Written Transmission in Rabbinic Judaism and Early Christianity.* Uppsala: C. W. K. Gleerup, 1961.
Gillespie, Thomas W. "A Pattern of Prophetic Speech in First Corinthians," *JBL* 97 (1978): 74-95.
———. "Prophecy and Tongues." Ph.D. diss., Claremont Graduate School, 1971.
Goppelt, Leonhard. *Theology of the New Testament.* 2 vols. Translated by John E. Alsup and edited by Jürgen Roloff. Grand Rapids: Wm. B. Eerdmans, 1981-1982.
Grabner-Haider, Anton. *Paraklese und Eschatologie bei Paulus: Mensch und Welt im Anspruch der zukunft Gottes.* Neutestamentliche Abhandlungen 4. Münster: Aschendorff, 1968.
Greeven, D. H. "Propheten, Lehrer, Vorsteher bei Paulus," *ZNW* 44 (1952): 1-43.

Grosheide, Frederick W. *Commentary on the First Epistle to the Corinthians.* Grand Rapids: Wm. B. Eerdmans, 1953.

Grudem, Wayne A. *The Gift of Prophecy in 1 Corinthians.* Washington, D.C.: University Press of America, 1982.

———. "A Response to Gerhard Dautzenberg on 1 Cor. 12:10," *BZ* 22 (1978): 253-70.

Gundry, Robert H. "'Ecstatic Utterance' (N.E.B.)?" *JTS* 17 (1966): 299-307.

Gunkel, Hermann. *Die Wirkungen des heiligen Geistes nach der populären Anschauung der apostolischen Zeit und der Lehre des Apostels Paulus.* Göttingen: Vandenhoeck & Ruprecht, 1888.

Güttgemanns, Erhardt. *Offene Fragen zur Formgeschichte des Evangeliums.* Beiträge zur Evangelischen Theologie 54. München: C. Kaiser, 1970.

Guy, H. A. *New Testament Prophecy: Its Origin and Significance.* London: Epworth Press, 1947.

Harnack, Adolf von. "Die Lehre der zwölf Apostel: Prolegomena," in *Texte und Untersuchungen zur Geschichte der altchristlichen Literatur*, vol. 2: 1-274. Leipzig: J. C. Hinrichs'sche Buchhandlung, 1884.

———. *Die Mission und Ausbreitung des Christentums in den ersten drei Jahrhunderten*, 4th ed., 2 vols. Leipzig: J. C. Hinrichs, 1924.

Harrelson, Walter. "Death and Victory in 1 Corinthians 15:51-57: The Transformation of a Prophetic Theme," in *Faith and History: Essays in Honor of Paul W. Meyer*, 149-59. Edited by John T. Carroll, Charles H. Cosgrove, and E. Elizabeth Johnson. Atlanta: Scholars Press, 1990.

Harrisville, Roy A. "Speaking in Tongues," *CBQ* 38 (1976): 35-47.

Hartman, Lars. "Some Remarks on 1 Cor. 2:1-5," *SEÅ* 39 (1974): 109-20.

Hawthorne, Gerald F., and Otto Betz. *Tradition and Interpretation in the New Testament: Essays in Honor of E. Earle Ellis for his 60th Birthday.* Grand Rapids: Wm. B. Eerdmans; Tübingen: J.C.B. Mohr (Paul Siebeck), 1987.

Hays, Richard B. *Echoes of Scripture in the Letters of Paul.* New Haven: Yale University Press, 1989.

Henneken, Bartholomäus. *Verkündigung und Prophetie im 1. Thessalonicherbrief.* Stuttgarter Bibelstudien 29. Stuttgart: Verlag Katholisches Bibelwerk, 1969.

Héring, Jean. *La Première Épitre de Saint Paul aux Corinthiens.* Commentarie du Nouveau Testament 7. Neuchatel: Delachaux & Niestlé, 1949.

Hill, David. "Christian Prophets as Teachers or Instructors in the Church," in *Prophetic Vocation in the New Testament and Today*, 108-30. Edited by J. Panagopoulos.

———. *New Testament Prophecy*. Atlanta: John Knox Press, 1979.

———. "On the Evidence for the Creative Role of Christian Prophets," *NTS* 20 (1973-74): 262-74.

Holtz, Traugott. "Das Kennzeichen des Geistes (1 Kor. XII.1-3)," *NTS* 18 (1971-72): 365-76.

———. *Der erste Brief an die Thessalonicher*. Evangelisch-Katholischer Kommentar zum Neuen Testament 13. Neukirchen-Vluyn: Neukirchener Verlag, 1986.

———. "Traditionen im 1 Thessalonicherbrief," in *Die Mitte des Neuen Testaments: Einheit und Vielfalt neutestamentlicher Theologie; Festschrift für Eduard Schweizer zum Siebzigsten Geburtstag*, 55-78. Edited by Ulrich Luz and Hans Weder. Göttingen: Vandenhoeck & Ruprecht, 1983.

———. "Zum Selbstverständis des Apostels Paulus," *TLZ* 91 (1966): 321-30.

Horsley, Richard A. "'How Can Some of You Say That There Is No Resurrection of the Dead?' Spiritual Elitism in Corinth," *NovT* 20 (1978): 203-31.

———. "Wisdom of Word and Words of Wisdom in Corinth," *CBQ* 39 (1977): 224-39.

Hurd, John C. *The Origin of 1 Corinthians*. Macon, GA: Mercer University Press, 1983.

Iber, Gerhard. "Zum Verständnis von I Cor 12.31," *ZNW* 54 (1963): 43-52.

Jenkins, C. "Origen on I Corinthians," *JTS* 10 (1909): 29-50.

Jeremias, Joachim. *New Testament Theology*. New York: Charles Scribner's Sons, 1971.

Jervell, Jacob. *Imago Dei*. Forschungen zur Religion und Literatur des Alten und Neuen Testaments 76. Göttingen: Vandenhoeck & Ruprecht, 1960.

Jewett, Robert. *A Chronology of Paul's Life*. Philadelphia: Fortress Press, 1979.

———. *The Thessalonian Correspondence: Pauline Rhetoric and Millenarian Piety*. Philadelphia: Fortress Press, 1986.

Joest, Wilfried. *Gesetz und Freiheit*. 2nd ed. Göttingen: Vandenhoeck & Ruprecht, 1956.

Johanson, B. C. "Tongues, a Sign for Unbelievers?: A Structural and Exegetical Study of I Cor. XIV.20-25," *NTS* 25 (1979): 180-203.

Johnson, Luke Timothy. "Norms for True and False Prophecy in First Corinthians," *ABR* 22 (1971): 29-45.

Juel, Donald. *Messianic Exegesis: Christological Interpretation of the Old Testament in Early Christianity.* Philadelphia: Fortress Press, 1988.

Käsemann, Ernst. *Commentary on Romans.* Grand Rapids: Wm. B. Eerdmans, 1980.

———. "A Critical Analysis of Philippians 2:5-11," *JTC* 5 (1968): 45-88.

———. *Essays on New Testament Themes.* London: SCM Press, 1964.

———. *Exegetische Versuche und Besinnungen.* 2 vols. Göttingen: Vandenhoeck & Ruprecht, 1960-1965.

———. "God's Righteousness in Paul," *JTC* 1 (1965): 100-110.

———. *Leib und Leib Christi: Eine Untersuchung zur paulinischen Begrifflichkeit.* Beiträge zur Historischen Theologie 9. Tübingen: J. C. B. Mohr (Paul Siebeck), 1933.

———. *New Testament Questions of Today.* Philadelphia: Fortress Press, 1969.

———. *Perspectives on Paul.* Philadelphia: Fortress Press, 1971.

Kennedy, George A. *New Testament Interpretation Through Rhetorical Criticism.* Chapel Hill, NC: University of North Carolina Press, 1984.

Kloppenborg, John. "An Analysis of the Pre-Pauline Formula 1 Cor. 15:3b-5 in Light of Some Recent Literature," *CBQ* 40 (1978): 351-67.

Koch, Klaus. *The Rediscovery of Apocalyptic.* London: SCM Press, 1972.

Koenig, John. *Charismata: God's Gifts for God's People.* Philadelphia: Westminster Press, 1978.

Koester, Helmut. Review of *Weisheit und Torheit*, by Ulrich Wilcken. *Gnomon* 33 (1961): 591-95.

———. *Introduction to the New Testament.* 2 vols. Philadelphia: Fortress Press; Berlin/ New York: De Gruyter, 1982.

Krämer, Helmut. "prophētēs," *TDNT* VI, 781-96.

Kramer, Werner. *Christ, Lord, Son of God.* Naperville, IL: A. R. Allenson, 1966.

Kümmel, Werner G. *Introduction to the New Testament.* Nashville: Abingdon Press, 1966.

Lambrecht, J. "Paul's Christological Use of Scripture in 1 Cor. 15.20-28," *NTS* 28 (1982): 502-27.

Lang, Friedrich. *Die Briefe an die Korinther.* Das Neue Testament Deutsch 7. Göttingen: Vandenhoeck & Ruprecht, 1986.
Leitzmann, Hans and Werner G. Kümmel. *An die Korinther I.II.* Handbuch zum Neuen Testament 9. 4th ed. Tübingen: J. C. B. Mohr (Paul Siebeck), 1949.
Levenson, Jon D. "Why Jews Are Not Interested in Biblical Theology," in *Judaic Perspectives on Ancient Israel.* 281-308. Edited by J. Neusner, B. A. Levine, and E. S. Frerichs. Philadelphia: Fortress Press, 1987.
Lightfoot, Joseph B. *St. Paul's Epistle to the Philippians.* London: Macmillan Co., 1878.
Lim, Timothy H. "'Not in Persuasive Words of Wisdom, but in the Demonstration of the Spirit and Power,'" *NovT* 29 (1987): 137-49.
Lohmeyer, Ernst. *Kyrios Jesus: Eine Untersuchung zu Phil. 2,5-11.* Heidelberg: C. Winter, 1928.
Louw, Johannes P., and Eugene A. Nida. *Greek-English Lexicon of the New Testament Based on Semantic Domains.* 2 vols. New York: United Bible Societies, 1988.
Lüdemann, Gerd. *Paul, Apostle to the Gentiles: Studies in Chronology.* Philadelphia: Fortress Press, 1984.
Lührmann, Dieter. *Das Offenbarungsverständnis bei Paulus und in paulinischen Gemeinden.* Wissenschaftliche Monographien zum Alten und Neuen Testament 16. Neukirchen-Vluyn: Neukirchener Verlag, 1965.
MacGorman, J. W. "Glossolalic Error and Its Correction: 1 Corinthians 12–14," *RE* 80 (1983): 389-400.
Mack, Burton L. *Rhetoric and the New Testament.* Minneapolis: Fortress Press, 1990.
Malherbe, Abraham J. "'Pastoral Care' in the Thessalonian Church," *NTS* 36 (1990): 375-91.
Maly, Karl. "1 Kor 12,1-3 eine Regel zur Unterscheidung der Geister?" *BZ* 10 (1966): 82-95.
———. *Mündige Gemeinde: Untersuchungen zur pastoralen Fuhrung des Apostels Paulus im 1. Korintherbrief.* Stuttgart Biblische Monographien 2. Stuttgart: Katholisches Bibelwerk, 1967.
Marshall, I. Howard. *1 and 2 Thessalonians.* The New Century Bible Commentary 52. Grand Rapids: Wm. B. Eerdmans, 1983.
Martin, Ralph P. *Carmen Christi: Philippians ii.5-11 in Recent Interpretation and in the Setting of the Early Christian Worship.* Cambridge: Cambridge University Press, 1967.

———. *Philippians.* London: Oliphants, 1976.
———. *The Spirit and the Congregation: Studies in I Corinthians 12–15.* Grand Rapids: Wm. B. Eerdmans, 1984.
———. *Worship in the Early Church.* Westwood, NJ: F. H. Revell, 1964.
———. *The Worship of God: Some Theological, Pastoral, and Practical Reflections.* Grand Rapids: Wm. B. Eerdmans, 1982.
Mauser, Ulrich. "Paul the Theologian," *HBT* 11 (1989): 80-106.
Meeks, Wayne A. *The First Urban Christians: The Social World of the Apostle Paul.* New Haven: Yale University Press, 1983.
Merklein, Helmut. "Der Theologe als Prophet: Zur Funktion prophetischen Redens im Theologischen Diskurs des Paulus," *NTS* 38 (1992): 402-29.
Metzger, Bruce M. *A Textual Commentary on the Greek New Testament.* 3rd ed. London/New York: United Bible Societies, 1971.
Michaelis, Wilhelm. *Die Erscheinungen des Auferstandenen.* Basel: H. Majer, 1944.
Michel, Otto. *Der Brief an die Römer.* Meyer Kommentar 4. Göttingen: Vandenhoeck & Ruprecht, 1955.
———. "Evangelium," *RAC* VI, 1107-59.
———. "oikodomein," *TDNT* V, 119-59.
Moffatt, James. *The First Epistle of Paul to the Corinthians.* London: Hodder and Stoughton, 1938.
Morris, Leon. *The First Epistle of Paul to the Corinthians: An Introduction and Commentary.* Grand Rapids: Wm. B. Eerdmans, 1958.
———. *The First and Second Epistles to the Thessalonians.* London: Marshall, Morgan and Scott, 1959.
Müller, Ulrich B. *Prophetie und Predigt im Neuen Testament.* Studien zum Neuen Testament 10. Gütersloh: Gütersloher Verlagshaus Mohn, 1975.
Murphy-O'Connor, Jerome O. P. "Tradition and Redaction in 1 Cor 15:3-7," *CBQ* 43 (1981): 582-89.
Myers, Jacob M., and Edwin D. Freed. "Is Paul Also Among the Prophets?" *Int* 20 (1966): 40-53.
Neil, William. *The Epistle of Paul to the Thessalonians.* London: Hodder and Stoughton, 1950.
Neufeld, Vernon H. *The Earliest Christian Confessions.* New Testament Tools and Studies 5. Leiden: E. J. Brill, 1963.
Neugebauer, Fritz. "Geistsprüche und Jesuslogien," *ZNW* 53 (1962): 218-28.

Newman, Carey C. *Paul's Glory-Christology: Tradition and Rhetoric.* Leiden: E. J. Brill, 1992.
Niederwimmer, Kurt. "Erkennen und Lieben," *KD* 11 (1965): 75-102.
Nock, Arthur D. *St. Paul.* London: T. Butterworth, 1938.
Osten-Sacken, Peter von der. "Die Apologie des paulinischen Apostolats in 1 Kor 15:1-11," *ZNW* 64 (1973): 245-62.
Painter, John. "Paul and the *Pneumatikoi* at Corinth," in *Paul and Paulinism: Essays in Honour of C. K. Barrett*, 237-50. Edited by M. D. Hooker and S. G. Wilson. London: S.P.C.K., 1982.
Panagopoulos, Johannes. "Die urchristliche Prophetie: Ihr Charakter und ihre Funktion," in *Prophetic Vocation in the New Testament and Today*, 1-32. Edited by J. Panagopoulos.
Parry, R. St. John. *The First Epistle of Paul the Apostle to the Corinthians.* Cambridge: Cambridge University Press, 1928.
Pearson, Birger A. "Did the Gnostics Curse Jesus?" *JBL* 86 (1967): 301-5.
———. *The Pneumatikos-Psychikos Terminology in I Corinthians.* SBLDS 12. Missoula: Scholars Press, 1973.
Pannenberg, Wolfhart. *Jesus, God and Man.* Philadelphia: Westminster Press, 1968.
Pfister, Friedrich. "Ekstase," *RAC* IV, 943-87.
Plank, Karl A. "Resurrection Theology: The Corinthian Controversy Reexamined," *PRS* 8 (1981): 41-54.
Poythress, Vern S. "The Nature of Corinthian Glossolalia," *WTJ* 40 (1977-78): 130-35.
Reiling, Jannes. *Hermas and Christian Prophecy.* Leiden: E. J. Brill, 1973.
———. "Prophecy, The Spirit and the Church," in *Prophetic Vocation in the New Testament and Today*, 58-76. Edited by J. Panagopoulos.
Reitzenstein, Richard. *Die Hellenistischen Mysterienreligionen nach ihren Grundgedanken und wirkungen.* 3rd ed. Leipzig: B. G. Teubner, 1927.
Rengstorf, Karl-Heinrich. *Die Auferstehung Jesu.* 5th ed. Witten/Ruhr: Luther-Verlag, 1967.
———. "sēmeion," *TDNT* VII, 200-269.
Richardson, William. "Liturgical Order and Glossolalia in 1 Corinthians 14.26c-33a," *NTS* 32 (1986): 144-53.
Ricoeur, Paul. *Interpretation Theory: Discourse and the Surplus of Meaning.* Fort Worth, TX: The Texas Christian University Press, 1976.
Roberts, Peter. "A Sign — Christian or Pagan?" *ExpTim* 90 (1978-79): 199-203.

Robertson, Archibald, and Alfred Plummer. *A Critical and Exegetical Commentary on the First Epistle of St. Paul to the Corinthians.* 2nd ed. Edinburgh: T. & T. Clark, 1961.

Robinson, D. W. B. "Charismata versus Pneumatika: Paul's Method of Discussion," *RTJ* 31 (1972): 49-55.

Robinson, James M. "Die Hodajot-Formel in Gebet und Hymnus des Frühchristentums," in *Apophoreta*, 194-235. Edited by Walther Eltester. Berlin: A. Töpelmann. 1964.

Robinson, James M., and Helmut Koester. *Trajectories Through Early Christianity.* Philadelphia: Fortress Press, 1971.

Robinson, William C., Jr. "Word and Power (I Corinthians 1:17–2:5)," in *Soli Deo Gloria: New Testament Studies in Honor of William Childs Robinson*, 68-82. Edited by J. McDowell Richards. Richmond: John Knox Press, 1968.

Sandy, William, and Arthur C. Headlam. *A Critical and Exegetical Commentary on the Epistle to the Romans.* The International Critical Commentary 45. 2nd ed. New York: Charles Scribner's Sons, 1896.

Schatzmann, Siegfried. *A Pauline Theology of Charismata.* Peabody, MA: Hendrickson Publishers, 1987.

Schlatter, Adolf von. *Die Korintherbriefe.* Stuttgart: Calwer Verlag, 1962.

———. *Erläuterungen zum Neuen Testament.* Stuttgart: Calwer Verlag, 1947.

———. *Gottes Gerechtigkeit: Ein Kommentar zum Römerbrief.* 3rd ed. Stuttgart: Calwer Verlag, 1959.

Schlier, Heinrich. "amēn," *TDNT* I, 335-38.

———. *Der Brief an die Galater.* Meyer Kommentar 7. 4th ed. Göttingen: Vandenhoeck & Ruprecht, 1965.

———. "Kerygma und Sophia: Zur neutestamentlichen Grundlegung des Dogmas," in *Die Zeit der Kirche*, 206-32. Freiburg: Herder: 1956.

Schlink, Edmund. "Gesetz und Paraklese," in *Antwort: Karl Barth zum siebzigsten Geburtstag*, 325-35. Edited by Ernst Wolf, Ch. von Kirschbaum, and Rudolf Frey. Zollikon-Zürich: Evangelischer Verlag, 1956.

Schmithals, Walter. *Gnosticism in Corinth: An Investigation of the Letters to the Corinthians.* Nashville: Abingdon Press, 1971.

———. *Paul and the Gnostics.* Nashville: Abingdon Press, 1972.

Schmitz, Otto. "parakalō," *TDNT* V, 773-99.

Schniewind, Julius. "Die Leugnung der Auferstehung in Korinth," in

Nachgelassene Reden und Aufsätze, 110-39. Berlin: A. Töpelmann, 1952.
Schulte, Hannelis. *Der Begriff der Offenbarung im Neuen Testament.* München: C. Kaiser, 1949.
Schürmann, Heinz. *The First Epistle to the Thessalonians.* New York: Herder & Herder, 1969.
Schütz, John Howard. "Charisma and Social Reality in Primitive Christianity," *JR* 54 (1974): 51-70.
⸻. *Paul and the Anatomy of Apostolic Authority.* London/New York: Cambridge University Press, 1975.
Schweitzer, Albert. *The Mysticism of Paul the Apostle.* New York: Seabury Press, 1968.
Schweizer, Eduard. "Observance of the Law and Charismatic Activity in Matthew," *NTS* 16 (1969-70): 213-30.
⸻. "pneuma," *TDNT* VI, 332-455.
⸻. "The Service of Worship: An Exposition of I Corinthians 14," *Int* 13 (1959): 400-408.
⸻. "Zum religionsgeschichtlichen Hintergrund der 'Sendungsformel'," *ZNW* 57 (1966): 199-210.
Scroggs, Robin. "The Exaltation of the Spirit by Some Early Christians," *JBL* 84 (1965): 359-73.
⸻. "Paul: *Sophos* and *Pneumatikos*," *NTS* 14 (1967): 33-55.
Sellin, Gerhard. "Das 'Geheimnis' der Weisheit und das Rätsel der 'Christuspartie' (zu 1 Kor 1–4)," *ZNW* 73 (1982): 69-96.
Sider, Ronald J. "St. Paul's Understanding of the Nature and Significance of the Resurrection in I Corinthians XV 1-19," *NovT* 19 (1977): 124-41.
Soden, Hans von. "Sakrament und Ethick bei Paulus," *MTS* 1 (1931): 1-40.
Soskice, Janet Martin. *Metaphor and Religious Language.* Oxford: Clarendon Press, 1985.
Stählin, Gustav. "paramytheomai," *TDNT* V, 814-23.
Stendahl, Krister. "Kerygma und Kerygmatish," *TLZ* 77 (1952): 715-20.
⸻. *Paul Among Jews and Gentiles.* Philadelphia: Fortress Press, 1976.
Strecker, Georg. "Entrückung," *RAC* V, 461-76.
Stuhlmacher, Peter. *Das paulinische Evangelium I.* Forschungen zur Religion und Literatur des Alten und Neuen Testament 95. Göttingen: Vandenhoeck & Ruprecht, 1968.

———. *The Gospel and the Gospels*. Grand Rapids: Wm. B. Eerdmans, 1990.

———. "The Hermeneutical Significance of 1 Cor 2:6-16," in *Tradition and Interpretation in the New Testament*, 328-48. Edited by Otto Betz and Gerald F. Hawthrone.

Sturm, Richard E. "Defending the Word 'Apocalyptic': A Problem in Biblical Criticism," in *Apocalyptic and the New Testament: Essays in Honor of J. Louis Martyn*, 17-48. Edited by Joel Marcus and Marion L. Soards. Sheffield: Sheffield Academic Press, 1989.

Sweet, John P. M. "A Sign for Unbelievers: Paul's Attitude to Glossolalia," *NTS* 13 (1967): 240-57.

Talbert, Charles H. "Tradition and Redaction in Rom. xii.,9-21," *NTS* 16 (1969-70): 83-93.

———. "Paul's Understanding of the Holy Spirit: The Evidence of 1 Corinthians 12–14," in *Perspectives on the New Testament: Essays in Honor of Frank Stagg*, 95-108. Edited by Charles Talbert. Macon, GA: Mercer University Press, 1985.

Theissen, Gerd. *Psychological Aspects of Pauline Theology*. Philadelphia: Fortress Press, 1987.

———. *The Social Setting of Pauline Christianity: Essays on Corinth*. Philadelphia: Fortress Press, 1988.

Thiselton, Anthony C. "The 'Interpretation of Tongues: A New Suggestion in the Light of Greek Usage in Philo and Josephus," *JTS* 30 (1979): 15-36.

———. "Realized Eschatology at Corinth," *NTS* 24 (1977-1978): 510-26.

Unnik, William C. van. "Jesus: Anathema or Kyrios (1 Cor. 12:3)," in *Christ and Spirit in the New Testament*, 113-26. Edited by B. Lindars and S. Smalley. Cambridge: Cambridge University Press, 1973.

Vielhauer, Philipp. *Oikodome: Das Bild vom Bau in der christlichen Literatur vom Neuen Testament bis Clemens Alexandrinus*. Karlsruhe-Durlach: Verlagsdruckerei Gebr. Tron, 1940.

Vögtle, Anton. *Die Tugend- und Lasterkataloge im Neuen Testament: Exegetische, religions- und form-geschichtlich Untersucht*. Neutestamentliche Abhandlungen 16. Münster: Verlag der Aschendorffschen Verlagsbuchhandlung, 1936.

Walter, Eugen. *Der Erste Brief an die Korinther*. Düsseldorf: Patmos-Verlag, 1968.

Wanamaker, Charles A. *The Epistles to the Thessalonians: A Commentary on the Greek Text.* Grand Rapids: Wm. B. Eerdmans; Exeter: Paternoster Press, 1990.

Wedderburn, A. J. M. "The Problem of the Denial of the Resurrection in I Corinthians XV," *NovT* 23 (1981): 229-41.

Weinel, Heinrich. *Die Wirkungen des Geistes und der Geister im nachapostolischen Zeitalter bis auf Irenäus.* Freiburg: J. C. B. Mohr (Paul Siebeck), 1899.

Weiss, Johannes. *Der erste Korintherbrief.* Göttingen: Vandenhoeck & Ruprecht, 1925.

Wendland, Heinz D. *Die Briefe an die Korinther.* Das Neue Testament Deutsch 6-8. 5th ed. Göttingen: Vandenhoeck & Ruprecht, 1948.

Wilckens, Ulrich. "Der Ursprung der Überlieferung der Erscheinungen des Auferstandenen," in *Dogma und Denkstrukturen,* 56-95. Edited by Wilfried Joest and Wolfhart Pannenberg. Göttingen: Vandenhoeck & Ruprecht, 1963.

———. "Zu 1 Kor 2,1-16," in *Theologia Crucis–Signum Crucis: Festschrift für Erich Dinkler zum 70. Geburtstag,* 510-37. Edited by Carl Andersen and Günter Klein. Tübingen: J. C. B. Mohr (Paul Siebeck), 1979.

———. *Weisheit und Torheit: Eine Exegetisch-religionsgeschichtliche Untersuchung zu 1. Kor. 1 und 2.* Beiträge zur historischen Theologie 26. Tübingen: J. C. B. Mohr (Paul Siebeck), 1959.

Wilder, Amos. *Early Christian Rhetoric: The Language of the Gospel.* Cambridge, MA: Harvard University Press, 1964.

Wills, Lawrence. "The Form of the Sermon in Hellenistic Judaism and Early Christianity," *HTR* 77 (1984): 277-99.

Wilson, Jack H. "The Corinthians Who Say There Is No Resurrection of the Dead," *ZNW* 59 (1968): 90-107.

Wilson, Robert McL. *Gnosis and the New Testament.* Philadelphia: Fortress Press, 1968.

Wire, Antoinette Clark. *The Corinthian Women Prophets: A Reconstruction Through Paul's Rhetoric.* Minneapolis: Fortress Press, 1990.

Wright, Nicholas T. *The Climax of the Covenant: Christ and the Law in Pauline Theology.* Edinburgh: T. & T. Clark, 1991.

Ziesler, John A. *Paul's Letter to the Romans.* London: SCM Press; Philadelphia: Trinity Press International, 1989.

Index

Adam-Christ typology, 231
Apocalyptic, 255-58; centrality of, 9-11; and Paul, 260-62
Apollos, 143-44, 146
Apostles: in the Didache, 3-4
Apostleship, Paul's: and revelation, 189
Aune, David E.: criticisms of Käsemann, 11-17; on ecstatic experiences, 44n.42; on 1 Corinthians 12:2, 80-81; on 1 Corinthians 15:51-52, 227; on 1 Thessalonians 5:19-22, 38; on forms of prophetic speech, 19-20, 24-25; on LXX background of *prophētēs*, 133-34; on Thessalonian prophesying, 48-50; on tongues, 111

Baker, David L.: on *ta pneumatika*, 73-74; on zeal, 125
Baptism: in the Corinthian church, 166-70, 249-50; for the dead, 216; metaphorical use, 120; and resurrection, 216
Barrett, Charles K., 75
Bassler, Jouette, 81-82
Baumann, Rolf, 176-77
Beker, J. C., 230, 254-55
Berger, Klaus, 13-15
Best, Ernest, 39-40, 45
Body metaphor, 54

Body of Christ, 118-22
Boring, M. Eugene: criticism of Berger, 14; criticism of Bultmann, 6; criticism of Käsemann, 12; on forms of prophetic speech, 17-19
Braun, Herbert, 176
Brockhaus, Ulrich, 55, 90-91
Brox, Norbert, 93
Bruce, F. F., 39
Bultmann, Rudolf: on denial of resurrection, 205, 211; on forms of prophetic speech, 5-6; on kerygma, 223; on "mind" in Paul, 154; on offices, 123

Charisma, 98, 102-3. *See also* Spiritual gifts
Collins, John, 255-56
Confessional formulas, 222-23
Conzelmann, Hans: on cursing Jesus, 92-93; on *diakonia*, 101; on 1 Corinthians 14, 131-32; on gifts and offices, 123-24; on grouping of gifts, 110; on *ta pneumatika*, 69-71
Corinthian church: divisive loyalties in, 168-69; elitism in, 115-17; immaturity of, 184-86; quarrels in, 166; social composition of, 173
Corinthian controversy: significance of, 34-35

Cranfield, Charles B. E., 51-52, 57-58
Dahl, Nils A., 166
Dautzenberg, Gerhard: criticisms of, 30-31; on prophecy and kerygma, 28-31; on speaking mysteries, 153
Death: defeat of, 232-34, 254
De Boer, Martinus C.: on baptism, 216; on resurrection, 205, 209-10, 217, 231-32
Diakonia, 101-2, 104
Didache, 41; Harnack on, 3-4; prophets in, 2-5
Discourse, 218, 238-41, 245-46
Dodd, C. H.: on preaching and teaching, 27
Dualism, anthropological: in Corinthian church, 206-11
Dunn, James D. G.: on confessing Jesus, 89; on cursing Jesus, 93; on measure of faith, 52-53; on restriction on prophecy, 57

Ebeling, Gerhard, 238, 243
Ecstasy, 153-55
Edification, 142-44, 149-50
Eichholz, Georg, 88-89
Ellis, E. Earle, 73-74
Encouragement, 148-50
Energēma, 100-101
Engelsen, Nils I. J., 138-39, 140
Exhortation, 144-48, 149-50

Faith: apportioning of, 54-55; gift of, 112-13; measure of, 51-54
Faith, the: Paul's use of, 59-61
Fascher, Erich, 133
Fee, Gordon D.: on baptism, 120; on discernment of spirits, 105-6; on distribution of gifts, 114; on elitism in the Corinthian church, 115-16; on 1 Corinthians 12:2, 80; on 1 Corinthians 15, 200-201; on grouping of gifts, 110-11; on *hoi pneumatikoi,* 75, 77; on knowledge and wisdom, 109

1 Corinthians: importance of, 33-36, 65
Funk, Robert: on modes of discourse, 238-39, 241

Galatian controversy, 190-93
Glory, 247
Glossolalia. See Tongues
Gnosticism: in Corinthian church, 92-93, 207-8
God: knowledge of, 260-61; uniqueness of, 259-60
Gospel: of Christ, 245-48; meaning of, 221-22; source of, 189
Grudem, Wayne, 31

Harnack, Adolf von, 3-4, 23
Harrelson, Walter, 228-29, 233
Harrisville, Roy, 137-38, 140
Hays, Richard B., 159, 261
Hill, David: criticism of Käsemann, 12; on prophecy and wisdom utterances, 188; on prophetic preaching, 24, 25-28; on purpose of prophecy, 141, 147
Holtz, Traugott, 36-38, 43, 44
Horsley, Richard: on Corinthian wisdom, 177; on denial of resurrection, 208-10
Hoti recitativum, 203

Iber, Gerhard, 125-26
Inspiration, 22-23

Jesus Christ: confessing, 85-89; cursing, 90-95; exaltation of, 232
Jewett, Robert, 46-48
Judd, Bo, 181-82

Käsemann, Ernst: on apocalyptic, 9-11, 255-57; on baptism in Corinthian church, 167-68; on the body of Christ, 119-20; on *charisma,* 103-4; on Christian prophets, 240; on confessing Jesus, 85-86, 87-88; criticisms of, 11-17;

INDEX

on denial of resurrection, 216; on forms of prophetic speech, 6-9; on the kerygma, 223, 243-44; on measure of faith, 51, 53-54; on Old Testament prophets, 135; *Sentences of Holy Law*, 6-11; on theology, 237-38, 239-40, 242-44; on wisdom, 175-76

Kerygma: as criterion of prophecy, 243, 248-49; Paul's interpretation of, 244-45; Paul's use of, 223-24; and power, 171-72; and prophecy, 28-31; and wisdom, 171-72, 175, 178-79, 186

Knowledge utterances, 107-9

Kramer, Werner: on confessing Jesus, 85, 86-87

Law of retaliation, 6-8
Logic, deductive: in Paul, 229-30
Lührmann, Dieter, 193

Malherbe, A. J., 148-49
Martin, Ralph P., 41-42
Mauser, Ulrich, 259-60
Merklein, Helmut, 219-20, 227
Ministry of Paul: power in, 174-75; weakness in, 173-74
Mirror reading, 202-3
Müller, Ulrich B.: on forms of prophetic speech, 23-24; on *Shepherd of Hermas*, 22
Murphy-O'Connor, Jerome, 224

Neil, William, 45
Neufeld, Vernon, 222-23
Niederwimmer, Kurt, 197-98

Offices, 123-24
Oracles, 21
Osten-Saken, Peter von der, 225-26
Paul: call of, 193-94; prophetic ministry of, 193-95. *See also* Ministry of Paul
Pearson, Birger, 208, 209
Philo, 208-11

Plank, Karl A., 212-13
Pneumatikōn: interpretation of, 67-78, 95
Promise, 134-35
Prophētēs: meaning of, 132-33
Prophetic speech: example of in 1 Corinthians 15, 202, 204-5, 235; forms of, 5-6, 6-9, 17-25, 140-41; function of, 8, 141-42, 197-98; problematic nature of, 49-50, 62-63; restriction on in Romans, 56-58; scope of, 49, 62; as a sign, 158; and the Spirit, 48-49, 62; test of, 50, 58-59, 61-62, 79, 88, 94-95, 127, 162-63, 263
Prophets (Christian): importance of, 2; relationship to Old Testament prophets, 134-36; task of, 262-63
Prophets (Old Testament): function of, 134-36; Paul's view of, 134-36

Reasoning, circular: in Paul, 230
Resurrection: of Christ, and believers, 230-32; of Christ, on the third day, 214-15; and death, 253-54; denial of, 202, 204-18; and glory, 252; nature of body in, 234-35; realized, 211-18
Revelation: in Dautzenberg, 29; eschatological dimension in, 189-90, 192-93; and the gospel, 194-95; and prophetic speech, 196-97
Ricoeur, Paul, 245-46
Robinson, D. W. B., 71-73, 74
Robinson, James M., 40-41

Schmithals, Walter: on cursing Jesus, 92, 95; on *hoi pneumatikoi*, 76-77; on Thessalonian resistance to prophesying, 45-46
Schütz, John Howard: on apostolic authority, 170; on baptism in Corinthian church, 166-67; on denial of resurrection, 213-14; on edification, 142; on kerygma, 223; on Paul's use of "gospel," 221-22

Scriptures: in Corinthian church, 250-51
Shepherd of Hermas, 22
Spirit, God's: and wisdom, 182-83
Spirits: testing of, 105-6
Spiritual gifts: distribution of, 114-15; as manifestations of the Spirit, 98-100; purpose of, 117-18; ranking of, 122-23, 127-28
Stuhlmacher, Peter, 189-90, 193

Talbert, Charles H., 131
Teachers: in the *Didache*, 3-4
Teaching of the Twelve Apostles. See *Didache*
Theology: and prophecy, 197-98, 237-38, 239-40, 242-44; and reflection, 241
Thessalonian church: resistance to prophesying in, 44-88
Timothy, 145-46
Tongues: in Acts, 138-39; depreciation of, 106; distinction from other gifts, 69-73, 83-84, 110-11, 124-25, 128, 130-31, 140; in Paul, 137, 139-40; as a sign, 156-60; unintelligibility of, 150-55

Tradition, Paul's use of, 43-44

Vielhauer, Philipp, 142

Wedderburn, A. J. M., 210-11, 217-18
Weinel, Heinrich, 22
Wire, Antoinette Clark: on Corinthian wisdom, 177-78; on 1 Corinthians 15, 248-51; on identity of God, 257-58; and mirror reading, 202-3; on Paul's authority, 226
Wisdom: and apocalyptic, 14-15; cognitive element in, 179; in Corinth, 175-78; and the kerygma, 171-72, 175, 178-79, 186; and mystery, 180-81; and power, 170-75; and prophetic speech, 187-88; soteriological character of, 176, 180, 182; and the Spirit, 182-83; utterances, 107-9
Worship: order in, 160-63
Wright, N. T., 231

Ziesler, John, 57